Personal Names and Naming from an Anthropological-Linguistic Perspective

Anthropological Linguistics

Edited by
Svenja Völkel and Nico Nassenstein

Volume 4

Personal Names and Naming from an Anthropological-Linguistic Perspective

Edited by
Sambulo Ndlovu

DE GRUYTER
MOUTON

ISBN 978-3-11-221398-8
e-ISBN (PDF) 978-3-11-075929-7
e-ISBN (EPUB) 978-3-11-075937-2
ISSN 2701-987X

Library of Congress Control Number: 2023935860

Bibliographic information published by the Deutsche Nationalbibliothek
The Deutsche Nationalbibliothek lists this publication in the Deutsche Nationalbibliografie; detailed bibliographic data are available on the internet at http://dnb.dnb.de.

This volume is text- and page-identical with the hardback published in 2023.
Cover image: _jure/iStock/Getty Images Plus
Typesetting: Integra Software Services Pvt. Ltd.
Printing and binding: CPI books GmbH, Leck

www.degruyter.com

Antje Dammel

Preface

Naming people and places is one of the few absolute universals of human language. How naming is done varies to a high degree and in fascinating ways in the languages of the world. This variation is closely linked to cultural realities of speech communities: As Sambulo Ndlovu and Svenja Völkel emphasise in their introduction: When language expresses, symbolizes and embodies cultural reality, naming is at the core of practices constituting cultural reality.

As a linguist interested in interrelations of socio-pragmatic, cultural, and grammatical aspects of names and naming, I have been observing a rising interest in these fields in recent years, but at the same time, I have been missing the bigger picture of in-depth case studies on naming practices in languages of the world beyond Indo-European languages. This bigger picture is exactly what the present volume provides in several respects, namely structure, granularity, diversity of disciplines, topics and authors. Sambulo Ndlovu, the editor of the present book, has been doing socio- and ethnolinguistic research on African urban youth languages and on the relations of onomastics, address terms, and pragmatics for a long time. In the overall structure of the book and in the introduction co-authored with Svenja Völkel, he highlights original and insightful perspectives on naming persons. Just to give readers a glimpse: The contributions of the first part titled *The ethnopragmatics of anthroponyms* focus on group constituting and consolidating naming practices in such diverse communities as Hinihon (Papua New Guinea), societies of western Paraná State in the South of Brazil, and Lithuanian youth cultures. The papers in the second section investigate the role of name changes performing transitions in time, space, and society in diverse settings: changing name inventories and children naming trends in Israel, multiple situation-dependent naming of individuals in doing relationship in Madagascar, as well as developments in naming of indigenious groups and their lects in Australia as essential part of positioning ingroup and others within social and geographical space and thus, of organising and cherishing diversity. Part three investigates naming as manifestation of religious belief and practice. The contribution on the Meso, a Tibeto-Burmese branch of Sino-Tibetan in the Southwest of China, reconstructs the diachronic layering of spiritual names as evidence of religious transition and assimilation. By naming children after animals, the Ibibio and Tiv people of Nigeria transfer onto the next generation the social, cultural, and religious convictions linked to their worship of characteristics attributed to these animals. The

Antje Dammel, University of Münster, e-mail: dammel@uni-muenster.de

https://doi.org/10.1515/9783110759297-202

contributions in the last part of the book start out from analysing structural (morphological, syntactic), semantic and sociolinguistic aspects of anthoponyms and ask in which ways these features of naming systems are crystallisations of social structures and hybridities. Again, the rich data comes from diverse speech communities such as the Azerbaijani naming system, which integrates names of Turkic origin, Saaroa personal names in Taiwan, names and naming in the Polynesian society of Tonga, Mazahuan personal names in contact with Spanish in Mexico, and doing gender with Ndebele personal names in Zimbabwe.

When I was asked to write a preface to this book, I felt very much honoured. While preparing it, I found my favorite thing about writing this preface was getting first access to all these in-depth case studies augmenting my onomastic worldview. I wish the same experience to as many linguist, onomastician, sociologist, anthropologist, politologist, and historian readers all over the globe as possible. The book will be an eye opener for each of these disciplines as it widens the perspective on what people, groups, and societies do with names, how naming practice is an essential factor constituting socio-cultural realities, and how naming systems are entrenchments of these practices and realities.

Münster, October 31, 2022
Antje Dammel

Contents

Section Two: **Personal naming and cultural transissions**

Section Three: **Anthroponyms as religious belief and practice**

List of figures

https://doi.org/10.1515/9783110759297-204

List of maps

https://doi.org/10.1515/9783110759297-205

List of tables

https://doi.org/10.1515/9783110759297-206

Sambulo Ndlovu & Svenja Völkel

Chapter 1
Introduction: The cultural aspect of personal names

The nexus between language and culture is grounded on the fact that language expresses, embodies and symbolises cultural reality (Kramsch 1998). Such a nexus falls within the ambit of anthropological linguistics. The majority of personal names are derived from words already in use in a language. Names also indicate language structure (Anderson 2007); hence, Utley (1963) argues them to be part of the grammar of a language. However, their meaning is socially constructed within a particular culture (Aceto 2002) and these cultural meanings warrant an anthropological-linguistic perspective that is concerned with relations among language, society and culture, involving speech communities, the performing of language and socio-cultural representations in language. In practice and literature, the domain of anthropological linguistics is interchangeable with that of linguistic anthropology (Foley 1997; see also Nassenstein and Völkel 2022 for a more detailed description of the framework of this book series). The study of names (proper nouns) is part of language studies and it, too, cannot be separated from cultural and social performance. An interrogation of anthroponyms (personal names), for example, goes beyond the structural appreciation of language into the domain of anthropological linguistics, which attempts to explain hidden meanings behind language use, different forms of language and the use of registers and style (Foley 1997). Different types of anthroponyms have been analysed in linguistics, anthropology and philosophy, and they have been proved to be referential, descriptive, symbolic and in some cases to have psychological effects and power.

From a cross-linguistic perspective, names are a typological universal. This means they are found in all human languages around the world, and they are used by people of all societies (Hocket 1963: 17). However, typological studies show that they differ in form, function and usage across languages and cultures. Therefore, Van Langendonck and Van de Velde (2016: 18) define a name on cross-linguistically shared semantic-cognitive grounds as "a nominal expression that denotes a unique entity at the level of established linguistic convention to make it psychosocially

Sambulo Ndlovu, University of Eswatini, Great Zimbabwe University, and University of Mainz, Germany, e-mail: matsilaneg@gmail.com
Svenja Völkel, University of Mainz/Germany, e-mail: svenja.voelkel@uni-mainz.de

https://doi.org/10.1515/9783110759297-001

salient within a given basic level category". As such, they are definite, mostly singular and without a defining sense (as compared to common nouns).

Anthroponyms, in particular, are proper names of humans, denoting individual persons or groups of people. Person-denoting names for individuals are, among others, given names, surnames, nicknames and pseudonyms. Some of these names include a relational component, i.e., a connection to another person is established, such as the mother in matronyms, the father in patronyms or the children in teknonyms. Apart from surnames, which also refer to a group of people based on family ties (just like clan names), other group anthroponyms denote communities based on other social criteria, e.g., ethnonyms (names for ethnic groups, such as tribal names) and demonyms (names for groups associated with a particular place, i.e., anthroponyms of toponymic origin). Such names often differ considerably depending on whether they are self- or third-party designations. According to Van Langendonck and Van de Velde (2016: 33), anthroponyms are the most prototypical type of names, and they are probably the best studied kind of onomastics. However, there is a strong bias towards research on Indo-European languages. Hence, a broader range of languages needs to be studied in order to gain a more comprehensive understanding of onomastics, and anthroponomastics in particular – an aim to which we want to contribute with this book.

A second objective of this publication is to focus on the study of personal names from an anthropological-linguistic perspective. Foley (1997) characterises anthropological linguistics as an inter-discipline of linguistics and anthropology, situating language in its social and cultural context, whereby it is both cultural practice and social structure. Names are not only a linguistic phenomenon in terms of their formal features, etymological meanings[1] and historical-linguistic developments, but there is also a strong cultural component (see also Bramwell 2016). The socio-cultural meaning and function of names, their use or non-use (e.g., name avoidance or taboo, honorific forms), naming and name change practices (e.g., at birth or marriage), and so forth, are aspects which make this clear. Anthroponyms describe social subjects, together with ideas of interpersonal relationships and social interaction, which are culturally constructed realities. As such, names and naming practices have developed in specific social contexts to fulfil particular functions beyond reference to or the address of specific persons. According to Alford

1 Most scholars agree that names as such have no lexical meaning but only reference (i.e., identifying function). The lexemes used as names might have lexical meanings (e.g. *Mr. Smith*) but not the name itself, because neither does every "smith" have this name, nor is every Mr. Smith still a "smith". This can be called the etymological meaning of names (Nyström 2016). Thus, meaning here is not understood as lexical meaning, but in terms of other kinds of meaning, such as the etymological or socio-cultural meaning of names and naming in general.

(1988), personal names are cultural universals that are reflective of the specific cultures that create them.

While, in the western tradition, names were established as meaningless beyond being individualising (Suzman 1994), later studies have established that even in these western traditions, personal names in fact carry social and cultural aspects such as gender, religion and history (Pilcher 2017). The cultural specificities of names and naming conventions make them part of active metaphorising, "a culture-specific speech practice which demands explication within an ethnopragmatic perspective" (Goddard 2004: 1211). This leads to the third aim of this volume, which is to demonstrate the communicative and cultural pragmatics in names. The use of names is embedded in social contexts; it varies according to the interpersonal relationships between the participants in communication (i.e., speaker, addressee and/or referent – be they namer, named person(s) or name hearer(s)[2]) and the situation (e.g., formal or informal contexts). Furthermore, the use, non-use and choice of alternative names for a person creates social meanings such as politeness, respect, disrespect, offense and even magic attack.

This book gives multiple illustrative examples of the broad cross-linguistic variety of anthroponyms and their cultural characteristics and meanings. It is an interdisciplinary and cross-linguistic ethnopragmatic exploration of personal names, which can only be understood when studied in the context of the culture that produces them. According to Goddard (2004: 1211), ethnopragmatics refers to "explanations of speech practices which begin with culture-internal ideas, i.e., with the shared values, norms, priorities, and assumptions of the speakers, rather than with any presumed universals of pragmatics". The ethnopragmatics of names speaks to their performative functions within cultural contexts; hence, this book incorporates the idea that names are part of speech acts as they perform specific cultural functions.

The volume is themed along Austin's (1975) idea of "How to do things with words". Here, the focus is more specifically: How to do (cultural) things with people's names. Anthroponyms fulfil certain communicative actions beyond the referential (Lynch 2016). Choices of personal names are functions of language choice which are

---

2 The speakers are generally also the namers, who decide which name they use for a named person. However, in narratives with direct or indirect speech, where narrator and speaker are distinct persons, the situation gets more complex. The named person(s) can be the speakers themselves, the addressee(s) or the referent(s). In name addressing, the relevant social relationship is that between the speaker (namer) and the addressee (named person), who is also the person intended to hear the name. In name reference, the interpersonal situation is more complex. The choice of name use reflects the relationship between the speaker (namer) and the referent (named person), wherein the personal relationship of the addressee (name hearer) to the referent assumed by the speaker also plays a role.

shaped by the motive, which can be expressive, appealing or representative (Hymes 1972). Leech (2003) identifies five functions of language in culture and society: 1. informative functions, referring to the subject matter (the name bearer); 2. expressive functions, referring to the speaker (the namer); 3. directive functions, referring to the listener (those addressed in the naming); 4. phatic functions, referring to the means of communication (names as a communication bridge); and 5. aesthetic functions, referring to the messages (the styling or typology of names). The various chapters in this book demonstrate how personal names, as part of language, perform culture. According to Duranti (2009), language use is constitutive of our social life. That is, speaking does not just happen in social interaction, speaking itself is social interaction. Names are part of action and are equivalents to action (Malinowski 1935), they are part of language which is a form of social interaction, and they are to be understood within particular activities (Wittgenstein 1953).

Personal names and naming are entwined in culture through naming ceremonies, practices and conventions. According to Lynch (2016), names and naming are essential practical rituals of everyday life. They go beyond the structure of language to index social structure and roles (Ndlovu 2022). Mensah and Rowan (2019) observe that names and naming interface with every facet of life; they are indicators of social structuring such as sex and gender (Pilcher 2017; Ngubane 2013; Koopman 1979), identity, status and class (Ndlovu 2022) and kinship structures and history (Mensah and Iloh 2021). Personal names also "do religion"; they are a communication bridge between people and their deities (Mensah 2015, 2020; Sagna and Bassène 2016; Mamvura 2021; Abubakari 2020). Research has also established that names perform cultural and social acts such as expressions of love and hate (Babane and Chauke 2017), coloniality (Mapara and Nyota 2016; Pongweni 2017), directing and appealing (Ndlovu 2015) and representing power dynamics (Neethling 2018).

Structure and topics of the volume

The volume draws chapters from different cultures across the globe to demonstrate how names as a linguistic phenomenon are deeply embedded in cultural contexts and how anthroponymy does culture. The chapters address the topic with studies from different linguistic and cultural areas: South America (Brazil), Central America (Mexico), Africa (Nigeria, Ethiopia, Madagascar, Uganda, Zimbabwe), North-Eastern Europe (Lithuania), the Middle East (Azerbaijan, Israel), Asia (China, Indonesia, Tibet), Oceania (Tonga, Papua New Guinea) and Australia. The book has eighteen chapters, including this introduction (Chapter 1), with the rest of the chapters falling into four thematic sections as described below.

Chapter 1: Introduction

The introduction explores theoretical concerns in the language culture nexus and demonstrates how onomastics, especially personal names and naming, are relevant in the study and understanding of culture and identity. It reviews literature to demonstrate how personal names are part of social practice in cultural contexts representing and expressing people's interpersonal living worlds, and how they also reveal intra- and inter-cultural relations.

Section One: The ethnopragmatics of anthroponyms

This section focuses on the socio-cultural functions of names and naming in societies. It comprises Chapters 2 to 5.

Chapter 2 explores the indigenous knowledge system performed by personal names and titles among the Hamar of South West Ethiopia. It demonstrates how the Hamar community and culture link their culture of agro-pastoralism to their titles and naming conventions. The chapter provides an overview of Hamar naming practices with a focus on the livestock-centred system of address and its interconnectedness with the pastoral indigenous knowledge system.

Chapter 3 is an exploration of the naming conventions of the Hinihon of Papua New Guinea. *Unim ate* ('big names') are powerful entities which are passed on from generation to generation within a clan. The name givers bestow their names on young recipients and create a relationship of care and affection as their personal inner essence is transmitted with the names. These bequeathed names express the people's deep connection with the land, and they are avoided as part of Hinihon pragmatics (naming taboo) to facilitate identity concealment. Instead, people are called by birth-ordinal names which make a person's identification obscure. They are *opu ondik* ('talk without meaning').

Chapter 4 correlates names, parental motivations for name giving and linguistic features of names, history and social class in the West of Paraná, a region in the south of Brazil. It establishes that surnames in that region corroborate the relationship between history, migration and family names. It also demonstrates that linguistic features of first names shed light on the influence of social class on innovative spellings.

Chapter 5, the last chapter in this section, explores nicknaming among Lithuanian youth. The key observations are that the nicknames created by young people are characterised by spontaneity, expressiveness, emotionality, representation of social identity and linguistic hybridity. Further, nicknaming as a socio-cultural phenomenon is associated with the youth subculture, which is characterised by distinctive norms and rules reflecting the processes of youth socialisation. Furthermore, the chapter asserts that nicknames help express certain attitudes towards other members of the same sociolect. Through nicknames, one can identify the social roles of Lithuanian youth, as well as the social and cultural identities they are building.

Section Two: Personal naming and cultural transitions

This section shows how personal names exhibit the characteristic of transitioning in time, space and societies. Chapters in this section analyse how personal names index political, social, physical and temporal boundaries. It comprises Chapters 6 to 9.

Chapter 6 presents qualitative research that was carried out in Israel regarding the choice of common versus unique given names for new-borns. The chapter engages the theory of ten basic human values and establishes that popular names are chosen as guided by either the security value or the conformity value, both motivated by conservativeness. On the other hand, the stimulation value is motivated by openness to change. The findings show that some Israeli parents who give unique names to their first-born children tend not to give them to their siblings.

Chapter 7 looks at naming in Madagascar, and especially the poetics and spiritual practices of naming and address. Speaking names out loud in these societies of primary orality brings into consciousness, and into continued existence, moments of poetic pronouncements and prosaic audacity. In this chapter, ethno-archaeologists and ethnographers are drawn into learning about and learning from the humour, beauty and blessing in naming individuals. It further discusses the practice of giving derogatory names to children to turn away the attention of envious evil-doers. The child is later sprinkled with a name of blessing. The chapter incorporates ethnopragmatic cultural transitions and rites of passage involving names and naming.

Chapter 8 describes the range of strategies Indigenous Australian communities use to divide up their local language ecologies, their practices for naming lects and the role of variation in the processes of differentiation and connection. The authors show that language and group naming systems are local ways of organising diversity, and that naming is at the very heart of the concerns of sociolinguistics and linguistic anthropology, linking the social, the political, the geographic and the linguistic. It is important because it has a bearing on how people see themselves and others, and on how they construct "same" and "different". By surveying group and language naming in four regions across Indigenous Australia, the chapter establishes that, contrary to the contemporary belief that diversity is a problem, names of people and their lects in Indigenous Australia open our eyes to other ways of understanding and valuing diversity.

The last chapter in the section, Chapter 9, engages with colonial transitions in eastern Zimbabwe through names. The chapter looks at the nicknames of white farmers in the area and how these names have remained part of the history and geography of the land even after political independence. The nicknames express nuances of colonial resentment by the Black name givers. However, there are some positive nicknames that indicate that there were some colonial farmers who integrated into the communities.

Section Three: Anthroponyms as religious belief and practice

This section focuses on the link between names and naming and spirituality in society. Chapters 10 to 13 look at the religious implications of personal names and naming.

Chapter 10 looks at death prevention names among the Bakonzo people of Western Uganda. The author argues that naming is an important aspect of communication between the Bakonzo and their spirits and reflects on the figurative nature of the names given to children born after the death of the sibling they follow. The chapter describes two aspects of this naming practice: the different themes carried in these names, and the figures of speech through which these themes are carried across to the listener and to the spirits. The names are analysed through semantic and contextual reading for insights on their meanings and the figurative resources used to develop the meanings. The chapter draws attention to the poetic nature of Konzo personal names, as well as to the spiritual logic behind the names.

Chapter 11 looks at the spiritual and historical implications of spirits' names among the Moso, a Tibeto-Burmese branch of the Sino-Tibetan language family of Southwest China. The Moso practise Dongbaism and Dabaism as their religions. The author avers that Dongba and Daba spirits' names show massive similarities to Tibetan Buddhism, but with different historical layers and styles that may be remnants of the Bon religion, the indigenous belief prevailing on the Himalayan plateau before Tibetan Buddhism. Through the analysis of morphological structures, the chapter explores the assimilation of Tibetan linguistic elements into

Dongba and Daba naming practices and reconstructs the transition from Daba to Dongba.

Chapter 12 explores the motivations for the adoption of animal names as personal names among the Ibibio and Tiv people of Nigeria. The chapter examines the physical connection between animals and humans, and the beliefs that influence the choice of animal names as personal names. The author asserts that in the two cultures, animals have a profound role as religious totems for worship and as objects of sacrifice for ritual purposes. Parents therefore give the names of certain animals to their children to project their social, cultural and religious leanings and ideologies. Others admire certain specific characteristics of these animals.

Chapter 13 describes how personal naming is a strategy for preventing death among the Basà people of North-Central Nigeria. The work focuses mainly on the grammatical structure of Basà personal names and how they perform death prevention. It shows how certain names and naming patterns are a way of preventing infant mortality. The chapter further explores how Basà death prevention names generate and maintain some level of assurance and security that are vital for the survival of a child, given the belief that certain spiritual forces are responsible for incessant child mortality. These names are believed to link the bearer with their past, with ancestors and deities.

Section Four: The linguistics of anthroponyms and their socio-cultural indices

This section focuses on the linguistic analysis of personal names and how their structure and semantics impact socio-cultural indices. Chapters 14 to 18 analyse the morphology, syntax, semantics and sociolinguistics of proper names and link the structures and meanings to cultural concepts of social structure.

Chapter 14 focuses on Turkic personal names and naming (borrowed names which have been used in the Azerbaijani language for a long time and have been adapted to the language) in Azerbaijan. The chapter considers the traditions and motives behind name giving in Azerbaijan and determines the principles of nomination therein. Further, the chapter engages with ways of forming personal names and the interlinguistic and extralinguistic factors influencing the development of the naming system.

In Chapter 15 the author demonstrates the link between the structures and characteristics of Saaroa personal names in Taiwan and their culture. The chapter engages with the names at different levels of linguistic analysis and demonstrates how these structures are, in fact, expressions of Saaroa cultural beliefs and practices.

Chapter 16 is an exploration of names and naming in the Polynesian society of Tonga. The chapter addresses different types of personal names and their historical development, naming practices and the grammar of *hingoa* ('name'). Through these grammatical aspects, the chapter shows that personal names and linguistic behaviour in Tongan are deeply embedded in the cultural context of this Polynesian society. Social aspects of kinship and stratification are conceptualised in grammatical features and naming practices.

Chapter 17 proposes a typology of Mazahuan personal names to trace cultural hybridities in the Mexican culture. It explores the modern way of nominating in modern Mazahua from lexicological and phonetic-phonological points of view and describes how the structure of these personal names is a clue to explaining the hybrid Spanish-Mazahuan culture that obtains today.

Chapter 18 extricates gender and patriarchal tendencies and practices from the morphology of Ndebele personal names in Zimbabwe. The chapter demonstrates how Ndebele personal names are morphologically constructed to do gender. The treatment of sex and gender in Ndebele culture can be read in the morphology of the preferred names for boy and girl children.

All these examples of personal names and naming clearly demonstrate that anthroponyms are a linguistic and a cultural phenomenon. To gain a comprehensive understanding of how linguistic and anthropological facts interact, interdisciplinary research on personal names is needed. This includes aspects of linguistic forms of names, naming practices and the cultural meaning of names. The present volume shows a wide range of cross-cultural and cross-linguistic diversity, as well as dynamics of cultural and linguistic practice over time.

References

Abubakari, Hasiyatu. 2020. Personal names in Kusaal: A sociolinguistic analysis. *Language & Communication* 75. 21–35.

Aceto, Michael. 2002. Ethnic personal names and multiple identities in Anglophone Caribbean speech communities in Latin America. *Language in Society* 31 (4). 577–608.

Alford, Richard D. 1988. *Naming and identity: A cross-cultural study of personal naming practices.* New Haven, CT: HRAF Press.

Anderson, John M. 2007. *The grammar of names.* Oxford: Oxford University Press.

Austin, John L. 1975. *How to do things with words.* Oxford: Oxford University Press.

Babane, Morris T. & Mkhacani T. Chauke. 2017. The sociocultural aspects of Xitsonga dog names. *Nomina Africana: Journal of African Onomastics* 31 (1). 59–67.

Bramwell, Ellen S. 2016. Personal names and anthropology. In Carole Hough (ed.), *The Oxford handbook of names and naming*, 263–278. Oxford: Oxford University Press.

Duranti, Alessandro. 2009. The relevance of Husserl's theory to language socialization. *Journal of Linguistic Anthropology* 19 (2). 205–226.
Foley, William A. 1997. *Anthropological linguistics: An introduction*. Malden, MA: Wiley-Blackwell.
Goddard, Cliff. 2004. The ethnopragmatics and semantics of 'active metaphors'. *Journal of pragmatics* 36 (7). 1211–1230.
Hockett, Charles F. 1963. The problem of universals in language. In Joseph H. Greenberg (ed.), *Universals of language*, 1–22. Cambridge, MA: MIT Press.
Hymes, Dell H. 1972. On communicative competence. In J. B. Pride & Janet Holmes (eds.), *Sociolinguistics. Selected readings*, 269–293. London: Penguin.
Koopman, Adrian. 1979. Male and female names in Zulu. *African Studies* 38 (2). 153–166.
Kramsch, Claire. 1998. *Language and culture*. Oxford: Oxford University.
Leech, Geoffrey. 2003. Modality on the move: The English modal auxiliaries 1961–1992. In Roberta Facchinetti, Frank Palmer & Manfred Krug (eds.), *Modality in contemporary English*, 223–240. Berlin: De Gruyter Mouton.
Lynch, Gabrielle. 2016. What's in a name? The politics of naming ethnic groups in Kenya's Cherangany Hill. *Journal of Eastern African Studies* 10 (1). 208–227.
Malinowski, Bronisław. 1935. *Coral gardens and their magic*. London: Allen & Unwin.
Mamvura, Zvinashe. 2021. An ethnopragmatic analysis of death-prevention names in the Karanga Society of Zimbabwe. *African Studies* 80 (1). 111–124.
Mapara, Jacob & Shumirai Nyota. 2016. Suburban blight: Perpetuating colonial memory through naming in Mutare, Zimbabwe. In Oliver Nyambi, Tendai Mangena & Charles Pfukwa (eds.), *The postcolonial conditions of names and naming practices in Southern Africa*, 289–306. Newcastle, UK: Cambridge Scholars Publishing.
Mensah, Eyo O. 2020. Name this child: Religious identity and ideology in Tiv personal names. *Names*. 1–15.
Mensah, Eyo O. 2015. Frog, where are you? The ethnopragmatics of Ibibio death prevention names. *Journal of African Cultural Studies* 27 (2). 115–132.
Mensah, Eyo O. & Queendaline I. Iloh. 2021. Wealth is king: The conceptualization of wealth in Igbo personal naming practices. *Anthropological Quarterly* 94 (4). 699–723.
Mensah, Eyo O. & Kirsty Rowan. 2019. African anthroponyms: Sociolinguistic currents and anthropological reflections. *Sociolinguistic Studies* 13 (2–4). 157–170.
Nassenstein, Nico & Svenja Völkel. 2022. Studying the relationship of language and culture: Scope and directions. In Svenja Völkel & Nico Nassenstein (eds.), *Approaches to language and culture*, 3–29. Berlin: de Gruyter Mouton.
Neethling, Bertie. 2018. Celebrities changing their names: For better or for worse? *Names*. 1–16.
Ndlovu, Sambulo. 2022. *Naming and othering in Africa: Imagining supremacy and inferiority through language*. London: Routledge.
Ndlovu, Sambulo. 2015. Names as indigenous knowledge for making meat edible and/or inedible: Implications on food security in Zimbabwe. In Oliviu Felecan (ed.), *Conventional/unconventional in onomastics*, 751–762. Baia Mare: Editura Mega.
Ngubane, Sihawukele. 2013. The socio-cultural and linguistic implications of Zulu names. *South African Journal of African Languages* 33 (2). 165–172.
Nyström, Staffan. 2016. Names and meaning. In Carole Hough (ed.), *The Oxford handbook of names and naming*, 39–51. Oxford: Oxford University Press.
Pilcher, Jane. 2017. Names and "doing gender": How forenames and surnames contribute to gender identities, difference, and inequalities. *Sex Roles* 77. 812–822.

Pongweni, Alec. 2017. The impact of English on the naming practices of the Shona people of Zimbabwe. *Nomina Africana* 31 (2). 101–116.
Sagna, Serge & Emmanuel Bassène. 2016. Why are they named after death? Name giving, name changing and death prevention names in Gújjolaay Eegimaa (Banjal). *Language Documentation & Conservation* 10. 40–70.
Suzman, Susan M. 1994. Names as pointers: Zulu personal naming practices. *Language in Society* 23 (2). 250–272.
Utley, Francis L. 1963. The linguistic component of onomastic. *Names. A Journal of Onomastics* 11 (3). 145–176.
Van Langendonck, Willy & Mark Van de Velde. 2016. Names and grammar. In Carole Hough (ed.), *The Oxford handbook of names and naming*, 17–38. Oxford: Oxford University Press.
Wittgenstein, Ludwig. 1953. *Philosophical investigations*. New York: Macmillian.

Section One: **The ethnopragmatics of anthroponyms**

Sara Petrollino

Chapter 2
'Father of the spotted cow': Hamar titles and their connection to cattle appearance

Abstract: The Hamar are agro-pastoralist people inhabiting the southernmost corner of Ethiopia. Like many other pastoralist groups in Africa, their language is rich in words and expressions referring to the appearance of their cattle and goats (colours and patterns, horn shapes, brands, and ear cuts). The classification system for cattle appearance is extremely complex and it allows herders to provide detailed descriptions of animals' appearances. This system is closely intertwined with livestock-centred naming practices, in particular with individual appellations designated for adult humans and for livestock, particularly cattle. By studying the livestock-centred terms of address we can understand the organising principles of the Hamar descriptive system for cattle appearance. Hamar titles and appellations are employed as identification devices and as such they help to individuate people and heads of livestock; their referential and pragmatic function allows speakers to individuate people's and animals' statuses within the community. In addition, these naming practices are key to understanding the categorisation system for cattle appearance, remember its structuring principles and transmit them to younger generations. Building on the existing anthropological literature and on the author's first-hand collected data, the chapter provides an overview of Hamar naming practices with a focus on the livestock-centred system of address terms and its interconnectedness with the pastoral indigenous knowledge system.

Keywords: cattle names, cattle colors, honorific titles, pastoral linguacultures

1 Introduction

The Hamar are agropastoral people who live in South West Ethiopia: like many other pastoral groups of East Africa, their society and culture shows traits of typical

Acknowledgments: This paper is the result of endless conversations with Hamar men and women from various villages, who patiently taught me their livestock-centred system of address. I am deeply grateful for the insights and explanations that Wengela Gedo, alias Baldámba (calf name), or Nabuíz (favourite animal name), shared with me during my stay in Shanqo Kalama.

Sara Petrollino, Leiden University Centre for Linguistics, e-mail: s.petrollino@hum.leidenuniv.nl

https://doi.org/10.1515/9783110759297-002

"East African Cattle Complex" societies (Herskovits 1926), whereby cattle is not only kept as a commodity but is a cultural theme; in these pastoral societies, cattle, as well as goats and sheep, play a fundamental role in shaping the identity of members of the society and are involved in rituals around death, birth and marriage.

The importance of cattle as a cultural theme is reflected in two domains which are of particular interest for an anthropological linguistic approach: lexical specialisation in the domain of animal appearance (the so called "cattle colours and patterns") and the livestock-centred naming practices for both humans and livestock.

In pastoralist societies, cattle are pedigreed animals and are considered members of the society and "mirror species" (Abbink 2003: 360). Humans identify with their livestock (Seligman and Seligman 1965: 169; Hazel 1997; see also Dubosson 2014: 88–89) and engage in naming practices that bind herders together with their favourite animals. Animals receive personal appellations on the basis of their physical traits, and herders derive terms of address (i.e. praise names and honorific titles) from the physical appearance and personal appellations of their livestock. These appellations have been referred to in the ethnographic literature under various lables, such as "calf names", "ox names", "bull names", "pet names", "favourite animal names", and so on.

This paper explores the relationship between Hamar terms of address and the pastoral knowledge system: a close analysis of the appellations assigned to both humans and cattle shows that these linguistic and cultural practices are inextricably intertwined with the descriptive system for cattle appearance. The formal and semantic relationships between appellations for cattle and humans and the descriptive linguistic terms for cattle coats highlight important aspects of the Hamar pastoral lingua-culture system: appellations for humans and cattle are not only identification devices with referential functions (i.e. individuating people, livestock and their statuses, creating a symbolic relationship between animals and people) but they also function as structuring principles for the descriptive system of cattle appearance. Appellations for humans and cattle derive their meaning from the cattle descriptive system: this allows members of the society to create meaningful associations and remember the principles underlying the indigenous categorisation system for cattle.

The paper is structured as follows: the next section provides an overview of livestock-centred linguistic and cultural practices in pastoral societies (§1.1), including a terminological note to distinguish descriptive terms for cattle appearance from "personal names" and "titles" in the context of East African livestock-centred terms of address (§1.2, §1.3). Next, the livestock-centred linguistic practices among the Hamar of South-West Ethiopia are presented (§2), with a brief explanation of the descriptive system for cattle appearance (§2.1), which is the starting point for understanding the principles regulating the assignment of titles to both humans and cattle. This is followed by a description of the titles for cattle (§2.2) and how they relate to the descriptive system for cattle appearance. Section 3 deals with terms of address for humans; after a brief outline of Hamar naming practices, it focuses on livestock-derived terms of address for adult Hamar men: the so-called calf names (§3.1) and favourite animal names (§3.2). The formal and semantic relations that link the descriptive system for cattle appearance to the terms of address for both humans and cattle will be explained and discussed. Given the history of contact among East African pastoralists, some of the links between the Hamar appellations and other languages will also be highlighted.

The plurality of names and titles that a Hamar man receives throughout his life, and their interconnection with cattle, will be exemplified here with a fictional male individual named Kála. Kála[1] is the birth name (*gáli náabi*) that the fictional individual received a few weeks after his birth (see §3). At a young age, Kála learns how to distinguish and describe the various colours and patterns on livestock's coats (see §2.1); while growing up (or even after his marriage), Kála may develop a special relationship with a cow or goat which will become his favourite animal. Kála will name his favourite ox (see §2.2) with a special appellation derived from the colour-pattern configuration of its coat. At the same time, Kála's age-mates will look at the physical traits of his favourite ox and they will come up with a new title for Kála, the so called "favourite animal name" (*qóle náabi*): this is a special title which will be used by friends and age-mates to address Kála in salutations and during dances (see §3.2). When Kála reaches puberty he is initiated into adulthood through various rituals, at the end of which he will leap over a row of cattle: at the end of this rite of passage (called *ukulí ɓulá* in Hamar), Kála becomes an adult man and he acquires the right to marry and build his own homestead, fields and herds. On this occasion he receives a new title, the so-called "calf name" (see §3.1). A calf name is a teknonymic title which evokes the appearance and physical traits of the heifer calf positioned at the beginning of the cattle row. During the ritual Kála stepped on a yellow calf, so he will be named *Burrémba*: 'father of the yellow cow'. From now on, he will be addressed as *Burrémbe* by his peers, age-mates, and by his mother.

1.1 Livestock-centred practices in pastoral societies

The lexical specialisation in the domain of animal appearance in the languages of East African pastoralists has been discussed in the anthropological and ethnographic literature in relation to cattle aesthetics, colour symbolism and its

1 Kála is also the numeral word for 'one'.

links with aspects of social organisation. Classic ethnographic works include Almagor (1983), Dubosson (2016), Dyson-Hudson (1966), Eczet (2018, 2019a, 2019b), Evans-Pritchard (1940), Fukui (1979, 1986, 1996), Galaty (1989), Lienhardt (1961), Ohta (1986), Tornay (1973, 1978), Turton (1980) and Wymeersch (1988), among others.

In addition to the descriptive terms for animal coats and animal appearances, the linguistic practices of pastoral societies include naming traditions for both animals and humans: pastoralists assign individual appellations to their animals and derive titles and terms of address for members of the society from the physical characteristics of their livestock (see Section 1.2). In the anthropological and ethnographic literature these livestock-centred linguistic practices are usually discussed in connection with the following topics: the "identification" of a man with livestock (Seligman and Seligman 1965), the cultural practice of animal beautification, which involves permanent body markings and horn training, and the phenomenon of the "favourite animal", a special human-animal relationship whereby a herder develops a particular relationship with a (usually) bovine or caprine animal; for an exhaustive overview and literature review on the topic of the favourite animal among the Hamar and other east African pastoralists see Dubosson (2014: 86–89, 2016, 229–54).

1.2 Livestock-centred terms of address in East Africa

Livestock-centred naming practices have been the object of study in ethnographic work among the Dhaasanac (Almagor 1972), the Dinka (Evans-Pritchard 1934; Seligman and Seligman 1965: 169–170; Lienhardt 1988, 1961: 12–16), the Nuer (Evans-Pritchard 1964, 1940: 18, 45–46), the Jie (Gulliver 1952), the Bodi (Fukui 1979) and the Murle (Arensen 1988, 1992, 70–76), among others; these works focus on livestock-centred terms of address for humans. Livestock names are also reported in the literature: Ohta (1986) provides a unique, comprehensive analysis of Turkana cattle names' etymologies; Seligman and Seligman (1965: 170) and Lienhardt (1961: 14–15) explain the meaning of a few Dinka cattle names, and Wolde Gossa Tadesse mentions livestock-centred naming practices among the Arbore (1999: 199); other works include Umesao (1966) for Datooga livestock names, Imai (1982) for the Gabra Oromo goat naming system and Galaty for Maasai cattle names (1989: 219–220). Lists of names and appellations can be found also in the linguistic literature; see for example the analysis of Iraqw cattle names in Rottland and Mous (2001), or the list of "bull names" (for humans) in Ik (Schrock 2014: 193); Tosco (2001: 581) provides a list of Dhaasanac "ox names" (for cattle); Storch (2005: 428–433) provides a detailed linguistic analysis of descriptive nouns for cattle appearance (also used as appellations for humans) in Dinka and Shilluk.

The literature on livestock-centred naming practices suggest that there are different systems of address in pastoralist lingua-cultures of East Africa. Some lingua-cultures have separate systems; appellations for animals and livestock-derived terms of address for humans do not coincide. This is the case for most of Hamar titles and appellations. In other languages, on the other hand, there might be a partial overlap between livestock-derived terms of address for humans and livestock appellations. In Hamar, for example, a small sub-set of cattle names correspond to titles for humans, see §3.1, Table 2.6. The overalp between appellations for cattle and titles for humans has caused some confusion in the use of labels such as "ox names", "bull names", "calf names" etc.: the labels are sometimes used with reference to both livestock and humans, so for languages in which the two systems are separate, the distinction between livestock-derived terms of address for humans and appellations for livestock is lost.

Another source of confusion is the overlap, in some lingua-cultures, between the system of address (for both livestock and humans) and the terms describing the physical traits of livestock: in Dinka and Shilluk, for instance, descriptive terms for cattle appearance become personal appellations for human beings and cattle (Storch 2005: 431, Martin 2018: 17). However, the function of cattle color and pattern terms as appellations in other languages is not always clearly described: Wymeersch (1988), for example, referred to the Turkana descriptive terms for cattle appearance as "names", although according to Ohta (1986), these are descriptive terms which are not used as appellations; similarly, the Karimojong's vocabulary for cattle appearance was described by Dyson-Hudson (1966: 96) in terms of "cattle names", but it is not clear whether these descriptive terms were used as appellations.

1.3 Names and titles

The appellations for animals and humans are usually referred to in the literature as "personal names". Ohta, for example, talks about "livestock individual names" (1986: 35) among the Turkana, and Lydall (1999) presented Hamar teknonyms, "calf names", "favourite animal names" and "killer names" as personal names.

Other authors have applied a refined distinction in pastoralists' systems of address and separated livestock-derived terms of address for humans from personal names. For example, in Nuer culture (Evans-Pritchard 1964), "ox names" are referred to as "titles" (ibid: 222), given their different pragmatic force in comparison to Nuer personal names. Similarly, Lienhardt (1988) compared Dinka ox names to Western personal names and concluded that "ox names" are praise names with different referential and pragmatic functions.

Concerning livestock appellations, some authors have distinguished cattle personal names from cattle titles: Seligman and Seligman (1965: 169), for example, noted an important difference between cattle personal names assigned to female cows and cattle titles assigned to oxen in Dinka culture; according to the authors: "(. . .) *the names of oxen are not individual names (as the names of cows are) but names which they share with all other bulls and oxen of the same class*" (p. 169), and "*. . . cows (not heifers) are given a personal name which they bear through life*" (p. 170).

In this chapter the Hamar appellations for cattle (§2.2) and the livestock-derived terms of address for humans (§3.1 and §3.2) will be analysed as titles rather than personal names.

Appellations for humans and cattle are centred on the appearance of livestock and are part of the knowledge system shared across pastoralists' lingua-cultures: the titles for Hamar men and for cattle, for example, are assigned according to rigid rules and are not decided arbitrarily by individual herders. The principles regulating the assignment of these titles are rooted in the descriptive system for cattle appearance: members of the Hamar society understand the cultural and pragmatic meanings of the titles because of their shared pastoral indigenous knowledge. The titles encapsulate speakers' attitudes and convey the specific status of the referent: the human titles referred to as "calf names" (§3.1), for example, individuate adult Hamar men who have been initiated in the presence of animals displaying specific colour-pattern configurations; livestock titles (§2.2) encapsulate the reference to the animals' physical traits and individuate parous female cows which are milked, draft oxen, or "favourite" animals, hence animals that play specific roles within Hamar culture and society. In some African societies (see Ameka 1991: 408), titles, praise names and other appellations are the most important categories of address; likewise, in many pastoralist societies the so called "calf names", "bull names" or "ox names" have a stronger pragmatic force than personal names.

2 Livestock-centered linguistic practices among the Hamar

Hamar culture has been thoroughly studied by the anthropologists Jean Lydall and Ivo Strecker, who have produced a rich corpus of academic literature and ethnographic documentaries on various aspects of Hamar culture and society (see for example Lydall and Strecker 1979a, 1979b, 1979c). Dubosson has worked on the phenomenon of the favourite animal among the Hamar and other pastoral societies and has written extensively on the social significance of the favourite animal (2013, 2014, 2016, 2018). Lydall has also written about aspects of the language (1976, 1988, 2002); for a descriptive grammar and linguistic work on Hamar see Petrollino (2016, 2019a, 2019b).

Lydall (1999) presented a paper on Hamar terms of address and illustrated some of their pragmatic functions, including the contexts in which "calf names" are used. Dubosson (2014) reports insightful information about Hamar favourite animal names, which will be discussed in the relevant sections below.

The Hamar data presented in this section were collected in the past few years in South-West Ethiopia by the author. The various titles for both cattle and humans, and their correspondence to the descriptive system for cattle appearance, were collected in different homesteads in order to check the consistency of the system across the Hamar society. Apart from some geographical variation, the core of the system as it is described in this paper seems to be shared across the Hamar society. This paper presents only part of the system, and many titles and appellations have been omitted.

In order to show the interconnectedness between the cattle descriptive system and livestock-centred naming practices, in the following section the Hamar descriptive terms for cattle are introduced (§2.1), followed by an account of livestock naming practices (§2.2). These two systems (cattle descriptive terms and cattle personal titles) are crucial to understanding how livestock-derived titles for Hamar men are assigned (§3).

2.1 The description of livestock appearance

Livestock appearance in Hamar (and in the languages of neighbouring pastoralist groups) is described in terms of four visual domains: coat (or phenotype[2]), horn shape, ear marks or cuts, and coat branding (tattoos). When describing an animal, a Hamar person refers first and foremost to the appearance of the coat. The terms used to describe the appearance of the animal's coat refer to the distribution of colour-pattern configurations on the body of the animal. These can be followed by a descriptor of the horns if these display a particular shape, or by a term describing special features of the tail, head, dewlap or legs.

The descriptors for coat appearance are nouns; as such they can be inflected for feminine or masculine gender, depending on the sex of the animal.

2 The coat phenotype refers to the animal's observable traits. There are overlapping descriptive systems for the phenotypes attested among cattle and among goats and sheep, with minimal differences, since some phenotypes are attested only in bovines and not in caprine or ovine species (and vice versa). The "calf names" discussed in §3.1 are derived from cattle appearance only, whereas the "favourite animal names" discussed in §3.2 can be derived from both bovine and caprine appearance.

Examples of descriptive expressions for cattle can be seen in (1) below.

(1) a. **deer labál**
red white.belly
'reddish with a white patch on the belly'

b. **t'itâ, qushumɓán-sa orgó**
blackish:M horn.F.OBL-GEN short
'blackish (ox), with short horns'

c. **bordí, alisɛ̂ taximɛ̂**
large.spots dewlap:M cut:M
'spotted, with a cut dewlap'

As illustrated in the examples above, these terms can be combined with each other as in (1a) in order to describe minimal variations in the colour-pattern configuration, or they can be combined with other descriptive terms referring to features of the head, tail, legs and dewlap (1c); the terms can also be accompanied by descriptors for horn shapes as in (1b).

The descriptors *deer, labál, t'iá* and *bordí* in the examples above individuate livestock according to coat pigmentation. These terms correspond to macro-categories for coat appearance, which are referred to as *dánta* in the Hamar language. The term *dánta* derives from the existential predicator *daa* (see Petrollino 2019b) and can be translated as 'way of being', both in the sense of 'appearance' and 'behaviour'.

The main macro-categories (*dánta*) for coat appearance are represented by 18 terms describing the variation in colour pigmentation, including sheen and (de)saturation, and the distribution, size and orientation of patterns on the animal's body. The term *labál* in (1a) above, for example, refers to a white underside patch that can extend to the flanks of the animal. A *deer labál* 'reddish with white underside patch' type of cattle (1a) belongs to the macro-category *labál*. Other "subtypes" of *labál* are *t'iá labál* 'blackish with white underside patch', *gal labál* 'yellowish with white underside patch' and so on, that is, types of coat appearance which combine the feature *labál* with other visual properties. For a coat to be described as such, the *labál* feature has to be visually predominant. The principles regulating the descriptive system for cattle appearance cannot be discussed here for lack of space, but the table below provides an overview of the most common terms defining the main macro-categories for appearance, accompanied by their glosses.

The 18 descriptors presented in the table above can be combined with each other into 152 expressions. Not all the logical combinations are possible: for example the inverse of *deer labál*, *labál deer* is not a grammatical expression and does not identify a cattle phenotype.

Table 2.1: Main categories for livestock appearance (*dánta*).

Term	Gloss
t'iá	blackish
c'aulí ~ c'ailí	whitish
deer	reddish
galáf	yellowish
guitá	iridescent
úlɔ	blueish
silbí	dark sheen
morá	desaturated
súra	pale grey
shamáj	roan
túrga	brindled
láala	colour sided
shɔ́ta	patched
bordí	large spots
zargí	small spots
labál	white belly
balá	forehead patch
gawá	bicolour pattern

The descriptive system for coat appearance described in this section will now be used to illustrate the connection with livestock naming practices: each *dánta* presented in Table 2.1 corresponds to a set of personal appellations for cattle (§2.2) and titles for humans (§3.1 and §3.2).

2.2 Cattle titles

The Hamar assign personal titles to a specific set of animals: parous female cows which are milked, draft oxen, and oxen which become the favourite animal of a herder. Several East African groups are known for naming cattle on the basis of their physical traits; the Turkana (Ohta 1986), the Maasai (Galaty 1989; Merker 1910), the Baggara (Reid 1930: 195), the Karimojong (Dyson-Hudson 1966: 96), (partly) the Iraqw (Huntingford 1953: 128; Rottland and Mous 2001: 380), the Datooga (Umesao 1966), the Gabra Oromo (Imai 1982) and possibly the Rendille and the Boraana (see Imai 1982) assign personal names to their livestock, and in some of these cultures livestock names are passed to the offspring along the matrilineal line. The Hamar naming system in this regard is special in that personal titles are assigned to both parous cows and draft oxen (or favourite oxen), regardless of the matrilineal line.

Cattle titles among the Hamar are used to call the animals when parous cows need to be paired with their calves at the end of the day, or to instruct the oxen on the direction to take while ploughing. Cattle titles are also used as praise names in cattle songs, when herders sing about their favourite animals; Dubosson (2014: 96) reports that herders whistle the names of their favourite animals in a specific way to call them.

Cattle titles are related to the cattle descriptive system discussed in the previous section: each macro-category of appearance (*dánta*) corresponds to a set of titles for female and male cattle.

An example of the correspondence between titles and appearance can be seen in Table 2.2 below: the titles that can be assigned to a parous female cow described for instance as *deer labál* will be *galtéʔ*, *labaléʔ*, or *kapél*; these titles are also assigned to other subtypes of *labál* (a few examples of subtypes are given under *labál*, preceded by a hyphen). Likewise, a ploughing ox described as *labál* will be assigned the titles *labbále* or *galtémbe*. These appellations are standard and are found across Hamar homesteads as titles for parous females, draft oxen and favourite oxen which fall under the *labál dánta*:

Table 2.2: Cattle titles for *labál* cattle.

dánta [gloss]	F cattle title	M cattle title
labál [white.belly]	galtéʔ; labaléʔ; kapél	labbále; galtémbe
- t'iá labál [blackish white.belly]		
- deer labál [reddish white.belly]		
- gal labál [yellowish white.belly]		
- silbí labál [dark.sheen white.belly]		

The majority of titles for parous female cows end in a glottal stop and/or carry a final accent, see Table 2.4 below. Sometimes the difference between titles for female and male cattle is only prosodic, as can be seen for the *shɔ́ta* cattle in Table 2.3:

Table 2.3: Cattle titles for *shɔ́ta* cattle.

dánta [gloss]	F cattle title	M cattle title
shɔ́ta [patched]	kolléʔ	kólleʔ
- t'iá shɔ́ta [blackish patched]		
- deer shɔ́ta [reddish patched]		
- c'ailí shɔ́ta [whitish patched]		
- galáf shɔ́ta [yellowish patched]		

Some of the ox titles, such as *galtémbe* in Table 2.2 or *garómbe* in Table 2.4 below, are morphologically derived from the titles for the female cows: the ox title *galtémbe* is thus derived from the parous cow title *galtéʔ*, *garómbe* from *garóʔ* and so on. These titles are identical to the teknonyms given to adult Hamar men and will be further analysed and explained in the coming section (§3).

In addition to cattle titles for female and male animals, a few *dánta* correspond to unisex titles that can be used for cattle of both genders. For example, cattle classified as *deer* can receive the title *déroʔ* regardless of the sex of the animal:

Table 2.4: Unisex cattle titles.

dánta [gloss]	F cattle titles	M cattle titles	Unisex title
deer [reddish]	ʔailó; sálleʔ; adaráʔ; béeziʔ; shardóʔ; nabír	díima; shardómbe; deerímbe	déroʔ
guitá [iridescent]	ɗilíp̓; gudán; láalaʔ	shálme; guitámbe	guíto
zargí [small.spots]	káiraʔ	kairámbe, wánc'o	atóle
gawá [bicolour.pattern]	garóʔ; tuljáʔ; gáuʔ	garómbe	luttéʔ
morá [desaturated]	digóʔ; bórkoʔ	mɔ́ra; digómbe	búle

Only a few cattle titles are morphologically derived from the descriptive terms for appearance. These are presented below; the titles follow the descriptive terms from which they are derived.

(2) a. deer (reddish) > déroʔ
b. guitá (iridescent) > guíto
c. silbí (dark sheen) > sílbo
d. shamáj (roan, fawn, beige) > shamóʔ

The titles *déroʔ* and *guíto* in (2a) and (2b) are unisex cattle appellations; *sílbo* in (2c) is a title for a male ox; *shamóʔ* in (2d) is a title for a female cow. These titles seem to follow the same pattern as some Hamar kinship terms (Petrollino 2016), which have a corresponding vocative form ending in *-o*: for example, *ímbo* is the vocative form of *imbá* 'father', *índo* of *indá* 'mother', *aakó* of *aaká* 'grandmother'.

In similar fashion, the Hamar masculine personal name *Túrgo*, used for people and not attested (so far) as a cattle title, could be a vocative form derived from the descriptive term for brindled cattle, *túrga*. It is worth mentioning that some cattle titles are sometimes attested as individuals' personal names: for example, the cattle title *Sílbo* in (2b) also exists as an individual's personal name, and *Káiraʔ* discussed below is a common personal name for a Hamar woman.

Some cattle titles correspond to terms referring to other animals or to natural objects displaying similar visual features; this is commonly reported in other studies on pastoralists' nomenclatures: descriptive terms for cattle appearance are often polysemic with terms referring to other animals, especially birds (see for example Evans-Pritchard 1940: 44–45, 1934; Lienhardt 1961: 12; Eczet 2019b; Ohta 1986: 40; Koopman 2019: 106–131; Oosthuizen 1996: 343–344; Poland et al. 2004: 34–79).[3] In the Hamar system, descriptive terms for cattle appearance are not polysemic and are not related to other terms.[4] Some cattle titles, however, can evoke their referential meaning through polysemy and point to visual features of cattle and other animals or natural objects. The cattle title *árka* for a *galáf* (yellowish) female cow also refers to the antelope species known as hartebeest. Likewise, the cattle appearance *zargí* (small spots) corresponds to the cattle title *Káira?* for a female cow, and *Wánc'o* for a male ox. These titles are polysemic with the terms *káira*, a type of lark displaying a spotted black and white pattern on the chest, and *wánc'o*, the star cluster known in Western astronomy as the Pleiades; see Figure 2.1 below:

3 Several authors have written about the rich colour analogies with other animals, and described them in terms of metaphorical processes. For example, Dinka cattle names were described in detail by Evans-Pritchard: "Their cattle are thus called by colour-analogy crocodile cow, fish eagle cow, leopard cow, and so on. The Dinka go even farther and make a double analogy in referring to their cattle by terms which suggest some activity associated with, or some attribute of, the creature that displays similar colouring to the cattle" (Evans-Pritchard 1934: 623); Fukui, among others, explained the link between cattle appearance and naming practices in terms of metaphorical extensions: "a girl who received a red (goloñi) morare [favorite ox] was named Lilinta (red dragonfly)" (Fukui 1979: 163); the metaphorical processes underlying Murle calf names were so elaborated that Arensen described them as riddles: "the boy takes a name based on the colour of his new calf. The name is a riddle based on the calf's colour" (Arensen 1988: 128).

4 Except for two terms: *labál* 'white belly' and *shamáj* 'roan, fawn, beige'. The first is related to the Hamar term for ostrich: *labalé*. The second, according to Lydall (1978: 577), derives from *sháami* 'sand'. The term could however be a borrowing from the cattle colour term *shimaji*, attested in neighbouring Surmic languages such as Bodi (see Fukui 1979).

Figure 2.1: (from left to right) *zargí* cattle coat (photograph by the author); a type of lark[5] called *káira;* the Pleiades[6], called *wánc'o.*

Some titles have been borrowed from other languages and a closer analysis can reveal the history of interethnic relations among East African pastoralists. The cattle title *gíto* for a male black (*t'iá*) ox, for example, is also attested in Datooga as a personal name for male black cattle (Umesao 1966: 184). The female cattle title *kapél* in Table 2.2 above is a borrowing from the Turkana descriptive term *-kapel(i)*, which refers to a type of coat pattern described as "small patches all over the body" (Wymeersch 1988: 130) or represented as a patched coat in Ohta's sketches (1986: 10); *-kapil-* is also reported for Nyangatom by Tornay (1973: 90). Further investigation descriptive terms borrowed from other cattle descriptive systems maintain their referential meaning to cattle appearance when they are adopted as terms of address in Hamar. Similar links can also be found among the Hamar "favourite animal names" described in section 3.2.

The system described in this section is the predominant naming practice for livestock. Other practices have also been observed and draft oxen and cows which are milked may be occasionally named after the people or place from which they have been acquired. Ohta (1986) reports similar naming practices among the Turkana: alongside the predominant naming system based on animals' physical traits, place names are also attested among the Turkana's cattle; Galaty (1989) also mentions "transaction names" for the Maasai; Iraqw cow names refer mostly to the way in which the animals were acquired and sometimes to the colour-pattern configuration (Rottland and Mous 2001).

5 Charles J. Sharp, CC BY-SA 4.0, via Wikimedia Commons, https://commons.wikimedia.org/wiki/File:Flappet_lark_(Mirafra_rufocinnamomea_kawirondensis).jpg

6 Juan lacruz, CC BY-SA 4.0, via Wikimedia Commons, https://commons.wikimedia.org/wiki/File:Pleiades_1.jpg

3 Personal names and titles for humans

Hamar naming practices consist of a plurality of terms of address: individuals receive various names, appellations and titles at different stages of their lives. Each term of address, to use Strecker's words, signifies "some specific aspect of their *persona*" (Strecker 1993: 126), constructing different social identities. Terms of address have various ethno-pragmatic interpretations and meanings. Lydall provided an overview of Hamar terms of address (1999) including the social and pragmatic norms regulating the use of some of them: husband and wife, for example, avoid calling each other by their birth names, and youngsters cannot address older people by their birth names.

A few weeks after birth, every individual receives a personal name, or *gáli náabi.*[7] *Gáli* refers to the name giving ritual and the plant used during the ritual (Lydall 1999; Lydall and Strecker 1979a: 33), whereas *náabi* can be translated as 'name' or 'appellation'.

Teknonyms characterise the addressee as a parent and are derived from the name of the first child. Like in other African languages, matronymics are formed from the name of the first child followed by the kinship term *indá* 'mother': thus, a matronymic such as *Bazónda* means 'mother of Bazo', *Barqínda* 'mother of Barqi' and so on. Likewise, patronymics are formed from the kinship term *imbá* 'father, owner': *Dambaitímba* translates as 'father of Dambaiti'.[8] As pointed out by Lydall (1999), these teknonyms are used in reported speech, or when referring to a person in absentia; the corresponding vocative form ending in *-e* is used instead when directly addressing a person by his or her teknonym. Thus, a woman known as *Barqínda* will be addressed as *Barqínde*, and so on.

In addition to personal names and teknonyms, Hamar men receive special titles such as the calf names (§3.1) and the "favourite animal names" (§3.2); these honorific titles are designated for people with a specific status and are given in the context of ritualised events.

Alongside the names and titles mentioned in this section, age-mates and hunting friends use nicknames recalling shared events and situations, and these may be used among friends as affectionate mockery. "Killer names" (Lydall 1999) are praise

7 Common Hamar personal names include circumstance names motivated by the event, period or place in which a child is born (*Goití* 'way', *Kánki* 'car', *Kerí* 'door', *Baqála* 'sprout', *Bɔ́na* 'drought'); animal derived names (*Walé* 'dove'); objects (*Álfa* 'knife'); name-sakes derived from neighbouring ethnic groups (*Áari*); placenames (*Turmi*); "number names"(Collard 1973) such as *Kála* 'one, first', *Óito* 'fourth', etc.

8 Jean Lydall and Ivo Strecker are known in the Hamar community as *Theoínda* and *Theoímba* respectively, after their first son's name.

appellations which were given in the past to somebody who had killed an enemy from a neighbouring group.

The next two sections are devoted to the description of Hamar calf names and favourite animal names. Among the Hamar, women do not receive calf names or favourite animal names, whereas in other groups such as the Mursi (Eczet 2013, 2018), the Bodi (Fukui 1979) and the Nuer (Evans-Pritchard 1964, 1937: 213), women receive cattle-derived titles at different stages of their life.

3.1 Calf names: *gaar náabino*

Calf names, or *gaar náabino* in the Hamar language,[9] are status titles which are given to Hamar men after the rite of passage into adulthood. During the ritual an initiated boy leaps over a row of cattle; the first cow of the row is a heifer calf referred to as *garró*[10]. The *garró* calf is carefully chosen because the colour-pattern configuration of her coat (i.e. the *dánta*; see §2.1) will determine the title given to the Hamar man once the ritual is over (see Lydall and Strecker 1979; Lydall 1999).

Within the Hamar system of address terms, calf names are status titles and their use is regulated by awareness addressee’s status within Hamar society. These titles are used to address Hamar men respectfully in large social contexts: a man can be addressed by his calf name by men of the same age-set (Lydall 1999); or a woman can address her firstborn by his calf name. The difference between calf names and favourite animal names, according to Dubosson (2014: 97), is that age-mates address each other by favourite animal names, whereas women should use the calf name when addressing adult Hamar men.

As mentioned earlier, a calf name is a teknonymic title: the calf name *Bordímba*, for example, is formed by the descriptive term *bordí* ‘large spots’ plus the kin term *imbá* ‘father, owner’, and it roughly translates as ‘father of the spotted cow’.[11] In principle, the title *Bordímba* is given to adult Hamar men who have leapt over a *bordí* calf (including the subtypes of *bordí*, for example *silbí bordí, t’iá bordí*, etc.); however the various *dánta* illustrated in §2.1 above may correspond to more than one calf name (see §3.1.1).

---

9 The form *náabino* is the feminine collective form of *náabi*.

10 As suggested by Lydall (1999), the terms *garró* and *gaar* are related and they translate as ‘grown up’. To be more specific, *gáar(i)* is the general form of a noun that means ‘big, grown up’ and *garró* can be analysed as the feminine inflected form (probably due to the fact that it refers to a female animal).

11 Livestock-derived titles for humans are usually teknonyms and translate as ‘father of’ in Dhaasanac (Almagor 1972: 87) and Turkana (Ohta 1986: 52). Ik (Schrock 2014: 193) has borrowed ox names from Teso-Turkana: for example, *Apá Lokiryon* translates as ‘father of the black bull’; the same can be said for Karimojong (Gourlay 1972: 245).

The association of calf names with the categories of cattle appearance can be self-evident, as illustrated by the example of *Bordímba.* Table 2.5 below shows the calf names which are derived from the corresponding descriptive terms for appearance:

Table 2.5: Calf names derived from descriptive terms for appearance.

dánta [gloss]	Calf name (gaar náabi)
deer [reddish]	Deerímba
c'ailí [whitish]	C'ailímba
guitá [iridescent]	Guitámba
súra [grey.pale]	Surámba
bordí [large.spots]	Bordímba

For other calf names, the link to the appearance of the calf can be understood by looking at the three systems (the cattle descriptive system, cattle titles and calf names) as a whole. A set of calf names, for example, is derived from one of the cattle titles designated for female cows. When a calf name is derived from one of the feminine cattle titles, the corresponding masculine cattle titles are identical to the teknonymic calf names (this was already pointed out above in §2.2). Table 2.6 provides an overview of these correspondences; titles for oxen are reported with the vocative form ending in *-e*:

Table 2.6: Calf names derived from feminine cattle titles. Calf names for humans derived from feminine cattle titles.

dánta [gloss]	F cattle title	M cattle title	Calf name for humans (gaar náabi)
balá [forehead.patch]	Annóʔ	Annómbe	Annómba
deer [reddish]	Shardóʔ	Shardómbe; Deerímbe	Shardómba
t'iá [blackish]	Qallóʔ	Qallómbe	Qallómba
silbí [dark.sheen]	Baldáʔ	Baldámbe	Baldámba
galáf [yellowish]	Laalóʔ	Laalómbe	Láalomba
zargí [small.spots]	Káiraʔ	Kairámbe	Kairámba
gawá [bicolour.pattern]	Garóʔ	Garómbe	Garómba
morá [desaturated]	Digóʔ	Digómbe	Digómba
labál [white.belly]	Galtéʔ	Galtémbe	Galtémba

A calf name such as *Annómba* thus translates as 'father of *Annóʔ*', but given the referential meaning of the cattle title *Annóʔ* and its connection to the cattle descriptive system, members of the Hamar society understand the meaning of the calf name *Annómba* and its reference to the *balá* type of appearance.

For other calf names, reference to cattle appearance is evoked through analogy. The calf name *Qaarímba*, for example, is composed of the term *qáari* 'python', given the association with the appearance *túrga* 'brindled, striped', which also describes the skin of the python. Likewise, the calf name *Shaalómba* was explained to me with reference to *sháalo*, the disease term for measles. *Shaalómba* is the calf name primarily associated with *shamáj*, a descriptive term which refers to a mixture of colours and is here roughly translated as 'roan, fawn, beige': the visual effect of measles on the skin of an affected person is described as *shamáj*; *shamáj* also describes the appearance (and the lumpy texture) of the traditional ale-gruel alcoholic drink *parsí*; an alternative name of the drink is *shamajâ*, 'the *shamáj* one'.

Other calf names were further analysed but the analogy with visual features could not be clearly established: the calf name *Silémba*, for example, refers to a *c'ailí* 'whitish' coat and could be derived from the term *silé* 'feather', but its link to a white appearance cannot be explained.

3.1.1 Name avoidance rule and alternative calf names

In the previous section it was mentioned that some categories of cattle appearance are associated with more than one calf name; to be more precise, a *dánta* usually corresponds to two or three calf names, one of which is considered the primary choice. Alternative options to primary calf names are necessary for cultural reasons, but also to account for minimal variations attested in coat pigmentation.

The appearance of the animals' coats is conceptualised as a continuum in which categories of appearance can have fuzzy borders: the appearance of a specific animal, thus, can be close to what is considered a prototypical example of a *dánta*, or it can diverge considerably and be considered closer to a contiguous category of appearance. When the coat of a specific animal is considered to be a good example of a category of appearance, the association will be with the primary calf name (indicated as calf name 1 in Table 2.7 and Table 2.8 below). However, if a type of appearance diverges from the prototypical pigmentation, an alternative calf name can be chosen that better conveys the visual differences of a specific animal's coat. In other words, calf names can accommodate to the actual visual continuum of animal appearance. In the case of spotted cattle, for example, the calf name assigned to a man can in principle indicates whether the types of spots are more similar to the category *bordí* 'large spots' or *zargí* 'small spots'. The choice of an alternative calf name is also dictated by strict cultural rules: within one family, the same calf name is avoided; thus brothers, or a father and his sons, cannot carry the same title. Despite the variety of coat phenotypes in Hamar herds, it can happen that the heifer calf chosen for the rite of passage falls into the same category as the cattle coat that determined the title of the boy's father or brothers. Let's take, as a fictional example, a man called *C'ailímba* after a *c'ailí* (whitish) cattle coat; if the son of *C'ailímba* leaps over a heifer calf which also classifies as *c'ailí*, the calf name *C'ailímba* will not be selected, and an alternative will be chosen. Usually, for each *dánta*, one or two optional calf names exist along with the primary calf name. The son of *C'ailímba* will receive the alternative title *Silémba* as illustrated in Table 2.7 below:

Table 2.7: Examples of alternative calf-names for *c'ailí*.

dánta [gloss]	Calf name 1 (gaar náabi)	Calf name 2	Calf name 3
c'ailí [whitish]	C'ailímba	Silémba	Annómba

The choice of an alternative name may be determined by the visual features on the coat of a specific calf: this aspect is very interesting because by looking at the choice of calf names with respect to the appearance of the calf, one can understand better the meaning of the categories of appearance and the similarities between contiguous categories; this will be further illustrated with 'spotted cattle', 'dark-blackish cattle' and other examples below.

The primary calf name associated with the category *zargí* 'small spots' is *Kairámba* (Table 2.8, third row), but depending on the name avoidance rule, and on the actual size of the spots on the animal's coat, the alternative title *Bordímba* could be used *Bordímba* (see the dashed arrow in Table 2.8) is the primary calf name associated with *bordí*, which is just another type of "spotted" appearance: the difference between the two is in the size (and distribution) of the spots on the animal's coat.

Table 2.8: Examples of alternative calf names. Examples of alternative calf names and their relation with animal's appearance.

dánta [gloss]	Calf name 1 (gaar náabi)	Calf name 2 (gaar náabi)
bordí [large spots]	Bordímba	Burrémba
– guitá bordí	Bordímba	Guitámba
zargí [small.spots]	Kairámba	Bordímba
guitá [iridescent]	Guitámba	Shaalómba
t'iá [blackish]	Qallómba	Baldámba
silbí [dark.sheen]	Baldámba	Qallómba

A similar example can be given for cattle described as *t'iá* (blackish) and *silbí* (dark sheen): *silbí* cattle can have sleek pigmentation and very dark coats, and display a mixture of blackish and reddish pigmentation (Figure 2.2, picture on the right). Similarly, *t'iá* cattle display a sleek, black coat (Figure 2.2, picture on the left):

Figure 2.2: (left) *t'iá* cattle coat; (right) *silbí* cattle coat, photographs by the author.

The visual difference between a coat described as *t'iá* and a coat described as *silbí* can in some instances be minimal, as illustrated in Figure 2.2, and the two categories *t'iá* and *silbí* are contiguous in the Hamar visual system.

Given this similarity, the primary calf name corresponding to a *silbí* cattle coat, *Baldámba,* can be used as the alternative calf name for a *t'iá* cattle coat, and vice versa; if the *silbí* coat displays a predominantly black pigmentation resembling more a *t'iá dánta,* it will be associated with the primary calf name for *t'iá*, *Qallómba* (see the black arrow in Table 2.8).

Another example illustrating the flexibility of the calf name system with respect to the actual appearance of the animal shows that in extreme cases a re-classification into another category of appearance is also possible. The coat *guitá bordí*, for example, belongs to the *bordí dánta* and is normally associated with the corresponding calf name *Bordímba* (Table 2.8, second row). If the calf name *Bordímba* has to be avoided, or if the visual feature *guitá* 'iridescent' is more visually predominant then the spots, the feature *guitá* will be looked at in order to determine the calf name, which will be *Guitámba* (see the blue arrow in Table 2.8).

Calf names can provide useful information about minimal variations in pattern configurations. The category for appearance referred to as *shɔ́ta* 'patched', for example, can describe patched coats, but also coats which fall between the appearance *túrga* 'brindled' and *bordí* 'large spots'. Depending on the orientation, size and shape of the patches with respect to the pigmentation of the coat, a *shɔ́ta* type of coat could be visually closer to either a *bordí* coat or a *túrga* coat. When choosing the calf name corresponding to a *shɔ́ta* calf, Hamar herders carefully observe the details of the coat, and in consultation decide whether the calf name associated with that specific animal should be *Bordímba* (after a *bordí pattern*) or *Qaarímba* (after a *túrga type of pattern*). Calf names are essential organising principles of the descriptive system for cattle appearance because they provide additional information about the physical appearance of the animal linked to a person's title. This is supported also by the fact that in explaining the meanings of the descriptive terms for cattle appearance, the Hamar people interviewed for this study often referred to the related calf names and explained the core meaning and referential range of the terms with the help of related calf names.

3.2 Favourite animal names: *qóle náabino*

Favourite animal names are referred to as *qóle náabino*. The term *qóle* refers to bovine, caprine and ovine livestock animals; these appellations are titles given to Hamar men by their age-mates, after a chosen favourite animal; this is usually a castrated ox or a castrated goat. The favourite ox undergoes a process of beautification which includes the training of the horns, ear cuts, branding, the incision of the dewlap, and a collar with a decorative bell (see Dubosson 2014 for a detailed description of the beautification ritual and the social signification of the favourite animal). A man is addressed by his *qóle náabi* in salutations, by his age-mates and members of the society who have taken part in the rituals connected to the beautification of the favourite animal, and by people with whom he has established confidence and intimacy.

Like cattle personal titles and calf names, each *qóle náabi* is linked to the appearance of the animal, in this case that of the favourite ox or goat. A few examples of *qóle náabi* can be seen in Table 2.9 below (a tilde ~ indicates inter- and intra-speaker variation, a semicolon indicates alternative titles):

Table 2.9: Examples of favourite animal titles.

dánta [gloss]	Favourite animal title (qóle náabino)
t'iá [blackish]	lukúrjɔi ~ lukúljɔi; lukurúʔ ~ lokurúk; lusikirjóno ~ lusikirjá
shamáj [roan]	lukuburáqo ~ lukuburráqo; ʄilabuíz; maccarɲáŋ
guitá [iridescent]	nabuíz; logíle; ɲakupurrát˺ ~ ɲakufurrát˺; logɔrráx̧
galáf [yellowish]	lɔɲabuá; lekkérz; lotiabuló; lokkemɛ́r
balá [forehead.patch]	naŋɔlɛamɔ́i; naŋɔlɛarúk
bordí [large.spots]	lusilbúq˺; korbók; lobokotɔ́la

The non-Hamar syllable structure and consonant clusters found in the favourite animal titles, together with the inter- and intraspeaker variation attested in the pronunciation indicate that these titles are not native to Hamar. According to Hamar elders, the titles have been adopted from the cattle descriptive systems and livestock-centred systems of address of neighbouring pastoralist groups, especially Nyangatom and Dhaasanac. This is confirmed also by Tornay (1981: 168), among others. A complete analysis of these titles cannot be presented here for lack of complete data about Dhaasanac and Nyangatom livestock-centred systems of address; however, it is worth mentioning that several titles display typical Teso-Turkana elements such as the masculine and feminine prefixes *lo-* and *na-*, and descriptive terms for cattle appearance such as *bok* 'pale reddish purple', *ɲaŋ* 'yellow-orange' and more. The titles *lokurúk* 'blackish', *nabuíz* 'iridescent', and *lekkérz* 'yellowish' in Table 2.9 above were also collected among the Dhaasanac with the same referential meaning.

The meaning of some of the titles corresponds to the meaning of the Teso-Turkana descriptive terms for cattle appearance; the association with a specific category for appearance has thus been correctly borrowed. The title associated with a black ox, *lusikirjóno* (Table 2.9), can be traced back to the Nyangatom colour term *-kiryon* for black cattle (Tornay 1973), attested also in the Ateso cattle colour term *lòkàkírjônón* 'the black one' (Barasa 2017: 78). In other cases, the association with cattle appearance and the semantic correspondence between the borrowed titles and descriptive terms in their original context is not always clear: the title *ɲakupurrát*, for example, corresponds to a blue roan coat with iridescent appearance called *guitá* in the Hamar system (Table 2.9). The title *ɲakupurrát*, however, includes the Teso-Turkana element *-kopurat* (Nyangatom) or *-kipʊra(t)* (Turkana), which is translated as 'pink' by Tornay (1973) and Dimmendaal (2015, after Barrett 1988).

Similar to calf names, favourite animal names can be derived from a corresponding cattle title: the title *naŋɔlɛamɔ́i*, corresponding to the *balá* appearance type in Table 2.9, is related to the cattle title assigned to a *balá* female cow, namely *naŋgulé?* (see the full correspondence in Table 2.10 below).

The list presented in Table 2.9 above is not exhaustive and does not show all the titles associated with the respective categories for appearance. Compared to the pool of *gaar náabino*, or calf names, the choice of a *qóle náabi* is made from among a much larger variety of titles.

Given the foreign origin of this naming practice, the relationship between titles and cattle appearance has to be memorised, and the system relies heavily on collective knowledge: the Hamar *qóle náabino* were in fact more easily collected in group discussions during which participants recalled a past history of multilingualism and contact with other pastoralist groups.[12]

4 Conclusions

The Hamar livestock-centred system of address and the descriptive system for cattle appearances have been juxtaposed and analysed to show their interconnectedness (see Table 2.10 below for an overview). The relationship between the system of address and the descriptive terms for cattle appearance has been mentioned in the anthropological and ethnographic literature; however, apart from Ohta (1986), detailed linguistic analyses are rare. We know from Evans-Pritchard's description of Nuer modes of address, for example, that "from its colors, distribution of markings, shape of horns, and other pecularities, he takes his *cot thak*, ox-name" (Evans-Pritchard 1964: 222) and for Hamar the literature reports that calf names are *derived* from the appearance of the *garró* calf (Lydall 1999; Dubosson 2014). This paper has tried to shed some light on the exact mechanisms by which titles and appellations are derived from the descriptive system for animal appearance. The relationship between terms of address for both humans and cattle and the descriptive system for cattle appearance has been analysed, and some of the processes that keep the systems connected have been explained: cattle titles and titles for humans are interconnected via the descriptive terms for cattle appearance, and meaningful associations are established through morphological processes, polysemy and analogy. This analysis has shown that in order to use and understand the livestock-centred systems of address, knowledge of the cattle descriptive system is necessary, and vice versa, titles (particularly calf names) are used as referential devices which can convey additional information about cattle appearance. These linguistic devices represent only part of a vast and fascinating knowledge system, whose intricacies and complexities are still far from being fully understood.

12 This resembles the case of Murle ox names, which have been borrowed from the Toposa language; Arensen (1988: 128–129) wrote about Murle ox names that "the words used are from the Toposa language so that most people do not know the components of the word and even less its true meaning".

Table 2.10: Examples of correspondences between cattle appearance and systems of address.

dánta [gloss]	Cattle titles (F, M, Unisex)	Calf names (1, 2, 3)	Favourite animal names
balá [forehead. patch]	F: annóʔ; pánəs; naŋuléʔ M: ʔárbo; wóle; annómbe	1: Annómba 2: Silémba	naŋɔlɛamɔ́i; naŋɔlɛarúk
gawá [bicolour.pattern]	F: garóʔ; tuljáʔ; gáuʔ M: garómbe Unisex: luttéʔ	1: Garómba 2: depends on combined colour	lutiʎabóʔ ~ lutiʎaɓóʔ ~ luciʎabóq˺~ luciljabóq; lutiljá ~ lutiljamɔ́i; loliɲabóq˺
deer [reddish]	F: ʔailóʔ; sálleʔ; adaráʔ; béeziʔ; shardóʔ;nabír; M: díima; shardómbe; deerímbe Unisex: déroʔ	1: Shardómba 2: Deerímba	lɔriáxɔ; loɲabə́r; lokopə́r ~ lokobə́r
galáf [yellowish]	F: laalóʔ; árka; nawíʔ; M: laalómbe	1: Burrémba 2: Laalómba	lɔɲabuá; lekkérz; lotiabuló; lokkemér

References

Abbink, Jon. 2003. Love and death of cattle: The paradox in suri attitudes toward livestock. *Ethnos* 68 (3). 341–364. https://doi.org/10.1080/0014184032000134487.

Almagor, Uri. 1972. Name-oxen and ox-names among the Dassanetch of southwest Ethiopia. *Paideuma* 18. 79–96.

Almagor, Uri. 1983. Colours that match and clash: An explication of meaning in a pastoral society. *RES: Anthropology and Aesthetics* 5. 49–73.

Ameka, Felix K. 1991. *Ewe: Its grammatical constructions and illocutionary devices*. Canberra: Australian National University PhD dissertation.

Arensen, Jon. 1988. Names in the life cycles of the Murle. *Journal of the Anthropological Society of Oxford* 19 (2). 125–130.

Arensen, Jonathan E. 1992. *Mice are men: Language and society among the Murle of Sudan*. Dallas, Texas: International Museum of Cultures.

Barasa, David. 2017. *Ateso grammar : A descriptive account of an Eastern Nilotic Language*. München : Lincom GmbH.

Barrett, Anthony. 1988. *English-Turkana dictionary*. Nairobi, Hong Kong: Macmillan Kenya.

Collard, Chantal. 1973. Les "Noms-Numéros" chez les Guidar." *Homme* 13 (3). 45–59. https://doi.org/10.3406/hom.1973.367358.

Dimmendaal, Gerrit J. 1983. *The Turkana language*. Dordrecht [etc.]: Foris.

Dimmendaal, Gerrit Jan. 2015. *The leopard's spots: Essays on language, cognition, and culture*. Brill's Studies in Language, Cognition and Culture 11. Leiden, Boston: Brill.

Dubosson, Jérôme. 2013. Esthétique et symbolique du bétail dans l'art rupestre: L'apport de l'anthropologie. *Les Cahiers de l'AARS* 16. 81–92.

Dubosson, Jérôme. 2014. Human 'self' and animal 'other'. The favourite animal among the Hamar. In Felix Girke (ed.), *Ethiopian images of self and other*, 83–104. Wittenberg: Halle an der Saale.
Dubosson, Jérôme. 2016. *Le bétail et sa représentation chez les pasteurs de l'Afrique du nord et de l'est. Une approche ethnoarchéologique*. Neuchâtel: Université de Neuchâtel.
Dubosson, Jérôme. 2018. The Hamar: Living by, for and with the cattle. In Timothy Clack & Marcus Brittain (eds.), *The river: Peoples and histories of the Omo-Turkana area*, 125–132. Oxford: Archaeopress Publishing Ltd.
Dyson-Hudson, Neville. 1966. *Karimojong politics*. Oxford: Clarendon Press.
Eczet, Jean-Baptiste. 2013. *Humains et bovins en pays Mursi (Éthiopie). Registres sensibles et processus de socialité.* Paris: École pratique des Hautes Études.
Eczet, Jean-Baptiste. 2018. Colours, metaphors and persons. In Timothy Clack & Marcus Brittain (eds.), *The river: Peoples and histories of the Omo-Turkana area*. Oxford: Archaeopress Publishing Ltd.
Eczet, Jean-Baptiste. 2019a. *Amour vache. Esthétique sociale en pays Mursi (Éthiopie).* Ethnologiques. Mimésis. *L'Homme*, (1), 161–163.
Eczet, Jean-Baptiste. 2019b. Ceci n'est pas une couleur. *L'Homme* 230 (2). 117–132.
Evans-Pritchard, E. E. 1934. Imagery in Ngök Dinka cattle-names. *Bulletin of the School of Oriental and African Studies* 7 (3). 623–628. https://doi.org/10.1017/S0041977X00138340.
Evans-Pritchard, E. E. 1937. Economic life of the Nuer. *Sudan Notes and Records* 20 (2). 209–245.
Evans-Pritchard, E. E. 1940. *The Nuer: A description of the modes of livelihood and political institutions of a Nilotic people*. Oxford: Clarendon Press.
Evans-Pritchard, E. E. 1964. Nuer modes of address. In Dell Hymes (ed.), *Language in culture and society*, 221–227. New York: Harper & Row.
Fukui, Katsuyoshi. 1979. Cattle colour symbolism and inter-tribal homicide among the Bodi. In Katsuyoshi Fukui & David Turton (eds.), *Warfare among East African herders*, 147–177. Osaka: Senri Ethnological Studies 3.
Fukui, Katsuyoshi. 1986. The cognition of nature through colours and patterns: From cases of the Narim in Southern Sudan. In Morimichi Tomikawa (ed.), *Sudan Sahel Studies: Vol. II*, 207–235. Tokyo: Institute for the Study of Languages and Cultures of Asia and Africa (ILCAA).
Fukui, Katsuyoshi. 1996. Co-evolution between humans and domesticates: The cultural selection of animal coat-colour diversity among the Bodi. In Ellen Roy & Katsuyoshi Fukui (eds.), *Redefining nature: Ecology, culture and domestication*, 319–85. Oxford: Berg.
Galaty, John G. 1989. Cattle and cognition: Aspects of Maasai practical reasoning. In Juliet Clutton-Brock (ed.), *The walking larder: Patterns of domestication, pastoralism, and predation*, 214–230. Southampton: World Archaeological Congress.
Gourlay, K. A. 1972. The ox and identification. *Man* 7 (2). 244–254. https://doi.org/10.2307/2799727.
Gulliver, P.H. 1952. Bell-oxen and ox names among the Jie. *Uganda Journal* 16. 72–75.
Hazel, Robert. 1997. Robes colorées et cornes déformées: Les pasteurs est-africains et leurs boeufs de parade. *Anthropologie et Sociétés* 21 (2–3). 67–85. https://doi.org/10.7202/015485ar.
Herskovits, Melville J. 1926. The cattle complex in East Africa. *American Anthropologist* 28 (1). 230–272.
Houtteman, Yvan. 2010. Murder as a marker of ethnicity. Ideas and practices concerning homicide among the Daasanech. In Echi Christina Gabbert & Sophia Thubauville (eds.), *To live with others. Essays on cultural neighborhood in Southern Ethiopia*,128–156. Köln: Rüdiger Köppe Verlag.
Huntingford, George Wynn Brereton. 1953. *The Southern Nilo-Hamites*. Vol. 8. Ethnographic Survey of Africa, East Central Africa. London: Oxford University Press for the International African Institute (IAI).
Imai, Ichiro. 1982. Small stock management and the goat naming system of the pastoral Gabra. *African Study Monographs* Supplementary Issue (1). 43–62.

Koopman, Adrian. 2019. *Zulu bird names and bird lore*. Pietermaritzburg: University of KwaZulu Natal Press.

Lienhardt, Godfrey. 1961. *Divinity and experience: The religion of the Dinka*. London: Oxford University Press.

Lienhardt, Godfrey. 1988. Social and cultural implications of some African personal names. *Journal of the Anthropological Society of Oxford* 19 (2). 105–116.

Lydall, Jean. 1976. Hamer. In M. Lionel Bender (ed.), *The non-Semitic languages of Ethiopia*, 393–438. Committee on Ethiopian Studies: Occasional Papers Series. East Lansing, Michigan: African Studies Center, Michigan State University.

Lydall, Jean. 1978. Le symbolisme de couleurs dans le rituel Hamar. In Serge Tornay (ed.), *Voir et nommer le couleurs*, 553–580. Nanterre: Laboratoire d'ethnologie et de sociologie comparative.

Lydall, Jean. 1988. Gender, number, and size in Hamar. In *Cushitic-Omotic: Papers from the International Symposium on Cushitic and Omotic Languages, Cologne, January 6–9, 1986*, 75.

Lydall, Jean. 1999. *The appealing use of terms of address among the Hamar in Southern Ethiopia.* Paper Presented at the Seminar: Social Interaction and Language Use in Africa. Leiden: African Studies Centre, Leiden University.

Lydall, Jean. 2002. Having fun with ideophones: A socio-linguistic look at ideophones in Hamar, Southern Ethiopia. In Yimam Baye et. al (eds.), *Ethiopian studies at the end of the second millennium: Proceedings of the 14th International Conference of Ethiopian Studies, November 6–11, 2000, Addis Ababa*, vol. 2, 886–911. Addis Ababa: Inst. of Ethiopian Studies, Addis Ababa University.

Lydall, Jean & Ivo Strecker. 1979a. *The Hamar of Southern Ethiopia (I), Work Journal.* Arbeiten Aus Dem Institut Für Völkerkunde Der Universität Zu Göttingen. Klaus Renner Verlag.

Lydall, Jean & Ivo Strecker. 1979b. *The Hamar of Southern Ethiopia (II), Baldambe explains*. Arbeiten Aus Dem Institut Für Völkerkunde Der Universität Zu Göttingen. Klaus Renner Verlag.

Lydall, Jean & Ivo Strecker. 1979c. *The Hamar of Southern Ethiopia (III), Conversations in Dambaiti*. Arbeiten Aus Dem Institut Für Völkerkunde Der Universität Zu Göttingen. Klaus Renner Verlag.

Martin, Amy. 2018. *The phonology, morphology and semantics of Shilluk cattle nouns.* Edinburgh: University of Edinburgh Master's dissertation. https://era.ed.ac.uk/handle/1842/37654.

Merker, M. 1910. *Die Masai: Ethnographische Monographie eines ostafrikanischen Semitenvolkes*. Berlin: Verlag von Dietrich Reimer (Ernst Vohsen).

Ohta, Itaru. 1986. Livestock individual identification among the Turkana: The animal classification and naming in the pastoral livestock management. *African Study Monographs* 8 (1). 1–69.

Oosthuizen, Marguerite Poland. 1996. *Uchibidolo: The abundant herds. A descriptive study of the Sanga-Nguni cattle of the Zulu people, with special reference to colour-pattern terminology and naming-practice.* Pietermaritzburg/Durban: Universty of Natal PhD dissertation. http://hdl.handle.net/10413/8490.

Petrollino, Sara. 2016. *A grammar of Hamar, a South Omotic language of Ethiopia*. Vol. 6. Cushitic and Omotic Studies. Köln: Rüdiger Köppe.

Petrollino, Sara. 2019a. Between tone and stress in Hamar. In Emily Clem, Peter Jenks & Hannah Sande (eds.), *Theory and description in African linguistics*, 287–302. Berlin: Language Science Press. https://doi.org/10.5281/zenodo.3367150.

Petrollino, Sara. 2019b. Existential predication in Hamar. *Nordic Journal of African Studies* 28 (4). https://njas.fi/njas/article/view/335.

Poland, Marguerite, David Hammond-Tooke & Leigh Voigt. 2004. *The abundant Herds: A celebration of the cattle of the Zulu people*. Fernwood: Vlaeberg.

Reid, J. A. 1930. "Some notes on the tribes of the White Nile Province." *Sudan Notes and Records* 13 (2). 149–209.

Rottland, Franz & Maarten Mous. 2001. Datooga and Iraqw: A comparison of subsistence vocabulary. In Dymitr Ibriszimow, Rudolf Leger & Uwe Seibert (eds.), *Von Ägypten Zum Tschadsee: Eine Linguistische Reise Durch Afrika: Festschrift Für Herrmann Junraithmayr Zum 65 Geburtstag*, 377–400. Heidelberg & Würzburg: Deutsche Morgenländische Gesellschaft.

Schrock, T.B. 2014. *A Grammar of Ik (Icé-Tód): Northeast Uganda's last thriving Kuliak language*. Utrecht: LOT-Netherlands Graduate School of Linguistics, Utrecht.

Seligman, Charles Gabriel & Salaman Brenda Zara Seligman. 1965. *Pagan tribes of the Nilotic Sudan*. London: Routledge & Kegan Paul.

Storch, Anne. 2005. *The noun morphology of Western Nilotic. Nilo-Saharan. Linguistic Analyses and Documentation 21*. Köln: Köppe.

Strecker, Ivo. 1993. Cultural variations in the concept of 'face.' *Multilingua – Journal of Cross-Cultural and Interlanguage Communication* 12 (2). 119–142. https://doi.org/10.1515/mult.1993.12.2.119.

Tornay, Serge. 1973. Langage et perception. La dénomination des couleurs chez les Nyangatom du Sud-Ouest éthiopien. *Homme* 13 (4). 66–94. https://doi.org/10.3406/hom.1973.367381.

Tornay, Serge. 1981. The Nyangatom: An outline of their ecology and social organization. In Lionel M. Bender (ed.), *Peoples and cultures of the Ethio-Sudan Borderlands*, 137–178. East Lansing, Michigan: African Studies Center, Michigan State University.

Tosco, Mauro. 2001. *The Dhaasanac language: Grammar, texts and vocabulary of a Cushitic language of Ethiopia*. Köln: Rüdiger Köppe.

Turton, David. 1978. La categorisation de la couleur en Mursi (Ethiopie). In Serge Tornay (ed.), *Voir et nommer les coulerus*, 347–368. Nanterre: Laboratoire d'ethnologie et de sociologie comparative.

Turton, David. 1980. There's no such beast: Cattle and colour naming among the Mursi. *Man* 15 (2). 320–338. https://doi.org/10.2307/2801674.

Umesao, Tadao. 1966. Families and herds of Datoga Pastoral Society: An analysis of the cattle system. *Kyoto University African Studies* 1. 173–206.

Wolde Gossa Tadesse. 1999. *Warfare and fertility: A study of the Hor (Arbore) of Southern Ethiopia.* London: London School of Economics and Political Science, University of London PhD dissertation.

Wymeersch, Patrick. 1988. Turkana cattle classification: Some preliminary notes. *Afrikanistische Arbeitspapiere* 16. 123.

Angella Meinerzag

Chapter 3
The shell and the essence: Name transfer among the Hinihon

Abstract: The investigation of the naming system of the Hinihon in Papua New Guinea and its analysis help to understand some central aspects of Hinihon culture. Their strong avoidance of pronouncing personal names, the use of birth-ordinal names instead, and the question "Why do usually not more than two living people carry the same name?", are key phenomena for analysis. The personal names always contain four pieces of information: which clan a person belongs to, the relevant birth-ordinal name, the person's gender and features within the landscape. The clans own a set of names that the members pass on from generation to generation. The name is directly transferred from name giver to receiver. Once the name givers bestow their names, they become empty and are merely shells of their names. The recipients become a dynamic continuation of former namesakes. Thus, the name is perpetual and it is only the name bearers who are replaced. The practice of avoiding these meaningful names results in identity concealment. This chapter explains further the deep connection Hinihon personal names have with the land and food.

Keywords: birth-ordinal names, food, land, namesakes, nomadic gardeners

> "Mi bai indai, tasol nem bai stap".
> [I will die, but my name remains], Hinihon 2001

1 Hinihon – empty villages and nomadic gardeners

Two circumstances were quite obvious when I first arrived among the Hinihon: they did not call each other by their personal names, but instead used birth-ordinal names like *Ipuhak* (first-born woman) and *Akom* (second-born man). Indeed, there were a lot of *Ipuhak* and identifying the right person was quite difficult.

Angella Meinerzag, Germany, e-mail: Angella@web.de

https://doi.org/10.1515/9783110759297-003

The other fact was that the villages where I conducted my research were more or less deserted. Only some of the Hinihon came back in the evenings. This seemed to me far from being a good starting point for doing fieldwork unless I decided to explore these two phenomena and find reasons why Hinihon do not use personal names and where they live if not in their village.

This article is based on a 14 months of research I conducted in the years 2000 and 2004. Prior to that, no ethnographic knowledge exists about the Hinihon people. Tok Pisin, the Neo-Melanesian Pidgin English, is the lingua franca of Papua New Guinea and is spoken across the country. Differences in school education, remoteness and location are facts that influence people's fluency of speaking and understanding Tok Pisin. The local language of the Hinihon is called Pamosu. Pamosu, which means 'language' and 'mouth', is a Papuan language belonging to the Trans-New Guinea family (Pawley 2006, Tupper 2014: 31, Z'graggen 1975: 27). Pamosu is spoken by approximately 1700 speakers (Tupper 2014: 9). Relevant linguistic work on the Pamosu language has been done by Liaw (2002) of the Summer Institute for Linguistics (SIL) and Tupper (2014). The Hinihon are one of the five groups that speak Pamosu and they number about 300 (Census Unit Register 2002). We communicated in Tok Pisin and I gradually learnt their language, Pamosu. Over time I focused on descriptions and key words that were used in different contexts, so that I could recognise conceptual connections.

The Hinihon live in a very remote area in the north of Papua New Guinea in a steep, ridged mountain landscape called the Adelbert Range. The range towers above the lowlands north of the town of Madang and has its highest elevation at an altitude of 1570m. The range is covered with dense tropical vegetation with a great diversity of animals and birds. Over 235 species of birds have been identified by Diamond (2021). To reach Hinihon villages, there is no access by road, only by foot paths. The paths lead among steep slopes, and two days' walk on average is necessary to reach the coast.

The two Hinihon villages are Aton and Avevete. It takes roughly half an hour's walk to get from one village to the other. The main impression of the two villages is the empty reddish-brown square surrounded by bamboo houses standing on wooden poles. At the time of my stay there were 14 bamboo houses in Aton and 6 in Avevete, but this number may change as they are regularly replaced or new ones are built as needed. The houses are made of natural materials, mainly from palm trees. On foggy days the nearby trees and palms disappear in wafts of mist and on sunny days one can see across the dark green tree canopies to the coastline and the sea.

However, Hinihon mostly do not live in their villages. They mainly live in their gardens and hamlets, which are dispersed throughout the region, several hours away from the villages. The houses in the hamlets are mostly on poles and are similar to the ones in the villages. At the time of my stay, there were ten hamlets within Hinihon region with two to four houses each. In addition, there were about 20 gardens, each with a single house.

Through garden work Hinihon can live self-sufficiently. Traditionally they harvest a large variety of yam, taro, bananas and pandanus; sweet potatoes, corn and onions were introduced later. As the region is very steep, there are different climatic zones. In the lower, warmer regions more food can be grown than in the colder ones. Hinihon have several garden plots dispersed in the different climatic zones. Their dispersed locations also reduce the risk of crop failure due to climatic causes, which would be devastating if Hinihon were dependent on a single garden only. Hinihon have established shifting cultivation, a technique of rotational farming in which plots of land are burned and cleared for planting. They farm only one year in an area, before moving to another and leaving the area to be reclaimed by the bush again.

A source of protein is ensured by hunting small mammals, mostly wallabies and possums. Hunting is mainly done by men with bows and arrows, but also by women and youngsters. Men use spears as well. On some occasions men and women go hunting together in a game drive system, where women drive the game out of the bush by beating sticks.

The gardens and hamlets are owned by patrilineal family groups, six in total in 2004. All brothers inherit land and have to divide it amongst themselves. However, the eldest living sons have a central position in the decision making. Although land remains the property of the sons, the men I talked to emphasised the custom of giving land access to their sisters. By this means, important relationships, namely with their nieces and nephews, can be established and maintained. The sisters will join with their families and help to clear the ground of dense vegetation and prepare it for planting. The whole terrain is divided into plots where the different families work. These plots can be redistributed to relatives or friends in further sections. The garden complex is, hence, like a garden patchwork as it comprises parts which are not only used by the owners, but also by many other people. The bonds that arise from working and living there together are long lasting, and one can remember and refer to common work from previous times. Having several garden plots dispersed in different locations allows Hinihon to be integrated within a large network of relationships across the territorial boundaries of the family groups. The garden is like a visible form of these networks where families and friends can work together. As gardens are newly laid out every year, new network constellations are possible.

Hinihon have to walk a lot to maintain their garden plots as they are not clustered in one place, but widespread throughout the region. Walking is a central aspect of the daily life and the capacity to walk long distances is required from childhood on. To express one's well-being, for example, it was commonly mentioned that health is a state in which walking is possible. Only healthy people can walk long distances to reach the remote gardens.

During our hikes, Hinihon regularly showed me where they had their old and new gardens. The newer ones were visible from afar due to less dense vegetation. They also pointed out hamlets and single houses, paths and hunting grounds, virgin bush, and the territories of the family groups, and explained who was living and working there. They sometimes drew my attention to trees or palms they had planted in memory of certain people or events. For Hinihon the bush also contains subtle information about the presence of other people and what they have done. I learned how to comprehend these signs only by walking along with them and experiencing common events. On our way back from a hamlet, for instance, *Andob Embam* and I crossed a stream with two big, flat stones on the bank. She told me that this was the place where she often cleans plates and pots with her sisters. Nearby, she showed me a bamboo cane channelling water from a source where we could fill up our bottles. Later on, we passed by an extinguished fireplace, which had been used by others. With a glowing piece of wood that she had carried with her, we wanted to light a fire for cooking, but we shortened the break because it began to rain. She cut two banana leaves with her machete to protect us from the rain. This episode demonstrates how human actions shape and make use of the natural environment. The traces left behind (e.g., the cut banana stems or the extinguished fireplace) are then observed and interpreted by following members of the community. Places are connected with events which are remembered when passing by. When accompanying people, I noticed that they often commented on the signs of human activity and knew who had been there before. Both individual and historical events are inscribed onto places, as has been observed in several societies in Papua (Bamford 1998: 32, Feld 1996, Kahn 1996: 168, Schieffelin 1976: 45, Sillitoe 1999). Walking through the bush with Hinihon led to conversations about several events and about the people's imprint there.

Migration and semi-nomadism are anchored in Hinihon history and present lifestyle. This can be retraced through Lutheran missionary and Australian patrol reports (Jordan 1952, Mackellar 1959, Read 1970). Hinihon migrated regularly from place to place where new settlements were constructed. One reason for their migration is their system of shifting agriculture and their widespread repartitioning of land. The land is possessed by small family groups with their leaders. The dispersion of small groups into the bush was mainly for reasons of protection against assault from enemies and fights with neighbouring villages. These fights occurred regularly in the past. Missionary and governmental work tried to regroup the dispersed Hinihon and encouraged them to build villages to facilitate school education, church services and aid posts. Faced with the lack of presence in these villages and the Hinihon's repugnance for communal settlements, they facilitated the Hinihon to maintain their lifestyle in scattered hamlets (Mackellar 1959). The Hinihon's resistance to settling together in one or two central villages is due to their need to remain nomadic in order to live self-sufficiently. The villages are not conceptualised as places to stay for a long time. There is no garden to plant and to work in; there is no bush for hunting. For Hinihon, it is the bush that is connected with health and that counts as a social place, not the village.

2 *Opu ondik:* 'talk without meaning'

As Hinihon avoid using personal names for referring to and calling each other, what do they use instead? Asking a Hinihon his or her name usually initiated reactions of shame, embarrassment and discomfort. The same happened when I asked for the names of other persons, such as parents, children or uncles. Hinihon either did not respond or lowered their voices when doing so. Faced with this discomfort, I very soon stopped asking for their personal names and used instead their naming system, which is based on birth-ordinal names. Even when I knew people's personal names, I didn't use them, as I respected their custom and adapted to their norm of using only birth-ordinal names.

The birth-ordinal name a person receives corresponds to a specific system that is absolute for the first- and second-born children and relative for the subsequent ones. The birth-ordinal names and the ranks to which they are attributed are listed in Table 3.1.

Table 3.1: Birth-ordinal names of the *Nembekal* clan.

	Male		Female
First rank	*Ame*	or	*Ipuhak*
Second rank	*Akom*	or	*Embam*
Third rank	*Fua*		*Ifua*
Fourth rank	*Enian*		*Omu*
Fifth rank	*Ulu*		*Kenav*
Sixth rank	*Masik*		*Masik umond*
Seventh rank	*Alekomu*		*Ninaku*

A first-born boy is named *Ame*, a first-born girl *Ipuhak*. These are the male and female birth-ordinal names for the first rank. A second-born boy is called *Akom*, a second-born girl *Embam*. A child receives a birth-ordinal name corresponding to the absolute birth order; this means that birth order corresponds to rank order. But for Hinihon, this system changes after the second rank to become relative when opposite gender pairs can be formed. Thus, opposite gender siblings fill the same rank if they are born consecutively. The third-born and fourth-born children both receive birth-ordinal names for the third rank if they are of opposite sexes. By contrast, two children of the same sex born successively will be consecutively ranked, as becomes clear in the example in Table 3.2.

Table 3.2: Example for the Hinihon birth-ordinal name system of the *Nembekal* clan.

	First-born	Second-born	Third-born	Fourth-born	Fifth-born	Sixth-born	Seventh-born
First rank	*Ipuhak (f)*						
Second rank		*Akom (m)*					
Third rank			*Ifua (f)*	*Fua (m)*			
Fourth rank					*Enian (m)*		
Fifth rank						*Ulu (m)*	*Kenav (f)*

In this example, the first-born child is a girl; she is called *Ipuhak*, the female birth-ordinal name for the first rank. The second-born child is a boy; he is called *Akom*. The third-born child is a girl; she is called *Ifua*, the female birth-ordinal name for the third rank. The subsequent fourth-born child is of opposite sex, a boy, and according to the changing system, he has the same rank as his sister. He is called *Fua*, the birth-ordinal name for the third rank. Herewith, the opposite gender pair for the third rank is filled; both have the birth-ordinal names for the third rank. The subsequent fifth-born child, being a boy, gets the birth-ordinal name for the fourth rank, *Enian*. The following sixth-born child, again a boy, does not form an opposite gender pair with his brother. Thus, he has the birth-ordinal name for the subsequent fifth rank and is called *Ulu*. The girl born after *Ulu* forms an opposite gender pair with him; she thus has the same rank as her brother and is called *Kenav*, the birth-ordinal name for the fifth rank.

Birth-ordinal names can follow a relative (Mimica 1991: 84) or absolute system (Geertz and Geertz 1964: 108). In Hinihon, we find a combination of both systems: while the first two ranks are absolute, the subsequent ones are relative and opposite gender pairs fill the same rank. Within an opposite gender pair, the birth-ordinal name does not necessarily reveal who is born first (e.g., *Ifua* or *Fua*).

In the past, the first two children had a special position for Hinihon as they were regarded as successors of the parents. The parents made sure that they had a second child only when the first could walk. In times of fights, which occurred regularly with other groups in the past, this was a precaution to facilitate escape. The mother could carry the younger child and the older one could run on its own. After these first two children, siblings were born without observing this time interval.

Each newborn child automatically receives a birth-ordinal name. As explained to me, children who die at a young age, even as young as several months old, keep their rank amongst their siblings. The next-born child will receive the corresponding rank, as if the deceased child were still alive. In contrast, stillborn children do not receive a birth-ordinal name. For Hinihon, essential socialisation did not occur, as stillborn children have not been fed and interactions did not take place. Feeding and sharing food is an elementary process for Hinihon and is central to establishing and maintaining relationships, as will be explained later.

The meaning of some birth-ordinal names derives, at least from what is known, from colours, such as 'white', 'red' and 'black', and from plants. Everything that has a white or light colour is called *fua*. The skin of the body, for instance, can be called *fuku fua* (*fuku* = skin; *fua* = white, light), 'white skin', and is used to describe white-skinned people. *Ulu* corresponds to a dark or black colour. *Fuku ulu* (*fuku* = skin; *ulu* = dark, black) 'black skin' is how the Hinihon describe their own skin colour. Other birth-ordinal names derive from bananas and palms. *Ipuhak* is a variety of banana. *Ame* is the first shoot that appears and the last to come up is called *masik*. All the others in the middle have the common term of *alek*. *Kenav*, *ifua* and *masik umond* refer to the different parts of a palm tree, which Hinihon use to make their bows. The palm is divided into different sections according to the hardness of the wood. Close to the roots is the hardest wood, described as *kenav*. Bows made from this part are very hard to draw and are mostly used by men. *Kenav* means 'hard, strong' and is also the term for human and animal bones. *Ifua* is the middle part of the palm. A bow made with this is easy to draw. *Masik umond* is the end part of the palm, where the wood is softest. The arrow will not fly as far as with a bow made from *ifua*, but can be easily used by women. Hence, the meaning of the birth-ordinal names derives from certain colours, adjectives, edible plants and palm trees, that played a central role for the Hinihon in former times.

To identify a specific person, birth-ordinal names are very imprecise, since there were, for example, 25 people called *Ipuhak* ('first-born woman') during my stay. To distinguish persons with the same birth-ordinal name, clan names can be added. The reference *Andob Ipuhak*, for instance, contains *Andob* as a short form of the clan name *Andobekal*. The suffix *-kal*, which means 'ancestors' house', is not used when the clan name is combined with the birth-ordinal name. Hence, *Andob Ipuhak* is the compound name for a first-born woman belonging to the *Andobekal* clan. This compound name referred to only14 women, which at least reduced the 25 potentialities when only the birth-ordinal name was used.

Kinship terms like *umbe* ('mother'), *inde* ('father') or *mamu* ('maternal uncle') are also widely used for identifying persons. Parents are mostly referred to in relation to their children, and younger and unmarried persons are mentioned together with their siblings. It was mainly through this embedding of persons into their kin networks that clear identification was possible.

Hinihon consider the references based on the birth-ordinal names or on the compound names as *opu ondik*, (*opu* = word, speech; *ondik* = empty, without sense or meaning). To illustrate the use of *opu ondik, Evakulok Ipuhak* gave me the following example (Hinihon statements were both in Tok Pisin and Pamosu, Pamosu being highlighted in italics): "Narapela man em tok wanem long yu na yu pilim hevi. Narapela bai tok: yu no ken harim na belhevi, em *opu ondik*, em tok nating". [Someone says something to you and you feel angry about it. Another will say: do not listen to that, it is *opu ondik*, it is nonsense, it is idle talk]. *Opu ondik* does not contain important meanings; it is nonsensical and empty talk. In this case, the birth-ordinal names or compound names are general reference forms which mark a person merely as a brother or sister amongst siblings. They substitute for the "true" personal names.

3 *Unim ate*: 'the true name'

In Pamosu, personal names are called *unim ate. Unim* means 'name' and *ate* is used to refer to something genuine, true, big and meaningful. *Opu ate*, for example, is in contrast to *opu ondik*, a meaningful, important and true speech.

Personal names are given directly from one adult person to a child. The name giver and the name receiver have to belong to the same clan. Thus, each of the Hinihon clans owns a set of personal names that the members pass on through time, from generation to generation. The members of a clan are matrilineally connected and they consider themselves as sharing the same blood. The word for 'clan' is the same as the word for 'blood' (*mabol*), and all children belong to the same clan as the mother. Each clan is connected with a specific animal and with a place of origin. The totemic animal is shared by all members of one clan and appears, for example, as carvings on digging sticks for gardening. Personal names belonging to the *Andobekal* clan are connected, for example, with the New Guinea harpy eagle, called *mambukom* in Pamosu. The bearers of these names identify with the properties of this eagle and it is unthinkable to have a personal name associated with another totemic animal. The same happens with single natural features specific to the place of origin, such as trees, rocks, stones, streams, birds, and edible plants like yams and bananas. Personal names anchor the bearers in their own places of origin. Therefore, just by hearing a name, Hinihon can deduce information such as to which clan a person belongs and where the corresponding place of origin is located.

By assigning a name, a person is marked as belonging to a clan. This has, amongst other things, the purpose of guaranteeing the continuation of the clan. Exploring cases of adoptions showed that clan leaders mainly use adoption to control the size of the clan and the balanced distribution of genders (Meinerzag 2015: 164–168).

Name giver and name receiver must moreover have the same gender and the same rank, i.e., they must have the same birth-ordinal name. A first-born woman (*Ipuhak*), for example, can only give her own name to her sisters' first-born daughter (also an *Ipuhak*) or to another first-born child within the same clan. It is impossible to give one's personal name to a child with another birth-ordinal name. The personal names are tied to them. Hence, all personal names are bound to a particular clan in combination with a specific birth-ordinal name.

The possession of names by clans is a common practice in Papua New Guinea and has been reported, for example, for the Nyaura (Wassmann 2001), for the Iatmul (Moutu 2013), for the Karawari (Telban 1998: 83–93) and for the Baruya (Godelier 1992: 7). For the Buang, it is the birth-ordinal names that are tied to the names (Hooley 1972: 502). That both birth-ordinal names and clan are bound to personal names is a specific trait of the Hinihon naming system. A similar rule has only been reported for the Bassari in West Africa (Cornevin 1954: 160).

For Hinihon it is important to preserve their personal names from disappearing. To achieve this, they creatively find solutions depending on the circumstances. In one case, *Evakulok Ifua* had once given her personal name to her granddaughter. According to the rules, this girl had the same birth-ordinal name *Ifua*, so both had the third rank. But this girl died at a very young age. The next child who was born after this incident was again a girl. Following the birth-ordinal name system, this girl should have had the fourth rank with the birth-ordinal name *Omu*. Since there were not many female descendants in the *Evakulokekal* clan in that time, the clan members decided in agreement with the parents that this newborn girl would take the place of her sister who died at a young age. Therefore, she was given the birth-ordinal name *Ifua*, which corresponds to the third rank. Hence, the original personal name could also be assigned to her. *Evakulok Akom* said in this context: "Tumbuna nem, mipela i no inap lus tingting. Mipela i no gat planti meri." [We should not forget our ancestral names. We don't have many women]. To prevent the personal name from being lost because there was no living person to whom it could be given directly, the traditional system was modified.

Evakulok Akom described the continuation of the names over time and generations with these words: "Mipela bihainim tumbuna, mipela bihainim clan. Tumbuna mipela i no save, tasol nem i stap. Mipela i mas kisim ples bilong tumbuna. *Unim saku* i kisim nem pinis, em bai kisim ples bilong mi" [We follow our ancestors, we follow our clan. We don't know our ancestors, but their names remain. We have to take their place. *Unim saku* has received my name, he will take my place].

The continuation of the clan and of the personal names are ensured by the name receiver, the so-called *unim saku* (*unim* = name; *saku* = palm of hand, leaf).

The name receiver is described as the open palm, into which the name giver can hand over the name. Together with the handover of the name, love and affection will also be transferred; this is called the *epiha elive* (*epiha* = inner essence, will, heart; *elive* = good) in Pamosu. *Sume Fua* explained this transfer with the following words: "Olgeta laik na amamas bilong mi i go wantaim. Olgeta laik i mas i go wantaim nem. Olgeta *epiha elive* i go wantaim" [All my love and my joy are sent along with. All my love has to go with the name. All *epiha elive* goes with it].

The *epiha* is the inner essence, in contrast to the *fuku*, the skin or shell which encloses it. This inner substance has several qualities. Applied to fruits, for instance, *fuku* is the skin or the shell and *epiha* is the inner flesh that can be eaten. When the term is applied to humans, e*piha* is conceptualised as being an inner essence; it is like a bodily knowledge of its own which is distinct from cognitive processes. In the context of naming, it is, above all, affection and care that are transferred. The more *epiha* an adult gives, the more the child is able to grow healthily. With this love, the child will be strengthened and a healthy growth is ensured.

From Hinihon statements, it became obvious that *epiha* is strongly linked with the sharing of food. Feeding, sharing food and sitting together are described as *epiha ene ekiav*, which is best translated as 'making affection apparent'. It is like a conversion of the invisible, inner essence *epiha* into a tangible and apparent form, and is even expressed as a duty. Food provision can also proclaim attachment, and statements about food are used to evaluate relationships. Discomfort or sympathy is expressed in terms of food quality and quantity.

The other significant facet of food is the land where it comes from. Talking about land always involves talking about the people who live on it, and a garden can be regarded as a concentrated form of people's networks. The products of the garden are harvested through the bodily effort invested by the people. Seedlings are transported from one place to another and Hinihon always know from which person they got them and from which garden they came.

Bestowing a name is, further, a transfer of knowledge and specific capacities. When talking about his name giver, *Sume Akom* told me: "Taim em i givim nem em tok, yu kisim pasin bilong mi. Mi man bilong painim abus, mi man bilong planim kaikai, mi man bilong lo, mi man bilong toktok. Orait dispela taim, ating mi mas kisim strong, paua tu, olgeta" [When he gave me his name, he said: "You must follow my behaviour. I am a good hunter, I am a good gardener, I am a person of law and I know how to speak". At this moment I think I received strength and also power, everything together]. The name giver acts like a role model for the name receiver. But the name receiver has the liberty of giving a new shape to the name. As *Sume Fua* explained, he had not yet bestowed his name, as he was waiting until he became older and had shaped the name. About the future name receiver, he said: "Senis bai kamap" [A replacement will come]; a successor will come for the name, and he will in his turn engage in a new namesake relationship with him.

Both namesakes develop a close dyadic relationship as they share an essential union composed of care, affection, food, knowledge, abilities and a formal union regarding their gender, their birth-ordinal name and their clan. The namesakes call each other using distinct nominations. The term *emave* is used for the namesakes. This term has no gender distinction and is similar to the "dyadcentric personhood" of the Korowai in West Papua described by Stasch (2002: 335–342). There, two persons carrying the same name are differentiated from others and form a social union. These names are not bestowed but invented by the two partners and allude mainly to commonly eaten food. The food, which is shared and incorporated by being eaten, serves to establish a close identification between the two partners. For Hinihon, this dyadic union with the namesake is not only intensified through commonly eaten food but also through the essential and formal similarities. This union also has a dynamic aspect, as the child will become a name giver him- or herself later, as an adult, and will then engage in a new dyadic union, this time with the future name receiver.

After the name transfer, the personal name is, as Hinihon put it, no longer with the name giver. Hinihon say that the name giver then remains only as the *unim fuku* (*unim* = name, *fuku* = skin, shell), the 'shell of the name', to describe the state after bestowing the name. *Evakulok Ipuhak* described it as being only the sheathing, the shell without content: "Mi stap nau, mi skin nating." [There I am now; I am only the blank shell.] She has given the personal name away, and now she remains only the empty shell. Therefore, she cannot pass on her name to another child, and no more than these two people can have the same name within the clan. Personal names are for Hinihon like entities that are handed over from generation to generation.

4 Avoiding the name – evading the person

From the first moment I met Hinihon it was obvious that referring to each other with personal names was avoided.

Not mentioning a personal name is primarily a matter of respect and of the modesty associated with respectful persons. The personal name of the *mamu* ('mother's brother'), for example, should not be pronounced by his *melek* ('niece' or 'nephew'; no gender distinction) regardless of whether or not he is present. Only the kinship terms *mamu* and *melek* will be used. The sister's children have to show humility to their *mamu* and a respectful distance must be shown towards him. This includes not calling him by his personal name. To utter the name would mean getting too close to him. *Sume Akom* explained it this way: "*Mamu* em bikpela samting, i no ken kolim nem. Na yu mas pret long en na yu no ken go klostu. Sapos, yu kolim nem, maus bilong yu i mas sem. Bilong wanem em bikpela man. Em kandere bilong yu, yu no ken kolim nem. Yu mas kolim em *mamu*" [The mother's brother is important; you cannot call his name. You must be afraid of him and you should not come too close to him. Should you call his name, you should feel ashamed as he is a big man. It is your uncle, you cannot call his name, you must call him *mamu*]. To avoid uttering a name reflects the intention to keep a respectful distance. In general, not to say people's names is the respect that people pay towards older persons and leaders. With this rule, however, I noticed an exception concerning the names of the two official leaders of the Hinihon, whose names were generally pronounced during my talks with the Hinihon. Both also introduced themselves without hesitation. They were more involved in public life, like, for example, through contacts with the administration. This also applies to a few people who had a school education on the coast.

In addition, it is forbidden to utter the personal names of the maternal cross-cousins, the mother's brother's children. They call each other either by the kinship term *napul* for the male cross-cousins, or *nomal* for the female cross-cousins. Marriage to maternal cross-cousins is tabooed; it is not possible.

A similar taboo relationship exists for all cross-sex in-laws; marriage is not possible. They will use the kinship term *nomal* or *nomil*, the latter being the term for the male in-laws. The avoidance of personal names reflects the behaviour of evading the person himself, either because the person is taboo or because a respectful distance has to be maintained.

The prohibition on uttering the names of a specific group of relatives or affinal kin is widespread in Papua New Guinea. An overview of various examples has been given by Aikhenvald (2021: 17–21).

Moreover, the avoidance of pronouncing names arises from the power inherent in names. Personal names include knowledge and history; they anchor the Hinihon in the past, present and future. A similar reluctance applies to the use of place names, particularly the names of places where people have their gardens and hamlets. People either say these names with lowered voices or they use the term for the climatic zone instead, which gives very imprecise spatial information as the zones, three in number, include a lot of different gardens.

Hinihon use *opu ondik* ('talk without meaning') as concealed speech to disguise and protect the true content. Protection was especially necessary in the past and has been incorporated as a norm that is still valid up to the present time. Disputes with neighbouring villages outside the Hinihon community took place frequently and were avenged via "sanguma", in Tok Pisin, a magical killing feared and practised in former times in the Adelbert Range and throughout Papua New Guinea.

Sorcerers were ordered to kill through magical manipulation, using, amongst other things the personal name of the person meant to be killed. Thus, the avoidance or very restricted use of personal names and the imprecision of names such as birth-ordinal names serves to avoid person identification and any powerful influence over them.

Overall, reasons for avoiding the personal name range from a respectful attitude towards elders and uncles to protection against outsiders and taboo relationships.

5 Conclusion

In general, personal names are very rarely used and instead people are called by their birth-ordinal names, or by their compound names (i.e., clan names and birth-ordinal names) or kinship terms. A correct identification of the person based solely on birth-ordinal names is difficult, and this is intentional. These kinds of *opu ondik* ('talk without meaning') are very general and non-precise. Hiding meaningful information through concealed speech is a common tendency among the Hinihon. Thus, birth-ordinal names, as a kind of *opu ondik*, conceal the powerful and meaningful knowledge inherent in personal names (*unim ate*). Personal names deeply connect people with their places of origin and with their associated totemic animals. They further anchor the Hinihon in a network of relatives and ancestors and irrevocably indicate that a child belongs to a clan.

These personal names are given from generation to generation, directly from an adult to a child. With the bestowing, the *epiha* ('inner essence of a person') is transmitted to the name receiver as care and affection and it contributes to the child's healthy development from this moment on. Sharing food objectifies the *epiha*; it is a tangible form of the bond among people, in which love and care become visible. Therefore, when Hinihon emphasise the importance of feeding their children, the following aspects are implied: their *epiha*, their bodily effort, the joint work and associated networks necessary for farming, and the individual and historical events that are inscribed in the land from which the food is obtained. Food for the Hinihon is much more than physical nourishment.

Once the name givers transfer their name, they remain merely as the shell of the name (*unim fuku*). They have passed the name, as they put it, into the receiver's flat open palm (*unim saku*). The name is no longer in their possession and cannot be given to another child. Thus, usually not more than two living people have the same name. The namesake relationship remains until the name recipient him- or herself becomes the giver and in turn establishes a new dyadic union. This is usually done when maturity is reached.

What is constant over time in these dyadic unions is the same personal name, the common clan, the same sex and the same birth-ordinal name, but what changes are the people who carry these names. This is similar to what land means for the Hinihon. Land is a continuous source of identity, strength, affiliation and self-sufficient nutriment that is passed on in a fixed succession. But the Hinihon, as nomadic gardeners, are also steadily on the move. Through new garden allotments and common garden work they are able to maintain but also to regularly redefine their network of relationships. Thus, a common trait of land and personal names is that they contain both a continuous and fixed aspect on the one hand, and a notion of being temporary and in flux on the other.

The name remains eternal, and it is only the name bearers who are replaced, as the often-expressed statement "Mi bai indai, tasol nem bai stap" [I will die, but my name remains] illustrates. The names enable the continual, dynamic connection between ancestors and descendants over time.

References

Aikhenvald, Alexandra. 2021. Names and naming in Papuan languages of New Guinea. *Academia*. 1–35. https://www.academia.edu/49076724/Names_and_naming_in_Papuan_languages_of_New_Guinea

Bamford, Sandra. 1998. Humanized landscapes, embodied worlds: Land and the construction of intergenerational continuity among the Kamea of Papua New Guinea. *Social Analysis. The International Journal of Anthropology* 42 (3). 28–54.

Census Unit Register. 2002. *2000 National census*. Madang Province. Port Moresby: National Statistical Office.

Diamond, Jared & David Bishop. 2021. Avifauna of the Adelbert mountains, New Guinea: Why is the Fire-maned Bowerbird *Sericulus bakeri* the mountains' only endemic bird species? *Bulletin of the British Ornithologists' Club* 141 (1), 9 March 2021. 75–108. https://doi.org/10.25226/bboc.v141il.2021.a8

Cornevin, R. 1954. Names among the Bassari. *Southwestern Journal of Anthropology* 10. 160–163.

Feld, Steven & Keith H. Basso (eds.). 1996. *Senses of place*. Santa Fe/NM: School of American Research Press.

Godelier, Maurice. 1992. Corps, parenté, pouvoir(s) chez les Baruya de Nouvelle-Guinée. *Journal de la Société des Océanistes* 94. 3–24.

Hooley, Bruce A. 1972. The Buang naming system. *The Journal of the Polynesian Society* 81. 500–506.

Jordan, J. 1952. *Patrol Report No 7 1951/52*. District Madang. Territory of Papua and New Guinea. Port Moresby: National Archives of Papua New Guinea.

Kahn, Miriam. 1996. Your place and mine. Sharing emotional landscapes in Wamira, Papua New Guinea. In Steven Feld & Keith H. Basso (eds.), *Senses of place*, 167–196. Santa Fe/NM: School of American Research Press.

Liaw, Yong Lam. 2002. *Pamosu organised phonology data*. Languages of Papua New Guinea (SIL). https://www.sil.org/resources/archives/42508

Mackellar, M.L. 1959. *Patrol Report No5 of 1958/59*. District Madang. Territory of Papua and New Guinea. Port Moresby: National Archives of Papua New Guinea.

Meinerzag, Angella. 2015. *Being Mande: Person, land and names among the Hinihon in the Adelbert Range, Papua New Guinea*. Heidelberg: Universitätsverlag Winter.

Mimica, Jadran. 1991. The incest passions: An outline of the logic of the Iqwaye social organization. *Oceania* 62 (2). 81–113.

Moutu, Andrew. 2013. *Names are thicker than blood. Kinship and ownership amongst the Iatmul*. Oxford: Oxford University Press.

Pawley, Andrew. 2006. Madang languages. In E. Keith Brown (ed.), *The Encyclopedia of Language and Linguistics*, 429–432. Amsterdam: Elsevier.

Read, W.R. 1970. *Patrol Report No. 9 of 1969/70*. District Madang. Territory of Papua and New Guinea. Port Moresby: National Archives of Papua New Guinea.

Schieffelin, Edward L. 1976. *The sorrow of the lonely and the burning of the dancers*. New York: St. Martin's Press.

Sillitoe, Paul. 1999. Beating the boundaries: Land tenure and identity in the Papua New Guinea Highlands. *Journal of Anthropological Research* 55 (3). 331–360.

Stasch, Rupert. 2002. Joking avoidance: A Korowai pragmatics of being two. *American Anthropologist* 29 (2). 335–365.

Telban, Borut. 1998. *Dancing through time. A Sepik cosmology*. Oxford: Clarendon Press.

Tupper, Ian. 2012. *A grammar of Pamosu*. Melbourne: Centre for Research on Language Diversity, La Trobe University.

Wassmann, Jürg. 2001. The politics of religious secrecy. In Alan Rumsey & James Weiner (eds.), *Emplaced Myth: Space, narrative, and knowledge in Aboriginal Australia and Papua New Guinea*, 43–70. Honolulu: University of Hawai'i Press.

Z'graggen, John A. 1975. *The languages of the Madang District, Papua New Guinea*. Pacific Linguistics B 41. Canberra: Research School of Pacific Studies, Australian National University.

Márcia Sipavicius Seide

Chapter 4
Personal names and motivations for name-giving in western Paraná state, Brazil

Abstract: This chapter sets out to correlate names, parental motivations for name-giving, linguistic features of names, history and social class in the West of Paraná, a region in the south of Brazil. It uses and qualitative methods to examine a sample of questionnaires administered in 2018 to undergraduate students of language teaching in a public university. The sample consists of respondents' names and their narratives about their parental name-giving process. While the analysis of surnames corroborates the relationship between history, migration and family names, some common motivations in the sample are independent of social class. However, the linguistic features of first names shed light on the influence of social class on innovative spelling.

Keywords: anthropological-linguistics, personal names, motivation for name-giving, West of Paraná, Brazil

1 Introduction

Cilac and Lalonde (2020: 131) argue that personal "names have the power to convey a lot of social and cultural information about its [*sic*] bearer, including gender, race or ethnicity and even socioeconomic status", and that choosing them is a "cultural act" on the parents' part. The authors proved these assumptions through research in bilingual communities in Canada. However, further research is needed in other communities, languages and cultures to provide empirical evidence in other contexts. This is the objective of the present study, which sets out to answer the following questions:

Note: I am thankful for the excellent translation by Professor Igor Antônio Lourenço da Silva (Universidade Federal de Uberlândia, ORCID 0000-0003-0738-3262), who received funding from the Brazilian Graduate Support Program (PROAP) by CAPES (Coordination for the Improvement of Higher Education Personnel). I am also thankful for the support provided by the Graduate Program in Letters (PPGL) at Unioeste, Brazil.

Márcia Sipavicius Seide, Western Paraná State University – Unioeste, e-mail: Marcia.Seide@unioeste.br

https://doi.org/10.1515/9783110759297-004

1. Can personal names reveal social, historical and economic information about the name givers and/or name bearers?
2. If name giving is a cultural act, by what means is it possible to shed light on the values behind the name givers' choices of first names?
3. Is there a correlation between name givers' social and economic status and their motivation for name giving?
4. Is it possible to find evidence of the social and economic status of name givers and, indirectly, of name bearers through their name spelling?

The research reported in this chapter is an attempt to provide answers to these questions. It is a quantitative and qualitative investigation that uses an interdisciplinary perspective to analyse a sample of data. Data were collected in 2018 through a survey of undergraduate students on a language training program at the Marechal Cândido Rondon campus of the Western Paraná State University – Unioeste, in Brazil. The research was approved by the university's ethics committee (Registration No. 84919518.6.0000.0107), and all participants provided informed consent.

Section 1 presents contextual and historical information about the region where data were collected and relates the respondents' surnames to its migration history. Findings confirm that studying the origin and distribution of surnames both facilitates mapping migration flows and requires considerations about the respondents' full name structure.

Section 2 focuses on the name givers' motivations for choosing a first name according to reports provided by the name bearers. It provides a classification of motivations, the frequency of each type of motivation mentioned in the sample, and text evidence for each, as extracted from the respondents' reports. Quantitative and qualitative data analyses indicate that aesthetic, honour, fictional characters, religion and uniqueness are the most frequent motivations in the sample.

Section 3 examines motivations by tapping into their distribution across social classes to find out whether and to what extent social class bears upon the motivations for choosing a first name. The data analysis points to few correlations between motivation and social class, as preferences oscillate in the sample.

Section 4 analyses whether the spelling of a name can reveal something about its bearer's social status. It describes and analyses a list of graphically divergent names according to the type of divergence: use of etymological spelling, use of foreign language spelling, pronunciation-based spelling and innovative spelling. Finally, the types of spelling divergences are correlated to the name givers' social class. Results of social and linguistic analyses point to one correlation in the sample: lower classes show a preference for innovative spelling.

The final remarks draw upon the previous sections to answer to what extent personal names carry historical, social and economic information. Investigations about motivations for choosing first names reveal that not all first names, by themselves, carry cultural, social and economic information, even though some motivations for choosing them can indeed shed light on the values and cultural traits of a given society. The same is not true for surnames, as their geographical origins reveal the history and migration flows of a given region. As for social information ascribable to a name, the study only found correlations between the use of divergent spelling forms and social class.

2 The West of Paraná, surnames and migration

The state of Paraná is located in the south of Brazil and is bordered to the north and northeast by the state of São Paulo (from which it was separated in 1853), to the south by the state of Santa Catarina, to the northwest by the state of Mato Grosso do Sul, to the west by Paraguay, and to the southwest by Argentina. The original indigenous population of the state of Paraná consisted mostly of Guarani people. Based on the 2010 census carried out by the Brazilian Institute of Geography and Statistics (IBGE), Mendonça and Sella (2020: 110) estimate that the current Guarani population is 52,000 people living in villages scattered over more than 100 Brazilian municipalities.

Once populated by indigenous peoples, the state of Paraná began to be inhabited by non-indigenous people through different migration processes that occurred at different times. As a result, the state is organised into 10 very heterogeneous mesoregions over its 77,174 square miles, with an estimated population of 11,516,8490 residents in 2020 according to the IBGE. One of the mesoregions is the West of Paraná, which has experienced the most recent colonisation process, starting in the mid-20th century (IBGE 2020). It comprises, among other areas, Foz do Iguazu, a municipality located on the triple border separating Brazil, Paraguay and Argentina. This municipality features the Iguazu Falls, one of the most internationally known tourist attractions in Paraná. The data analysed in this chapter were collected in the municipality of Marechal Cândido Rondon, which is ca. 100 miles away from Foz do Iguazu.

Although the settlement of the West of Paraná dates back to 1930, its colonisation increased in 1950 through a movement known as “March to the West”, promoted by the government of President Getúlio Vargas. It aimed to secure the Brazilian borders and spur agriculture by occupying demographic voids and nationalising vast tracts of land that had been sold to foreign groups. One of these lands was Fazenda Britânia, which the Brazilian government purchased from English owners and resold to the company Maripá. In turn, the company listed the lands aimed at farmers in the states of Santa Catarina and Rio Grande do Sul. These farmers happened to be mainly of Italian, German and Polish descent (Vescovi 2015: 45–46).

At the beginning of colonisation, Maripá was managed by a man of Italian descent who overtly sold the land preferentially to Catholics of Italian descent in the states of Santa Catarina and Rio Grande do Sul. Its management thereafter was in the hands of a man of German descent. He changed the colonisation strategy by focusing on those of German descent and seeking to unite people of the same ethnic origin and religion in the same location: Italian Catholics on one side, German Lutherans on the other (Grespan 2014: 56–57). Eventually, some towns had predominantly people of Italian descent, others had mostly descendants of Germans, and some had both lineages, from the 1950s through to the 1970s.

A process of agricultural modernisation and mechanisation started in the 1970s following an international movement called the Green Revolution (Horlings and Mardens 2011; Pingali 2012), which aimed at increasing the world's agricultural production through mechanisation, strengthened agricultural cooperatives and the implementation of agro-industries in the countryside. In the West of Paraná, the Green Revolution resulted in an increased heterogeneous population, with people migrating to the region in general and to the municipality of Marechal Cândido Rondon in particular (Frai 2016).

The establishment of higher education programmes also contributed to the development of the region in the 1980s. In 1990, the isolated universities and colleges that had been founded in the previous decade were joined together as a single public, multi-campus state university, the Western Paraná State University. Data collection for this research was carried out on the Marechal Cândido Rondon campus with undergraduate students of language teaching.

Considering that surnames are inherited from parents, its analysis can reveal the origins of its bearer's ancestors; in addition, analysing the surnames in a given region can provide a map of migration flows. This shows in the qualitative analysis of the surname origin questionnaire administered in 2018 amongst undergraduate students of language teaching on the Marechal Cândido Rondon campus.[1]

In total, 86 students answered the questionnaire. Their full names consist of different numbers of surnames as follows: one single surname (42 cases), two surnames (41 cases) and three surnames (3 cases) (see Tables 4.1–4.3, respectively). The tables show 85 surnames because two female students were twins who shared the same surname.

---

1 This questionnaire was also given to faculty members in Unioeste. Total responses are analysed in Seide (2020) and Butkuvienė et al. (2021).

Table 4.1: Family names containing a single surname.

Albrecht	Bourscheidt	Festner	Lansel	Rosa	Schulz
Alves (2 occurrences)	Burtet	Hoff	Luft	Sabady	Stenzel (2 occurrences)
Anton	Crespin (Graebin)[1]	Hoffmann	Machado	Salvini	Strenske
Antonin	da Silva[2]	Hoss	Machado	Sanches	Ullmann
Barella	da Silva[2]	Johann	Massirer	Scarabonatto	Vorpagel
Boesing	de Lima[2]	Kerkhoven	Oliveira	Schell	Walker
----------	de Mello[2]	Kissler	Rolim	Scherer	Zimmermann

Notes: 1) the surname in parentheses is in its original form as given by the respondent; 2) the forms *de* and *da* are considered equivalent – the first is a single preposition, the second is a preposition plus a feminine definite article; as prepositions, they only work in combination with the following word.

Table 4.2: Family names containing two surnames.

Alves Dalmas	da Silva Costa	Hoffmann Marczinksi	Marcos Verissimo	Queiroz da Silva	Tierling Defreyn
Alves de Oliveira	Dall´Anora Ferreira	Kerkhoven Lourenço	Martins Mentges	Schroder Hoffmann	Tischner Duarte
Ames Lima	de Araújo Moreira	Koelzer Gonçalves	Martins Wentz	Schroeder Apparecido	Torres Bedin
Antunes Borges	de Oliveira Mombach	Krockhecke Bonoldi	Massine Fontanive	Seabra Batista	Tristão Schulz
Caetano Buzzo	Feiber Stein	Lust Much	Melo dos Santos	Tandini Pedro	Yumi Uno
Campos Lambert	Godoi de Oliveira	Maas dos Santos	Mendes Schurmann	Ten Caten	Fauston Koch
da Costa Serra	Hahn Scherer	Mackmillan Brião	Minski Portal	Theodoro Rossetti	----------

Table 4.3: Family names containing three surnames.

Rodrigues Costa Oliveira
Kipper Bona de Borba
de Oliveira Rodrigues Marques

While the binary structure of a personal name plus a paternal surname follows the usual name-giving model in Germany and northern Europe, the structure formed by a personal name plus two surnames (the first as in the mother's family, the second as in the father's family) is the standard model in both Portugal and Brazil. Personal names containing more than two surnames are rare in the sample and reminiscent of times prior to the law for civil registration instituted in France and elsewhere following Napoleon's Civil Code (Lawson, 2016: 174).

Three names were registered in Paraguay, according to the students' birthplace. This finding shows another migration pattern in the region: people from the states of Paraná and Rio Grande do Sul had been attracted there by a migration policy instituted in Paraguay by President Alfredo Stroessner in the 1960s. This policy was concomitant with the "March to the West" promoted by Brazilian President Getúlio Vargas (Lucas, 2019: 67). Some of these families returned to their country of origin; consequently, some young people living in the municipality of Marechal Cândido Rondon were born and registered in Paraguay, where they also spent part of their lives.

One of these respondents was recontacted in January 2021 to collect further information. The female bearer of the surname "de Oliveira Mombach" informed us that "de Oliveira" stems from her paternal grandfather and Mombach stems from her maternal grandfather. This indicates that the paternal surname occupies the first position while the maternal surname stands in the second position. This arrangement follows the anthroponomic system in the Spanish language. Were her name registered in Brazil, it would probably be Mombach de Oliveira, following the Portuguese language system. This divergence causes misunderstandings as, in the eyes of Brazilians, "de Oliveira" would be the paternal surname, rather than the maternal surname.

The analysis of surnames according to their geographical origin also corroborates the colonisation history in the region: the names have German, Italian, Portuguese-Brazilian and Hispanic origin, and there are also names of other minority ethnic groups that live in the municipality of Marechal Cândido Rondon and/or in the West of Paraná. It also indicates a return migration movement, with people returning from Paraguay to the state of Paraná.

To better understand the relationship between surnames and migration, a complementary analysis was made based on the geographical information provided by a survey on the website Forebears.[2] The analysis focused on the country where the surname is more frequent, i.e., with the highest numbers of records, also considering spelling variants. Table 4.4 shows the most frequent origins of the surnames in the sample (spelling variants are provided in parentheses).

2 This is a statistical survey with data retrievable from https://forebears.io/surnames (accessed 12 February 2021).

Table 4.4: Origins of surnames in the sample.

Germany	Italy	Portugal and Brazil
Albrecht	Salvini	Oliveira
Burscheidt (Bourscheidt)	Barella	Machado
Stenzel	Rossetti	Silva
Zimmermann	Bedin	Alves

The structure of the surnames in the sample and their geographic origins confirms what is known about the colonisation history of the West of Paraná and the municipality of Marechal Cândido Rondon. It shows the intrinsic relationship between anthroponomastic studies and historical studies, especially when it comes to migration movements.

3 Motivations mentioned in the sample

Based on Leibring's (2016: 212) initial proposal, Butkuvienė et al. (2021) developed a classification of motivations for choosing a first name. Their classification framework was used to categorise the motivations mentioned in the questionnaire applied in this study. Table 4.5 lists the motivations and provides a brief definition for each of them.

Table 4.5: Motivations for choosing a first name.

Motivations	Definition
1. Uniqueness	The selection process is motivated by the name giver's belief that the first name chosen or created is unique, i.e., the only one of its kind or extraordinary, rare. It includes neologisms.
2. Honour	A name given in one's honour is a name of a person who is named after another person, including relatives, family friends and famous people (celebrities).
3. Religion	A religious name is one given for a religious reason, usually after a saint.
4. Chance	A chance name is one which is chosen either randomly or without clear motivation.
5. Meaning	A semantically meaningful name is one chosen because of its semantic load.
6. Belief	The anthroponomic choice is based on the belief that the name has traits that influence the personality of the named person.
7. Aesthetic	An aesthetic name is one which is chosen because the name giver finds it 'nice'. This category includes its phonetic features, length (long or short), good match with the surname, attractive graphical form, etc.
8. Popularity	A popular name is one which was popular in the social environment of the name giver when the child was born—or in a period significant to the name giver(s).

Table 4.5 (continued)

Motivations	Definition
9. Fictional Character	A name given after a character from a piece of literature or music, film, soap opera, etc.
10. Resemblance	A name in this category is one which resembles, or is similar to, a family member's name in terms of spelling or pronunciation.

Source: Butkuvienė et al. (2021: 15–19).

Butkuvienė et al. (2021) analysed the most recurrent motivations in a broader sample that also included faculty members and students' children. Overall, the major motivations are found independent of whether such data is included or excluded. The most mentioned motivations were the following, in descending order of frequency: aesthetic, honour, fictional character, religion and uniqueness. Table 4.6 shows an example of each of the most frequently mentioned motivations in the sample.

Table 4.6: Examples of the most frequently mentioned motivations in the sample.

Motivation	Example
Aesthetic	The second name "Caroline" was chosen for aesthetic reasons only. My parents thought the name would fit with the first name and decided on it.
Honour	My mother had a friend who was a very promising, intelligent woman. My mother honoured her by choosing her name because she wanted to pass all these qualities on to me.*
Religion	"Maria" was chosen by my mother when she had pregnancy complications. She made a promise to Our Lady Mary that she would name me Maria if I were born healthy.
Fictional character	My first name "Joice" was my mother's choice. She watched a [Brazilian] soap opera when she first watched television (she was about 12). There was an actress Malu Mader who played the role of a character named "Joice" in that soap opera.
Uniqueness	My mother told me that the day I was born she knew three other Andressas had been born in the hospital and decided to change the name. So I was renamed.

Note: *This answer is also indicative of the belief that characteristics of the honouree's personality would have a positive influence on the child's personality.
Source: Butkuvienė et al. (2021: 24–34).

4 Motivations, culture, history and social class

Santos (2005: 38) proposes a classification of social classes for the Brazilian population following a descending order of income, from landholders and capitalists to household employees. This classification framework was used to identify the social classes based on the professional occupation of the respondents' parents, as reported by them in the questionnaire. If a student's parents occupied different social classes, the highest class was considered.

They reported professions and occupations compatible with 10 out of the 13 classes described by Santos (2005). Based on economic characteristics of the region, the classes were grouped into strata as shown in Table 4.7, in which the number indicates their hierarchical position in Santos's (2005) list.

Table 4.7: Social classes of students' parents.

Category name	Stratum	Sample
3. non-agricultural self-employed	Upper	03%
4. agricultural self-employed	Upper	19%
5. self-employed specialists	Middle-Upper	16%
6. managers	Middle-Upper	05%
7. field specialist employees	Middle-Upper	05%
8. qualified employees	Middle	16%
9. supervisors	Middle	01%
10. workers	Middle	17%
11. elementary workers	Lower	16%
13. household employees	Lower	02%

Source: Santos (2005: 38).

Subsequently, a correlation was found between the motivations mentioned and the social class of the students' family, as shown in Table 4.8. Motivations are provided in decreasing order of mentions.

Table 4.8: Name givers' social classes and motivation for name giving.

Parents' social class	Reasons for choosing first name
3. non-agricultural self-employed	chance, aesthetic, uniqueness, fictional character
4. agricultural self-employed	chance, fictional character, religion, honour, uniqueness, aesthetic
5. self-employed specialists	fictional character, aesthetic, honour, meaning, chance, religion
6. managers	aesthetic, honour, others
7. field specialist employees	uniqueness, belief, aesthetic
8. qualified employees	aesthetic, honour, meaning, belief, popularity, uniqueness, chance
9. supervisors	religion

Table 4.8 (continued)

Parents' social class	Reasons for choosing first name
10. workers	honour, aesthetic, fictional character, religion, belief, uniqueness, others (dreams of the name)
11. elementary workers	honour, chance, fictional character, uniqueness, religion, aesthetic
13. household employees	aesthetic

Relating data on the parents' social class to the name-giving motivations reported by the students shows that the most frequent motivations are mentioned in almost all social classes. This data scattering shows no correlation between these variables. This is the case for the motivations of honour and aesthetic. The same applies for chance, which was not mentioned in all classes, but in classes 5, 8, and 11, each class corresponding to a different stratum. As for the less mentioned motivations, meaning was present in classes 5 and 8, i.e., in the middle and upper strata, while popularity was found only in class 8, in the middle stratum.

Uniqueness was mentioned in social classes 3, 4, 7 and 8, which indicates that a unique name is desired by the middle to upper classes, although not exclusively (considering that there was one occurrence in the lower-class stratum). Fictional character was mentioned by classes 3, 4, 5, 10 and 11, with a slight predominance in the upper stratum. Belief was mentioned in three classes – 7, 8 and 10 – indicating preference by the middle classes, which, however, is not exclusive, as this motivation is also mentioned in the lower classes. Religion was mentioned in classes 3, 7, 8 and 9, that is, both in the middle-upper and middle strata.

In general, social class and motivation are not interrelated in the sample. Considering that the most frequently mentioned motivations in this sample are the same as those in the broad sample analysed in a previous study (i.e., Butkuvienė et al. 2021), the authors' cultural explanation presented in the paragraph below also applies to the present data.

Honour and fictional character are usually related to Brazilian literary authors, sportsmen, fictional characters and music, which indicates a preference for national mass culture and less appreciation for international celebrities. While religion can be related to the fact that Catholicism is the most practised religion in Brazil, the preference for aesthetic and uniqueness motivations seems to be indicative of a more general trend of decreasing traditionalism and increasing individualism as part of cultural modernisation in general (Butkuvienė et al. 2021: 37–38); it is suggested that "the parents wish to 'personalise their creations' in a completely fresh manner, so as to satisfy their proud claim to singularity" (Felecan 2014: 134).

5 Linguistic features of students' first names and social class

This study also addresses another explanatory hypothesis related to social class: that choices of spelling forms that do not follow the spelling rules of Portuguese language will be more frequent in the lower strata. To test this hypothesis, names with divergent spellings as compared to standard spelling were identified. 22 out of the 86 names in the sample had this type of spelling, i.e., 1 in every 4 names, approximately. Divergence was analysed linguistically and correlated to the name givers' social strata. Table 4.9 provides the results.

Table 4.9: Analysis of names with non-standard spelling.

Parents' social class and stratum	Name	Classification
3 – Upper	Giovanna (double n)	Name according to Italian spelling
4 – Upper	Cleidi	Pronunciation-based spelling: final "e" in standard spelling
4 – Upper	Lizandra Tatiani	Pronunciation-based spelling: final "e" in standard spelling of the second name
4 – Upper	Márcia Elaini	Pronunciation-based spelling: final "e" in standard spelling of the second name
4 – Upper	Thaís	Innovative spelling: the name has no "h" or diacritic in standard spelling
5 – Upper	Angela Karina	Innovative spelling: use of the letter "k" instead of "c" in the second name
5 – Upper	Djeine Joyce	Pronunciation-based spelling in the use of "dj" in the first name; the second name is in English spelling
5 – Upper	Heloisa Emanueli	Pronunciation-based spelling: final "e" in standard spelling of the second name
5 – Upper	Keila	Innovative spelling: use of the letter "k" instead of "q"
5 – Upper	Manoeli	Pronunciation-based spelling: etymological "e" is replaced with "i"
5 – Upper	Yasmin Regina	The first name follows the English spelling
8 – Middle	Christian	Spelling according to the Latin etymology or the English (and German, etc.) language
8 – Middle	Lucas Matheus	Spelling according to the Latin etymology or the English language

Table 4.9 (continued)

Parents' social class and stratum	Name	Classification
8 – Middle	Jheinifher	Innovative spelling of the English name Jennifer with the addition of letters not corresponding to phonemes in Portuguese
8 – Middle	João Victor	Spelling according to the Latin etymon or the English language
10 – Lower	Camila Giovana	The second name, Giovana, is an Italian.
10 – Lower	Daiane Cristina	The spelling of the first name simulates its pronunciation in English, "Diane"
10 – Lower	Talita Emanoeli	Pronunciation-based spelling: final "e" in standard spelling of the second name
10 – Lower	Thaynara	Innovative spelling: the name has no "h" or "y" in standard spelling. The standard spelling is Tainara
11 – Lower	Aurielly Lohaine	Both names have an innovative spelling: the first name uses "ll" and "y", the second name uses "h"
11 – Lower	Danielly Mayara	Both names have innovative and creative spelling: the first name uses "ll", both names use "y"
11 – Lower	Natalie Cristiane	The first name uses English spelling

Table 4.9 shows that, contrary to the research hypothesis, the use of non-standard spelling is present in all social strata. However, the uses are concentrated in the upper stratum with 10 occurrences, and in the lower stratum with 7 occurrences. In addition, a correlation was found between the parents' social class and the type of non-standard spelling. Upper strata predominantly use spelling that follows pronunciation in linguistic contexts where writing would otherwise be difficult due to the grapheme-phoneme relationship in Portuguese. The middle strata predominantly use etymological spelling or English language spelling. The lower strata predominantly use innovative spellings.

6 Final remarks

In the Introduction, some questions were posed drawing on Cilac and Lalonde's (2020: 131) assumptions, namely that names carry in themselves much information about their bearer (gender, race, ethnicity and social and economic status), and name giving is a cultural act.

The first question was whether all types of personal names would carry such information. The analysis of geographical origin in Section 1 showed that the surname carries historical and ethnic information about the name bearers, as it is hereditary and indicative of migration movements. Research like this sheds light on such aspects.

The second question was whether name giving is a cultural act and by what means it is possible to shed light on the values behind the name givers' choice of first names. The motivations described in Section 2 unveiled the most appreciated cultural values when it comes to name giving: the beauty of the name (aesthetic motivation); admiration for others, whether they are ancestors, friends or acquaintances (honour); preference for the national culture through tributes to Brazilian poets and artists and through names inspired by Brazilian songs and fictional works (fictional character); professed religious belief (religion); and some level of individualism in the search for a unique name (uniqueness).

The third question was whether the name givers' social and economic status correlates with their motivations for name giving. The analysis described in Section 3 pointed to no correlation between motivation and social class in the sample, as the most frequent motivations were scattered across various social strata.

The fourth and final question was whether it is possible to find evidence of the name givers' social and economic status and, indirectly, of the name bearers in the spelling of their first names. To answer this research question, graphically divergent names were analysed from a linguistic point of view and according to the name givers' social strata. Findings pointed to the influence of social and economic status in the first names as evidenced by their spelling – more specifically, innovative spellings are a linguistic resource mostly used in the lower social strata.

All in all, what can be revealed by an anthroponomic study varies both according to the type of name under scrutiny (i.e., whether it is a first name or a surname) and according to the community, language and cultures involved (in this case, those related to undergraduate students of language teaching in a public university in the West of Paraná, Brazil), as well as the object of study (e.g., the linguistic constitution of names, or motivations for anthroponomic choice). However, as much as the results may vary according to the scope and type of research, both Cilac and Lalonde (2020) and the present study bring out the richness and potential of interdisciplinary anthroponomastic research. As a caveat remains that it is still debatable what is hidden behind names and name-giving practices, further research is needed to fully address this issue.

References

Butkuvienė, Karolina, Lolita Petrulionė, Marcia Sipavicius Seide & Edita Valiulienė. 2021. Name-giving motives in Lithuania and Brazil: A comparative view. *Domínios de Lingu@gem* 15 (3). 1–42. (accessed 12 February 2021).

Cilac, Jorida & Richard N. Lalonde. 2020. Motivations for baby-naming in multicultural contexts. In Ali. H. Al-Hoorie & Peter. D. Mac Intyre (eds.), *Contemporary language motivation theory: 60 years since Gardner and Lambert (1959)*, 130–152. Bristol, UK: Multilingual Matters.

Felecan, Oliviu. 2014. Unconventional first names: Between onomastic innovations and illustrious models, In Oliviu Felecan & Daiana Felecan (eds.), *Unconventional anthroponyms: Formation patterns and discursive function*, 133–155. Newcastle upon Tyne: Cambridge Scholars Publishing.

Frai, Patricia Helena. 2016. *Motivação para a escolha de um segundo nome na antroponímia rondonense* [Motivation for choosing a surname in the anthroponymy of the state of Rondônia]. Cascavel: Western Paraná State University MA thesis.

Grespan, Taiana. 2014. *Antroponímia de Toledo-Paraná – 1954–2004: aspectos inovadores* [Anthroponymy of the municipality of Toledo in the state of Paraná – 1954–2004: Innovative aspects]. Cascavel: Western Paraná State University MA thesis.

Forebears. 2021. Surnames – meanings, origins & distribution maps. https://forebears.io/surnames. (accessed 12 February 2021).

IBGE – Instituto Brasileiro de Geografia e Estatística. [Brazilian Institute of Georaphy and Statistics]. 2020. Paraná / Cidades e Estados / IBGE. https://www.ibge.gov.br/cidades-e-estados/pr/ (accessed 12 February 2021).

Horlings, Lummina G. & Terry K. Mardens. 2011. Towards the real green revolution? Exploring the conceptual dimensions of a new ecological modernisation of agriculture that could 'feed the world'. *Global Environmental Change* 21 (2). 441–452. https://research.wur.nl/en/publications/towards-the-real-green-revolution-exploring-the-conceptual-dimens-2 (accessed 12 February 2021).

Lawson, Edwin D. 2016. Personal naming systems. In Carole Hough (ed.), *The Oxford handbook of names and naming*, 169–198. Oxford: Oxford University Press.

Lucas, Patrícia. 2019. *Nomes comerciais em Naranjal – Paraguai* [Commercial names in the municipality of Naranjal – Paraguay]. Cascavel: Western Paraná State University MA thesis.

Mendonça, Sônia Cristina Poltronieri & Aparecida Feola Sella. 2020. Atitudes linguísticas de falantes bilíngues em aldeia guarani no oeste paranaense: avaliação em relação ao ensino de línguas na escola indígena [Linguistic attitudes of bilingual speakers in a Guarani settlement in the West of Paraná: Assessing language teaching in the indigenous school]. In Isis Ribeiro Berger & Elisângela Redel (eds.), *Políticas de gestão do multilinguismo: práticas e debates* [Multilingualism management policies: Practices and debates], 109–132. Campinas: Pontes.

Pingali, Prabhu. 2012. Green Revolution: Impacts, limits, and the path ahead. *PNAS – Proceedings of the National Academy of Sciences of the United States of America* 109 (31). 1–7. https://www.pnas.org/content/109/31/12302 (accessed 12 February 2021).

Santos, José Alcides Figueredo. 2005. Uma classificação socio-econômica para o Brasil [A socio-economic classification for Brazil]. *Revista Brasileira de Ciências Sociais* 20 (58). 27–206.

Seide, Márcia Sipavicius, 2020. A Antroponomástica Comparada [Comparative Anthroponomastic]. *Revista Onomástica desde América Latina* 1 (2). 83–102. https://doi.org/10.48075/odal.v1i2.25488 (accessed 12 February 2021).

Seide, Márcia Sipavicius. 2021. Prenomes cristãos: constituição, etimologia, motivação para a escolha antroponímica e conhecimento onomástico [Christian first names: Constitution, etymology, motivation for anthroponomic choice and onomastic knowledge]. Revista de Estudos da Linguagem 29 (1). 49–76. http://www.periodicos.letras.ufmg.br/index.php/relin/article/view/16765 (accessed 12 February 2021).

Vescovi, Jéssica Paula. 2015. *Prenomes e sobrenomes em Palotina-PR: um estudo comparativo* [First names and surnames in the municipality of Palotina, State of Paraná: A comparative study]. Cascavel: Western Paraná State University MA thesis.

Ilona Mickiene & Rita Baranauskiene

Chapter 5
Nicknames as a socio-cultural phenomenon among Lithuanian youth

Abstract: The 20th century saw an increase in the number of informal onym studies in both Lithuanian and foreign linguistics. Closely linked to youth sociolects, nicknames are created and used by young people to express their individuality, creative abilities, socio-cultural attitudes, or to convey a certain symbolic message. Typically, the nicknames created by young people are characterised by spontaneity, expressiveness, emotionality, representation of social identity and linguistic hybridity.

Nicknaming as a socio-cultural phenomenon is associated with the youth subculture, which is characterised by distinctive norms and rules reflecting the processes of youth socialisation. Furthermore, nicknames help express certain attitudes towards other members of the same sociolect. As a rule, nicknames created by Lithuanian young people tend to carry positive connotations. However, some can be used to offend, humiliate and hurt other members of the youth subculture. They are also used to mock, tease or make fun of a person by highlighting their negative features.

The aim of this study is to analyse nicknames used by the Lithuanian youth as a socio-cultural phenomenon, to identify the socio-cultural factors that determine the use of nicknames and to form a socio-cultural characterisation of nicknames, based on socio-onomastic theory. Nicknames can be classified into several semantic and cognitive groups, based on physical, psychological and social characteristics. Using the questionnaire survey method, the socio-cultural analysis of nicknames reveals certain trends within different groups of young people, depending on their sex, age and cultural environment. This analysis also identifies the social roles young people tend to assign themselves, as well as the social and cultural identities they are building.

Keywords: Lithuanian youth subculture, socio-cultural phenomenon, nicknames, socio-onomastics, perception of nicknames

Ilona Mickiene, Vilnius University, Lithuania, e-mail: ilona.mickiene@knf.vu.lt
Rita Baranauskiene, Vilnius University, Lithuania, e-mail: rita.baranauskiene@knf.vu.lt

https://doi.org/10.1515/9783110759297-005

1 Introduction

Studies of informal onyms gained popularity in 20th century linguistic research. Informal onyms are specific names that are created in an informal spoken environment by language users themselves. One of these informal groups of onyms is nicknames. In Lithuania, nicknames were traditionally analysed by region, focusing on nicknames used by rural residents of different age groups (Butkus 1995, 2007; Aleknavičienė 2005; Baranauskienė and Mickienė 2018). One example of this approach is a dictionary of nicknames collated and published by the Lithuanian linguist Alvydas Butkus between 1976–1990 (Butkus 1995). *Lithuanian Nicknames* contains the nicknames collected in rural areas and towns across the entire territory where Lithuanian is spoken. The same nicknames were later published as *The Reverse Dictionary of Lithuanian Nicknames* (Butkus 2007) in order to perform a structural analysis. However, there has been no detailed comprehensive analysis of the nicknames used specifically by young people in Lithuania until now. This category of nicknames has never been separately recorded or compiled before, nor have the dictionaries of A. Butkus been supplemented with new data. This suggests that contemporary Lithuanian linguistics should focus more on researching the nicknames currently used in the country, which could help identify the cultural and social changes people in Lithuania are experiencing. This study is one of the first attempts to unravel the links between present-day nicknames and the youth culture, potentially filling this gap in Lithuanian linguistics. The chapter analyses the nicknames created and used by young people in their immediate surroundings.

Personal development is influenced by the individual's social environment. Therefore, a young person's self-development depends on their informational interaction with their micro-environment (family, friends, school, university, classroom, art and sports clubs), the macro-environment (society, its culture, politics, media, state language policy) and the meta-environment (the world of spiritual values) (see Jovaiša 2002: 75). The environment and its changes, particularly in the surrounding micro-environment, affect the individual's linguistic behaviour. Therefore, linguistic behaviour depends on a certain determined programme, since language is essentially developed, promoted and modified by the linguistic environment. By denoting a person's connection with their macro- and micro-environments (birthplace, community, school, group, class, family), nicknames form a link with a particular place and community, acquiring the status of alternate names to the person's first name or surname. The social environment can be understood as a particular cultural model that is part of the knowledge, values and social relations prevailing in the community, encompassing linguistic behaviour and communication in different situations (see Rodney 2012: 18).

Informal environment and language are important because they act as tools which help describe the society and various social groups and their values. Informal linguistic acts can be associated with distinctiveness. They can highlight individuality and the need to preserve the functional, social and stylistic diversity of the language. Furthermore, youth culture is described as a distinct sociolect characterised by the use of informal youth language and its elements such as slang, nicknames, online (screen) names and English loanwords. It is important to note that this reflects the identity of a separate social group rather than of the entire nation. Nicknames are one of the most rapidly changing groups of onyms. Constant changes are driven by the need of nickname users, as a certain subcultural group, to distinguish themselves from other groups. It is also a way of expressing solidarity with other members of the same group, as well as highlighting certain popular trends and the need to be original. It is therefore important to capture and study this changing part of the youth sociolect by looking at the ways in which nicknames reflect new language realities, culture, the views of young people and their attitudes towards the language used in informal environments.

One of the most essential elements in analysing the use of any language is the age of the people speaking it. The language of speakers differs according to age as well as to gender, social class and roles, social groups and race/ethnicity (see Eble 2005; Sociolingvistika 2022). Generally, the language used by older generations tends to be more conservative, while middle-aged speakers often adhere to the rules of the standard variant. However, the language spoken by young people stands out for being grammatically and lexically innovative (Vakhtin et al. 2004: 79). Čekuolytė (2017: 65), in her dissertation "Adolescents' social order: An outsider's look inside an ethnographic and sociolinguistic study of social categories and stylistic practices among Vilnius Adolescents" also argues that their ages matter when working with them. German sociolinguist R. Fiehler (2002) argues that language behaviour varies according to age-relatednchanges occurring in human life. These include the shifting social roles within the family, the society and/or professional activities. Age is therefore one of the most important extra-linguistic factors in constructing a certain personality within an informal environment when communicating with peers. Thus, in this contribution, age is one of the crucial criteria representing the differences in linguistic behaviour of the youth from the secondary schools and from the universities/collegues.

The relationship between the language and the nation using it – as well as the local customs, worldview and geographical territory – is one of the reflections of linguistic landscape. First of all, through language, a person feels connected to a particular community or nation (see Karaliūnas 1997: 163), observing and building their relationships with the world, with other people as well as with themselves. The image of the world in the consciousness of a particular nation is linked to the worldview of their language, which, in its turn, captures and gives names to the features and elements of reality most important to the members of a certain community. Since the nation itself builds its collective character, the latter is understood as a specific set of common features. The national identity of Lithuanians, as one of the oldest Indo-European nations, has been shaped over many centuries and is associated with language, folklore, myths, customs, history, folk music and a nature-friendly worldview. It is important to note the relationship between language and culture as an expression of the culture characteristic to a person or a group of people. In order to create something, one needs to feel free within the language – to be able to use one's linguistic skills properly, to choose the necessary means of expression and to create new language features (see Pupkis 2005). Lithuanian youth, feeling free in the world and in language, create their sociolect and the nicknames by using both regular and irregular forms of lexemes and constructions.

When analysing a person's individuality, it is important to note not only the national character traits but also the individual characteristics of the person reflected in the nickname. When naming a person, i.e., giving them an invented name, we show that we know him/her well and can give some additional information or a more accurate description of that person. A nickname describes a person differently – it interprets and changes their name, i.e., their first name or surname. The naïve creators of nicknames unknowingly summarise the experience of introspection accumulated over many generations. To be more precise, when creating nicknames, the capabilities of the internal language system are being used and the creative powers of the language are being revealed. This means that nicknames can be systematic and creative, depending on each person's attitude and their individual relationship with a particular nickname. That is why additional naming or creating nicknames allows mutual understanding and communication among young people.

2 Theoretical framework

Giving a nickname is associated with *reference*, i.e., the relationship between the nickname, as a sign, and the nicknamed person, i.e., the bearer. Newertheless, given reference is a linguistic action that can be understood only by knowing the specific situation around the speech act, the first name or last name (if we assume that there is only one person who has the same first name and last name) clearly identifies the person. A nickname also has a specific reference and identifies one particular individual. According to J. R. Searle (1971), reference is not a relationship between the nickname (carrying a certain meaning) and the nicknamed person but rather a link between the addresser and the addressee. For a reference to be successful certain conditions are required: the addressee and the interlocutor must identify the referent who is being addressed by the addresser in the speech act, so the addresser must use an appropriate nickname to implement his or her reference intentions (see Meibauer 2001: 19). When using nicknames, all participants must respect the principle of cooperation with any associated maxims and strategies. Broadly speaking, there are two kinds of strategies – involvement strategies and independence strategies. They can both be used to negotiate our identities and relationships during interaction (see Rodney 2012: 25). "Involvement strategies are strategies people use to communicate friendliness or solidarity, and independence strategies are strategies people use to communicate respect or defence" (Rodney 2012: 73). The face strategy "we use to establish or maintain 'closeness' with the people with whom we are interacting – to show them that we consider them our friends. These include things like calling people by their first names or using nicknames, using informal language" (Rodney 2012: 25). This face strategy corresponds to fundamental social needs that young people experience: they want to be liked (sometimes referred to as our *positive face*) (Brown and Levinson 1987; see also Rodney 2012).

In this study, nicknames are analysed as a means of reference and as markers of cultural, social and interactive situations as well. According to Paul L. Leslie and James K. Skipper, "[n]ames are not just arbitrary symbols; they signify status, achievement, privilege, and meaningful social organization. They may mean ethnicity, social status, and social prestige, all of which may be understood as meaningful within social contexts" (Leslie and Skipper 1990: 280). A nickname indicates that the individual who is being nicknamed belongs to the same social community as the person using the nickname. Therefore, nicknames have a socio-cultural function – they are a means of social classification, i.e., identifying different individuals, indicating to which community they belong and what is their position within that community (see Ainiala and Östman 2017: 3–4). Nicknames can indicate social status, i.e., whether the individual belongs to the category of nickname creators or those who are being nicknamed. The socio-cultural values held by young people (their nationality, mother tongue, region, subculture, social position) play an important role in creating nicknames.

In this research nicknames are not being studied from a traditional – typological or etymological – perspective, but in accordance with socio-onomastics theory[1] and related linguistic pragmatics in order to find out how social identity

1 The term socio-onomastics was first used by Hans Walther in 1971. He defined the two main missions of socio-onomastics: (a) the study of the social origin and use of different variants of proper names within various situations and contexts, (b) taking into account the name giver, name bearer and name user (see Ainiala & Östman 2017: 7; Walther 1971: 45).

is constructed, in what everyday situations nicknames are used and how they are assessed. Nicknames, as one of the elements of the Lithuanian youth sociolect, created and used by young people, reflect their individuality, creative abilities and socio-cultural attitudes, or convey symbolic messages. Nicknames created by young people are characterised by spontaneity, expressiveness, emotionality, representation of social identity and linguistic hybridity. A nickname "is a unit which simultaneously includes an expression made up of form (sound, writing, gestured sign), some cognitive content or meaning, as well as an extralinguistic counterpart, that is, a referent" (Ainiala and Östman 2017: 5). Therefore, from a pragmatic perspective, the meaning of the nickname as a motivational element can also be determined by the environment in which that nickname is being used. To understand the meaning of nicknames, the environment must be evaluated. In certain realistic situations the use of nicknames can help achieve communicative goals, i.e., to show either a positive or negative attitude of participants towards one another.

The previous investigations of nicknames in Lithuania show (Butkus 1995; Aleknavičienė 2005), that mostly when creating nicknames, a particular person's unusual, atypical, uncharacteristic, substandard or even undesirable traits (within a particular community) are usually chosen. In this case, the nickname indicates the community's attitude towards unacceptable behaviour (for example, *Bitė* 'bee' – 'angry'; *Šakalas* 'jackal' – 'pander'), inappropriate language (*Barabanas* 'drum' – 'speaks loudly') or external appearance (*Karpukė* 'little wart' – 'skin defects'; *Kablys* 'hook' – 'a hooked nose'). At the same time certain requirements within the community or particular standards are being reflected. Therefore, the creation of nicknames can be understood as the labelling of community members, a certain reaction to a stimulus while seeking social control (see Butkus 1995: 24). The literary sources of the 18th and 19th centuries testify that by giving nicknames people in Lithuania were actually reacting to certain undesirable personality traits, and, in this way, controlling the behaviour, appearance and language of other community members (Aleknavičienė 2005: 49). Martin Ludwig Rhesa (1776–1840), who studied the Lithuanian language, noted that Lithuanians give ingenious nicknames to their neighbours based on their good or bad qualities (Rhesa 1818: 155; Aleknavičienė 2005: 49). In contrast, the Scandinavians, the Germans, the Romans and the English would mostly coin mocking nicknames (see Bach 1981). For example, the people of ancient Rome used nicknames (cognomen) referring to certain physical or character flaws, e.g., Lat. *Flaccus* (Horace) 'floppy'; *Naso* (Ovid) 'Big nose'; *Plautus* 'big foot'; Lat. *Brutus* 'fool', etc. (AŽ 1998: 57–58; Aleknavičienė 2005: 50). However, the contemporary nicknames of Lithuanian youth can be given both according to the historically formed traditions in Lithuania and by new models, determined by foreign cultures and languages; therefore, the analysis of Lituanian nicknames should reveal the motives.

It is important to stress that by giving each other nicknames, young people are also creating a distinctive identity and a sense of belonging to a particular group, in this way expressing their solidarity and friendship (see Gustafsson 2018: 231). Therefore, an assigned individual identity, as well as the collective identity, may affect the self-image of the name bearer (Gustafsson 2018: 231). Nicknames used by young people (within family, among friends, at school, in after-school clubs, in colleges/universities) are perceived as a sign of belonging to a particular social micro-group (micro-group (or micro-social) nicknames) that forms an opposition to a macro-group, where common and publicly used nicknames might be found (see Tsepkova 2018: 243). Micro-group nicknames used in a close private environment can denote several things, such as the relationships between the individuals involved in the nicknaming practices. These nicknames can also perform the functions of identification or differentiation, characterisation, evaluation, conceptualisation, integration, status tagging, social adaptation, emphatic communication, means of reducing social distance, entertainment, propaganda (discredit or praise) or commemoration (see Tsepkova 2014: 391). With the afore-mentioned aspects in mind, a study of present-day nicknames used by young people in Lithuania can be expected to return some interesting results and reveal the main characteristics of these nicknames.

The study of nicknames used by the Lithuanian youth is presumed to reveal universal and culturally-specific features of Lithuania's ethnic culture, the socio-cultural aspects of nicknaming and the main usage tendencies. In addition, the analysis of the links between the nicknames used by young people and their own identities could potentially confirm that nicknames are given for reasons of inclusion or exclusion.

3 Research methodology

Nicknames given by the Lithuanian youth in a socio-cultural context were analysed using the following research methodology: 1) data for analysis were collected using a questionnaire survey, based on closed and open questions; 2) the nicknames and motives for their use were analysed and assessed; 3) the attitudes of the respondents (pupils and university students) towards nicknames were studied; 4) the environments of nickname usage (schools or universities/colleges) were analysed in order to establish whether they determined the characteristics of nicknames and the relationships among their users.

The study is based on socio-onomastic theory, which states that "[n]ames or name systems are not to be understood as static, constant or non-variable but as variable and changing" (Ainiala and Östman 2017: 9). The study also follows Paul L. Leslie's and James K. Skipper's statement that "names cannot be understood without revelation of situational and contextual exigencies" (Leslie and Skipper 1990: 274). Therefore, the meaning of the nickname a person is given "can only be determined by first understanding the social conditions within which the term emerged" (Shumsky 2016: 7). When studying nicknames, it is essential to assess situational variation and the youth sociolect, which is associated with nickname competence (cf. toponymic competence, as described by Ainiala and Östman 2017: 8). During the analysis of nickname competence, an attempt was made to determine how many and which nicknames were used by pupils or students belonging to the socio-status of youth of different ages and genders. It should be noted that, depending on the situation (see Section 4.3.2), sometimes people's official first names/surnames are used, while in other cases nicknames or their variants may be favoured.

The data for this analysis was collected via a questionnaire survey in Lithuanian, completed by secondary school and university students during the period 2020–2021. The respondents were selected for this study based on several relevant socio-linguistic variables, including age and gender. The questionnaires were distributed to schools, universities and colleges in electronic form. The respondent target groups were also selected in order to cover different types of educational institutions: secondary schools, training centres, vocational schools, universities and colleges (also known in Lithuania as "universities of applied sciences"). The questionnaires were distributed to the respondents by their teachers or lecturers and completed anonymously during remote classes or lectures. The case study is based on the following data samples: 1) nicknames used by pupils (further referred to as "sample of data 1" or "SD1") and 2) nicknames used by university/college students (further referred to as "SD2") (cf. Tsepkova 2018: 243). The questionnaire survey consists of 4 parts which cover: 1) the demographic data, 2) the concept of nicknames, 3) the nicknames used by pupils and university/college students, and 4) the perception of nicknames. In order to answer the closed questions the respondents had to provide demographic data, including the situation in which the nicknames were used. The open questions disclosed the attitudes of respondents to the nicknames, the concept of the nicknames, the reasons for nicknaming and giving the nicknames, the origins of the nicknames, etc. Using the questionnaire survey method, based on open and closed questions, the socio-cultural analysis of nicknames revealed certain trends within different groups of young people, depending on their sex, age and social environment. This analysis also revealed the social roles young people tend to assign themselves, as well as the social and cultural identities they are building.

4 Analysis

4.1 The demographic characteristics of participants

In order to obtain the demographic data of the respondents who participated in the survey, they were each asked to specify their educational institution. Out of 164 respondents representing secondary education institutions, 146 (89%) were secondary school pupils and 18 (11%) came from training centres. Meanwhile, higher education institutions were represented in the study by 50 (61%) university students and 32 (39%) students of colleges (universities of applied sciences).[2] The data on secondary school pupils was collected from across the country, while the university/college students were mainly surveyed in two of Lithuania's biggest cities – Kaunas and Vilnius. Interestingly, secondary school pupils were more likely to fill out the questionnaire, which suggests that nicknaming is more common within this particular social group.

The gender difference between SD1 and SD2 is significant: 137 girls (83.5%) and 27 boys (16.5%) in schools, and 70 girls (85%) and 12 boys (15%) in higher education institutions. The ratio of girls to boys is 5:1, which reflects gender-related trends within Lithuanian educational institutions. It also shows that girls are more likely to take responsibility for and perform additional tasks assigned by their teachers or lecturers which are not directly related to their school subjects. The largest age groups within SD1 are 16 years (37%) and 17 years (36%), followed by 18 years (18.5%). The SD2 survey shows that the largest age groups here are 19 (33%) and 20 years (32%), followed by 21 years (28%). The demographic data reveals that adolescents aged 16 to 17 years and young adults aged 19 to 20 years are the most active respondents. This is the time when the value system, worldview and self-awareness are forming within young adults, which in turn helps build their mature personalities.

4.2 The concept of nicknames

The respondents were asked to complete the following sentences:[3] "a nickname means . . ." and "pupils/university students use nicknames because . . .". These sentences were completed by 158 out of 164 respondents in the SD1 group and 80 out of 82 respondents in SD2.

2 Due to data protection law, the exact names of secondary schools, training centres, universities and universities of applied sciences are not indicated.

3 The questionnaire was conducted in Lithuanian, and in the study translations into English are provided.

When describing a nickname, the respondents provided their own original definitions. Some described nicknames as onyms by providing simplified versions of the definitions used in linguistics ("a fake, unofficial name of a person"; "another – unofficial – way of naming a person"; "a made up name"; "a more amusing identification of a person if he/she is not angry about it"; "a title or name given to one person by another"; "a name given to a person by another person, often with the aim of teasing/ of picking up on some interesting or funny story/of highlighting a certain characteristic of the person"). Other participants associated nicknames either with the (unique) history of the nation ("Our uniqueness, our history, our distinctiveness"), with the person's uniqueness ("if it is not insulting, it is a unique business card of a person"; "distinguishing a person from others"; "at school children like to distinguish certain features of other children, to show their distinctiveness") or with the inclusion of the person into a certain social group ("proof that you are a member of the community, you will attract attention . . .", "a form of addressing your acquaintance"). Some of the respondents described nicknames as funny, playful, kind, humorous, offensive, mocking and abusive. The motives behind the creation of nicknames were also identified relatively precisely: according to certain external/physical or internal characteristics of the person, a specific event, behaviour, language or uniqueness. It is interesting to note that some respondents referred to specific nicknames rather than their definitions (*Bartė* is the female form made from the male form Bart, which is the character of animated film *The Simpsons*; *Džiuga*, the female form, which could be associated with one of the giants, named Džiugas, in the Samogitia region of Lithuania. From 1999 Džiugas has become a common name for boys).

When completing the statement "pupils/university students use nicknames because. . .", the respondents identified mostly positive reasons. A smaller group of respondents used nicknames for both positive and negative reasons, while the smallest group indicated only negative reasons (see Table 5.1).

Table 5.1: Reasons why pupils and university students use nicknames.

	For positive reasons (%)	For negative reasons (%)	For both positive and negative reasons (%)
SD1	51	22	27
SD2	73.7	8.8	17.5

Among the "positive reasons for use", the pupils indicated that using nicknames is more fun, entertaining, interesting, easier, more amusing or convenient. Using nicknames makes communication more playful and expressive, and it is easier to remember friends. Nicknames are also given when friends have the same names so it is easier to distinguish one person from another. Economy is another common reason, i.e., when the name is long, shorter and more convenient forms of nicknames can be used instead of the official first name or surname. Similar insights are observed in the work of the researchers who analyse place names (see Ainiala and Östman, 2017: 11).

Nicknames given for positive reasons are used in a friendly environment to establish closer relationships which, according to the respondents, "enrich a boring life routine and lead to a better mood". University students tend to place greater emphasis on the sense of commonality within the social group. When using nicknames, they feel closer; they can communicate in a more familiar and vivid way, i.e., "by giving a nickname to a person, they take him/her into their closest circle of friends".

When listing "negative reasons for nicknaming", the pupils mainly emphasised the intentions to mock, to tease, to make fun of others, to insult, gossip or embarrass, because "they think it is funny and entertaining". It is worth pointing out that when giving negative reasons, the pupils specifically described nicknamers as insecure and weak, trying to draw attention to themselves, seeking to be superior to others. It suggests that a certain distance exists between the nicknamer and the nicknamed, as reflected by the use of distal pronoun *they* ("they want to offend, to mock, to humiliate others"). The university students indicated very few negative reasons, mainly highlighting pride, anger at lecturers or classmates, and wishing to offend. This group of respondents associated negative nicknames with a certain age ("because they are still young and stupid"), which people grow out of eventually ("too old for nicknaming").

When analysing the use of nicknames, some respondents provided two possible reasons based on both positive and negative emotions: "wishing to offend or because the nickname suits and appeals to the person", and "wishing to offend or it is simply a friendly name used among people when they are all together". This indicates a more mature, comprehensive approach to the nicknames used by young people. The analysis of the reasons for using nicknames reflects the current socio-cultural situation in Lithuania, which, compared to the previous research on nicknames, is obviously changing. Today nicknames tend to be used more as a way of confirming a person's inclusion into a common social group in order to build a unique sense of identity and friendship.

4.3 Nicknames of pupils and university students

4.3.1 Nicknames and their origins

In the questionnaires each of the respondents was asked whether they had a nickname or nicknames in order to find out if the pupils and university students surveyed knew their own nickname(s). There is an assumption that if the respondent knows his/her own nickname, it generally carries a positive connotation, signifying solidarity with a certain micro-social group (see Table 5.2).

Table 5.2: Responses of pupils and university students on having/not having nicknames.

	SD1 (%)	SD2 (%)
Yes	54.3	48.8
No	32.9	29.3
Do not know	12.8	22

The analysis of responses to nicknames known and used among classmates/fellow-students, peer friends and groups showed that nicknames are less common in higher education institutions. However, the university students tend to use them more frequently when interacting with their peers and friends outside of their schools or higher education institutions (see Table 5.3).

Table 5.3: Responses of pupils and university students on their friends/group having/not having nicknames.

	SD1 (%)			SD2 (%)		
	Classmates	Peer friends	Group	Fellow-students	Peer friends	Group
Yes	68.3	55.5	28	43.2	62.2	11.1
No	10.4	13.4	33.5	21	13.4	27.2
Do not know	21.3	31.1	38.4	35.8	24.4	61.7

In order to explore the diversity of nicknames among young people, pupils and university students were asked to provide their own nickname(s) and explain their origins. A particular nickname is most likely to be related to age, gender, situational diversity, socio-cultural environment, identity or activities the bearer is interested or engaged in. When asked "What reasons encourage you to create nicknames", the respondents were most likely to mention movie characters (SD1 – 45.5% and SD2 – 50%), book characters (SD1 – 21.6% and SD2 – 34%), athletes (SD1 – 12.5% and SD2 – 19.6%) and politicians (SD1 – 11.4% and SD2 –9%). A more thorough analysis of the nicknames provided and the reasons for their emergence revealed that several other bases for nicknames were typical of both groups of respondents. Usually pupils create nicknames in the spoken language or give metaphorical nominations based on certain physical characteristics (*Pončka* 'donut' – "due to round shape"; *Pudelis* 'poodle' – "because of curly hair"; *Troliukas* 'Little troll' – "because of being the shortest in the group of friends"; *Nutella*[4] – "due to dark complexion"), personal characteristics (*Ateivis* 'alien' – "behaviour as if I were from another planet"; *Šventoji Marija* 'the Holy Virgin Mary' – "because I do not use bad language like others do"; *Mama Vaiva* 'Mother Vaiva' – "because of being caring"; *Sidas* 'Sid' – "because of stupidity"). Less frequently, nicknames may refer to semantic associations (*Kopūstina* 'Cabbage Girl' – "because my name, Justė, sounds like *kopūstė* ('cabbage')"; *Ugniagesys* 'Fireman' – "because others associate it with the name *Ugnė* ('fire')"), an activity or hobby (*Knygų žiurkė* 'Bookworm' – "because I used to read a lot of books"; *Švietėja* 'Copyist' – "because during the lessons I used to go to copy the exercises given by teachers"), language peculiarities (*Rusė* 'Russian (fem.)' – "because knows the Russian language"; *Lenkas* 'Polish (masc.)' – "because knows the Polish language"), or the place of residence (*Ispanė* 'Spanish (fem.)' – "because lived in Spain"). The pupils surveyed indicated that their nicknames were given to them by their classmates and other friends, less often by teachers or sports coaches. This statement was confirmed by the people referred to by the pupils to whom the nicknames had been given: their classmates (53.4%), friends (86.4%), children in other school years (25%), teachers (19.3%), parents (2.3%) and siblings (31.8%). According to the respondents, derogatory nicknames are given by non-friends to non-friends.

The university students indicated the use of abbreviated forms of names. This group of respondents tend to create nicknames with mostly positive connotations based on particular communicative situations (e.g., *Šarka* 'magpie' – "because I like make-up, to wear nice clothes", *Sėmka* 'sunflower' (slang form) – "was created while eating sunflower seeds with friends and one friend called me by that name", *Morkytė* 'Little carrot (fem.)' – "I was called so because of the colour of my car". Like the pupils in this study, the university students usually created nicknames for their fellow students (58.2%) and friends (53.7%), less often for teachers (25.4%), parents (4.5%) or siblings (20.9%). However, according to 93% of university students, they used to create nicknames for others when they were at school and only 7% of them used these nicknames in higher education institutions. It can therefore be argued that, unlike secondary school pupils, university students are less likely to create and use nicknames in higher education institutions.

The analysis of group nicknames reveals that people who stand out from the normal standards of the common social group are given a group nickname by other members of the same community. Group nicknames indicate group identity – when a person is being identified or is self-identifying with features specific to a certain

4 This nickname was provided in English.

micro-group. The review of group nicknames revealed that pupils created these nicknames mainly based on particular activities or hobbies (*Smuikai* 'violins' – "because they are learning to play violin"; *Sportininkai* 'athletes' – "because they like to play sports"; *Fermeriai* 'farmers' – "according to their hobby"; *Braškiniai* 'strawberries' – "friends who buy strawberries"; *Rūbininkės* 'cloakroom attendants (fem.)' – "had a key to the cloakroom"; *Skateriai* 'skaters' – "according to their hobby") or based on character traits (*Moksliukai* 'nerds' – "because they study a lot"; *Vištos* 'chickens (fem.)' – "victims of attention"; Populiariosios 'popular ones (fem.)' – "because of their behaviour"; *Elitas* 'elite' – "because of their behaviour"; *Žiurkytės* 'little rats (fem.)' – "because they are behaving so"; *Tenerifės* 'Tenerifes' – "isolated"), and less frequently based on physical characteristics (*Rudžiai* 'browns' – "all three children in the family are redheads"; *Lietuvaitės* 'Lithuanians (fem.)' – "friends with long blond hair"; *Zuikiai* 'bunnies' – "because both brother and sister are buck-toothed"), or the place of residence (*Pušynas* 'pine forest' – "according to the district"; *Rajoniniai* 'Districters' – "living in a district").

University students tend to give common group names according to specific activities in realistic situations (*Atstovybininkai* 'associationists' – "working in students' association"; *Fuksai* 'freshers' – "because they are first year students"; *Pirmas suolas* 'front desk' – "diligent girls who were sitting at the front") and according to character traits (*Atsiskyrėlės* 'isolated' – "the girls who did not talk to anyone, used to sit further away from their groupmates"; *Bitch Club* – "because of their communication among themselves"; *Auksiniai* 'golden ones' – "think that they are very good").

The difference in reasons as to why pupils and university students tend to choose nicknames (students use more positive, situational nicknames or abbreviations of official names) can also be explained by studies of other linguists. They suggest that the characteristics of juvenile nicknames are different from those used by adults (see Ainiala and Östman 2017: 9; Van Langendonck 2007: 317–320). The nickname competence of pupils and university students thus differs and it mainly depends on age and situation.

When studying the Lithuanian "nicknamescape", it is important to consider the language contact situation, i.e., the relationship between the official language (Lithuanian), the mother tongue (Lithuanian and minority languages) and popular foreign languages used in this linguistic community. History shows that Lithuania has been affected by language contact for several centuries now (e.g., Lithuanian and Polish in the Polish-Lithuanian Commonwealth, Lithuanian and Russian in Soviet Lithuania, Lithuanian and English after Lithuania joined the European Union). Therefore, today's Lithuania should be considered as a multilingual contact area of Lithuanians, minority languages and the English language.

Lithuania's nicknamescape has also been shaped by other people living here, their languages and cultures. For instance, the nickname analysis by A. Butkus reveals that during the period of Soviet Lithuania the people who lived in rural areas were often nicknamed according to first names and surnames of Soviet politicians – *Stalin, Lenin, Khrushchev* (Butkus 1997). The current nicknames used by young people in Lithuania are more focused on Western European and American culture through films, books, sports and politics. Words from other languages are adapted to the Lithuanian language system by adding the suffix *-as* for a male form and *-ė* for a female form; they are written in Lithuanian characters in the questionnaires (Eng. *Ken* > Lith. *Ken-as*, Eng. *Marge* > Lith. *Mardž-ė*), or spelt in their original form (Eng. *Bitch Club*). The choice of nickname is therefore often determined by a particular trend in popular culture, prevalent during the period analysed. The research on youth nicknames has shown that pupils and university students are increasingly more likely to create nicknames in English (SD1 – 29.5% and SD2 –22.4%), probably because they use a lot of English words and phrases when communicating with each other. Furthermore, as a result of globalisation, English has become the *lingua franca* in the European Union. Not surprisingly, it is seen as a fashionable, popular and modern language by the young linguistic community in Lithuania.

The respondents in this study also indicated that they created nicknames in Russian (SD1 – 18.2%, SD2 – 20.7%), probably due to the large Russian community living in Lithuania. There are 35 schools in Lithuania where Russian is the language of instruction, with mixed schools also operating in the country. In addition, more than 12 Russian-language newspapers and news programmes are still available in Lithuania. This allows the country's Russian community to preserve and cherish their identity. However, the Lithuanian pupils and university students tend to use Lithuanian-language nicknames (SD1 – 65% and SD2 – 81 %.).

4.3.2 The situations where nicknaming occurs

The frequency and the kinds of social environments nicknaming can occur in – at school or outside of school – were also analysed. The data collected showed that both groups were more likely to use nicknames outside of school (92%) or university (81.5 %.) than at school (79.8 %) or within higher education institutions (61%). An assumption was made that the respondents would use nicknames more frequently when talking about others (see Table 5.4).

In order to identify the situations in which nicknames are being used, the respondents were asked to specify the social environment (several options were available) at school or outside of school where they were likely to use nicknames. Both groups

Table 5.4: Use of nicknames by pupils and university students depending on their social environment.

	SD1 (%)		SD2 (%)	
	At school	Outside of school	In higher education institutions	Outside of higher education institutions
Constantly	8.5	7.3	1.2	4.9
Often	18.3	26.8	15.9	23.5
Sometimes	53	57.9	43.9	53.1
Never	20.1	7.9	39	18.5

of respondents normally used nicknames when communicating with friends both outside of school (90.2% of pupils and 95.8% of university students) and at school (84.1% and 87.1%, respectively) (see Table 5.5). Many nicknames "strengthen the identities of their user community. Group identity is reinforced by using the group's own names as part of the group's own language" (Ainiala and Östman 2017: 11).

Table 5.5: Use of nicknames by pupils and university students depending on specific situations.

	SD1 (%)		SD2 (%)	
	At school	Outside of school	In higher education institutions	Outside of higher education institutions
With friends		90.2		95.8
With classmates/fellow students	84.1		87.1	
During breaks	68.9		56.5	
During classes/lectures	34.8		21	
During events organised by educational institution	25		6.5	
With pupils/students in junior years	21.3		14.5	
With pupils/students in senior years	25.6		16.1	
With teachers	2.4			
With girlfriend/boyfriend		27.4		47.9
With sibling(s)		26.8		53.5
With parents		12.2		31
During training/extra-curricular activities		25.6		18.3
Do not use	9.7	7.2	11.2	4.2

The analysis of specific situations in the school or university social environment shows that nicknames are used more often when communicating with friends from senior years at school (25.6%) and university (16.1%), compared to communicating with junior years at school (21.3 %) and university (14.5%). It is likely that this trend occurs due to the prestige around making friends with those who are older. Due to pupils/students being able to communicate more intimately and openly, nicknames were more likely to be used during breaks (68.9% of pupils and 56.5% of university students) than during lessons (34.8%) or lectures (21%). A considerably higher frequency of nicknaming during school events (25%), compared to university events (6.5%), can be explained by the fact that many traditional celebrations, such as 1st September (start of the academic year in Lithuania), Teacher's Day, the Harvest Festival, Christmas Eve, the public holidays of 16th February and 11th March, the Last One Hundred Days and the Last Bell, take place in schools. These events are often organised by pupils themselves, which is an opportunity for self-expression, showcasing their creative abilities, and a chance to communicate freely in their usual sociolect.

In order to examine the use of nicknames outside of school and higher education institutions, the respondents were asked to choose from the following situations: within family (with parents and siblings), with a girlfriend or boyfriend, in training, or during the extra-curricular activities. The survey revealed that university students were more likely to use nicknames within their family when communicating with siblings (53.5% of university students and 26.8 % of pupils), and parents (31% and 12.2%, respectively). It is possible this is due to the changing relationships between parents and their children, who are able to communicate in their sociolect with their parents and other family members more openly as they become adults. A more frequent use of nicknames demonstrated by university students (47.9%) when talking to their girlfriend or boyfriend, compared to 27.4% of pupils, may be explained by the fact that the relationships between members of the younger age group are less likely to be considered romantic. It is assumed that pupils attend sports training or extra-curricular activities together with their friends. Therefore, their leisure environment allows these young people to communicate in their own language code and use nicknames (25.6%). Because university students are less involved in sports or cultural activities (basketball or football teams, folk singing or choirs, drama groups), they do not have as many opportunities to speak in such environments in the youth language of university students (18.3%).

4.4 The perception of nicknames

Informal onyms relate to different user attitudes towards them, so the respondents in this study were asked to rate their nicknames according to nickname characteristics provided in the questionnaire (see Table 5.6). To assess the user attitudes on a differential semantic scale of 1 to 5, the respondents were asked to choose one of the options, where, for example, 1 – nice, 2 – more nice than unpleasant, 3 – neither nice nor unpleasant, 4 – more unpleasant than nice, 5 – unpleasant.

Table 5.6: Perception of own nicknames.

	SD1 (%)					SD2 (%)				
	1	2	3	4	5	1	2	3	4	5
Nice – unpleasant	20	7.8	27.8	21.1	23.3	2.5	2.5	22.5	25	47.5
Stylish – not stylish	23.3	11.1	35.6	13.3	16.7	7.5	7.5	30	32.5	22.5
Interesting – boring	26.7	4.4	28.9	21.1	18.9	2.5	7.5	15	32.5	42.5
Memorable – not memorable	8.9	7.8	5.6	30	47.7	5	0	10	20	65
Original – unoriginal	25.6	6.7	25.6	25.6	16.5	12.5	10	27.5	17.5	32.5
Playful – not playful	27.8	14.4	11.1	20	26.7	7.5	7.5	17.5	17.5	50
Insulting – not insulting	52.2	18.9	7.7	5.6	15.6	70	17.5	7.5	2.5	2.5
Like – dislike	26.7	2.2	25.6	23.3	22.2	2.5	5	17.5	20	55

The respondents also rated nicknames as either positive or negative (see Table 5.7) as well as indicating their perception of ethical/unethical, popular/unpopular, offensive/non-offensive, playful/non-playful nicknames (see Table 5.8).

Table 5.7: Perception of nicknaming as positive or negative.

	SD1 (%)	SD2 (%)
Positively	66.5	83.6
Negatively	33.5	16.4

The respondents were asked to comment on their positive or negative assessment of nicknames. According to the respondents, positively perceived nicknames are convenient "and interesting to use in the company of friends, they are playful, they make communication more vibrant, bring people closer, create stronger connections between friends, and allow distinguishing between namesakes". Summarising the respondents' comments, it becomes obvious that using nicknames in close social environments is encouraged because "nicknames have always been and are something that brings people closer and strengthens relationships, just a 'fun game', they appear as soon as they disappear". Negative comments provided by the respondents reveal that insulting, mocking nicknames are associated with their remote use and hierarchical relations among the people who are communicating, "because distant people come up with nicknames only because of physical otherness, which can offend, less familiar people give nicknames for malicious, wicked purposes (to insult, highlight the person's physical or character 'imperfections', show their own superiority over another, etc.)".

Table 5.8: General perceptions of nicknames among pupils and university students.

	SD1					SD2				
	1	**2**	**3**	**4**	**5**	**1**	**2**	**3**	**4**	**5**
Ethical – unethical	12.8	23.2	48.8	11.6	3.6	7.5	8.8	60	18.7	5
Popular – unpopular	4.9	6.7	22	34.1	32.3	3.8	7.5	22.5	35	31.2
Insulting – not insulting	6.7	21.3	50.6	10.4	11	11.3	15	57.5	11.2	5
Playful – not playful	5.5	9.8	38	25.2	21.5	3.8	5	27.5	35	28.7

When assessing nicknaming according to given characteristics, the respondents mostly commented on the purpose of using nicknames ("friendly jokes without humiliating or insulting a person") and attitudes towards nicknames ("some people may like nicknames, others may be offended"; "a nickname means that you were noticed by a person and it is not understood as bullying"; "it is important to know the right place and time and not to take yourself too seriously, then there will be no thoughts of being offended or concerns over ethics").

In response to the question of whether nicknames were specific only to young people, 81.1% of pupils and 86.1% of university students responded negatively, arguing that "older people also have nicknames, especially famous people – athletes, politicians, teachers"; "nicknames are used by the respondents' parents, friends of parents, grandparents". It is interesting to note that, according to the respondents, "nicknaming has no age limit"; "the nicknames of older people can be brought from their youth or created due to various life situations".

The respondents usually cite the following reasons for giving nicknames: due to unique character traits (SD1– 47%, SD2 – 61%), in order to distinguish the person from others (SD1 – 51%, SD2 – 61%), due to a similarity to the person's surname or first name (SD1 – 58%, SD2 – 57%). The most commonly chosen answers to the question "Why do young people need nicknames?" show that nicknames are needed for brevity, playfulness, wishing to stand out/distinguish, to name someone more accurately, and because they are understood as a distinctive language code, a sociolect (see Table 5.9). This is also confirmed by the fact that the majority of respondents (78% of pupils and 66.2% of university students) associated nicknames with the habit of using them in the language of young people.

Table 5.9: Reasons for giving nicknames to pupils and university students.

	SD1 (%)	SD2 (%)
Need to stand out/distinguish	50.6	55.4
For more accurate naming	48.8	64.9
For playfulness	59.8	73
For stylishness	28.7	32.4
For originality	47	43.2
For brevity	63.4	63.5
Wish to humiliate others	34.1	28.4
Wish to praise others	12.8	13.5
Wish to speak in language not everyone understands	86	51.4

Summarising the respondents' perceived reasons for nicknaming, the main functions of this practice in young people can be either affective, relationship-building or positioning. All of these show that nicknames denoting interactional aspects are favoured among young people and allow the expression of their feelings, determine their approach towards each other and reflect individual value systems.

5 Conclusions

This research was conducted in order to identify the socio-cultural aspects of nicknames used by young people in Lithuania. A total of 246 respondents – students of secondary schools, training centres, universities and colleges – were interviewed using the questionnaire survey method. Significant differences relating to age and gender were identified between the two data sets used in this study (the SD1 and SD2 age groups). Nicknaming tends to be more open and common within the social group of pupils, while the female respondents from both social groups demonstrated more willingness and responsibility in filling out the questionnaires. The socio-cultural changes currently taking place in Lithuania can be observed by analysing the reasons for using nicknames. The data collected during the survey confirm that nickname use indicates inclusion into a particular common micro-social group, which helps build unique identities, friendships, close relationships and mutual communication rules. Positive or group nicknames also reflect solidarity within a particular community.

The analysis of nickname origins showed that nickname competence displayed by the respondents was dependent on their age. Therefore, motivations for nickname use given by pupils were usually related to certain external and internal attributes as well as to the metaphorical nominations of the nickname chosen, while university students were more likely to draw on particular situational aspects when selecting alternative ways of distinguishing a person. Thus, young people get called by different nicknames when they leave school and enter university. The study of Lithuania's nicknamescape revealed strong links between Lithuanian as a state language and English as a popular foreign language (and sometimes Russian as a national minority language) in the young linguistic community of Lithuania. The nicknames popular today are more focused on Western European and American culture and are mostly presented in adapted forms using Lithuanian characters. The study also revealed that nicknames were mostly used when communicating with friends both during school and outside of school hours. This allows young people to showcase their creative abilities and express themselves within their usual sociolect without much restriction. Nicknames, as a unique language code, are accepted by young people, who associate their use mainly with symmetrical communicator relations within a close social environment. Nicknames also allow their users to be concise, playful, and to distinguish or describe other people more accurately.

Contextual analysis of the data revealed that referring to a person by their nickname is highly context-sensitive. This confirms that the main functions of nicknaming are related to interactional aspects within the youth subculture. The use of nicknames strengthens the community of young people and reflects the identities of its members. The research confirmed that assigning a nickname is a value-based process. Furthermore, a young person's self-perception reveals their relationship with themselves and their worldview. So in some situations nicknames can teach young people to look at their own imperfections with humour and accept them. The study also highlighted the link with the socio-economic theory on the diversity of nicknames. The study of nicknames used by young people in Lithuania was the first in the country, so it is not yet possible to compare this data to other trends. This research could therefore potentially be used to develop a database of nicknames in order to track the changing nicknaming trends in Lithuania.

References

Ainiala, Terhi & Jan-Ola Östman (eds.). 2017. *Socio-onomastics: The pragmatics of names*. Amsterdam & Philadelphia: John Benjamins.

Aleknavičienė, Ona. 2005. Tauragniškių pravardės [Nicknames of Tauragnai village people's nicknames]. *Lituanistica* 63(3). 47–70.

AŽ – *Antikos žodynas* [Dictionary of antiquity]. 1998. Vilnius: Alma Littera.

Brown, Penelope & Stephen Levinson. 1987. *Politeness: Some universals in language usage*. Cambridge: Cambridge University Press.

Bach, Adolf. 1981. *Deutsche Namenkunde*. Heidelberg: Carl Winter Universitätsverlag.
Baranauskienė, Rita & Ilona Mickienė. 2018. Structure of Lithuanian nicknames. *Onomastica Uralica* 13. 317–326.
Butkus, Alvydas. 1995. *Lietuvių pravardės* [Lithuanian Nicknames]. Kaunas: Aesti.
Butkus, Alvydas. 1997. Lietuvių pravardės, kilusios iš įžymių asmenvardžių [Lithuanian Nicknames derived from personal names of celebrities]. *Acta Baltica* 94. 19–23.
Butkus, Alvydas. 2007. *Lietuvių pravardžių atvirkštinis žodynas* [Inverse dictionary of Lithuanian nicknames]. Kaunas: Aesti.
Čekuolytė, Aurelija. 2017. *Vilnius adolescents' social order: An outsider's look inside. An ethnographic and sociolinguistic study of social categories and stylistic practices among Vilnius adoliscents*. Vilnius: Institute of the Lithuanian Language PhD dissertation.
Eble, Connie. 2005. What is sociolinguistics? *Sociolinguistics Basics*. http://www.pbs.org/speak/speech/sociolinguistics/sociolinguistics/.
Fiehler, Reinhard. 2002. Sprache und Alter. Wie verändert sich das Sprechen, wenn wir älter werden? *Sprachreport* 2. 21–25.
Gustafsson, Linnea. 2018. Modern nicknames in Sweden. *Onomastica Uralica* 10. 229–242.
Jovaiša, Leonas. 2002. *Edukologijos įvadas* [Introduction to Education]. Vilnius: Vilniaus universiteto leidykla.
Karaliūnas, Simas. 1997. *Kalba ir visuomenė: Psichosociologiniai ir komunikaciniai kalbos vartojimo bruožai*. Vilnius: Lietuvių kalbos institutas.
Leslie, Paul. L. & James K. Skipper. 1990. Toward a theory of nicknames: A case for socio-onomastics. *Names* 38 (4). 273–282.
Meibauer, Jörg. 2001. *Pragmatik. Eine Einführung*. Tübingen: Stauffenburg-Verl.
Pupkis, Aldonas. 2005. *Kalbos kultūros studijos* [Study of language standardisation]. Vilnius: Gimtoji kalba.
Rhesa, Liudwig. 1818. *Das Jahr in vier Gesängen* [The year in four cantos]. Königsberg: Königliche Hartungsche Hofbuchdruckerei.
Rodney, H. Jones. 2012. *Discourse analysis: A resource book for students*. Abingdon/New York: Routledge.
Searle, John R. 1971. *Sprechakte: Ein sprachphilosophischer Essay*. Frankfurt/M.: Suhrkamp.
Shumsky, Neil Larry. 2016. Toponyms of a different type: Metaphors as place names and place nicknames. *Names* 64(3). 127–137. http://dx.doi.org/10.1080/00277738.2016.1118857
Sociolingvistika. 2002. http://www.sociolingvistika.lt/sociolingvistika--kas-tai.htm
Tsepkova, Anna. 2014. Cognitive and cultural peculiarities of nicknaming in macro-social groups "politics", "sport" and "entertainment". In Oliviu Felecan (ed.), *Unconventional anthroponyms–formation patterns and discursive function*, 389–405. Cambridge: Cambridge Scholars Publishing.
Tsepkova, Anna. 2018. Pragmatic and motivational peculiarities of contemporary Russian nicknames (case study: Novosibirsk school, college, university contexts). *Onomastica Uralica* 10. 243–262.
Vakhtin, Nikolaj Borisovich & Evgenij Vasilevich Golovko. 2004. *Sotsiolingvistika i sotsiologiya yazyka* [Sociolinguistics and sociology of language]. St. Petersburg: Izd. tsentr Gumanitarnaya akademiya, Evropeyskiy universitet v Sankt-Peterburge.
Van Langendonck, Willy. 2007. *Theory and typology of proper names*. Berlin & New York: Walter de Gruyter.

Section Two: **Personal naming and cultural transissions**

Shlomit Landman

Chapter 6
The naming gamble: Unique versus common given names

Abstract: Proper names are words used to identify human beings who are affiliated to social and personal subjective representations. Many scholars have proposed a relationship between a person's name and her or his sense of identity and self. Our qualitative semi-structured interviews of 45 secular Israeli parents examined their attitudes towards the naming process. Based on Shkedi (2010), the interviews were analyzed thematically, and later compared with Schwartz's (2012b) theory of ten basic human values. Analysis showed that the selection of names that were popular was guided by the execution of the security value or the conformity value, both motivated by conservativeness. In contrast, the stimulation value may be applied, motivated by openness to change, which leads to the selection of unique proper names. One of the interesting findings was a tendency to name mainly the first-born children of the family with unique proper names. Most of the parents that had given unique names to their first child were reluctant to use such names for the next children of the family. These phenomena can be explained as a case of the conservative social changing of the linguistic habitus, according to Bourdieu (1991).

Keywords: uncommon given names, common names, basic values, motivators, linguistic habitus

1 Introduction

The present article aims to illuminate the motivations behind the choice of unusual names, compared with the motivations for selecting common names. According to Israel's Central Bureau of Statistics, since the late 1970s the number of uncommon names given to Jewish newborns in Israel, those found at a frequency of 3–10 per year, has been rising. This suggests that more and more Israeli parents are choosing unusual names, though most infants do receive common names.

Like nouns, given names seem to have arisen from the need to identify objects, in this case people, so as to facilitate everyday communication (Foucault 2011).

Shlomit Landman, Achva Academic College, e-mail: shlomitlnd@gmail.com

https://doi.org/10.1515/9783110759297-006

Indeed, from a philosophical point of view the definition of given names is grounded in the knowledge of a relevant language: "The Reference of a proper name is the object itself that we thereby designate; the idea we have when we do so is wholly subjective. (. . .) The Sense essence of a given name is grasped by anyone who has sufficient knowledge of the language (. . .)" (Frege 1984: 366). At the same time, the unique quality of given names is perhaps "single-purpose" and, therefore, possessed as well of an extraordinary, almost mystical, emotional charge, as Wittgenstein noted (1953). The mystical charge of names emphasised in the Jewish religion, and thus the naming act, is still part of "the act of creation", even for secular parents in Israel. The fact that most Hebrew given names are words in the language, and therefore transparent to the speakers (Rosenhouse 2003), places a responsibility upon the naming parents.

The name's emotional charge is especially influential at the start of life, as a first sign that the mother-child symbiosis has been disrupted: "A name is the first gift given us by others, and also the first symbol of the fact of another's existence – since who would actually need to call us by name if not the other?" (Amir 2013: 30). As such, the repetition of the infant's name is a key means by which the parents' feelings towards him/her are mirrored. According to Kohut (1984), this mirroring of the parents' feelings, especially those of the mother, has a decisive impact in terms of building self-esteem. The child's given name is a major recurring element and essentially serves as a key tool for mirroring (Nadav et al. 2008). It has been suggested that the younger the child, the greater the given name's potential for having a negative impact on identity formation and the development of self-esteem (Dion 1983).

Various studies have explored the consequences of given name stereotyping on the course of people's lives. The studies have looked at desirable and undesirable names, and have found, for the most part, that desirable names are common names, and vice versa, uncommon names are less desirable (Mehrabian 2001; Lawson 1980). Ellis and Beechley (1954) found a significant tendency towards severe emotional disturbance among boys with peculiar names in the case histories of 1682 children at an emotional therapy clinic. According to Anderson and Schmitt (1990), American men with unusual names show a significantly higher incidence of psychopathology than do women with such names.

A widely-cited study on this topic found that primary school children with "desirable" names reach school readiness earlier, and at higher levels they perform better scholastically, and even score higher on I.Q. tests. More importantly, the analysis indicated that parental educational and ethnic variables were irrelevant to the outcomes (Busse and Seraydarian 1978). Erwin and Calev (1984) showed that grade differences between male/female pupils bearing different types of names persist into adulthood, which is consistent with the information presented above about the impact of names on identity-building and self-esteem.

Harari and McDavid (1973) found that essays evaluated by primary school teachers received grades that were different to a statistically significant degree, in accordance with the (imaginary) pupils' given names as written on the essays. Essays bearing such names as *David* and *Lisa* received higher grades than did those bearing uncommon given names, such as *Elmer* and *Bertha*.

On the other hand, Kang et al. (2020: 462) note that "CEOs with uncommon given names tend to develop a conception of being different from peers and accordingly pursue strategies that deviate from industry norms. (. . . .) the positive relationship between CEO name uncommonness and strategic distinctiveness is strengthened by the CEO's confidence, power, and environmental munificence."

Lieberson (2000) states that it is implausible for parents who choose unique or common names for their infants to be aware of the research findings noted above or the frequency of the names at the time of giving them to the infants. Naming is a social act, and as such "(. . .) those who name are generally in positions of power, names reflect the ideologies of the dominant group" (Vanguri 2016: 4).

Most researchers have examined the impact of the names; few investigate the givers of the names – the parents. Ephratt (2006) found that the naming act and the attributed essences of given names are highly significant for the parents, since they charge the names with personal meanings, even if the chosen names are very common at the time of the naming. Adminien'e and Naus'eda (2009) demonstrate that socially important texts are a factor in name giving. They found that in certain instances parents give unique names out of a desire to connect to texts that they deem culturally significant – for instance, the name *Jedi* from a film, or the name *Mowgli* from a book. Nevertheless, the issue of uniqueness might be crucial.

2 Theoretical background

The new Jewish communities were founded in the Holy Land during the late 19th century by the Zionist movement, a national movement with roots in a distant common past. This reference to the past dictated a cultural awakening similar to what occurred in European nation states that were occupied for centuries, such as Hungary, the Netherlands and others. Local elites that had been reared in the dominant, occupying culture and were disappointed by the status accorded them in 19th century Europe turned to their national cultures and worked to revive them (Hroch 1985). This cultural awakening had an onomastic element: foreign names were abandoned in favour of names from the national language, e.g. in Hungary the German *Stefan* was replaced by the Hungarian *István*. Political Zionism sparked a similar development in the late 19th century, as it presented world Jewry with the vision of a nation state in an ancient land. The language of the Biblical past – Hebrew – was revived, while non-Hebrew names reflecting attachment to foreign cultures, including traditionally Jewish names symbolizing exilic life, were discarded in favour of names from the Bible discovered afresh, and names derived from spoken Hebrew. According to Whiteman (1988), who studied the names of Jewish newborns in Palestine/Israel from 1882–1980, the names in the early part of that period were generally traditional, but the relative percentage of such names dwindled as the number of new and renewed Biblical names rose.

The Zionist awakening of the late 19th century invested the given names of Jewish newborns, especially in the Holy Land, with an emotional, social, extra-linguistic charge. For example, choosing the Biblical name *Avshalom*, which traditional Judaism had rejected for generations, over the name *Shalom*, reflected an identification with Zionism that replaced the former identification with the Jewish religion. This process is consistent with Barthes' (1998) discussion of words that deviate from their immediate lexical meaning in each society and take on a dual meaning, both denotative and connotative, that points to sensitive issues in the relevant society. Today, one can detect the hyper-charge connected with Israeli given names in the controversy over the current trend of giving foreign names, especially English ones, to Israeli newborns (Landman 2020).

2.1 Basic human values theory: Choosing common names vs. uncommon names

Basic values are what guide our actions, and they are linked to attitudes, norms, opinions and actions determined by social and individual motivations rooted deeply in the consciousness of individuals in a given society (Rokeach 1973; Schwartz 1992). The aim of these motivations is to allow the choice of basic values on all possible issues that will ensure maximum wellbeing for the choosing individual as a member of the group.

Schwartz's theory of "basic human values" explains humans' behaviour as a choice of basic values motivated by anxiety over the results or as a choice to confront anxiety by choosing basic values, motivated by an individual motivator. As shown in Figure 6.1, Schwartz found ten basic human values that are motivated by four different motivators. Two of the motivators are social motivators and the other two are individual. The theory was validated by: "(. . .) data from hundreds of samples in 82 countries around the world. (. . .) The samples include highly diverse geographic, cultural, linguistic, religious, age, gender, and occupational groups (. . .)". (Schwartz 2012a: 12). Schwartz's theory was validated worldwide since it mainly applied in intercultural research. However, the theory was applied in the current research in order to identify basic human values as a tool to analyse the qualitative data.

Figure 6.1: Theoretical model of relations among ten motivational types of value according to Schwartz (2012a: 9).

In this article, interviewee explanations of the considerations that guided the naming process indicated that parents may have social or individual motivations and, accordingly, motivate their behaviour according to a certain set of values, while rejecting other value sets. Most of the children of the interviewees have common names as a result of a choice of names based on the security basic value or the conformity basic value, both values motivated by the social motivator of conservation; as such, the choice was driven by anxiety. This is the "secure" choice, meant to keep children from being conspicuous. In sharp contrast to this is the choice of the unique name based on the stimulation value, driven by the individual openness to change motivator; this choice is free from anxiety. This value encompasses the objectives of excitement, innovation and challenge. Implementation of this value stems from a desire to maintain an optimal level of challenge in life, and the social challenge of an unusual name meets these conditions.

3 Methodology

This study is based on interviews held from 2012 to 2014 in various places around Israel. All of the interviewees were native Hebrew speakers; that is, they were born in Israel or in Palestine-Eretz Israel. The youngest interviewees were in their twenties, while the oldest were in their eighties. I interviewed 22 mothers and 23 fathers, not necessarily spouses. The interviewees resided in different Israeli localities within the Green Line, from Eilat to Karmiel, from Jerusalem to Haifa and Tel Aviv.

The interviewees belonged to different socioeconomic strata and were ethnically diverse. I interviewed academically-trained professionals, self-employed people and blue-collar workers. The parents defined themselves as secular; I refrained from interviewing people who self-identified as religious, as I did not wish to address issues of adherence to traditional naming practices. The interviewees were recruited spontaneously; I interviewed people I met under a variety of circumstances – professional, social or other. I asked the prospective interviewees if they were Israeli-born and if they had children, and requested their participation in an interview as part of a linguistics research project pertaining to the process of choosing baby names. Most of the interviewees in the study were members of a nuclear family, but there were also couples that had not married, divorced people (some of whom had second families), people of different sexual orientations, single mothers who had become pregnant via sperm donation, parents of children born after lengthy periods of fertility treatment, and parents of children adopted at various ages.

Throughout the article, interviewees will be referred to via male or female pronouns even if the group in question is mixed gender, for the sake of readability. The interviewees are identified by false initials to safeguard their privacy. The names mentioned in the interview statements are accurate only to the degree that they are prevalent Israeli names. Less common names are denoted by initials or replaced by other names.

4 Analysis

Qualitative research strives to understand real world processes via the stories of interviewees who have experienced these processes (Denzin 1995). The present study aimed to reach the broadest possible understanding of the various aspects involved in baby naming processes, on the assumption that the interviewees represent only themselves (Shkedi 2010). The choice of a qualitative approach reflected a desire to give interviewees the opportunity to tell their stories freely, without the sense of obligation that can arise from a detailed questionnaire embodying assumptions about the process, thereby leading the stories in directions that are irrelevant to the interviewees (Maykut and Morehouse 1994).

The research tool chosen was the semi-structured interview, which allows interviewees' themes to be explored and developed relatively easily (Denzin 1995). This kind of interview includes several fixed questions, but when interviewees raise new categories or express themselves in unusual ways, it is possible to deviate from the initial interview format and ask other questions, until the issue has been fully explored.

With the intention of trying to reconstruct processes involved in baby naming, a preliminary interview consisting of 13 questions was developed. A pilot study found that the initial questionnaire was too detailed and hindered the free flow of interviewees' speech. In the interview as actually conducted, the first three questions related to interviewee biographical information – age, place of birth and the circumstances in which the interviewee was given his/her own names. The latter question elicited openness and greater detail on the part of the interviewees, which essentially made the rest of the interview a monologue on the naming of their children, with numerous tangential discussions of issues specific to the interviewees. Where necessary, the interviewees were asked additional questions, whether to clarify their stories or because they offered other details that took the naming process into new places. Interviewee questions such as "I'm not sure what the name means, you must know, right?" were answered with a nod and a smile. In cases where interviewees insisted, they were told that it would be possible to return to the topic when the interview was over. Only two interviewees, a woman and a man, did this; based on this one may assume that for most of the interviewees their children's names are a closed issue.

Only the interviewer and interviewee were present at each interview, even when couples living together were interviewed. At the second stage of the study, the recordings were transcribed in an effort to organise and structure the data collected, so I could interpret it and understand the meanings in it (Shkedi 2010). The transcripts revealed two categories, the linguistic properties of the names, and a social category. The categories were reviewed laterally, and themes encompassing similar messages were grouped together. Later, the themes were compared to the theory of basic human values developed by Schwartz (2012a). In the present study, statements on topics related to the prevalence of names, common and unique, are presented.

Name choices were associated in many instances with parental concerns about the name's impact on their children's status among their peers. This concern was sometimes explained in terms of the parents' personal experiences, and sometimes mentioned as a known fact: "People make fun of names". The fear of ridicule relates to the issues of the use of unusual given names.

4.1 Acting upon the conservation motivation: The security value

The choice of common names embodies the choice of security or conformity values. The social motivator of both values is conservation (Schwartz 2012b). Conservatively motivated interviewees, whose choices were influenced by the fear of ridicule, fulfilled the security value. According to Schwartz (2012b), the security value encompasses the objectives of achieving a sense of safety, harmony and stability in all possible relational spheres – social, conjugal/romantic and personal. Adherence to this value stems from individuals' basic need to meet society's demands. Some of the interviewees admitted that unusual names they liked during the naming process were rejected because they feared their children would suffer ridicule, especially during childhood, as A. said when discussing the choice of his eldest son's name when in his late twenties:

> Yes, Israelis, the culture, have fashions and there's a set of names. *A name that's, like, unusual, I think is a good thing.* I mean, I really enjoy introducing myself as A. and there aren't many of us, especially my age, now there are more. My brother's name is R-m, that's also an unusual name, and also when he introduces himself people stop and listen, and a lot of times they mention the name, that they find it interesting. So, I think there's a kind of advantage to it, *but I wouldn't have wanted any kind of distress to come from it. I mean, not to traumatise a child over strange names,* and I didn't have my parents' talent for finding something that would fit in.

A.'s comments clearly convey the fear, which recurs in the statements of other interviewees, of his children being ridiculed. This fear is the *anxiety* which, according to Schwartz (2012b), serves as the regulator acting on the preference for motivators that drive certain specific values. B. related an argument she had with her spouse about a unique name she wanted to give her eldest son, now in his forties: "(. . .) but my husband was *totally against* it, *he said people would laugh at him, and I caved* (. . .)". C. also reported this same fear about the names of her children, now in their twenties: "We played around with names *before we made the final decision that they shouldn't be laughed at, that they shouldn't suffer abuse during their childhood*". Another mother related, with regard to the name of her baby daughter: "But *I was afraid of how other people would react. I have a lot of trouble with the opinions of the people around me*".

D., who throughout the interview maintained that his wife alone had decided on the names of their now-teenage children, and that he had acquiesced and was altogether uninterested in names, suddenly said, at the end of the interview:

D: I didn't think, but I couldn't have given them a very unusual name that isn't out there.

S.L.: Why?

D.: Because *that isn't us, we're regular people. Daria,* for instance [accent on last syllable – S.L.], is a wonderful, beautiful name, but *I couldn't call my daughter that,* I don't know, *I'd need guts.*

4.2 Acting upon the conservation motivation: The conformity value

Other interviewees also acted out of the social motivation of *conservation*, but the value that comes across from their statements is that of conformity. The main difference between these interviewees and those of the previous section is a sweeping denial of the advantage of unique names, a byproduct of which is lack of anxiety.

According to Schwartz (2012b), the conformity value encompasses the objectives of achieving restraint in everyday interactions, generally with people who are close to us, as well as meeting/adhering to social expectations and norms. This value stems from the demand that the individual internalises social requirements so as not to subvert them. In accordance with the aversion to social conspicuousness that is embodied in the conformity value, E. said, regarding the choice of names for his children, now in their twenties: "I so don't like unique names (. . .)". With regard to rejecting "inappropriate" names, E. said:

E: Yes, there were names I wouldn't have wanted my child to have.

S.L.: Which ones?

E.: Not so much, not so much, my wife came up with all kinds . . . I guess it was these kinds of new names that I don't . . . No, that's not for me.

S.L.: Unusual names?

E.: Yes, I don't much care for them.

A similar message is conveyed by F., a mother of young children, who also poked fun at unique names: "(. . .) I'm not looking for unique names, *I don't need them to be called Shmoki Ben* [spoken mockingly – S.L.] (. . .) That's not important (. . .)"

F.'s statement illustrates the ridicule that unique names can elicit – thereby clearly demonstrating that the interviewee statements in Section 4.1 are based on "real life".

4.3 Acting upon the openness to change motivation: The stimulation value

The choice of the stimulation value, which is opposed to the security and conformity values, is what drives the desire to give newborns unusual names. According to Schwartz (2012b), choosing the stimulation value means choosing renewal and challenge in life. It is worth asking to what degree the naming process can be said to encompass the stimulation value with regard to the name givers, the parents, inasmuch as, on the face of it, it is the infants who will be experiencing renewal and challenge as they go through life with the unusual name, and not their parents. The obvious answer is that, during the symbiotic stage of life, infants are perceived by their parents as an inseparable part of them (Amir 2013). Thus, all decisions made about newborns are personal.

Schwartz (2012b) describes the stimulation value, driven by the individual motivator of openness to change, as a value oriented towards achieving objectives of excitement, renewal and challenge; its implementation stems from a desire to live life to the fullest. The openness-to-change motivator requires confrontation with the anxiety to which the interviewees in the security value section succumbed. This comes across in G.'s explanation of why she bothered to verify that the name she had chosen for her young daughter was indeed unique:

> *We were actually happy to give her a name that was less mainstream, less conventional, it builds a strong character.* Before I became pregnant, I thought I really liked the names *Alma* and *Meeka*, but then I discovered that I'm not the only one who likes those names. We wanted something that would be less common.

There were interviewees who related to the fact that they had chosen their children's names mainly for their uniqueness, as with H., who said, regarding the search for unique names for her 20-year-old twins: "Because we felt it was hard to find a name [for the second twin – S.L.] that would compete *with this name's 'wow' factor*".

> S.L.: A--- [the first twin's name – S.L.] is 'wow'?
>
> H.: *Because it's so rare. . .*

I., whose name is unusual, as is its diminutive/nickname, but whose eldest daughter, now in her thirties, was the only one of his children to be given an unusual name, spoke favourably about unique names:

> I'll say it again, *names have power.* First of all, *your name is different and special,* maybe you are too. (. . .) *Maybe you're also different and special.* But memory, I meet people, just now

> I met someone, we worked together in ’88, so if I’d been called *Yossi* or *Danny* or *Shlomo*, that fades out over the years, with the memory, since over the course of your life you meet a lot of Yossis and Dannys and Shmuels and the like. But S., people meet once in a lifetime.

All the interviewees who bear unique names said their names had proven advantageous over the years, though some maintained that the names had been a burden in childhood. One interviewee even mentioned that she had intended to change her name on reaching adulthood, as her name was always being confused with a common traditional name. But by the age of 18 she realised that her name had upsides, and she also gave her baby son a unique name, though she commented: “I hope they won’t mess it up”.

J., an interviewee in her thirties who bears a unique name and gave her baby daughter a name that she does not consider unique, made similar remarks about the issue of uncommon names: “(. . .) Because you immediately have to be a special person, or because the fact of the uniqueness already raises connotations about who I am”. Later in the interview she returned to her own name, but this time she talked about its advantages, especially concerning her career: “(. . .) *It’s also a name people remember, and I never have to explain who I am after being interviewed for a new job*”.

The toughening experience is related to societal attitudes, as can be seen in the statements of one interviewee regarding his extended family’s opposition to a unique name: “We [he and his wife – S.L.] wanted the name *Azgad* [a very uncommon Biblical name – S.L.], . . . *and they vehemently objected*, even within the family, I had two uncles – ‘why on earth Azgad? *They’ll call him Misgad (mosque)’. And they kept saying all this nonsense*”.

Attitudes regarding the choice of a unique name shed light on the amount of knowledge about name popularity available to parents during the naming process. Lieberson (2000) argues that parents are entirely unaware of name popularity levels at a given time. However, interviewees whose choices were guided by the stimulation value affirmed that the names they were choosing were indeed unique. Other interviewees, who claimed that they had chosen unique names and only afterwards discovered that the names were not unique, were not guided by the stimulation value. Had they been guided by the stimulation value, they would have checked the popularity levels of the names selected, as did those interviewees whose primary goal was to choose unique names.

There were interviewees who said that, after their children were born, they started hearing the names more often. As K. said about the names of her young children: “I like unique things; more widely-used names like *Ido*, *Tal*, (very common names at the time – S.L.) didn’t interest me. After I gave them the name, I suddenly started hearing it a lot”. Similarly, L. said: “At that time I didn’t think the name was as popular as it turned out to be later on, but it also sounded unusual to me". With a smile, another interviewee said about the name of her teenage son: ". . . So, the name *Etai* spoke to me, and I was sure it was so unique, I didn't know it was the most popular name in those years". Another interviewee had this to say about the name of his young son: "I thought it was pretty unique, then I realised it wasn't. A lot of people named their kids that . . .".

Certain interviewees got their onomastic knowledge from their older children's educational frameworks, though such knowledge is likely to be less accurate for the newborn's age group, as Lieberson (2000) noted. This can be seen in M.'s remarks about her choice of name for her baby daughter: "*Alma; I'm totally against very popular, I won't do something like that* (. . .) In Ofer's class [her eldest son – S.L.] there are six Almas, *six Almas*!"

The statement of the next interviewee, the father of a teenage son, sheds light on the frustration felt by a parent who did not choose his/her child's name on the basis of the stimulation value. In retrospect, he found he'd chosen a very popular name for his son and realised too late that the stimulation value was important to him: "But whenever I hear the name *Ido*, and I hear it a lot, I feel dissatisfied. (. . .) Because, because, because a name should be personal in some way, it should be unique. (. . .) *There are a lot of Idos, so it's . . . It's a problem. The signifier should be specific*".

5 Discussion

Most of the interviewees named their children on the basis of the conservation motivation and chose commonly used names. The interviewees could be divided into two categories. There were those who named their children based on the security value; they acknowledged the upsides of unique names, but their statements conveyed the restraining effect of anxiety in terms of deciding on socially accepted names. Other children were named based on the conformity value, in which case no mention was made of the advantages of unusual names; rather, aversion was expressed regarding the attempt to stand out that unique names embody. In sharp contrast, there were some interviewees who named their children in accordance with the stimulation value, motivated by openness to change; they had verified, at the time of naming, that the names they were giving their children were unusual.

The question that arises here is what, exactly, a unique name is. The interviewees in this study defined unique names intuitively as names that "aren't often heard", but that is not an empirical definition. Characterizing such names entails trying to understand the ways in which given names spread within a specific society. Kripke (1994) defines given names as rigid designators that gain popularity in the society in two different steps. In the first step, the new given name enters the language via an initial baptism, effected by its being pointed out or described as such. In the next step, the given name is known to more than few speakers, and its use is transmitted within social circles until it spreads throughout society as a whole. In cases where the name is transmitted via the media, it is characterised by particularly rapid prevalence curves, as found by Lieberson (2000). Thus, unique names are those that are at Kripke's (1994) baptism stage, and they are names whose statistical distribution in a given society is low. As we have seen above, low statistical dispersion can be checked, which is what interviewees did when their goal was to choose unique names.

Unusual names were chosen on the basis of the stimulation value, whose motivator is openness to change; a minority of interviewees went in this direction. These interviewees were aware that the names would make their children stand out, and they also referred to the strengthening of the children's character that would occur as a result of the automatic conspicuousness conferred by the names. As indicated by interviewees who bear unique names, these names have benefits. For example, they make those who bear them stand out, but the advantages come at later stages in life. Most of the interviewees with unusual names spoke appreciatively of their names and of the economic advantage they embody, particularly in monetary terms – acquaintance with useful people who don't forget the bearer of a unique name, or standing out at job interviews. However, most of these interviewees did not give their children such names, indicating that their own experiences were not entirely positive. In general, interviewees who chose unusual names also gave them mainly to their eldest sons and daughters. The younger children of these interviewees received popular names.

The rift between these two motivators – the openness-to-change motivator (naming their children with names according to Kripke's first step), and the conservation motivator (naming their children with names according to Kripke's second step), can be understood in terms of the action of a given society's linguistic habitus. According to Bourdieu (1991), linguistic habitus is shaped by small changes over time, starting in the centre of the society, and is adapted to market conditions and subject to considerations of profit and loss. Bourdieu maintains that individuals produce discourse under the expectation of social sanctions, and this unconscious expectation tends to shape the sense of social containment with regard to linguistic products – in our case, the names given to babies. The finding that most of the interviewees who acted in accordance with the conservation motivator reported fear of social sanctions verifies Bourdieu's observation (1991) regarding the social mechanisms that influence the production of the individual's linguistic products in society.

The path of action of the linguistic habitus can also be seen in the behaviour of those parents who introduced small linguistic changes by the very fact of choosing unique names for their eldest children. Most of these parents are indeed, as Bourdieu claimed, from the "social centre" – living in the geographical centre, well-educated and with a good socio-economic status. Social changes are not plain acts, even at the centre. The degree to which this effort was traumatic, that is, the degree to which confronting the resultant social sanctions proved difficult, can be seen in the fact that only the eldest children were given unusual names. The children who followed them received common and, for the most part, quite popular names.

Choosing names for infants is similar to decision-making in risk situations, as defined by Kahneman and Lovallo (2005: 126): "Decision-makers (. . .) Their approaches to risk demonstrate risk aversion and near-proportionality. The unwillingness to bear explicit responsibility for possible losses is very strong (. . .)". According to Kahneman and Lovallo (2005), the term "near-proportionality" refers to risk aversion at a proportional level, that is, the cash equivalent of rising bets stands (nearly) in direct relation to the outcomes. Large gambles are taken by parents who are influenced by the openness-to-change motivator, as they are aware of the high level of profit associated with unique names; that is why they confront the risk embodied by their choice. Parents who choose names on the basis of the security value are aware of the high sums that unusual names can yield, but fear the consequences of the bet for their offspring during childhood. Parents influenced by the conformity motivator deny the chance of profit that unique names represent.

A special case of naming process gambles is the choice of a unique name with attributes that soon make it popular. Harari and McDavid's (1973) study, mentioned in Section 1, found that primary school teachers evaluated essays in accordance with the children's names that appeared on them. Essays bearing common names received higher grades than did essays bearing unusual names. Surprisingly, the most uncommon girl's name at the time the article was published, *Adele*, received a high grade.

Adele's good grade and the name's growing prevalence since that time can be attributed to its phonological composition – the combination of a sonorant consonant, /l/ with a stop consonant and a vowel whose vocalisation level is very low: /d/. The sonorant consonants – /l/, /m/, /n/ and /r/ – sound particularly pleasant to American ears (Smith 2007, 1999, 1998). Furthermore, the name *Adele* ends with the sonorant consonant /l/, a very desirable sound for the Israeli ear (Landman 2016). Phonological analysis of the Israeli names that have been the most popular in the long term indicated that the interaction created by the sonorant consonants /l/, /n/ and /r/, whose sounds are especially sonorous when combined with sounds whose vocalisation is particularly low, such as the /a/ and /d/ in the name *Adele*, are exceptionally pleasant to Israeli ears, as demonstrated by the names *Hila* and *Daniel*, two of the most popular names of the past thirty years in Israel (Landman 2016). Given the surging popularity of the name *Adele* in the United States, one may assume that this combination of sounds is also pleasant to American ears. Regarding the choice of the name *Adele*, the parents made a naming bet that proved successful even in childhood; they chose a name that was unique at the time of naming, so that the girls stood out because of the name. However, thanks to the name's phonological properties, it spread quickly and became prevalent, so that the girls benefited from a name with striking phonological advantages that soon became popular and, hence, socially desirable (Lawson 1980; Mehrabian 2001).

The most significant practical implications of social attitudes towards different types of given names seem to be related to the way in which teachers and caregivers of young children pronounce names that are considered to be socially problematic, i.e., unique names, particularly as, in recent years, children's given names have served as one of the more effective early literacy tools (Yaffe-Gur 1996; Levin et al. 2003). The most effective means of preventing unnecessary harm to young children is to inform student teachers about the complexity of the issue, so they can show appropriate caution with regard to children's names, as the name represents the child's identity (de Pina-Cabral and Lourenço 2019).

References

Adminien'e, Vilija & Naus'eda, Aurimas. 2009. Sociolinguistic tendencies of baby names in English speaking countries. *Acta Humanitarica Universitatis Saulensis* 8. 329–336.

Amir, Danah. 2013. *Te'hom Safa* [Cleft tongue]. Jerusalem: Magnes Press, Hebrew University.

Anderson, Timothy & Paul R. Schmitt. 1990. Unique first names in male and female psychiatric inpatients. *Journal of Social Psychology* 130 (6). 835–837.

Barthes, Roland. 1998. *Mitholog'yoth* [Mythologies]. Tel Aviv: Babel Publishing.

Bourdieu, Pierre. 1991. *Language and symbolic power*. Cambridge: Polity Press.

Busse, Thomas V. & Louisa Seraydarian. 1978. The relationships between first name desirability and school readiness, IQ, and school achievement. *Psychology in the Schools* 15 (2). 295–302.

Denzin, Norman K. 1995. Symbolic interactionism. In Jonathan A. Smith, Rom Harré & Luk Van Langenhove (eds.), *Rethinking psychology*, 43–58. London: Sage Publications.

de Pina-Cabral, Joao & Lourenço, Nelson. 2019. Personal identity and ethnic ambiguity: Naming practices among the Eurasians of Macao. *Social Anthropology* 2(2). 115–132.

Dion, Kenneth L. 1983. Names, identity, and self. *Names* 31 (4). 245–257.

Ellis, Albert & Robert M. Beechley. 1954. Emotional disturbance in children with peculiar given names. *The Journal of Genetic Psychology* 85. 337–339.

Ephratt, Michal. 2006. Personal names as condensation and displacement. *Ha'ivrit We'ahyoteha* [The Hebrew and Its Sisters] 6–7. 55–72.

Erwin, Philip G. and Avraham Calev, Avraham. 1984. The influence of Christian name stereotypes on the marking of children's essays. *British Journal of Educational Psychology* 54. 223–227.
Foucault, Michel. 2011. *Hammilim Ve'haddvarim: Archeologia shel Mad'ei Ha'adam* [The Order of things: An archaeology of the human sciences]. Tel Aviv: Resling.
Frege, Gottlob. 1984. Sense and reference. *Iyyun* [Examination] 33. 364–382.
Harari, Herbert & John W. McDavid. 1973. Name stereotypes and teachers' expectations. *Journal of Educational Psychology* 65. 222–225.
Hroch, Miroslav. 1985. *Social preconditions of national revival in Europe: A comparative analysis of the social composition of patriotic groups among the smaller European nations*. Cambridge: Cambridge University Press.
Kahneman, Daniel & Dan Lovallo. 2005. Careful choices and daring forecasts: A cognitive perspective on risk-taking. In M. Bar-Hillel (ed.), *Rats'yonaliuth, Hognuth, Osher* [Rationality, equity, happiness]. Haifa & Jerusalem: University of Haifa Press & Keter Publishing House.
Kang, Yungu, David H. Zhu & Jan Anthea Zhang. 2021. Being extraordinary: How CEOS' uncommon names explain strategic distinctiveness. *Strategic Management Journal* 42. 462–488.
Kohut, Heinz. 1984. *Keitsad Merapp'eth Ha'analiza?* [How does analysis cure?] Tel Aviv: Am Oved.
Kripke, Saul. 1994. *Shemoth We'hechre'ach* [Naming and necessity]. Ra'anana: Mif'alim Universitaim le'Hotza'a la'Or.
Landman, Shlomit. 2016. Onomastics in a melting pot society with common roots: Israeli Jews in the second half of the twentieth century. *Annales de Démographie Historique* 1. 131–149.
Landman, Shlomit. 2020. *Anie Hallishz Hay'chida Ba'olam: Tahalichei Mattan Shemoth Lethinokoth* [I Am the Only Lishaz in the World: Naming Newborns]. Tel Aviv: Resling Publishing.
Lawson, Edwin D. 1980. First names on the campus: A semantic differential analysis. *Names* 28(1). 69–83.
Levin, Iris, Linnea Ehri, Orit Hamuj & Liat Peled-Haim. 2003. The ability of preschool children to read and write their first names and the names of their classmates: The contribution of knowledge about letters. *Or'yanuth Wesafa* [Literacy and Language] 3. 47–70.
Lieberson, Stanley. 2000. *A matter of taste*. New Haven & London: Yale University Press.
Mehrabian, Albert. 2001. Characteristics attributed to individuals on the basis of their first names. *Genetic, Social, and General Psychology Monographs* 127 (1). 59–88.
Maykut, Pamela & Richard Morehouse. 1994. *Beginning qualitative research: A philosophic and practical guide*. London: Falmer Press.
Nadav, Meir, Rabin, Shiber Stanley, Ben Asher, Yitzhak Zion and Binyamin Maoz. 2008. *Ha'atsmie Bemar'ath Hashem* [The self in the mirror of names]. Tel Aviv: Hakibbutz Hameuchad.
Rokeach, Milton. 1973. *The nature of human values*. New York: Free Press.
Rosenhouse, Judith. 2003. First names in contemporary Hebrew. In D. Sivan & P. Halevy-Kirtchuk (eds.), *Kol le'Yaakov* [Jacob's Voice], 341–357. Beersheba: Ben-Gurion University.
Schwartz, Shalom H. 1992. Universals in the content and structure of values: Theory and empirical tests in 20 countries. In Mark P. Zanna (ed.), *Advances in experimental social psychology* 25. 1–65.
Schwartz, Shalom H. 2012a. An Overview of the Schwartz Theory of Basic Values. *Online Readings in Psychology and Culture*, Unit 2. Retrieved from http://scholarworks.gvsu.edu/orpc/vol2/iss1/11
Schwartz, Shalom H. 2012b. Value orientations: Measurement, antecedents and consequences across nations. In Roger Jowell, Caroline Roberts, Rory Fitzgerald & Gillian Eva (eds.), *Measuring attitudes cross-nationally: Lessons from the European social survey*, 169–203. London: Sage.
Shkedi, Asher. 2010. Te'oria Hame'uggeneth Benarativim: Havnayath Te'oria Bemechkar Eichuthanie [Theory anchored in narratives: Constructing theory in qualitative research]. In Leah Kassan &

Michal Krumer-Nevo (eds.) *Data analysis in qualitative research*, 436–461. Beersheba: Ben-Gurion University Publishing.
Smith, Grant W. 1998. The political impact of name sounds. *Communication Monographs* 65. 154–172.
Smith, Grant W. 1999. Effects of name sounds in the congressional elections of 1998. *Names* 47. 325–335.
Smith, Grant W. 2007. The influence of name sound in the congressional elections of 2006. *Names* 55 (4). 465–472.
Vanguri, Star M. 2016. *Rhetorics of names and naming*. Basingstoke: Taylor & Francis Ltd.
Whiteman, Sasha. 1988. First names as cultural indices: Trends in the national identity of Israelis, 1882–1980. In Nurit Graetz (ed.), *Nekudath Tatspith: Tarbuth Wechevra Be'Eretz Israel* [Observation point: Culture and society in the land of Israel], 141–151. Tel Aviv: The Open University.
Wittgenstein, Ludwig. 1954. *Chakiroth Philosophiyoth* [Philosophical investigations]. Jerusalem: Magnes Press, Hebrew University.
Yaffe-Gur, Talyah. 1996. *Estrateg'yoth Keri'a bekekrv Yaldei Haggan* [Reading strategies among preschool children]. Haifa: University of Haifa M.A. thesis.

Susan Kus & Victor Raharijaona

Chapter 7
From "sprinkling" a blessing to audaciously appropriating a name: Some reflections concerning personal names and naming in the central highlands of Madagascar

Abstract: Roaming the central highlands of Madagascar as archaeologists (one indigenous and one off-islander), we continue to be charmed by the beauty, humour and "prosaic" historical force of names one comes to use to "orient" oneself on the history-laden landscape. There is 'A place not in the heavens' (*Tsiandanitra)*, carrying the sense of 'The closest one can come to heaven (on-earth)'. There is 'The place of beautiful blue ginger' (*Antsakaviromanga*). There is also the place, humorously called, 'finally, a boy child (has been born)' (*Sambolahy*). Yet, there are also places such as *Maromiandra*, 'Where the many wait (for the arrival of the sovereign)'. Speaking such names out loud in societies of primary orality and of sensitivity to oral poetics continues to bring into consciousness, and into continued existence, moments of poetic pronouncements and prosaic audacity. In such societies, it is also the case that ethno-archaeologists and ethnographers are drawn to learning about and learning from those same dimensions of humour, beauty and blessing in naming individuals, and audacity in "self-naming". It is considered that keeping a name private among family members or assigning a humorous "detractive/distractive" name, such as 'Healthy young dog', to a child can turn away the attention of the envious adult "evil-doer" from a new young child. But later the child can be "sprinkled" with a name of blessing such as 'The one of radiant beauty' or 'Blessed and bestowed upon us by the creator'. Each time it is pronounced, the name re-enacts the blessing and offers continuing beauty in a society sensitive to the power of words to enact, remind and delight those whose ears and sensitivities have been

Acknowledgements: We would like to express our gratitude to Dr. Clarisse Rasoamampionona, Deuxième Vice-présidente de l'Université de Fianarantsoa, Madagascar, not only for her practical help, but also for sharing her many insights into the subtleties and complexities of her Betsileo heritage. We are also grateful to the Merina and Betsileo people who have taught us so much in the field with such grace, kindness and patience.

Susan Kus, Rhodes College, Memphis, Tennessee, U.S., e-mail: Kus@Rhodes.edu
Victor Raharijaona, Chercheur Associé Université de Fianarantsoa, Madagascar, e-mail: v.raharijaona143@gmail.com

https://doi.org/10.1515/9783110759297-007

duly cultivated to appreciate oral poetry. Yet it is also the case that historically some "leaders" have audaciously assumed names such as *Andrianampoinimerina*, 'The noble desired in the heart of Imerina (the kingdom/state)' This contribution seeks to offer an appreciation of the "art" of personal names in the central highlands of Madagascar.

Keywords: oral poetics, ethno-archaeology, Madagascar, trope, appropriating a name

1 A place not in the heavens

Exploring and experiencing the landscape of central Madagascar as ethno-archaeologists (one a foreigner and the other indigenous), we have been charmed and fascinated by the Malagasy poetic proclivity in naming villages we have visited, valleys we have explored, and hills we have climbed. We have lived at *Tsiandanitra*, 'Not in the heavens', whose name carries the sense of 'the closest place to heaven on earth'. It lies across a small river from 'At-the-place-of-beautiful-blue-ginger',*Antsakaviromanga*, and 'The-hill-like-a-pearl', *Ambohiboahangy*. Lying to its north is the village of *Sambolahy* or 'So happy for a boy'. As the story goes, living in the village was a couple who had a series of girl children. Very late one evening there was a loud cry heard coming from the village. It was the husband, who cried out, in his delight, a phrase that could roughly be translated as: 'Finally we have been graced with a boy child!' Subsequently, the village was renamed to continue to recall that moment past of delight and humour. To be clear, the word for 'name' in Malagasy is *anarana*. This term is used in the same way as its English equivalent when speaking not only of individuals but also of objects, animals, plants, places, etc.

There is a saying in the highlands of Madagascar that 'one captures a bull by its horns, a butterfly by its tongue, and a human being by their ears'.[1] Certainly, we, the authors, continue to be captured by the arresting poetic descriptiveness, as well as by the descriptive playfulness, that can be found not only in place names, but also in names for everything from hairstyles to hats to protective and curative beads. There is the hairstyle of numerous hanging braids that is called *kilavoambary* or 'that bend over like the ripe stalks of rice'. There is a hat called *trafon'omby kely* or 'the hump of a little (zebu) calf'; another hat for a young child carried on its mother's back bears the delightful name of *tsiminohanatra* or '(the little one) who will not listen to-advice'. During one field season we collected over 80 names for

1 *Ny ombalahy rohizana amin'ny tandrony, ny lolo samborina amin'ny lelany, ny olombelona azo amin'ny sofiny.*

beads used for medicinal and protective purposes. One bead is named 'the palm of the hand that is never empty' or *felatananatsifoana.* To hear a mother calling out the name of her young daughter, *Mirana*, which translates as 'Radiant beauty', or a young child being called by a parent, *Sitraka*, 'With whom-one-is-well-pleased', is to be offered a poetically powerful pause for reflection. The conferring of a personal name and the taking on of a new personal name in the central highlands of Madagascar, as the reader might suspect, is worthy of fuller discussion in order to render "honour" to the oral poesis of the Malagasy people who have allowed us to work with and among them in the field. They have added cross-cultural bearing to our appreciation of Gertrud Stein's (1935) words:

> Poetry I say is essentially a vocabulary. . ..
> . . . So that is poetry really loving the name of
> Anything and that is not prose.
> *Lectures in America*

2 Food for thought in a society of primary orality

The Malagasy have a saying: *Ny vavasoa sakafo*. The "literal" translation of this trope is 'The beautiful/pleasing/delightful mouth [is] food/nourishment'. However, a less prosaic and more indigenous lyrical effort to translate into English the intended sense of this proverb would be: 'A mouth offering sweet/beautiful speech offers nourishment for thought and feeling'. Such an understanding and sentiment is certainly experienced in a society of primary orality.

To be clear, we are not trained as linguists, though the co-author, Raharijaona, is a native speaker of Malagasy. Yet, as anthropologists we have come to appreciate, over numerous years of fieldwork, aspects of living in a world of primary subsistence and traditional and substantial orality. In such a world, 'thinking through the body' (á la Jackson 1983) renders embodied experience mnemonically effective and affective. To live in such a world allows one to create and share rich concrete imagery, metaphors, metonyms and tropes drawn from communal cultural practices and personal experiences, as many anthropologists have come to understand (e.g., Fernandez 1986). Both traditional and "novel" tropes can be used to think about not only the practical and the social, but also the philosophical and the aesthetic. Such a world is also a whole whose "wholeness" is revealed in material and sensuous symbols, metonyms, metaphors and tropes. As we have learned in the central highlands of Madagascar, conferring a personal name in a world of primary or substantial orality can bless and/or protect a newly recognised individual. To change one's name or accept a name change in such a society can signify a recognition or revelation of "character" in many senses of the term. In such a society it can be the case that to pronounce the name of a deceased individual might call their spirit into one's presence. Yet, before we begin to discuss our appreciation and understanding of "bearing" personal names in highland Madagascar, let us clarify some matters concerning this island, which after Greenland, New Guinea and Borneo is the fourth (or fifth) largest island in the world.[2]

3 "The Big Red Island"

Madagascar has been called "The Big Red Island" because of the red lateritic soil that covers most of the island. The east coast sees tropical rains for most of the year. The central highlands area sees a seasonal weather pattern which can reach temperatures as low as 40° F (4° C) during the austral winter. The highlands influence the passage of winds and rains across the island to the west. The west coast has distinct rainy and dry seasons.

The current population of Madagascar is estimated to be more than 28 million, and the people of Madagascar recognise approximately 18 ethnic groups among themselves. The Malagasy language[3] is a Malayo-Polynesian language whose closest "relative" is Ma'anyan, spoken in Borneo. Madagascar has two major dialect groupings (central north east and south west) and the Malagasy language has anywhere from 11 to 23 dialects, according to what source one consults. The Malagasy language family and its dialectical "nature" across the island testify to the island's relatively late occupation, estimated to be between 50 and 500 CE (Burney et al. 2004; Beaujard 2011) by Austronesian voyagers/explorers traveling across the Indian Ocean.

As one might suspect there are a number of loan words from other early voyagers and settlers of the island, particularly from Malay and Javanese, as well as Arabic and Bantu. The north and west coasts of the island saw significant trade as early as the 11th century CE from across the Indian Ocean (Burney et al. 2004). Words borrowed from French and English are also found in the Malagasy language, evidence of the island's later history involving European trade and subsequent colonization.

Given the size of the island, its large population and number of "ethnic" groups, its environmental diversity, and its numerous dialects, we obviously cannot purport

2 If one counts Australia as an island, rather than a subcontinent, then Madagascar ranks fifth.

3 Malagasy is also spoken on the island of Mayotte. There are also Malagasy speakers on the islands of Reunion and Mauritius.

to speak of the island as a singular whole. Our primary fieldwork has been concentrated in the Betsileo countryside outside the regional capital of Fianarantsoa and in the countryside of Imerina, where the present-day capital of the country, Antananarivo, is found. The Betsileo region lies to the south of Imerina. That is to say, we have worked in the central highlands of the island and it is from there that we draw our examples and our "tales" of personal names.

Besides drawing from our experiences in the field, we will be referring to several "classical" works on Malagasy culture. These include works by both Malagasy and non-Malagasy scholars. We would like to draw our readers' attention to an underlying "attitude" of the approach that was often brought to the study of Malagasy culture under colonial rule.

Henri-Marie DuBois was a Jesuit missionary in Madagascar (from 1902–1924) who understood himself as someone sent "to educate" the indigenous population of Madagascar. However, as a Jesuit scholar, he understood his need to "understand" the indigenous language and indigenous predispositions, customs and beliefs, as he states in the introduction to his work, *Monographie des Betsileo*. He goes on to explain this further by saying:

> . . .[this is to be done] to the ends, no doubt, in order to redress their deformations, to correct their errors, to fill in their deficiencies, but underlying all this so as to provoke, support, direct and develop their movement upward. (DuBois 1938: vii, our translation from the original French][4]

This stance might further explain DuBois' "appreciation" of orality and Betsileo oration (as well as Betsileo personal names). He writes near the end of his monograph, which is of "epic" size (more than 1,500 pages):

> To summarise, the Betsileo orator, like the Betsileo themselves in all their speech, like every common man in his phrases, is before all else concrete. Abstract ideas do not please him and he doesn't completely seize [or understand an idea] except in the form of an image, of something concrete seen or experienced. (DuBois 1938: 1259, our translation from the original French)[5]

We bring DuBois' assertions in the above quote to the reader's attention in order to emphasize its contrast with our attempt to appreciate societies of primary orality and of substantial orality as we discussed above and will illustrate in the sections below. Yet, before we move our focus to the actual topic of naming and personal

4 ". . .a fin, sans doute, d'en redresser leurs déformations, d'en corriger les erreurs, d'en compléter les déficiences, mais par-dessus tout d'en provoquer, soutenir, diriger et développer l'essor".

5 "En somme l'orateur betsileo comme le Betsileo, dans tout son langage, comme tout homme du peuple faisant des phrases, est avant tout 'concret'. L'idée abstraite ne lui plaît pas et il ne la saisit complètement que sous forme d'image, de chose vue ou vécue."

names in the highlands of Madagascar, we wish to briefly mention an additional source concerning Betsileo names and naming practices.

The indigenous Betsileo scholar, Jessé Rainihifina (1888–1980), also discussed naming among the Betsileo (Rainihifina 1975: 48–56). In his study of Betsileo "heritage of the mind/spirit" (*lovantsaina)*, which might be equivalent to "cultural and intellectual heritage" and custom (*fomba*), he said he followed DuBois' example of inquiry and study. He, however, published in the Malagasy language as a way of "protecting" cultural heritage for the Malagasy. It should be noted that he was a catechist who later became a Protestant pastor.

4 Names to designate, to describe, to delight, to express delight, to bless, to protect and, in some cases, to demonstrate the art of stringing beads

During one's lifetime in central Madagascar, one might undergo several name changes, or at least two, according to Rainihifina (1975: 47). Included among the ways personal names can be acquired are the bestowing of a name on an infant, acquiring a replacement "nickname" as a child, "earning" a name as one moves into adulthood, and, in some cases, appropriating a name for oneself. In death, in traditional practice in the highlands, a person's name is no longer uttered aloud in public (though there are some exceptions, as the reader will come to learn). As we will see in the examples offered below, some personal names are single syllables. However, Malagasy are reputed for bearing very long names. The Malagasy language is agglutinative, as the reader might already have deduced from the examples of names offered above that we have translated into English as "strings" of English words. There is a Betsileo saying, found not only in the literature concerning their culture (e.g., Michel-Andrianarahinjaka 1987), but a saying that we have heard in the field used by an oral historian:[6] *Ny taroña fihengo vakaña eko ny mañendrika ro hatao* – "Speech is like (the art of) stringing beads" (It is done to render beautiful one's knowledge and thoughts.). The sense of this proverb is that, while all may delight in the beauty of individual beads, and indeed may know the individual names of different beads, not everyone has the ability to arrange them into a necklace to render beautiful the one who wears it. In cultures of primary orality and of significant orality, as we have come to appreciate in the central highlands of Madagascar, proverbs and sayings can be used to think *with and about* past

6 This Betsileo oral historian from the village of Ambondrona was named *Ranaivozanany Joseph*.

situations *and* about new situations. We have brought this proverb to our reader's attentions so as to help them appreciate the talent and thought that often underpins the creation of long Malagasy personal names, certainly in history. It is also the case that these names of "strings" of words/beads are not pronounced (or written[7]) as phrases or sentences of individual words. As single words they are each pronounced with a slightly different cadence.[8]

4.1 A child's name

In the field we have met children with names ranging from lovely to cute to funny. As we mentioned above, the name *Mirana* can be translated as "Radiant beauty". This name, pronounced out loud, can be understood as both a description and a flattering. Other children's names are bestowed both based on early observation and as a wish to continue to be realized, such as the name *Landy*. *Landy* can be translated as 'silk', but it also carries the image of a chrysalis unfolding its beauty for the world. While in the field, we also met a little boy who answered to the personal names of *Ingahipasy* and *Rapasy*, when villagers addressed him. His "given" personal name as an infant was Pascal (a French and Christian first name). Pasy is a nickname for Pascal (analogous to using Suzy for Susan). Because he was so precocious from a very early age, he came to be called, by some, Ingahipasy, or "Monsieur Pasy". Others called him *Rapasy*. This is a nickname that can be understood as the "malgachisation" of "Monsieur Pastor". This is a deliberate humorous play on words concerning his given Christian first name. Other names for children, we were told, were sometimes given in consultation with a ritual specialist, to protect the child from bad fortune or from jealous and maliciously intentioned individuals. Once, while doing field work in the countryside of Imerina, we were told by elders in the village where we were staying that we should not call out the name of a toddler or young child to grab the child's attention (as one might do in the U.S.). To do this might also grab and direct the attention of a *mpamosavy* ('a-caster-of-evil-spells') in the immediate area towards the child. This would also explain why children would not immediately answer or recognise us when we first called out their

7 The name of the location/village that we lived in while doing fieldwork, that we mentioned in our opening paragraph, *Tsiandanitra*, 'Not-in-the-heavens', if written (and spoken as a phrase), would be *tsy any amin'ny lanitra*.

8 We are tempted here to try our "hand" at concrete metaphor and imagery in the fashion of the highlands by suggesting the alternative image for the pronunciation of long names as the image of a stringed instrument where one might pluck each string individually OR one might play several strings together as a cord.

names. A young child is taught not to answer to their name on its first or second calling so as to be sure of who is calling and what their intentions are.

An "infant" new to the world will be recognised as an individual, but will not necessarily be immediately given their "real name" (*tena anarany*) that they will usually bear through childhood. Instead, they will be given a "baby-name" (*anaranjaza*) in the interim (Ravelojaona and Rajonah 1937–52: 52). Such names can range from a generic reference to a humorous appellation. Rainihifina (1975: 47) points out that the "newness" of the new arrival can be seen in such names as 'The new little girl' (*Ikalavao*), 'The new little boy' (*Ilahivao*) and "The new arrival" (*Ivaoavy*). It should be pointed out that the Malagasy language does not mark gender in third person singular pronouns or in certain nouns. Take the example of the term of respectful address, *Tompoko*, which is used for both males and females. However, gender can be marked if needed for clarification or specificity. Consequently, one can add the term *vavy* (female/feminine) or the term *lahy* (male/masculine) to the term *Tompoko* to create the English equivalents of 'Madame' (*Tompokovavy*) and 'Sir' (*Tompokolahy*). Consequently, not all personal names are gender specific.

As a child continues to grow and mature it begins to reveal its individual character and the characteristics that will allow it to acquire a first "real name". Rainihifina (1975: 47) says that just as each person has a different face, they also bear an individual name to not only help distinguish them, but also to grant them respect. Rainihifina (1975: 47–56) offers an extensive discussion of names with numerous examples from the Betsileo. He also arranges the names into categories so as to offer his readers an insight into the poesy of naming practices among the Betsileo. Below we cite some of his categories with a sampling of the examples he offers.

There are names such as 'The yellow one' (*Imavo),* which might refer to the colour of a person's skin or complexion, 'The-shrimp' (*Ipatsa*), referring to a child's small size, and 'The bottom of the basket' (*Ivodiharona*) referring to a child's appearance as wrinkled or crushed, like an item at the bottom of a basket. Names such as these he understands to be ones of "physical appearance" (*araka ny endrika),* which sometimes, as we have come to appreciate during our fieldwork, involve a bit of humor and perhaps even protection from envious/malicious ones.

There are names such as 'The little boy (considered as the) plaything (of-his-parents)' (*Lahianakisa*),[9] 'The binding (that ties/unites the members of the family)' (*Ifehy*), and 'Who is not a stranger/visitor' (*Tsivahiny*). It should be noted that the term of negation, *tsy (*not), is often used to reinforce a positive interpretation. We remind the reader of the name of the village we noted in our introduction, 'Not in

9 The term *kisa* in Betsileo means 'toy' or 'delight'. In the Merina dialect this term means 'chicanery'.

the heavens’, as an example of the use of the term *tsy*. As we have come to understand, this term can be interpreted in English as not only “the closest to, but not exactly” and “anything but”. Rainihifina (1975: 47) categorises names such as these as “terms of endearment” (*mihantahanta*)

There are names such as ‘The one who makes you lift up your head’ (*Imampiandra*) and ‘The one who wipes away tears’ (I*mampihiratsa*). There are also names such as ‘Who brings one joy’ (*Imaharavo*) and ‘Who makes you happy’ (in the sense of the one who wipes away sadness) (*Imahafaly*). Such names Rainihifina (1975: 48) classifies as “names of memory” (*anarana fahatsiarovana*), names recalling sad memories of the past that have been replaced by intervening lovely moments of new life.

One might be given a name such as ‘S/he of the sowing of rice seedlings’ (*Iketsa*), ‘S/he of the harvest’ (*Ivokatsa*), ‘S/he-of-the-famine’ (*Imosa*) or ‘S/he of the troops’ (*Itafika*), recalling a moment when military troops invaded the village. Rainihifina (and we, the authors) would classify these as names as “moments of memory”, of seasonal routine, seasonal disruptions, and exceptional historical events around when the birth took place. One might even receive a name from a visitor passing by at the time of birth (DuBois 1938: 38). Such names include ‘The new one’ (*Ravao*) and ‘The good finish’ (*Rasoavita*).

An obvious classification used in naming, that Rainihifina (1975: 48) points out, is the “place where the child was born” (*toerana nahaterahana*). Examples of such names are ‘S/he born on the side of the-road’ (*Iandalana*) and ‘S/he born in the courtyard’ (*Iandrindrina*).

The Malagasy year has 12 months and each month contains 28 days (a system of calculation evidently borrowed from Arabic traditions). The months and their days of the year are used to understand one’s destiny upon birth.[10] One might be named for the day of the week on which one is born. Someone born on Sunday (*Alahady*) might be named *Iady* or *Ikalady* or *Ialahady* (where gender may or may not be marked). (A former head of the Betsileo Province of Fianarantsoa was named Ralahady Samuel.) Someone born on Tuesday (*Talata*) might be named *Itala* or *Italata*. If one is born in the first month of the year, *Alahamadyl*, one might be “blessed” with the name ‘The strong one’ (*Imady*) or ‘The healthy one’ (*Isalama*). Born in the last month of the year (*Alohotsy)* one might receive a name such as ‘S/he living in fullness (like the moon)’ (*Ivelonoro*) or the name “S/he whose destiny has been corrected” (*Ivitankazar*y) (Rainihifina 1975: 49).

Sometimes the names of both the mother and the father are used in gratitude for the child coming to “fruition”. DuBois (1938: 384) makes a comment about very

10 This calendar is additionally used to choose appropriate days for festivities and for funerals.

long names in the Malagasy language using the following example. *Randriatsara* ('Mr. the good noble'), the father's name, and *Rampizafy* ('Mme. The grandchild'), the mother's name, were used to create the name of their son, *Rampizafindrandriatsaravola.*

In some cases, a ritual specialist, who understands how to read destinies, such as an *ombiasa (*or *ombiasy* in Imerina*)* or a *mpanandro* ('maker of days'), will be consulted to choose a name to distance nefarious forces and/or confer protection and/or good fortune. Some names that ritual specialists suggest might be considered by the reader as "insulting". There are names such as 'S/he the dog' (*Iamboa*), 'S/he the rat' (*Ivoalavo*) and 'S/he the weed' (*Ibozaka*). Such "bad" (*ratsy*) names are disliked by bad spirits (*tsy hotian'ny fanahy ratsy*) (Rainihifina 1975: 49). If a child is born on a day of bad destiny (taking into account the day of the week as well as the month of the year), they may be offered names such as 'S/he whose day (of bad destiny) has ended' (*Ivitanandro*), 'S/he of renewed destiny' (*Ivaombita),* 'S/he that lives joyfully' (*Ivelonoro*), or 'S/he the amulet of life' (*Ivelonkazary*). Another type of "naming strategy" to distance bad fortune is to offer a name "twisted/distorted/inverted" from its "real" meaning.[11] Examples of such names include 'The slave of the dog' (*Indevonamboa*), and 'The little girl" (*Ikampela*) used to refer to a boy (Rainihifina 1975: 49).

In some cases of bad destiny that significantly threaten the child and/or the parents, the mother in particular, a ritual specialist will suggest that the child be abandoned. In such cases, another individual from the village might retrieve the child, or the actual parents themselves might even retrieve the child after "ritual" abandonment. Names that such a child would be given include the place of abandonment and the manner of "disposal". Such names include 'S/he (left) on the road' (*Iandalana*), 'S/he the chaff' (which is tossed away, in some cases for domesticated fowl or pigs to eat) (*Iampombo*) and 'S/he in the corner' (the corner being where one leaves a hoe or a pounding stick when entering the house after the task of digging, pounding rice, etc. is completed) (*Ianjoro*). Working in the Betsileo countryside, we met a young girl who was named *Zanadahy.* This name is translated as 'Child of a male'. Her mother, a ritual specialist, after understanding her daughter's problematic destiny, chose this name for her daughter after ritually abandoning her and arranging for her daughter to be retrieved by her (the ritual specialist's) brother. Later, as Zanadahy, who was actually raised by her own mother, approached the age of marriage her name was changed to *Fara* ('The last one' or 'The youngest one').

Rainihifina (1975: 51) offers examples of Christian names that have undergone adjustments in pronunciation. He refers to these names as "names that come from

11 *Anarana ampifamadihina amin'ny tena marina.*

the sacred writings" (*anarana avy amin'ny soratra masina*). These names include *Rapetera* ('Sir Peter'), *Rajaona* ('Sir John'), and *Rafilipo* ('Sir Philip').

As we see above, there are many sources of inspiration for giving names to children as they enter the world, begin to "reveal" their individuality, and move into adulthood. When a child is conferred their first "real name" it is often accompanied by a ceremony.

4.2 Naming ceremonies in youth

As stated above, an infant "new" to the world will be recognized as an individual, but traditionally the name it first bears will almost invariably be temporary. As the child continues to grow, he or she will begin to reveal the character and characteristics that will allow him or her to acquire a "real" "first" name. That name, as discussed above, can range from a wish, to a comment on physical or behavioral traits, to a protection, etc. According to DuBois, the naming of a child is considered the most important rite of social initiation. It is during the ceremony of the *hazary* that a "first" real name is conferred and made public. DuBois (1938: 378–379) discusses the ritual of the *hazary* bath in much detail. It is a complex rite that demands much skill on the part of the *ombiasa* (ritual specialist). We offer here a quick resume of this ritual for the curious reader. Along with various "medicinal" plants, a grasshopper and a whirling beetle are placed in the water that will be used for the ritual bath. The grasshopper and the beetle should be kept alive during the ceremony so as to be returned alive to the places where they were caught. The grasshopper is called a *kimbeferofero*, which can be translated as '(a-wish-that-you)-continue-to-move-forward-and-upward'. The whirling beetle is called *fandiorano*, which translates as 'cleaner-of-the-water(-source)'. Certainly, these names carry several metaphorical and symbolic interpretations, among which we should not ignore those of water, earth and sky.

For this ritual naming ceremony, pieces of banana plants and sugar cane are placed outside at the four corners of the house where the bath will take place. The *ombiasy* takes six sips of the *hazary* bath water using six different banana leaves. Six is a critically significant number. A phrase in the Malagasy language is *enin'oro enin-kahavelomana*. This translates as 'surrounded by happiness, (and) fully alive'. The term *enina* is both the number 'six' and the qualitative adjective meaning 'surrounded by' or 'wrapped in'.

After the bath the child is passed to an individual who has explicitly walks outside the house to receive the child, and it is this person who pronounces or bestows the name of the child, doing so publicly. The *hazary* water is thrown out through the door by the *ombiasa*, who pronounces a blessing. DuBois, the Jesuit priest, said that some people may equate this naming to a "*baptême idolâtrique*" (1938: 378), but he does clarify that the ritual should *not* be equated with sorcery. Nevertheless, in his text he uses the terms *sorcier* and *devin* interchangeably when referring to an *ombiasa*.

Ceremonies such as the *hazary* bath and, in some cases. a first haircut (Ravelojaona and Rajonah 1937–70: 529) are moments for the "real" first name of a child to be announced publicly to the family, friends, and members of the immediate rural community. Yet, as we discussed above, in the Malagasy highland societies of significant orality one must be careful in calling out names, certainly of young children. It is also the case that a young child might have a name change after being accorded their "real" first name. This might be because the funny sobriquet that served as the first name is no longer pleasing to them or others, or it might be the case that a misfortune took place and a ritual specialist was consulted both for healing and for seeking a new name to bring good destiny. DuBois (1938: 384–385) explains a ceremony that can take place when a young individual takes a new name. They tell their new personal name to the person who is directing the ceremony. It is at the moment of the "immolation" or sacrifice of a cow or steer that the new name is announced publicly by the "director of ceremonies", who is carrying the young child on his shoulders. The newly acquired name is pronounced out loud while he strikes the ground with a cane or baton.

4.3 Names in adulthood

As a child grows it may receive other names, as discussed above, from an amusing nickname to a blessing to a protective wish. In adulthood one might additionally come to be called by another name or even take a new name for oneself. As the reader might suspect, some names that come to be used as personal names to address an individual in adulthood are funny nicknames. Some nicknames or names of humour (*anaram-bosotra*) are gentle ones and others might be bordering on critique or insult. Examples include *Rasola* or 'Sir/Madame-the-bald-one', *Ravavany* or 'Sir/Mme.-big-mouth' (analogous to *blabbermouth* in English), and *Ralavasofina* or 'Sir/Mme.-the-long-eared-one'. The last name carries the image of someone who, after listening to others, is always offering comments to show that they know more than others do (Rainihifina 1975: 50).

In some cases, one seeks the help of a ritual specialist if one is undergoing misfortune. The person may be counseled to take a name to replace the one received at the time of the *hazary* bath ceremony *(anarana nohazariana)* (DuBois 1938: 20). One misfortune is the loss of a child, another is that of sterility. Not only a wife, but the husband as well, might be given a personal name that was given to a child during the *hazary* ceremony, the ritual bath ceremony discussed above. The child whose name is used does not necessarily have a relationship with the adult taking on the name. A similar name of a child who has benefited from the medicinal *hazary* bath might be accorded by an *ombiasa* to an adult who is continuing to suffer from an illness, and who is said to suffer ostensibly because their name does not "fit their well-being". In another case, a person seeking help from an *ombiasa* might be given a talisman (*ody*) to correct a life situation and they will be offered a name change to increase the effectiveness of the talisman. It should be noted that such talismans bear names as well, including such names as 'surrounded-by-prosperity' (*soamanodidina*) and 'fully-alive' (*tafita*).

A form of respect for an adult will be to use, as their personal name, a name that includes the name of (their) child (*anarana tamin-jaza*). DuBois says that it is said that you lose your name (*very anarana*) (1938: 31). One will come to be called the 'The-mother-of-Radiant-beauty' (*Reninimirana*), for example. One of the authors cited in this paper, *Rainihifina*, offers his own name as an example, as it means 'The-father-of-the-one-thrown-away'. This name was a name given by an *ombiasa*. Other personal names of respect required as an adult include a name given to one with many children, who has lived a long time (*anaran'ny maro anaka sy ela velona*). There is *Ramarozafy* or 'Sir/Mme.-with-many-grandchildren' and even *Ratrajafinafy* or 'Sir/Mme.-having-lived-to-see-her/his-fourth-generation-of-offspring'.

There are additional reasons offered in the works of DuBois (1938), Rainihifina (1975) and Ravelojaona and Rajonah (1937–70) concerning earning a name and deliberately choosing a new name for oneself. A ritual specialist such as an *ombiasa* or a *mpanandro* ('maker-of-days') (most often a male, but not exclusively) might earn a name based on their skill (Rainihifina 1975: 49). One *mpanandro* ('maker-of-days') was called *Rafanidy*, 'Sir-who-(is-singularly-capable-and)-protects-(all-things)'. In situations of joyfulness an individual might change her/his name. The name *Ratsaraony* means 'Mme.-who-has-crossed-the-river', referring to having been able to leave a highly problematic situation behind. In other cases, they will take the name of an ancestor to perpetuate the name and memory of the ancestor (DuBois 1938: 386–387). A person might also appropriate the name of an ancestor in an effort to seek their blessing. This is a name breathed or sprinkled, (*mitsioka anarana)* (Ravelojaona and Rajonah 1937–70: 529). While doing field work over numerous seasons, we (Kus and Raharijaona) have been sprinkled and blessed, *nitsioka (*past tense of *mitsioka*), to help us bring our work/research projects to fruition.

The ceremony for taking on a new name as an adult in the Betsileo region is accompanied by a celebration (*lanonana*) with family, friends and fellow villagers. According to Ravelojaona and Rajonah (1937–70: 529), during this celebration an *omby* (a steer or a cow) is sacrificed. There is a particular manner in which the beast is sacrificed. Its stomach is slashed with a large knife or hatchet called a *lelan'ny kalaza*. This word translates as the 'tongue of the hatchet'. With each strike of the knife or hatchet the current name of the individual is called out, before the person is accorded or appropriates their new name. The meat of the slaughtered beast is cooked and shared with those attending the *lanonana*.

In some cases, after the death of an individual, their name will rarely be pronounced out loud. Ravelojaona and Rajonah (1937–70: 529) remark that while a body disintegrates in death, the name is not corrupted (*ny anarana tsy mba lo*). Yet, most often when the name of one who has passed is pronounced, it is attached to past honours or accomplishments. Both the naming ceremony and the care taken with the name of those past underline again the need to appreciate the traditional and primary orality of the highland cultures we are discussing.

Rainihifina (1975: 50), in his work, offers a discussion of historical names and, in particular, names of nobility. We would like to take a moment to introduce our reader to additional words of "value" that have been used in names given to or assumed by members of the "noble caste" in the central highlands. This is so as to be able to offer a short historical tale in order to contextualize the assignment, acceptance and appropriation of a series of names in a society of primary orality.

In creating and sustaining a social hierarchy in the central highlands of Madagascar, names of nobility were certainly chosen with both care and audacity. There is the term *Andriana* that has been traditionally translated as 'The Noble'; when referring to the head of a ruling elite it would be analogous with 'King' or 'Queen'. As the reader has often read in this article, Malagasy names are "long strings of words" and, certainly in an oral society, a ruling noble's name would be crafted to attract and retain attention and respect. To allow us to offer our naming tale from the past, we present a quick oral taste of "powerful" images from Rainihifina's (1975: 49–50) fuller discussion. Among the terms that have been used in the names of past rulers (and in some cases, their residences) are terms like '1,000' (*arivo*), '10,000' (*alina*), 'sun' (*masoandro*), 'gold' (*vola mena*), 'silver' (*vola fotsy*), 'sparkling' (*manarana* or *mamiratra*), 'river' (*ony*) and 'deep waters' (*antara*). Clearly these words carry images of preciousness, singularity and indomitability.

5 An historical tale of names

If one does a casual search concerning Malagasy history, one's attention will be quickly brought to the figure of *Andrianampoinimerina*, who came to politically control two thirds of the island and whose successors went on to rule over the entire island. His dates of rule are traditionally given as 1787–1810. We have done research on this sovereign over the years, including his "power to name, and claim to dominion" (Kus and Raharijaona 2002). The short tale below draws from more extensive work, but here we focus on the various personal names that he bore during his lifetime. We have access to the tales of his name changes because of the research of the Jesuit priest, François Callet, whose published work (1908) of over 1,000 pages contains oral traditions he collected in the Malagasy language from elders in the central highlands during the mid-19th century. Some of his informants actually witnessed the last days of this sovereign.

As a young child, Andrianampoinimerina, was accorded the personal name of 'The vigorous/healthy (little) dog', *Imboasalama*. Certainly, as we have learned, this is a name of humour, observation and protection. One day when he was tending to grazing cattle, 'The vigorous/healthy (little) dog' decided he would pay his great-aunt a visit as she lived nearby at the site of *Ambohidratrimo* ('The height of Mr. Crocodile'). This was not just any "great-aunt", it was *Ramorabe*, 'Mme. of much gentleness'. She was married to the ruling noble of the village. Yet it was she who was descended from a sovereign who had reigned over a united kingdom of Imerina. This kingdom was now divided. Her marriage to her husband was a marriage of alliance. When she saw her grandnephew in dirty clothing (as he had been tending to cattle), she told her "attendants" to bathe 'The vigorous/healthy (little) dog' and she told her husband to give the child one of his clean silk "wraparounds" and a silk loincloth. Silk is the material of nobles and this gesture of having her husband give these clothes of silk to their grandnephew was her symbolic gesture designating this grandnephew as having a claim to rule Imerina.

Imboasalama went on to become a reputed warrior in his efforts to reunite the kingdom of Imerina. He was consequently given the name of *Ombalahibemaso* or 'The big-eyed bull', which carries the sense of a person with both force and a perspicacious glance, that is to say, astutely observant. This 'Big-eyed bull' went on to reunite the 12 sacred mountains of the kingdom of Imerina and established his residence at the central site of Antananarivo or 'The town of 1,000'. (1,000 carries the notion of "incredibly numerous"). He also went on to appropriate the name of *Andrianampoinimerina* for himself. This name can be translated as 'The noble desired in the heart/navel of (the kingdom) of Imerina'. Certainly, to pronounce his name out loud was to propagate political propaganda in that early state. (For a fuller discussion see Kus and Raharijaona 2002.)

There is an additional tale about this "desirable" noble. On each of the 12 sacred mountains of his reunited kingdom resided a wife from a marriage of alliance he had made. The following tale, found in the oral traditions collected by Callet, still exists in popular traditions of today. This is a tale of one of the wives of 'The big-eyed bull' who became 'The noble desired in the heart/navel of Imerina". In the recounting of the tale below, we will use the shortened personal name of *Desiré* to refer to *Andrianampoinimerina*.

This tale complements the proverb cited above about how a bull can be ensnared by a rope, a butterfly caught by its tongue and a human being mesmerized by words. Desiré began his rise to political power at the sacred height, *Ambohimanga*, 'The blue height' (where "blue" signifies beauty as well as the colour). A young woman, *Miangaly*, tradition has it, lived on a high mountain (*Ambohipoloalina* or 'The height of the darkness of 10 nights') covered in forest and mist. This height was to the west of Ambohimanga. Being so beautiful, Miangaly excited passion in many. The term *ngaly* can be translated as 'shiny black' and when used in a reduplicated form (*ngalingaly*) it is analogous to 'the colour of ebony'. This name is thought to refer to the beautiful colour of her dark skin. Desiré, 'The desired one', desired her and took her for one of his wives. However, 'The capricious one' taunted 'The desired one' by constantly seeking excuses to return to the home of her parents, like a bird that swoops down to lightly touch the water's surface only to fly away again ("*Manifi-drano ny ngita, Misai-mandro, ravorona*") (Ramalagasy 1961: 29).

One day in the early morning light, Desiré sat at the boulder *Ambatomiatendro* ('At the boulder from where all the lesser heights are visible'). This boulder is in the town of Ambohimanga. From that location Desiré turned his gaze to the west. The formerly named 'Big eyed-bull', ensnared in the ropes of Miangaly's charms and ploys, sighed: "How I long for Miangaly!" ("*Manina an'I Miangaly aho izany!*"). *Hagamainty* ('He who wears a hat with a black-rim'), the sovereign's wise and faithful counselor, recognized that sexual desire and love can mix badly with politics. Hagamainty commented that: "It is rather Miangaly that longs for you!" ("*I Miangaly no manina re*!"). The 'Noble desired in the heart/navel of Imerina' recognized his counselor's wisdom that the paramount sovereign of the land should not be captive to his emotions. Coming to his "senses", Desiré commissioned his musicians to compose the song, *I Miangaly no manina*. The term *miangaly* took on two meanings, both that of 'capriciousness', and of 'having a talent for singing or playing songs of a melancholy or plaintive nature'. The song, *I Miangaly no manina*! is said to have been a favourite of Desiré. A version of it continues to exist in popular folksongs in the highlands of Madagascar. (For a fuller discussion of the Miangaly tale see Raharijaona and Kus 2010.)

6 To "toss a few seeds" by way of conclusion

The colonial heritage of Madagascar and the expanding bureaucratic apparatus of the country of Madagascar have and are continuing to "influence" naming practices across the island. Certainly, there is the "fixing" and "registering" of identity through personal names, including family names and personal names that do not change, except in the case of marriage. In some cases, one can observe a "shortening" of names to facilitate administrative needs. We have observed some localized resistance to such prosaic and persistent assaults on naming traditions. In the villages where we undertake our fieldwork, we come to know people by the names they are known by in their village. One striking discovery was that if you look at their official ID cards, they will sometimes have not only an additional "last name" but an entirely different "first name".

The Malagasy have an expression, *fampariahitsa*. This carries the sense of 'spreading/tossing the seeds of grass [that they may take root]'. The metaphorical image carries the wish that one's words/speech may offer moments and incentives for further reflective thought. We are grateful for the experiential seeds we have received during our seasons in the field. There are seeds from beginning to understand embodied experience in the highland countryside of Madagascar. There are seeds of an appreciation of the humorous, poetic and philosophical skills of many individuals in a society of substantial orality. There are also the seeds of appreciation of the Malagasy language as agglutinative, allowing the creation of names, including personal names, from a range of images, from amusing to thought-provoking to "striking". We hope these seeds will contribute to the larger discussion of personal names contained in the contributions to this volume.

References

Abinal, Antoine. 1955. *Dictionnaire malgache-français par Abinal et Malzac*. Paris: Éditions maritimes et d'outre-mer.

Beaujard, Philippe. 2011. The first migrants to Madagascar and their introduction of plants: linguistic and ethnological evidence. *Azania* 46 (2). 169–189.

Burney, David, Lida Piggot Burney, Laurie Godfrey, William Jungers, Steven Goodman & Henry Wright. 2004. A chronology for late prehistoric Madagascar. *Journal of Human Evolution* 47 (1–2). 25–63.

Callet, François (1908) 1972. *Tantara ny andriana eto Madagasikara: documents historiques d'après les manuscrits malgaches*. Antananarivo: Imprimerie Nationale.

DuBois, Henri-Marie. 1938. *Monographie des Betsileo (Madagascar)*. Paris: Institut d'Ethnologie.

Fernandez, James. 1986. *Persuasion and performances: The play of tropes in society*. Bloomington: Indiana University Press.

Jackson, Michael. 1983. Thinking through the body: An essay on understanding metaphor. Social Analysis 14. 127–149.

Kus, Susan & Victor Raharijaona. 2002. The power to name and the claim to dominion of a Malagasy sovereign. In Maria O'Donovan (ed.), *The dynamics of power*, 362–383. Center for Archaeological Investigations Occasional Paper No. 30, Carbondale: Southern Illinois University.

Michel-Andrianarahinjaka, Lucien S. 1987. *Le système littéraire betsileo*. Fianarantsoa: Amboaontany.

Raharijaona, Victor & Susan Kus. 2010. Longing, lust and persuasion: powerful and powerfully sensuous women in Imerina Madagascar. Amour et sexualité du côté de l'océan Indien occidental (Comores, Madagascar et île Maurice). *Etudes Océan Indien, INALCO* 45. 51–65.
Rainihifina, Jessé. 1975. Lovantsoina II: Fomba Betsileo [Cultural Heritage II: Betsileo Customs]. Fianarantsoa: Ambozontany.
Ramalagasy [alias used by P. Rasamison]. 1961. I Miangaly no manina. *Teny voakendry firaketana ohabolana aman-pitenenana malagasy, boky II* [A collection of well-chosen words and proverbs from Malagasy oral discourse, Volume II.], 25–30.
Ravelojaona & Gabriel Rajonah (eds.). 1937–70. Boky firaketana ny fiteny sy ny zavatra Malagasy [Encyclopedia of Malagasy language and culture]. Antananarivo: Imprimerie Industrielle.
Stein, Gertrude. 1935. *Lectures in America*. New York: Random House.

Jill Vaughan & Ruth Singer

Chapter 8
Organising diversity: Naming groups and their languages in Indigenous Australia

Abstract: This paper builds an understanding of the diverse naming practices in Indigenous Australian communities through an examination of group and language naming in four regions: Cape York Peninsula in north-eastern Australia, the Western Desert region in western Australia, and among speakers of two language groups of coastal northern Australia (Yolŋu Matha varieties in eastern Arnhem Land and Burarra in north-central Arnhem Land). These descriptions draw from the literature and from the authors' community-engaged fieldwork in Arnhem Land. We describe the range of strategies speakers use to divide up their local language ecologies, practices for naming lects and the role of variation in the processes of differentiation and connection. Naming practices across these areas show some interesting similarities, but also striking differences. Language and group naming systems are local ways of organising diversity. The study of naming is at the very heart of the concerns of sociolinguistics and linguistic anthropology: linking the social, political, geographic and linguistic. It is important because it has a bearing on how people see themselves and others, and on how they construct "same" and "different". In the contemporary world, where diversity is seen by states and institutions as a problem – a "logistical headache" (Migge and Léglise 2013: 1) – studying local perspectives can open our eyes to other ways of understanding and valuing diversity. A key benefit for researchers is that it provides an opportunity to come face-to-face with our own erroneous assumptions. In this paper, we highlight the value of bringing to the fore speakers' conceptions of differentiation and of divisions within the language ecology, and the importance of attending to the views of all relevant social actors in grasping locally salient sociolinguistic processes.

Keywords: Indigenous Australia, multilingualism, naming, endangered languages, linguistic variation

Jill Vaughan, Monash University, e-mail: jill.vaughan@monash.edu
Ruth Singer, University of Melbourne, e-mail: rsinger@unimelb.edu.au

https://doi.org/10.1515/9783110759297-008

1 Introduction

1.1 Naming as a way of organising diversity

The names and borders of groups of people and their languages as conceived of by anthropologists and linguists are sometimes incommensurable with the lived social reality of the speakers themselves. The process of drawing such borders and assigning names is not neutral, trivial or objective; it is a highly political process driven and shaped by understandings of group identity, similarity and difference (Ionnàccaro and Dell'Aquila 2001; Léglise and Migge 2006). In the Australian context, the relationships between individuals, social groups and languages can be somewhat indirect. It is a common tendency (e.g. in northern Australia) for the individual to patrilineally inherit allegiance to a clan group, with each clan owning its own tract of land (e.g. Merlan 1981). Languages belong to the land rather than to clans directly, and so the relationship between individuals and "their" languages is mediated. Languages are sometimes named after the clan associated with the land, or some aspect of that social group, but many other language naming strategies exist.

Typically, a language gains wider public acknowledgement through "artefactualisation" as a dictionary or grammar, the "birth certificates" of a language (Blommaert 2008). However, the linguist's conception of a discrete language, often an artefact of the language documentation process (a "doculect" in Cysouw and Good's 2013 term), may not reflect the ways in which speakers divide up their own local language ecology. This "doculect" may be just one of a number of closely related varieties that, through chance or circumstance, happens to have been documented while others have not. Australia is no exception, with linguists working on Australian languages usually classifying and naming language and codes in a community (or relying on someone else's classification), and then getting on with whatever else it is that they want to research. It is easy to forget or fail to realise, however, that the people who identify as speakers of Australian Indigenous languages often name and classify codes in very different ways to linguists. Understanding local perspectives on language naming offers important insights into ideologies around social and linguistic differentiation.

This paper builds an understanding of the diverse naming practices in Indigenous Australian communities through an examination of group and language naming in four regions: Cape York Peninsula in north-eastern Australia, the Western Desert region in western Australia, and among speakers of two language groups of coastal northern Australia (Yolŋu Matha varieties in eastern Arnhem Land and Burarra in north-central Arnhem Land). These descriptions draw from the literature and from the authors' community-engaged fieldwork in Arnhem

Land. We describe the range of strategies speakers use to divide up their local language ecologies, practices for naming lects and the role of variation in the processes of differentiation and connection. Naming practices across these areas show some interesting similarities, but also striking differences.

Language and group naming systems are local ways of organising diversity. The study of naming is at the very heart of the concerns of sociolinguistics and linguistic anthropology: linking the social, political, geographic and linguistic. It is important because it has a bearing on how people see themselves and others, and on how they construct "same" and "different". In the contemporary world, where diversity is seen by states and institutions as a problem – a "logistical headache" (Migge and Léglise 2013: 1) – studying local perspectives can open our eyes to other ways of understanding and valuing diversity. A key benefit for researchers is that it provides an opportunity to come face-to-face with our own erroneous assumptions. In this paper, we highlight the value of bringing to the fore speakers' conceptions of differentiation and of divisions within the language ecology, and the importance of attending to the views of all relevant social actors in grasping locally salient sociolinguistic processes.

1.2 Languages and groups in the Australian context

A rich literature addresses how languages, dialects, varieties, special signed and spoken registers and other ways of talking can be named in Australia (e.g., Sutton 1979; Walsh 1997; Wood 2016). This literature reveals great diversity in language naming and classification processes across the region. Within the diversity of ways of conceiving of languages, there are two common tendencies that seem to be widespread around Australia. The first is the distinction between "owning" a language and "speaking" a language (Merlan 1981; Rumsey 1989; Sutton 1978, 1997). A person might well speak a language they do not "own", and equally might "own" a language they do not speak (or do not speak fluently). For example, in a language survey carried out by the Warruwi School in the early 1990s, participants were asked to write down their languages. Most wrote down a single language. This is rather surprising given that Warruwi Community is highly multilingual and most adults speak two to eight Indigenous languages (Singer 2018). In the survey, however, people reported their language *ownership* rather than all the languages they spoke. As Biddle (2012) notes, this is common in language surveys in the Australian context. The language that an Indigenous person owns in Arnhem Land is the language of their patrilineal clan, inherited via their father's father. Thus the Warruwi survey had not, as intended, collected information on language use in the community, but rather on an aspect of participants' social and language identity.

The second common tendency found across many communities is the way that language ownership, land ownership and clan membership intersect. Merlan (1981), reviewing relevant literature from around Australia and drawing on her own research in the Roper River region, reconstructs a traditional conceptualisation in which languages are associated primarily with an area of land, and only secondarily with a social group, as shown in Figure 8.1. It seems likely that this formulation predates White contact, and, as Merlan notes, there is no "neat line [that] can be drawn anywhere in Australia between 'traditional' and 'post-contact' Aboriginality" (1981: 133).

Figure 8.1: The indirect relationships between individuals and "their" languages (based on Evans 2003; Merlan 1981).

Although this conception of language identity is referred to in the literature as "language ownership" because of the authority it bestows on the "owner", it is not meant to imply that a person or clan owns a language directly. Rather, the clan owns an area of land, a clan estate, which has some language that belongs to it. Therefore that clan has authority over that language and responsibility for it (Figure 8.1). The idea that the language belongs to the land, rather than to the clan directly, is supported by creation myths from quite disparate areas in which creation spirits "planted" languages in the land during the Dreamtime. In doing so, they created an association between specific languages and specific areas of land (see Merlan 1981; Sutton 1997; Evans 2010).

1.3 Locals vs. linguists?: Conflicting motivations in language naming practices

In the process of language documentation, linguists need to decide on the name they will use for the language or "doculect" they are focusing on. Sometimes this is straightforward, but very often it is not. The processes linguists and other (community outsider) stakeholders undertake when "naming" a variety may be subject to social and political pressures very different from those acting on local community naming practices. Typically, linguists are guided by a universal approach based on structural differences (i.e., phonology, syntax, lexicon) and degrees of mutual intelligibility between varieties.

Haspelmath (2017) outlines a set of principles for linguists making decisions about naming varieties which drive towards standardisation and uniformity. In doing so he reveals some significant divergences from local community naming practices observed in Australia and around the world. Some important divergences include his recommendation that each language should have a unique name, and that while sometimes multiple names are in concurrent use for one variety, "this cannot be a general solution" (2017: 83). As we will see, it is frequently the case that one variety is referred to locally with various epithets due to politically motivated social processes (e.g. Sutton 1979). Haspelmath outlines an additional "non-principle": that the language name need not reflect the name speakers use for their own language (the autoglottonym) (2017: 90). This is justified, it would seem, by the fact that closeness to the autoglottonym is not required of major world languages like German and Chinese, and the author believes languages with small numbers of speakers should be treated in much the same way. This ignores, however, the power structures within which linguists operate when working in small speaker communities, and the importance of centring local preferences in language naming (although of course this is often not straightforward).

Local approaches to language naming and dividing up the linguistic space, on the other hand, often adopt a maximalist perspective on linguistic differentiation. In other words, local models of linguistic boundaries may describe larger numbers of language varieties than the linguist's dialectology (Garde 2008: 147). This is certainly the case in Indigenous Australia (see, e.g., Miller 1971; Sutton 1978; Wilkinson 1991). Walsh (1997) recognises this in his distinction between what he terms "language$_{1a}$" for "geographical dialects" and "language$_{1b}$" for other named varieties or registers within some particular language$_{1a}$ (while "language$_2$" refers to the linguist's approach based on mutual intelligibility). He observes that Indigenous perspectives on linguistic diversity can be primarily about social groupings and affiliations with the land. These are then extended to describe diversity in linguistic space. Linguists, on the other hand, may start from linguistic features and work up from there to make connections with social groups and through them, to the land.

This is not to say that local perspectives always tend towards the maximalist, however, as speakers may want to either maximise or minimise differences between varieties depending on the context of a conversation (Lüpke 2018). In many communities, this is possible due to inherent flexibility in language naming processes – a range of levels of "granularity" may be available for sociolinguistic group identification (e.g. Garde 2013). This flexibility can be altered or undermined, however, through interaction with linguists' endeavours or other political processes (e.g. strategic essentialism deployed as a strategy in claims for land rights – Rumsey 1989).

2 Language and group naming in Australia: Four examples

The literature on language naming in Australia attests to the confusion often experienced by researchers when trying to interpret names offered by language speakers. Early researchers erroneously assumed that Indigenous Australians were organised into groups of around 500 people who spoke a single language (Merlan 1981; Sutton 1991). But clear "ethnolinguistic groups" bounded by language were not present. Instead, Indigenous people moved around in smaller groups which were multilingual or multi-dialectal. The primary unit of social organisation in much of Australia is the small patrilineal clan. Groups of people who live together come from multiple clans, because people always marry someone from another clan (Sutton 2003). Language naming provides insight into Indigenous perspectives on linguistic diversity within highly complex regional systems of social organisation.

Walsh (1997) provides evidence that in pre-contact times there were often very fine-grained systems for naming linguistic varieties, such that a variety spoken by 30 speakers or even fewer could have its own name. However, in some cases what has been analysed as a "language name" has in fact been a one-off description of a variety rather than an established label. In addition, we should not assume that language naming is entirely systematic in every region. It is possible that some, or even many, varieties had no name at all (Sutton 1979: 90). Early researchers often recorded fine-grained terms, but no overarching term that would group all the varieties perceived by linguists as similar, i.e. as a language. The names that missionaries, linguists and anthropologists used to refer to what they perceived as a single "language" have since been taken up by speakers in many areas (Walsh 1997).

In this section, we overview four local language naming systems in Cape York, the Western Desert and Arnhem Land (eastern and north-central) (Map 8.1).

2.1 Cape York Peninsula

In many regions around Australia there is a linguistic ideology that designates a unique linguistic variety to each clan, or land-owning descent group. Sutton (1978) studied the connections between land owning groups, other social categories and linguistic variation in the Cape Keerweer area of western Cape York Peninsula (see also Smith and Johnson 1986; Johnson 1991; Rigsby 2005; Sutton 1991, 2001). He recorded the local language ideology that "all clans have at least slightly different

Map 8.1: Key regions and locations featured in Section 2 (Map: Jill Vaughan).

dialects" (Sutton 1978: 183). These clan-affiliated dialects are referred to here as "clanlects". Another ideology recorded by Sutton was that every clanlect should have a distinctive name such as *Wik-Ngathárra*, where *wik* is the classifier for "language" and *Ngathárra* is a language name, not just the name of a clan. In practice, Sutton observed that clanlects people perceived to be similar were often referred to by the same name. For the 26 clans of the Cape Keerweer area Sutton studied, he lists 13 names for clanlects (1978: 180). From the linguist's perspective the named varieties are in some cases quite similar, with 90% similarity in a list of 100 basic vocabulary items. For other pairs of named clanlects the lexical similarity was only 41% (1978: 178). Sutton found that older people in the Cape Keerweer area were highly multilingual/lectal, speaking and understanding a number of varieties in addition to their own. This, he observes, reflects a life lived closely together with people who used varieties different from their own.

As in many regions of Australia, language naming in Cape York is not straightforward. Names for linguistic varieties can vary in their meaning depending on the context of use. In the southeast corner of the peninsula, now known as the Kuku Yalanji area, over 60 different "tribal names" have been recorded by researchers since the late 19th century (Sutton 1978, 1979). Wood (2016) demonstrates that most of these so-called "tribal names" in fact referred to language varieties. The term *Kuku Yalanji* is a good example. It contains the classifier for language *kuku* combined with a demonstrative *yala* 'this, here' and is translated by speakers as meaning 'the language spoken here, our language'. As Wood (2016) points out, this term is a classic shifter, in Jakobson's (1957) sense, as the meaning changes depending on who uses the term and where they are located in the landscape and in historical time. Other terms used in the Kuku Yalanji area are tied to the landscape, such as *Kuku Yalunyu*, which refers to a language variety shared by people who lived along the same river. Even these terms referring to geographic range are used along a sliding scale (Wood 2016; cf. Carr and Lempert 2016). *Kuku Yalunyu* was used to refer to a small, core group at the mouth of the river, but could also be extended to include people upriver, or even to contrast the language varieties used on the coastal side of the Great Dividing Range with those on the inland side. Furthermore, Sutton (1979: 100) explains that a great deal of language name confusion has been due to the fact that languages do not really have names "in the usual sense" in the region. Instead, speakers might well offer some name for their language when asked for it, but this might be a place-name, a patriclan name, or even a phrase like *uuku malayi ngathun* 'my own language'. These terms may be mistaken for reified language names by those documenting the language or culture.

2.2 Western Desert

The term "Western Desert language" is sometimes used by linguists to refer to language varieties used across a large area in the very centre of Australia, including areas of the Northern Territory, Western Australia and South Australia. The varieties covered by this term are quite similar in structure but often very different in vocabulary. Miller (1971) investigated linguistic variation at Warburton mission from 1969–1970. He found that the use of nine variables was correlated with the geographic affiliation and life history of speakers. The differences in use of the variables were mainly a matter of degree, as many speakers used more than one variant. One way that speakers classified the varieties was through reference to the demonstrative 'this'. So the western variety associated with the Warburton mission is referred to as *Ngaanya-tjarra* (this-HAVING) while the variety to the east is known as *Ngaatja-tjara* (this-HAVING). This is similar to naming practices in north-east Arnhem Land, where the term for the demonstrative 'this' is also used to distinguish varieties at a higher level than clanlects.

However, once we look more closely the practices among speakers of the Western Desert language are quite different. In part, these differences stem from distinct social structures in the Western Desert and distinct ideologies around the connections between language, land and social identity. For example, the notion of the patrilineal clan is not clearly applicable in this region, and "dialect variations (. . .) [have] no direct territorial significance" (Berndt 1959: 93) but are instead more related to kin connections. Miller surveyed around 100 people at Warburton mission, asking them "What is your language?" Interestingly, most people offered multiple language names, but some offered none. In the areas of western Cape York and north-central Arnhem Land discussed above and below, people will usually answer this question with one language. This primary language identification is with the clanlect associated with their clan. After that, they may list other languages that they can speak. Miller found that this was not the case at Warburton. The language names given to Miller in his survey were constructed using words that differed across varieties, such as the demonstrative 'this' or the terms for 'come' and 'go'. He also observed that the same person might use different language names to refer to the same variety, across different interviews. Miller came to the conclusion that language naming in this area is largely contextual.

> The primary purpose of the dialect names is, I would suggest, a means of identifying 'us' vs. 'them'. (. . .) It is useful to have more than one set of contrasts, so that one can take a narrow or broad view, depending on which the situation calls for. (Miller 1971: 73)

The words used to construct language names depended on the context, as people highlighted selected linguistic variables to distinguish varieties. Despite the variation in the form of the names people used, their naming practices, taken together, circumscribed coherent "dialects" or "varieties" – which were also distinguished by the nine linguistic features Miller identified. Miller reports on one discussion he had with a man about three terms for 'sit' found in the east, west and north (Miller 1971: 75). By the end of their discussion, they were using three emergent language names: *Nyinanyi-tjara-nya, Nyinara-tjara-nya* and *Nyininpa-tjara-nya*, each having the structure: 'sit-HAVING-NAME'. Miller points this out to demonstrate how easily language names can come into use for a specific purpose in a specific context without necessarily ever being used again.

2.3 Eastern Arnhem Land: Yolŋu Matha

In eastern Arnhem Land, varieties of the Yolŋu Matha language group are spoken. Variation exists along two main axes: moieties (kinship-based social groups) and clans (land owning groups) (see, e.g., Amery 1993; Evans 2003; Keen 1995; Morphy

1977; Schebeck 1968; Wilkinson 1991). As in the Cape Keerweer area, each person has a relationship of "ownership" to the clanlect of their patrilineal clan. In Wilkinson's (1991) grammar of the Yolŋu variety Djambarrpuyŋu, she summarises the connections between clans and language varieties at Galiwinku:

> there is an important social correlation between one's inherited territorial affiliation and a particular language variety [*clanlect*]. In terms of Yolŋu language ideology this affiliation is paramount. There is a single variety considered one's "own" and which should ideally be acquired by all its members. Furthermore each of the named land owning groups, which I will refer to here on as clans, is held to speak a variety distinct from that of any other (Wilkinson 1991: 3)

In this region, there is a tendency for all named varieties to be considered distinct, unique languages, even when closely related and mutually intelligible (1991: 5). In this way the Yolŋu Matha speakers' ideologies about language ownership and language naming are similar to those at Cape Keerweer. The clanlect naming practices are different, however, as each clanlect of Yolŋu Matha is named simply by using the name of the clan. So, for example, the clanlect associated with the Galpu clan is also called "*Galpu*". We find a further axis of variation in the so called Dhuwal-Dhuwala group of Yolŋu Matha varieties, sometimes referred to as a dialect of Yolŋu Matha, which is associated with a large area of coastal north-east Arnhem Land. The difference between the Dhuwal and Dhuwala varieties relies on a single rule that deletes the final vowel in certain conditions; thus the demonstrative 'this' is *dhuwala* in the Dhuwala variety but *dhuwal* in the Dhuwal variety (Morphy 1977). Half the clans in the Dhuwal-Dhuwala area speak Dhuwal and the other half are affiliated to the Dhuwala variety. The distinction corresponds to the difference between two patrimoieties, Dhuwa and Yirritja, which are connected to marriage rules. Morphy observes that the vowel-deletion rule "operates as a socially perceived and consciously maintained marker of social differentiation" (Morphy 1977: 51) and has much greater salience to speakers than the much more extensive east-west variation in clanlects.

2.4 North-central Arnhem Land: Burarra

Speakers of the Burarra language live on, and own, country to the east of Maningrida, a highly multilingual township in north-central Arnhem Land. Burarra is a non-Pama-Nyungan language, but has long been in contact with Pama-Nyungan languages to the east. Some among the Burarra group align socially and culturally with the strongly patrilineal Yolŋu groups of the north-east, while others reflect a localised interweaving of eastern and western Arnhem Land orientations (Carew 2016).

"*Burarra*" has come to be used widely as a macro label for all varieties of the language, captured, for example, by a single ISO639-3 code (bvr), but this term masks various sociolinguistic complexities. Carew (2016: 17) suggests that the designation probably originated as an eastern exonym for the language group (see also Borsboom 1978; Glasgow 1994; Mirritji 1976). Viewed from within, however, the sociolinguistic space may be divided in a number of ways. As in the examples above, contextual factors play a role in determining how language boundaries are drawn and varieties named in any particular interaction.

Other designations for the entire language group and its sub-varieties have been favoured at different times and by different people – both speakers and outsider stakeholders, such as linguists and anthropologists. These differing schemas highlight the co-existence of interacting naming systems that do not necessarily fit within a neatly hierarchical model. They also point to the diverse social, cultural and epistemological positions of scholars and the Burarra speakers they have worked alongside.

One of the earliest published delineations of the language is found in linguist Arthur Capell's regional survey of linguistic groupings, *Languages of Arnhem Land, North Australia* (1942). He describes three close dialects ("Burera" (Burarra), "Gudjälavia" (Gu-jarlabiya) and "Gunaidbe" (Gun-nartpa)) (Figure 8.1), claiming it to be "an arbitrary matter which dialect is taken as standard" (1942: 374). *Gu-jarlabiya* means something like 'it moves along steadily' (from *gu-* 'it' + *jarlabiya* 'walk'), while *Gun-nartpa* is a demonstrative variant (*gun-* 'thing of land/neuter noun class' + *-nartpa* 'that (in focus)') which can function as a shibboleth identifying speakers from clans in the Cadell River region.

Figure 8.2: Attested varieties in Capell (1942).

The variety labels reproduced in Capell are replicated in the accounts of several scholars, but in varied configurations. In most cases, however, Burarra is given as a superordinate category encompassing the others as sub-varieties or more minor alternative labels (Figure 8.2). Some sources also note the term *Gu-jingarliya* ('it with tongue'). Green (1987: 1) observes that, along with *Gu-jarlabiya*, this label is both interchangeable with Burarra to refer to the entire language group, and available as an endonym to designate the non-Gun-nartpa speakers of Burarra.

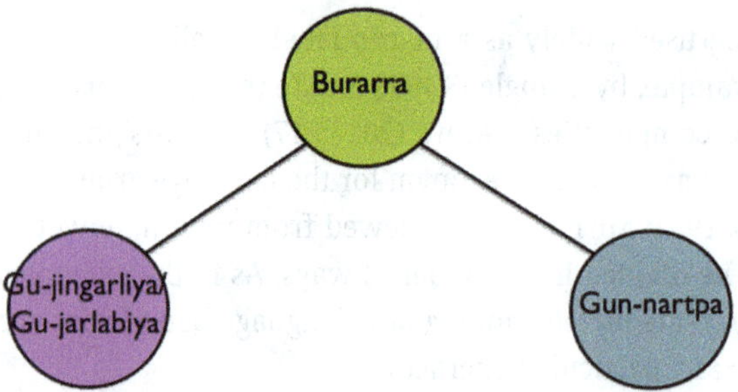

Figure 8.3: Attested varieties in Green 1987; Jones and Meehan 1978; Gurrmanamana et al. 2002.

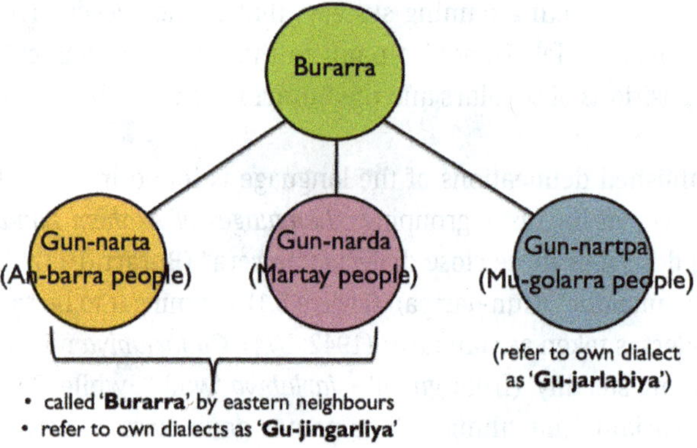

Figure 8.4: Attested varieties in Glasgow 1994.

Glasgow's *Burarra-Gun-nartpa Dictionary* (1994), based on decades of Bible translation and language and literacy work in Maningrida, reflects further subdivisions within the Burarra varieties (Figure 8.3, 8.4). She distinguishes Burarra/Gu-jingarliya from Gun-nartpa, and divides the former into two further dialect groups: *Gun-narta*, also known by the regional tribe name *An-barra*; and *Gun-narda*, also known by the regional tribe name *Martay*. *Gun-narta*, *Gun-narda* and *Gun-nartpa* are regional variants of the same demonstrative, and can function as shibboleth terms, socioterritorial identity markers for varieties spoken, respectively, in the coastal region west of the Blythe River, to the east of the Blythe River, and further south in the Cadell River region. *An-barra* derives from *barra* 'base/bottom', perhaps referring to associated coastal sites that are under water (Carew 2016: 60; Gurrmanamana et al. 2002), while *Martay* refers to the stringybark flower which blooms in the dry season, an emblem of the *Marrangu* clan cluster with which this group is affiliated (Elliott 1991). Glasgow describes the varieties as "three very close dialects (. . .) or two, depending on perspective" (1994: 7), with little linguistic variation distinguishing the An-barra and Martay varieties at least (see also Vaughan 2018). Glasgow notes, however, that each group is proud to have a distinct identity. This set of "shibboleth" language labels (*Gun-narta, Gun-narda* and *Gun-nartpa*) reflects the operation of "Ausbau" within the Burarra space. Ausbau refers to the creation of intentional linguistic differentiation to shore up perceived social and political differences between groups (Garde 2008; Kloss 1967). This schema also reflects the operation of a kind of "fractal recursivity", whereby "an opposition, salient at some level of relationship, [is projected] onto some other level" (Irvine and Gal 2000: 38) – in this case the projection of a salient socio-political division into the linguistic field. Additionally, Glasgow positions Gu-jarlabiya somewhat differently from Green (1987), as an endonym for Gun-nartpa speakers instead. This gives a limited indication of the inherent instability or flexibility which characterises the use of some of these terms.

Other scholarly works identify further varieties of names in use among the Burarra groups. In his work on local organisational structures in Arnhem Land, Hiatt (1962) additionally lists the eastern sub-groups *Mariŋa* (Maringa) and *Marawuraba* alongside An-barra and Martay as "four loose common residence groupings" (1962: 280). These terms have sometimes been drawn on to label perceived linguistic varieties by speakers and scholars (e.g. Carew 2016: 16–17; Hamilton 1981: 3). Carew (2016: 140–141) further notes the terms *gun-nyarlkuch* (soft speech) and *gun-derta* (hard speech) in use as secondary terms to distinguish between the Burarra lects, with Gun-nartpa speakers claiming their own variety as *gun-nyarlkuch*. Recent fieldwork conducted by author Vaughan in Maningrida has found these terms still in limited use, but not in a strictly consistent way.

The variations in Burarra naming schemas attested here highlight a range of pertinent factors acting on local naming processes. Published naming systems typically only present a single perspective characterising a single point in time: there is "no view from nowhere, no gaze that is not positioned" (Irvine and Gal 2000: 36). The situated positionalities of scholars are relevant – for example, Hamilton (1991) worked with An-barra people, while Carew (2016) worked predominantly with the Gun-nartpa group. Schemas also change over time, with historical events impacting the changing fortunes of specific language labels. The "artefactualisation" (Blommaert 2008) of Burarra in the Glasgow (1994) dictionary – a well-known text frequently used in the community – may, for example, have further promoted and stabilised the use of "Burarra" (e.g. rather than "Gu-jingaliya").

2.5 Comparing the examples

This review of language naming, group naming and linguistic variation illustrates how different systems of naming can be. Local patterns of language naming tend to take a fine-grained view of variation, often reflecting ideology as much as practice. Linguists tend to focus on broader measures, at the level where typological profiles diverge and lexical differentiation makes mutual intelligibility difficult. This review also points to the usefulness – but also ultimately to the limitations and the highly situated nature – of scholarly artefacts of language naming practices.

Some of the languages discussed here, such as the Wik languages of western Cape York, are no longer spoken as much as they were, while others, such as the Yolŋu Matha languages of north-east Arnhem Land, are still widely spoken. Changes have occurred in recent decades in the kinds of variation found in these languages, the way that this variation is deployed and how boundaries between varieties are drawn and named.

Systems of language naming in Indigenous Australia are quite variable. Their meanings may be context-bound, even emergent, or alternatively quite clear-cut and fixed. In some cases, a single name may designate both a clan group and the language spoken by its members (e.g. in eastern Arnhem Land), while in other cases group and language names are distinct, with languages named for elements of the landscape, clan emblems, shibboleth terms or linguistic qualities distinguishing the varieties of different groups, or employing “shifter” labels.

Multiple systems may be in operation, even if they are apparently conflicting because the meaning of the names is tied to the context of their use. There is no reason to assume that in the pre-contact era everything was neat and orderly and that the more contextual systems represent some kind of decay. In many cases greater “orderliness” seems to have developed through the pressures of interaction with White society (e.g. Walsh 1997). It is also important to keep in mind that Indigenous Australian language names do not necessarily prioritise linguistic features, i.e. features of the languages themselves. A linguist’s view of linguistic diversity is oriented towards distinctive linguistic features, e.g. phoneme inventories, or towards certain variables being used more than others. This is apparent in the quote from Urciuoli (2013) below, which reflects on the process of naming languages:

> When people name a language, what is being named? In what ways are people even imagining something nameable? How do people abstract the conception of a coherent set of forms from the perception of sounds coming out of mouths? All these points precede the question of how the namer’s authority enters into the process of naming and how that authority is constituted. All these points also suggest how emergent and contingent a construction is a named language. (Urciuoli 2013)

As Walsh (1997) points out, “languages can be named for properties of their speakers rather than properties of their language use”. Sutton (1991) gives the example of the use of the language name *Wik-Ngenycharr* to refer to the languages used by a group of clans south of the Kendall River. These clans are affiliated with languages that are linguistically quite different from one another, and that have more similarities to languages in other areas than to one another. Regardless, the term *Wik-Ngenycharr* is used to refer to this set of languages because this group of clans is seen as having something important in common. It is a linguistic term, but "regionally and politically selective" (Sutton 1991: 51).

3 Discussion and conclusions

In this paper, we have outlined several ways in which the processes of naming groups and their languages provide a productive lens into the role of language in social and cultural life, as illustrated by four examples from language groups in northern and western Australia. Language naming tells us especially about how variation is dimensionalised into the geographical and social cosmos (Evans 2013), and about local strategies for dividing up the social space. The four examples illustrate how different approaches to language naming can be within Indigenous Australia.

Tamsin Donaldson questions why we should expect Indigenous classifications to create discrete or hierarchical groupings, drawing on Ngiyampaa people's classification of their languages in western New South Wales (Donaldson 1984). In western Arnhem Land a range of cross-cutting social groups of different scales are simultaneously available and language names are part of this assemblage of categories (Singer 2018). Language names emerge from social life, not language form, so claims to speakership are claims of social identity. Accounts of language names that refer to linguistic features are in some sense always post hoc. The fluidity of language identities and the flexibility with which people use language names does not, however, render language names or the categories they invoke meaningless. Speakers may make different distinctions depending on their aims in a specific time and context. Diversity is the bedrock of social, cultural and political life and skilled social actors index their various memberships and alliances with care. They can also both obscure and create distinctions via language.

We have explored the significant role of scholars and other stakeholders in language naming processes, and seen examples of the impact of delineating and "artefactualising" a doculect. In the case of the Burarra varieties, this has contributed to a proliferation of language naming schemas. Because Indigenous language names are often fluid, flexible and not discrete or hierarchically nested, there is indeterminacy in how language names and group names are mapped to linguistic units as perceived by linguists. The naming schemas in the literature arise from specific collaborations involving a team of researchers and Indigenous people (mainly Elders) working together at a certain place at a certain time.

As noted in the introduction, Australian Indigenous people tend to distinguish varieties down to a fine-grained level of analysis, such as clanlects. Linguists tend to be "lumpers", coining names for larger categories such as Murrinhpatha, which were not previously recognised by Indigenous people. Today, Indigenous Australians' social and political networks extend over a greater area of land than ever before and names for larger categories have been taken up as terms for larger political units, for example in land claims (Rumsey 1989), or for sharing resources for language support. Ultimately language naming reflects what language is understood to be, i.e. what its nature is.

The accounts in this chapter show that Indigenous languages are understood as a part of Indigenous people and their social groups and as a part of tracts of land. The diversity of approaches to language naming around the world reflects a diversity of understandings of what language is. As the "ontological turn" that emerged from work in anthropology is felt more in linguistics we can expect to see more accounts of the different "philosophies of language" that underlie language naming schemas (Chernela 2018; Demuro and Gurney 2021). Like other aspects of Indigenous people's lives in Australia, understandings of what a language is are also in flux and merit close attention (Hauck 2016).

The picture that emerges from across the Australian region is one of great diversity in naming practices. Assumptions of uniformity can be traced to erroneous methods in language and anthropological documentation. Sutton (1979: 101) gives the example of linguists asking locals "what is your tribe?" and "what is your language called?" and then fitting the responses neatly into a traditional European model of one-to-one language-tribe linguistic nationalism (see also Irvine and Gal 2000). Many scholars have wrongly assumed language to be the sole or primary basis for sociality, rather than one of the many cultural indexes that are available for identity construction – one that often crosscuts key social groupings in Indigenous Australia. We have shown that language naming practices are diverse across the Australian region, but that two key characteristics define most local processes: (i) inherent fluidity and social strategy in the deployment of language names, and (ii) strong interconnections between language, people and country.

References

Amery, Rob. 1993. An Australian koine: Dhuwaya, a variety of Yolngu Matha spoken at Yirrkala in North East Arnhem Land. *International Journal of the Sociology of Language* 99. 45–64.

Berndt, Ronald M. 1959. The concept of 'the tribe' in the Western Desert of Australia. *Oceania* 30 (2). 81–107.

Biddle, Nicholas. 2012. *Indigenous language usage*. Canberra: Centre for Aboriginal Economic Policy Research, Australian National University. http://caepr.anu.edu.au/sites/default/files/cck_indigenous_outcomes/2012/09/2011CensusPaper01_IndLangUsage.pdf.

Blommaert, Jan. 2008. Artefactual ideologies and the textual production of African languages. *Language & Communication* 28 (4). 291–307.

Borsboom, A. d. 1978. Dreaming clusters among Marangu clans. In Lester Richard Hiatt (ed.), *Australian Aboriginal concepts*, 106–120. Canberra: Australian Institute of Aboriginal Studies.

Capell, Arthur. 1942. Languages of Arnhem Land, North Australia. *Oceania* 12 (4). 364–392.

Carew, Margaret. 2016. *Gun-ngaypa Rrawa 'My Country': Intercultural alliances in language research.* Melbourne: PhD Thesis, Monash University.

Carr, E. Summerson & Michael Lempert. 2016. Pragmatics of scale. In Summerson E. Carr & Michael Lempert (eds.), *Scale: Discourse and dimensions of social life*, 1–22. California: University of California.

Chernela, Janet. 2018. Language in an ontological register: Embodied speech in the Northwest Amazon of Colombia and Brazil. *Language & Communication* 63. 23–32. https://doi.org/10.1016/j.langcom.2018.02.006.

Cysouw, Michael & Jeff Good. 2013. Languoid, doculect, and glossonym: Formalizing the notion "language." *Language Documentation & Conservation* 7. http://scholarspace.manoa.hawaii.edu/handle/10125/4606 (accessed 9 December 2020).

Demuro, Eugenia & Laura Gurney. 2021. Languages/languaging as world-making: The ontological bases of language. *Language Sciences* 83. 101307. https://doi.org/10.1016/j.langsci.2020.101307.

Donaldson, Tamsin. 1984. What's in a name? An etymological view of land, language and social identification from central western New South Wales. *Aboriginal History* 8 (1/2). 21–44.

Elliott, Craig. 1991. *"Mewal is Merri's name": Form and ambiguity in Marrangu cosmology, North Central Arnhem Land*. Canberra: MA thesis, Australian National University.

Evans, Nicholas. 2003. Context, culture, and structuration in the languages of Australia. *Annual Review of Anthropology* 32. 13–40.

Evans, Nicholas. 2010. *Dying words: Endangered languages and what they have to tell us*. Malden, MA: Wiley-Blackwell.

Evans, Nicholas. 2013. *Multilingualism as the primal human condition: What we have to learn from small-scale speech communities*. Plenary presented at the International Symposium on Bilingualism 9, Singapore, 10–13 June 2013.

Garde, Murray. 2008. Kun-dangwok: "clan lects" and Ausbau in western Arnhem land. *International Journal of the Sociology of Language* 191. 141–169.

Garde, Murray. 2013. *Culture, interaction and person reference in an Australian language*. Amsterdam & Philadelphia: John Benjamins.

Glasgow, Kathleen. 1994. *Burarra–Gun-nartpa dictionary with English finder list*. Darwin: Summer Institute of Linguistics.

Green, Rebecca. 1987. *A sketch grammar of Burarra*. Canberra: Honours thesis, Australian National University.

Gurrmanamana, Frank, Lester R. Hiatt & Kim McKenzie. 2002. *People of the Rivermouth: The Joborr texts of Frank Gurrmanamana.* Canberra: National Museum of Australia and Aboriginal Studies Press.

Hamilton, Amanda. 1981. *Nature and nurture.* Canberra: Australian Institute of Aboriginal Studies.

Haspelmath, Martin. 2017. Some principles for language names. *Language Documentation* 11. 81–93.

Hauck, Jan David. 2016. *Making language: The ideological and interactional constitution of language in an indigenous Aché community in eastern Paraguay.* Los Angeles: PhD thesis, University of California Los Angeles.

Hiatt, Lester R. 1962. Local organization among the Australian Aborigines. *Oceania* 32 (4). 267–286.

Ionnàccaro, Gabriele & Vittorio Dell'Aquila. 2001. Mapping languages from inside: Notes on perceptual dialectology. *Social & Cultural Geography* 2 (3). 265–280.

Irvine, Judith T. & Susan Gal. 2000. Language ideology and linguistic differentiation. In P. V. Kroskrity (ed.), *Regimes of language: Ideologies, polities and identities*, 35–84. Santa Fe: School of American Research Press.

Jakobson, Roman. 1957. *Shifters, verbal categories, and the Russian verb.* Cambridge, Mass.: Harvard University Russian Language Project.

Johnson, Steve. 1991. Social parameters of linguistic change in an unstratified Aboriginal society. In Philip Baldi (ed.), *Patterns of change, change of patterns: Linguistic change and reconstruction methodology*, 203–217. Berlin & New York: De Gruyter Mouton.

Jones, Rhys, & Betty Meehan. 1978. Anbarra concept of colour. In Lester Richard Hiatt (ed.), *Australian Aboriginal concepts*, 20–29. Canberra: Australian Institute of Aboriginal Studies.

Keen, Ian. 1995. Metaphor and the metalanguage: "Groups" in northeast Arnhem Land. *American Ethnologist* 22 (3). 502–527.

Kloss, Heinz. 1967. Abstand-languages and Ausbau-languages. *Anthropological Linguistics* 9 (7). 29–41.

Léglise, Isabelle & Bettina Migge. 2006. Language-naming practices, ideologies, and linguistic practices: towards a comprehensive description of language varieties. *Language in Society* 35. 313–339.

Lüpke, Friederike. 2018. Multiple choice: Language use and cultural practice in rural Casamance between convergence and divergence. In Jacqueline Knörr & Trajano Wilson Filho (eds.), *Creolization and pidginization in contexts of postcolonial diversity: Language, culture, identity*, 181–208. Brill: Leiden.

Merlan, Francesca. 1981. Land, language and social identity in Aboriginal Australia. *Mankind* 13. 133–148.

Migge, Bettina & Isabelle Léglise. 2013. *Exploring language in a multilingual context: Variation, interaction and ideology in language documentation.* Cambridge: Cambridge University Press.

Miller, Wick R. 1971. Dialect differentiation in the Western Desert language. *Anthropological Forum* 3 (1). 61–78.

Mirritji, Jack. 1976. *My people's life.* Milingimbi: Milingimbi Literature Centre.

Morphy, Frances. 1977. Language and moiety: sociolectal variation in a Yu:lngu language of North-East Arnhem Land. *Canberra Anthropology* 1(1). 51–60.

Rigsby, Bruce. 2005. The languages of eastern Cape York Peninsula and linguistic anthropology. In Bruce Rigsby & Nicolas Peterson (eds.), *Donald Thomson: The man and scholar*, 129–142. Canberra: Academy of the Social Sciences in Australia with support from Museum Victoria.

Rumsey, Alan. 1989. Language groups in Australian Aboriginal land claims. *Anthropological Forum* 6 (1). 69–79.

Schebeck, Bernard. 1968. *Dialect and social groupings in North East Arnhem Land.* Unpublished manuscript, Australian Institute of Aboriginal Studies, Canberra.

Singer, Ruth. 2018. The wrong t-shirt: Configurations of language and identity at Warruwi Community. *Australian Journal of Anthropology* 29(1). 70–88.

Smith, Ian & Steve Johnson. 1986. Sociolinguistic patterns in an unstratified society: the patrilects of Kugu Nganhcara. *Journal of the Atlantic Provinces Linguistic Society* 8. 29–43.

Sutton, Peter. 1978. *Wik: Aboriginal society, territory and language at Cape Keerweer, Cape York Peninsula, Australia*. Brisbane: PhD thesis, University of Queensland.

Sutton, Peter. 1979. Australian language names. In Stephen Wurm (ed.), *Australian Linguistic Studies*, 87–105. Canberra: Pacific Linguistics.

Sutton, Peter. 1991. Language in Aboriginal Australia: social dialects in a geographical idiom. In Suzanne Romaine (ed.), *Language in Australia*, 49–66. New York: Cambridge University Press.

Sutton, Peter. 1997. Materialism, sacred myth and pluralism: Competing theories of the origin of Australian languages. In Francesca Merlan, John Morton & Alan Rumsey (eds.), *Scholar and sceptic: Australian Aboriginal studies in honour of L. R. Hiatt*, 211–242. Canberra: Aboriginal Studies Press.

Sutton, Peter. 2001. Talking language. In Jane Helen Simpson, David Nash, Mary Laughren, Peter Austin & Barry Alpher (eds.), *Forty years on: Ken Hale and Australian languages*, 453–464. Canberra: Pacific Linguistics.

Sutton, Peter. 2003. *Native title in Australia: An ethnographic perspective*. Cambridge: Cambridge University Press.

Urciuoli, Bonnie. 2013. Is Spanglish a bad term? *Anthropology News*, 1 August 2013. Available at: http://linguisticanthropology.org/wp-content/uploads/2014/10/Aug.-2013-Vol.-54-Issue-8.-Is-Spanglish-a-Bad-Term-Bonnie-Urciuoli1.pdf (accessed 20 October 2020).

Vaughan, Jill. 2018. "We talk in saltwater words": Dimensionalisation of dialectal variation in multilingual Arnhem Land. *Language & Communication* 62. 119–132.

Walsh, Michael. 1997. How many Australian languages were there? In David T. Tryon & Michael Walsh (eds.), *Boundary rider: Essays in honour of Geoffrey O'Grady*, 393–412. Canberra: Pacific Linguistics.

Wilkinson, Melanie. 1991. *Djambarrpuyngu: a Yolngu variety of Northern Australia*. Sydney: PhD thesis, University of Sydney.

Wood, Ray. 2016. The problem of "tribal names" in Eastern Australia: The Kuku Yalanji example. In Jean-Christophe Verstraete & Diane Hafner (eds.), *Land and language in Cape York Peninsula and the Gulf Country*, 337–360. Amsterdam & Philadelphia: John Benjamins.

Willie Lungisani Chigidi

Chapter 9
Names they left behind: Remembering the times with the White farmers in some parts of Chimanimani and Chipinge in Zimbabwe

Abstract: For nearly a century while the people of Zimbabwe lived under colonial rule, they interacted with White people in all sorts of manners. Black-White relationships were characterised by, among other things, name labelling, whether the interaction took place in urban, rural or farm environments. This chapter intends to focus attention on the lasting impact of the interactions that existed between White people and Blacks who worked on or lived next to White owned farms. The argument raised here is that Black people reacted in their own way to the treatment they received and to the behaviour and habits of the White people who lived in their neighbourhoods, who employed them or who carried out commercial business in the vicinity. The African people's powerful reaction to what they regarded as misdemeanours was to give Whites names and the interesting thing about those names is that they have become a permanent feature in the lives of the people long after those targeted by the linguistic onslaught are gone. This chapter will discuss names given in response to the kind of treatment Blacks received from White farmers, names that defined Black people's perceptions of the qualities and behaviour of some White individuals, and names given based on the reconstruction of the White men's original names to fit into the phonology of the local language. Most of the names to be discussed in this chapter are obtained from Rusitu Valley, in Chimanimani and Chipinge, where they have become part of the history and geographical terrain of the Eastern Highlands of Zimbabwe.

Keywords: Ndau, nicknames, Rusitu, Melsetter, transphonologisation

1 Introduction

It is standard practice all over the world that people are given names by their parents or by whoever else is authorised to do so. But it is also possible that, as people grow older and even in their old age, they can be given other names, this

Willie Lungisani Chigidi, Midlands State University, e-mail: chigidiwl@staff.msu.ac.zw

https://doi.org/10.1515/9783110759297-009

time by other "unauthorised" persons, which are known as nicknames. The question to ask is "who gives them, to whom and for what reasons" (Awedoba and Owoahene-Acheampong 2017: 147). In Zimbabwe, for nearly a century that Black people lived under colonial rule they interacted and related with White people in all sorts of manner. These Black-White interactions took place in urban, farming, mining or rural environments. The focus of this chapter is on the lasting impact of the interactions that took place between White people and the Blacks who worked for them or who lived next to some White-owned farms in the Rusitu Valley between Chimanimani and Chipinge. The dominant relationship that existed is that between employer and employee which, regrettably, took the form of a master-servant relationship. This relationship often, if not usually, resulted in the master or employer ill-treating the servant or employee. In some cases the White farmers behaved in ways that seemed to be unusual in the eyes of the Black person. Black people therefore reacted strongly to the treatment they received from, and to the behaviours displayed by, the White people who employed them or those who carried out commercial businesses in the vicinity. The powerful reaction of the Black people to what they regarded as White farmers' misdemeanours or strange ways of doing things was to give them nicknames and the interesting thing about those sobriquets is that they have become a permanent feature of the people long after those targeted by the linguistic onslaught are gone.

Names that will be discussed in this chapter are of three types: (i) those that resulted from the reconstruction of the original White farmer's name so that it fitted into the phonology of the local language, which in this case is Ndau; (ii) names that were given in response to the nature of the treatment received from White farmers; and (iii) names that defined Black people's perceptions of other qualities and behaviours of certain White individuals.

The area where the names to be discussed are found covers parts of what today are known as Chimanimani and Chipinge districts. These districts are found on either side of Rusitu River as it meanders between the lands of Chiefs Mutema, Ndima and Ngorima on its way to join the Haroni River, which flows all the way to the Indian Ocean. These lands made up the district that was known as Melsetter (including Chipinga) from 1927 (Jollie 1927). The original village of Chimanimani was founded by Thomas Moodie in 1892, but in 1895 moved to its current site and was officially named Melsetter after the Moodie family home in the misty Orkneys of Scotland (Jollie 1927); the name changed to Mandidzudzure in 1982 and later to Chimanimani. The Whites who settled in Melsetter (Chimanimani and Chipinge) were led by Moodie and included both Dutch and the English. Jollie (1927) further explains that many of the English left, leaving behind just a few, but the Dutch had "stood the pioneer conditions best and most of those who remained were of this breed". This is the calibre of the White settler who inhabited the area, which, for our purposes here, stretches from Charter Junction near Chimanimani to parts of northern Chipinge. The Boer has been regarded as a more difficult employer and neighbour than the British and represents the majority of the bearers of the names to be discussed here. Most of the Africans who created the nicknames given to the White farmers were the original inhabitants of the lands occupied by those White farmers, but some of them ended up going back to work on the lands they had lost to the invaders. Some had their cattle confiscated or bought for a few coins, so that in the end the White farmers owned cattle and land and Blacks owned nothing – they had lost all: land, cattle, freedom and dignity. They were an angry lot and they were best placed to start fighting back in the war of words called nicknaming.

2 Naming the "good" White farmer

The White farmers who employed Black workers were not of like character. Some were reasonably good to their workers while others were bad and sometimes outright cruel. Black workers gave nicknames to their White employers according to how they perceived them, that is, whether they perceived them as good or as bad.

The White farmers with whom Black workers had no issue were simply called by their original European names. The use of the White farmer's formal name is an indication that the relationship was cordial. If the White farmer had a case to answer it was because s/he had come and assumed a dominant and superior position on the African man's land. Some farmers had dispossessed the Blacks of their land but proceeded to relate well to their workers and Black neighbours. Black people did not go out of their way to create new names for such invaders. Instead, they just used the formal name of the White colonial master. However, since they were not able to pronounce the names properly, they tamed the linguistic environment by "ndaulising" the sounds of the English/Boer names. In other words, "the majority of Blacks resorted to transphonologising foreign sounds as a subtle response to domination" (Ndlovu and Mangena 2013: 348). "For the indigenous Zimbabweans, the English people brought 'strange sounding' names that needed to be adopted to indigenous phonological systems" (Ndlovu and Mangena 2013: 348) and they succeeded in indigenising them. In a way, the indigenous people were not "defeated" as they did not fail to name the stranger. As Williams says, "Once you can name something, you're conscious of it. You have power over it. You're in control. You own it" (Williams 2015). In that sense, Blacks owned the space, they controlled it, they had power over it. It is like when one owns a vicious dog: once it has been given a name, it answers to the name, barks at nothing when ordered to do so and lies down when required to do so by the name giver. The owner has power over the vicious dog. So once they gave the White farmer a nickname, they could name the farmer, they could name his farm, they could name the road to his farm, they could name his wife, dog, lorry, cattle, etc. If they wanted, they could prefix that with *Baas*, like *Baas Mare (Murray).*

3 The transphonologisation of foreign sounds

Names of White farmers in the Rusitu area with foreign sounds that were transphonologised include names such as Peacock. Peacock's name was simply reduced to *Pikoko*. The farm was *purazi raPikoko* 'Pikoko's farm', the store was *chitoro chaPikoko* 'Pikoko's store' and so on with everything else that was owned by Peacock. It became something possessed by Pikoko, resulting in possessive phrases in which *Pikoko* became the possessive stem of a possessive phrase. Further down the road was Murray's farm. Murray's name was also reduced to *Mare* because the locals were not able to properly pronounce Murray with the final '*-ray*', so they simply called him *Mare*, which coincidentally was the same word the locals used for the English word 'money', which in Ndau language is *mare*. The last White farmer along the road parallel to Nyahode River going down to Kopa in Rusitu at that time was the White tomato grower called Warring, who was called *Warangi*. His farm was later managed by Gilson and the locals were equal to the task and phonologised the sounds of this name to *Girisoni.* Today this farm is owned by ARDA (Agricultural Rural Development Authority), but locals still identify the place as *kuAdha' kwaGirisoni* 'at Girisoni's ARDA'. ARDA owns many farms all over Zimbabwe and in this case the place is known as *kwaGirisoni* 'at Girisioni', to differentiate it from other ARDA farms in the area. The other White farmer in the area known by his personal name was Green. The locals demonstrated their ability to control the situation by simply calling him *Girini.*

At every strategic point along each road on these farms, there were signposts indicating where 'Baas' so and so resided and the name of the farmer was written on a piece of metal hung by a chain on a vertical iron pole. However, most of the locals could not read (and write) so they relied instead on their sense of hearing. For that reason, what was written on the signposts did not matter. They could not read and decipher what was written there. The sounds that made up the names were the sounds that they heard and dealt with in demonstrating their resistance to the establishment of the White man's empire. What made their resistance to the establishment of the White man's empire more complete is that the locals rarely, very rarely, transphonologised the White man's first names. They always phonologised the sounds that made up the surnames. For example, if it were the case of

Thomas Moodie, they phonologised the sounds that made up Moodie (*Mudhii*), the family name, thereby ensuring that their power over the family was complete, not only on the Moodie home in Melsetter, but also on the "old home of his family in the Orkneys (in Scotland)" (Jollie 1927). The locals even had the temerity to transphonologise names of missionaries, men of God who ministered to them. For example, one White missionary at Rusitu Mission, Reverend Evans, was generally known as *Mufundisi Evhenesi.* The Ndaus had lost their land, independence, cattle and freedom, but they would not allow themselves to be completely overwhelmed by strange names. They at least retained their linguistic freedom and used it to transform the strange "words" into something they could manage and share among themselves.

It is significant to note that these names whose sounds the Ndaus transphonologised to fit into local sound systems are the names that have been used ever since to identify and name places. Commuters who travel along the road from Kopa in Rusitu Valley to Chimanimani and back know that the next place to stop to drop or pick passengers is *Mare* 'at Mare' or *Pikoko* 'at Pikoko' or some other place. At Mare and at Pikoko there are no more relics of the departed White farmers (except perhaps for the pine trees that grow there) – there is no name Murray or Peacock written on a metal signpost, no store or shop apart from vendors selling bananas and avocado pears, and no more farmer's homestead. What has persisted and defied "death" are the Ndaulised names *Mare*, *Pikoko*, *Girini*, *Girisoni* and *Warangi.*

4 Nicknaming the unpopular employer

We have so far discussed White farmers' names which were transphonologised into the Ndau sound system and became the names that some places are known by. We now turn to names given to White farmers which are indicators of the local people's creative abilities. Most such names were given to White farmers because there were variants between behaviour and expectations. As Mashiri (2004: 13) argues, "Generally speaking, Shona people seem to rely mostly on nicknaming practices for defining inappropriate or excessive behaviour, uphold cultural ideals and politely rebuking deviant behaviour or personalities (. . .) There is power potential embedded in nickname systems which speakers can exploit in dynamic ways at any given discoursal instance".

The locals did not have any problem coming up with appropriate nicknames. In giving White farmers nicknames they were merely doing what they were used to doing in their own culture and communities when they intended to bring anyone whose behaviour was unbecoming into line or to condemn someone for an unacceptable cultural doing. Examples can be given here to provide background to the discussion of what used to happen on the farms. Very often, names that were given to dogs in Ndau communities were commentaries on human behaviour. In one homestead in the Dzingire area there was once a dog named *Mareyokurasha* 'Wasted money'. The background to this was that after a night of drinking traditional beer and dancing, there was an elderly woman in her 80s who expected to be given a hot meal of *sadza* 'thick mealie-meal porridge' and roasted meat that was well salted, early the following morning. This lady was the most senior paternal aunt in the family and so she expected her brothers' wives to perform their traditional role and prepare her a hot meal at sunrise, since as sister to their husbands she too was their "husband" from a cultural perspective. One could be divorced for failing to fulfil this obligation. After all, in the event of problems with their husbands, the wives would also go to the aunt to ask for her intervention and she would oblige. Now, when the meal was not provided by any of the brothers' wives as expected, the old lady went mad and approached her elder brother:

Aunt: *Yee baba!*
[Excuse me father]

Brother: *Mwatii?*
[What is it?]

Aunt: *Pano hapana imbwa doko here pano apa?*
[Is there no puppy here?]

Brother: *Iyo iripo iyo.*
[There it is.]

Aunt: *Imbwa iyo zita rayo ndiMareyokurasha.*
[The name of that dog is *Mareyokurasha*]

From that moment till the day it died that dog was called, and would answer, to the name *Mareyokurasha* 'Wasted money'. In Ndau culture, as in many other Bantu traditions, when a woman is married, *lobola* is paid to her family; in turn she is expected to bear children and perform wifely duties in her adopted home and family. Then people will say *"Hamuchionizve. Ndikwo kunozwi kuroora uku"* 'That is what it means to be married'. If the woman disappoints then people say *"Hapana zvekuroora apa"* 'Useless wife'. That means *lobola* was wasted. Because none of her brothers' wives prepared a hot meal for the aunt it meant that the wealth from the family that was used to pay *lobola* for each and every one of them was a waste, hence the little dog was named *Mareyokurasha* 'wasted money' up until its death. *Mareyokurasha* is not just a label, but "a highly communicative facet" (Makaudze 2016: 14). The Ndau people call this *kugadzikira* 'heaping unkind words on someone'.

Here, "the dog's name is used to admonish relatives and to shame them into carrying out whatever responsibilities they have been neglecting" (Tatira 2004: 95).

In other homesteads in the same community there were also dogs that were named in the same way. One dog was named *Hunematura* 'You have lots of poisonous stuff used in practising witchcraft', to imply that someone had a lot of substances used for witchcraft because she was responsible for the bewitching of many people who were dying in the area. Another dog was named *Ramwiwa* 'Beer has been taken in excess', to depict the behaviour of the father of the family who, when he came home drunk, would sing at the top of his voice at night when the neighbourhood was asleep, harassing women and children. Yet another dog was named *Zvepanomutikapu* 'Strange things happening here are for the eyes to see while the mouth remains shut because they are so bad you can't even comment'. This name defined the inappropriate and unbecoming behaviour of some of the family members. The behaviours were so outrageous that one ran out of words to describe them; the name thus advised people that, when it comes to things that people do there, "just watch and keep quiet". *Kapu* is an ideophone that expresses the action of just looking at something happening without saying a word (because it is so terrible). This is a case of *kugadzikira* 'saying unkind words about someone'. This confirms the point that "Through the institution of dog-naming, members of society engage in accusation and counter-accusation with each other on sensitive issues" (Tatira 2004: 88).

Some of the people who had the tradition of such nicknaming practices of *kugadzikira* 'saying unkind words about someone' were the same people who went to work on the farms in the Rusitu Valley. Mashiri (2004: 18) observed that "some workers refer to their unpopular employers or superiors by scathing nicknames when talking among themselves or when the name bearer is within over-hearing range". The White farmers who employed local Blacks were given nicknames by their unhappy workers in the same way the same Black workers nicknamed their dogs back at home. In all cases there was something unbecoming. The only difference was that at home in the rural areas some nicknames were not given to the culprits; names defining behaviour were often bestowed on dogs and whenever the dog was called by the name people knew that it was not the behaviour of the dog that was being corrected or the dog that was being reprimanded or scolded, but a human being. Maybe this can be regarded as nicknaming by proxy – you name a dog to name a person. The dog bears the name on your behalf, like someone who votes by proxy.

4.1 Farmers who denied workers food

When White employers ill-treated their Black employees, they encouraged them to engage their nicknaming skills, which they had perfected when naming dogs in their communities, as explained and exemplified above. The nicknames that were given to the White farmers carried lots of meanings in them. They were forms of *kugadzikira* 'saying unkind words about someone' by a people who were angry. As Makaudze (2016: 13) observes, "Naming among the traditional Shona has been a very conscious activity. Most of the names convey rich layers of meaning about either the bearer or the name givers (. . .) the names are actually books in miniature". The nicknames tell sad stories about how White farmers treated their Black employees. One such name is *Biyarendongwe* 'Clay pot full of locusts'. The story behind this nickname, given to the White farmer who owned Albany Farm, situated on the edge of the Rusitu Valley, is that the farmer was very mean when it came to providing his employees with food. It was standard practice in those days that White farmers gave their workers weekly rations of mealie-meal and some form of relish. Usually the relish was in the form of dried beans, milk or the more popular dried fish called *bakayawe* that came from Mozambique (formerly Portuguese East Africa). Some workers supplemented this with dried cow-peas leaves called *mupfutswa*, which they brought from their rural homes if they went there at the weekend or month end. But others had no such provisions to supplement with, as they came from far away Mozambique. However, the White farmer would not give relish to his workers, demanding that they eat the staple *sadza* 'Thick mealie-meal porridge' with a kind of locust called *ndongwe* in Ndau language. There were swarms of such locusts which often destroyed crops and the locals would catch them in large numbers, roast them and then store them in big clay pots as a fall-back on when relish became hard to come by, especially in winter. The White farmer would not give his workers relish at times, calling upon them instead to eat the locusts they had preserved and stored in their big clay pots, and that earned him the nickname *Biyarendongwe* 'Big clay pot full of roasted locusts'. This is the rich layer of meaning about the bearer of the name that Makaudze (2016) talks about. The road from Rusitu Valley, which runs parallel to the Nyahode River as it stretches up to Charter, passes through Temurai's Farm before it gets to Mare, Pikoko and beyond. Temurai's Farm was so named because the owner of the farm was also guilty of not providing his farm workers with food. In Ndau language, *temurai* means 'eat your staple *sadza* without relish'. *Sadza* is good and palatable if it is taken with suitable relish. The owner of this farm was notorious for giving his workers mealie-meal and then requiring them to supply their own relish, or, better still, to eat it without any relish. His explanation would always be that people should eat *sadza* without relish, for which the Ndau word is *temurai*, and so he was nicknamed Temurai. Unfortunately, any name that a White farmer was given by his workers was also taken on by the surrounding communities.

On the other side of the Rusitu River, approximately fifteen kilometres from Chipinge at the Chipinge-Mutare-Chimanimani road junction, at a place commonly known as Jopa, is another former White man's farm. The White owner of the farm was nicknamed *Mutakura* 'cooked maize seed' by his employees and the local community. Again, this is a nickname which had to do with the way the White farmer handled his workers with regard to food matters. Instead of providing his workers with mealie-meal and relish, the former White farmer expected his workers to eat maize seed boiled until soft in water and salt, called *mutakura* in Ndau. Sometimes the maize seed was mixed with beans and then boiled. Because of this behaviour and practice the White farmer was nicknamed *Mutakura*, because he made people eat the unpopular *mutakura* (boiled maize seed).

Each of these names, Biyarengongwe, Temurai and Mutakura, is a social statement reflecting the bearer, the namer and the social environment (Pfukwa 2016). The name is a social statement about the cruel and mean individual who did not feed his employees well, although they worked very hard to produce wealth for him; it is a social statement about the namer who was an abused individual who was not properly fed by the employer; and also about the social environment, which was one of capitalist exploitation in a colonial set up. As Pfukwa (2016) declares, while writing on guerrilla fighters of the Second Chimurenga, the "Second War of Liberation in Zimbabwe", each name was a rich metaphor in itself, a narrative that effectively summarised an aspect of the struggle. Since the nicknames Biyarendongwe, Temurai and Mutakura predate the Second Chimurenga that Pfukwa is commenting on, we assume that this nicknaming is an unofficial extension of the First Chimurenga, especially if we consider that *Biyarendongwe* connects the events on this farm with one of the causes of the First Chimurenga, which was an outbreak of locusts which was blamed on the White settlers.

4.2 The farmers who beat up workers

Closely related to the nicknames denoting food deprivation are those nicknames that were consciously created to describe the physical harassment of farm workers by White farmers. Masaka, Gwaravanda and Mukusha (2012: 488), who studied the nicknames of White farmers and employers in parts of Masvingo Province, put it aptly:

> Nicknames given to White farmers and employers were often a reaction against all types of abuses, including physical, psychological and verbal. Nicknaming was, therefore, a political process, because names created a group consciousness for the purpose of warning, reminding, describing, evaluating, and resisting the exploitation of Black people on White farms.

Abusive White farmers and employers were given witheringly scornful and severely critical nicknames. There were White farmers and employers who used abrasive words and others who used mere physical power to abuse their workers. In some cases these were young White farmers who physically or verbally abused employees much older than themselves. Blacks detested this dehumanising behaviour and attitude on the part of the White farmers. They therefore resorted to giving nicknames that defined the nature of their abuse. In fact, this was a mode of defiance, resistance, retaliation and, ultimately, an expression of their struggle for freedom. As Masaka, Gwaravanda and Mukusha (2012: 489) explain, "The nicknaming of White farmers indicated an emotional reaction and dislike of the exploitative and brutal nature of White farmers". The Blacks reacted with equally brutal verbal responses.

One such brutal verbal response of Blacks is indicated by the nickname given to the White farmer whose farm was situated next to Biyarendongwe's farm. The farmer was nicknamed *Madhonora* 'one who hits hard with a fist' by his Black workers. The White farmer was in the habit of hitting his workers using his fists. He used to warn his workers, "*Mina dhonora wena*" 'I will hit you hard with my fist', using a mixture of Ndau and Nguni words, resulting in a kind of *Chilapalapa* that the locals could understand. The Ndau use the verb *kudhonora* from the verb radical *-dhonor-* 'to hit hard' when referring to hitting hard with a fist, especially on the chest. Because of this habit of threatening and in some cases actually carrying out the threat, his Black workers nicknamed him *Madhonora*, implying someone who hits others hard, especially on the chest. Madhonora lived next door to Biyarendongwe who, besides having been given this more well-known nickname, was also nicknamed *Manduku* 'User of a knobkerrie'. Biyarendongwe was quite advanced in age by the 1960s and walked with the help of a stick shaped like a knobkerrie at one end. Incidentally, the farmer nicknamed *Manduku*, the language called Ndau, and the stick called *nduku* all had some kind of relationship with the Nguni. The White farmer came from South Africa, *nduku* (*induku* in Nguni languages) is a Nguni knobkerrie, and Ndau people interacted with the Gaza-Nguni sometime in the early 19th century. *Nduku* 'knobkerrie' was a weapon used by the Nguni when fighting or when beating up people. Biyarendongwe was well-known for beating up workers with his *nduku* 'knobkerrie' when they had displeased him. This is what earned him a second nickname, *Manduku*, and now he had two. Biyarendongwe or Manduku was a second generation owner of the farm. Biyarendongwe's father, who first owned the farm, came with his trusted Black foreman of the Xhosa tribe from South Africa. When Biyarendongwe inherited the farm after his father's death, he also inherited the foreman, who was equally advanced in age. The Black foreman also used *nduku* to deal with his subordinates on the farm, although the term Manduku was never used as a nickname to refer to him. So the *nduku* tradition was quite strong on Biyarendongwe's farm. It was quite a feat to be one employer and then have two nicknames from his Black workers, neither of which was pleasant or neutral – a far cry from *Pachedu* 'We are together', a nickname for Roy Bennett, a former policeman turned farmer who was very much liked by his workers and the surrounding communities.

In the southern part of the Rusitu Valley, closer to Chipinge, was a White farmer called *Chibhakera* 'fist'. *Chibhakera* is a Ndau word shared with Shona to mean a 'fist'. Here was a White farmer who thought he had a right to hit adult Black workers with his fist (like Madhonora) whenever he thought they had erred or performed their duties badly. For that reason his workers and surrounding communities nicknamed him *Chibhakera* 'fist'.

One White farmer in the Chipinge area was nicknamed *Babaarinane* 'The father is better'. This was a nickname given to a White farmer who was more vicious than his father. When people complained that the young White farmer was cruel, those in the know would say "*Babaarinane*" 'The father is better', implying that the son was worse. The younger of the White farmers was more vicious than his father and so he was nicknamed *Babaarinane.* This farmer was notorious for harassing his employees and the latter hated him. "Nicknames encapsulated a dislike for the exploitative tendency of White farmers – a resistance against dehumanising experiences at the hands of the White employers" (Masaka, Gwaravanda and Mukusha 2012: 488–489).

Machongwe 'Cocks' was nicknamed thus because he was in the habit of personally going around his Black workers' compound in the early hours of the morning, waking them up and ordering them to go to the fields to start the day's work. These are the dark hours when the cocks begin to crow to signal approaching daybreak. For this hated habit his Black employees nicknamed him *Machongwe* 'cocks'. Obviously, this was an expression of resistance and protest. Although the nickname does not imply beating anyone, the act of waking up Black workers so early in the morning even in very cold winters borders on using excessive force.

Each time the Blacks used these names they were hurling unpleasant and angry insults at their White employers. These names show that there were no cordial relations between White employers and their Black employees because "Names that people call each other are sometimes powerful indicators of social relations" (Allen 1993; Herbert 1999, quoted in Barnes and Pfukwa 2007: 431).

5 Neutral and complementary nicknames

While the nicknames that have been discussed so far show nothing positive about the bearers, there were other nicknames that were neutral and sometimes complementary. Some of them show that the name givers actually had a lot of admiration for the named because of their ability to perform certain feats. The nicknames given to such White farmers would thus bestow positive qualities on the bearer. In cases like that, "A name is a full social statement that ascribes to the bearer certain attributes and values" (Pfukwa and Viriri 2011: 427). Chimanimani is such a hilly and mountainous country that driving along some of its roads is sometimes like dicing with death. Two nicknames for White farmers are associated with the introduction of automobiles in the area. One White farmer was nicknamed *Mututu* 'Strong and fast-moving wind' for his driving skills along the long, curvy and winding dusty road from his homestead to Chimanimani, or to other White farmers' homesteads. The Black people who also walked on the same gravel roads with their bare feet would watch in awe as the White man's Land Rover, which had no doors, sped past them while they waved it down in desperate attempt to get a lift. Others, who were going nowhere far and did not need a lift, would simply wave their hands to greet the awesome White man as he sped past them, raising a huge cloud of dust in the process. The speed with which he drove along this winding gravel road raised so much dust that it was possible to trace the route followed by the vehicle for 2 or 3 kilometres, merely by seeing the stretch of rising dust following the direction the car had taken, without actually seeing the car itself. Such were the driving habits of this White farmer that locals nicknamed him *Mututu*, which means 'strong and fast-moving wind'. There was nothing hateful or derogatory about the name. It was an expression of a mixture of admiration and hopelessness of a people witnessing a fast-moving automobile on a dangerous rugged road while engulfed in a cloud of dust which they had no choice but to inhale. There is also another nickname whose creation was inspired by a White farmer's ability to drive a motor vehicle in dangerous terrain. The nickname was *Chikwiramakomo* 'One who climbs mountains'. It has already been mentioned that Chimanimani is a mountainous country and this White farmer was in the habit of manoeuvring his Land Rover up the hills and mountain slopes. His homestead was on top of a hill and it was approached by a very straight road stretching for almost two kilometres from the main Kopa to Chimanimani road. The entire two kilometres stretch was straight, and awestruck locals and Black farm workers watched as the vehicle climbed up the rising road to the homestead, or down the hill, if it was leaving the homestead to join the main road. This, combined with his habit of driving his jeep up the hills even where there was no road, when checking on his herd of cattle, rightfully earned the White farmer the descriptive nickname *Chikwiramakomo* 'One who climbs mountains'. *Chikwiramakomo* was a neutral nickname that merely registered the local people's preoccupation with the White farmers driving antics. Indeed, *Mututu* and *Chikwiramakomo* were nicknames that ascribed to the bearers certain attributes. There was nothing hateful about them.

Sharing a common border with Biyarendongwe is *Manyoka* 'Owner of snakes'. This nickname was given to this White farmer because he loved snakes and kept a large number of them at his homestead. If there is anything that an average African fears it is a snake. If Africans see a snake the first thing they want to do is to kill it, even if it means no harm to anyone who does not disturb it. Any Ndau person who keeps a snake is thought to be a witch or wizard and no one likes to be associated with her/him. The White farmer who kept snakes was not admired, although neither was he hated. The snakes were his and Blacks had no business getting near them, but were just as uncomfortable as they would have been with a known witch among themselves. After all, the White man's home was a no go area, so they left him alone with his snakes but nicknamed him *Manyoka* 'Owner of snakes'. Maybe the safest thing that can be said is that the nickname expressed people's fears of the farmer and his snakes. If this is so then neutrality in this case becomes questionable.

On the eastern side of the Nyahode River between Temurai and Mare lived an old White woman who ran a shop at her homestead. The old lady was affectionately nicknamed *Chimbuya* 'A small old woman' because she was old, maybe in her 80s in the 1960s, small bodied and lived alone (with her domestic workers) on that forest covered mountain slope. This was a nickname that showed that the old lady lived harmoniously with the Black community that lived there and with others who came to buy from her shop, the type of shop owner who endeared herself with mothers by giving sweets to the babies strapped on their backs when they visited the shop. She may also have been nicknamed *Chimbuya* 'a small old woman' because she was old and behaved like a grandmother to Black children. Nicknames like *Mututu, Chikwiramakomo* and *Chimbuya* were given "to individuals who were famous for some social behaviour" (Makaudze 2016: 20). As Awedoba and Owoahene-Acheampong (2017: 157) point out, "in some cases nicknames are associated with affection and endearment even if they do not seem to praise".

6 Naming places after the departed White farmers

Zimbabwe became independent from British rule in 1980. Since then, some colonial names of places that had been in use for almost a century were replaced by those that were historically, culturally, socially and linguistically relevant to the local people. Names like Masvingo (Fort Victoria), Chegutu (Hartley), Chivhu (Enkeldorn), Chimanimani (Melsetter) etc came into use. However, there are places within Chimanimani District which came to be identified by the nicknames given to the colonial White farm owners during those Melsetter heydays. Some places are still known today by their former White farmers' European names, albeit in their transphonologised forms, such as Mare, Pikoko, Girini, Girisoni etc, while others are still known today by the nicknames that were given to the former White farmers. While many of these areas have since been occupied by Black people under the Land Resettlement Programme, nothing is being done to obliterate the nicknames given to these places by Black employees. Ndlovu (2018: 4) has noted that names that the youth have been giving in the city of Bulawayo have stood the test of time and are now being passed from generation to generation. Equally, the names that the Black people gave to their White employers in parts of Chimanimani and Chipinge have become a permanent feature of the topography. As Bosch (1994, quoted in Ndlovu 2018:5) points out, "nicknames are not necessarily regarded as permanent as proper names. But historically nicknames in some cases have acquired a more permanent function". The name *Biya* 'clay pot' (the possessive stem *-rendongwe* was dropped long ago) has become a permanent feature in the area. The White farmer was nicknamed *Biyarendongwe,* and since then the place which was officially called Albany Farm has been known by people in the surrounding communities as *kwaBiya* 'at Biya'. Very few people seem to know that officially the farm was called Albany Farm. This former farm, now resettled, has, is and is likely to remain known forever as *kwaBiya* 'at Biya', Albany Primary School as *kuchikoro kwaBiya* 'at Biya School', the road as *pato rekwaBiya* 'Biya Road', the wetlands as *dimba rekwaBiya* 'Biya wetlands', etc.

People in the Rusitu Valley also refer to a place they call *kwaMututu* 'at Mututu', *pato rekwaMututu* 'Mututu Road', *komboni yekwaMututu* 'Mututu Compound', etc. That place will be known for the unforeseeable future by the nickname of the White farmer who used to speed along the winding dusty roads of Chimanimani. Again, decades after the White owner left the place at the Chipinge-Mutare-Chimanimani Road junction, the farm is still known as *kwaMutakura* 'at Mutakura'. To this day people still refer to places by nicknames given to departed White farmers and so they refer to *Chibhakera, Manyoka, Machongwe* etc. *Machongwe* is fast growing into a busy "growth point" with an urban outlook and urban facilities. We may end up with a town called *Machongwe* in future. What this shows is that these names have become a permanent feature of the landscape long after the White farmers who were given those nicknames departed and, ultimately, passed on or have been replaced as a result of Zimbabwe's Fast Track Land Reform Programme. The names themselves are a record of the trajectory through which the Ndau people of Chipinge and Chimanimani have travelled. They are a reflection of the events and interactions that took place in colonial times in some parts of Chipinge and Chimanimani Districts. Thus, the "act of naming is an act of recording histories, cultures and values" (Pfukwa 2018: 37). As Ndlovu (2016: 39) would say, it is history that was frozen in names. Indeed, these names "keep the history of the people because of their connection with historical period or historical activity or event" (Ndlovu 2013: 2).

7 Conclusion

This chapter has discussed nicknames that were given by Black workers to the White farmers who had occupied their space, parcelling out pieces of land to farm, and to others who engaged in other commercial activities in the neighbourhood of the Rusitu Valley in Chimanimani and Chipinge Districts. White farmers came with their own personal names which the Ndau people could not pronounce correctly, so they resorted to the option of phonologising foreign sounds as a way of dealing with the situation. Those White farmers who were called by their names but with their sounds fitted into the Ndau linguistic system were the relatively nicer ones of the White farmers whose conduct and attitude Black workers could at least tolerate. However, cruel and unpopular White farmers were given nicknames that were indicators of the uneasy relations that existed between them and their Black workers or neighbouring communities. In a sense, such names were indicators of the will and determination of Black workers to fight back and resist domination and ill-treatment. Yet there were also nicknames that were at least neutral and, at most, indicators of admiration. These were more or less like praising nicknames, given because the Blacks were mesmerised by the actions of certain White farmers like *Mututu.* Interestingly, the names that were given by the Ndaus to White farmers as response to ill-treatment and cruelty have become part of the landscape. For nearly forty years after the White farmers departed, various aspects of landscape remain identified and known by the departed White farmers' nicknames. These names are now being passed on from generation to generation by a people with a strong oral tradition. Some of the names that were there before colonialism have also been obliterated. The conclusion that one arrives at is that it would require an event of monumental proportions, bigger than colonialism and bigger than the liberation struggle, to obliterate these names which were the Ndau people's expressions of anger, hostility, resistance, power and determination to liberate themselves.

References

Awedoba, Albert Kanlisi & Stephen Owoahene-Acheampong. 2017. What is in a nickname: Ghanaian nickname cultures. *Ogirisi: A New Journal of African Studies* 13. 146–165. https://www.ajol.info/index.php/og/article/view/161161 (accessed 31 August 2021).

Barnes, Lawrie A. & Charles Pfukwa. 2007. Ethnic slurs as war names in Zimbabwe Liberation War. *Names* 55 (4). 427–436.

Jollie, Tawse. 1927. The romance of Melsetter. Available at rhodesia.me.uk/melsetter/ (accessed 27 August 2021).

Makaudze, Godwin. 2016. Naming the landscape: Oronyms in Chief Nyashanu area as books in miniature. *IGAMA: African Journal of Onomastics Studies* 1 (1). 13–22.

Masaka, Dennis, Ephraim Taurai Gwaravanda & Jowere Mukusha. 2012. Nicknaming as a mode of Black resistance: Reflections of Black indigenous peoples' nicknaming of colonial White farmers in Zimbabwe. *Journal of Black Studies* 43 (5). 479–504.

Mashiri, Pedzisai. 2004. More than mere linguistic tricks: The sociopragmatic functions of some nicknames used by Shona-speaking people in Harare. *Zambezia* 31 (1–2). 22–45.

Ndlovu, Sambulo & Tendai Mangena. 2013. Selected transphonologised Zimbabwean toponyms. In Oliviu Felecan (ed.), *Name and naming onomastics in contemporary public space*, 347–354. Baia Mare: Editura Mega.

Ndlovu, Sambulo. 2013. Historicity of some Ndebele toponyms in Zimbabwe. *Greener Journal of Social Sciences* 3 (5). 292–298.

Ndlovu, Sambulo. 2016. The Bulawayo linguistic landscape as linguistic heritage: Hodonyms and oikonyms. *IGAMA: Journal of African Onomastics Studies* 1 (2). 96–108.

Ndlovu, Sambulo. 2018. Characteristics and social impact of urban youth languages on urban toponymy: S'ncamtho toponomastics in Bulawayo. *Literator* 39 (1). 1–7.

Pfukwa, Charles. 2016. "We died for this country" (sic): Claiming space through the name in the Second Chimurenga. In Ruby Magosvongwe, Obert B. Mlambo & Eventhough Ndlovu (eds.), *Africa's intangible heritage and land: Emerging perspectives*, 82–90. Harare: University of Zimbabwe Publications.

Pfukwa, Charles. 2018. (Re)writing an urban landscape: Street names in Harare's CBD after 1980. *Nomina Africana* 32 (1). 37–45.

Pfukwa, Charles & Advice Viriri. 2011. Wasu to Samaz: Collective identity in Manyika nicknames. In *Proceedings of the 10th LASU Conference, Roma, Lesotho, 25–27 November 2009*, 427–437. Roma: National University of Lesotho.

Tatira, Liveson. 2004. Beyond the dog's name: A silent dialogue among the Shona people. *Journal of Folklore Research* 41 (1). 85–98.

Williams, Robin. 2015. *The non-designer's design book: Design and typographical principles for the visual novice.* Pearson Education. https://www.goodreads.com/author/quotes/90817.Robin_P_Williams (accessed 29 August 2021).

Section Three: **Anthroponyms as religious belief and practice**

Danson Sylvester Kahyana

Chapter 10
This baby's name is 'Leaf' or 'Garbage heap': Reading the figurative in selected death prevention names among the Bakonzo

Abstract: Among the Bakonzo people of Western Uganda, naming is an important aspect of communication, as names denote or connote several meanings. From someone's name, for instance, one can glean several pieces of sociological information, including gender, birth order and the context of birth (famine, war, epidemics, death, etc.). This chapter reflects on the figurative nature of the names given to children born after the death of the sibling they follow, for instance *Kyabu* ('garbage heap or rubbish pit'), *Kithi* '(leaf') and *Bahwere* ('they are finished'). There are two aspects of this naming practice that the study is interested in: the different messages or themes carried in these names, and the figures of speech through which these messages or themes are conveyed to the listener. For each name, the researcher performs a semantic and contextual reading for insights into its meaning and theme, as well as the figurative resources used to develop this meaning and theme. He supplements the insights gained from this exercise with some interviews with selected elders, who are renowned for their deep knowledge of the Konzo language and culture. It is hoped that this chapter will shed light on the poetic nature of Konzo names, as well as draw attention to related aspects of Konzo culture.

Keywords: Bakonzo, naming, figurative language, death prevention names

Acknowledgements: I thank Professor Sambulo Ndlovu for his wonderful contribution to this paper. Without him, I would not have thought of writing about this fascinating subject of death avoidance or prevention names. I also thank the anonymous peer reviewers for the insights that helped me improve the paper. Finally, I thank Marita Muukkonen and Ivor Stodolosky of Perpetuum Mobile/Artists at Risk for giving me a space (Väinämöisenkatu 21 B 17, 00100, Helsinki) where I could rest and write as I recovered from the attack I suffered in Uganda on 26 April 2022.

Danson Sylvester Kahyana, Makerere University/Stellenbosch University,
e-mail: dkdan76@gmail.com / danson.kahyana@mak.ac.ug

https://doi.org/10.1515/9783110759297-010

1 Introduction

The Bakonzo live in Western Uganda at the foothills of the Rwenzori Mountain, mostly in the districts of Kasese, Bunyangabu, Kabarole, Ntoroko and Bundibugyo. Their population is in excess of 1,000,000 people (Matte 2021). They share a lot with the Banande of the Democratic Republic of Congo, who number about 7,000,000 people. Both groups, for instance, "speak the same language, have the same clans, and the same economic and family organisation" (Facci 2009: 352).

The subject of names is central to the Konzo identity. This is perhaps because the Bakonzo were subjugated by the Tooro Kingdom for decades, both before and after Uganda's independence on 9 October 1962. During this period of subjugation, the Bakonzo were forced to take on a Tooro identity, including the Lutooro language and Tooro names (Balyage 2000: 13). The Bakonzo Life History Research Society, founded in the 1950s to "instill patriotism among the Konzo people and have them unite together" (Peterson 2012: 964), was tasked with researching the history and culture of the Bakonzo as a means of valorising the Konzo identity. In a letter to the chairperson of the society, Mr. Mukirane, one Mukonzo, called Swalehe Musyenene, set out a research programme for the society to pursue with regard to the subject of names:

> How should we know the real names of the Konzo children from the 1st to the 12th born?
> What are the equivalent Konzo names for West, North, or South?
> What is the Konzo name for [the] Rwenzori Mountains?
> What is the Konzo name for the River Semliki? (Peterson 2012: 964)

In Appendix 2 of their *Kinande/Konzo-English Dictionary with an English-Kinande Index* entitled "The Personal Names of the Nande", Mutaka and Kavutirwaki (2008: 400) observe thus:

> In the Nande [and Konzo] culture, the name a child is given upon his birth is ordinal in that it indicates the sex and the rank he occupies among the other children born from the same womb (. . .). Apart from the name a child gets at his birth, he may also have other names, for example a name he gives himself, a name given to him because of the circumstances in which he was born, a spiritual name in that it bears the name of a spirit, and a proverbial name.

The above observation shows that personal naming processes among the Bakonzo/Banande people are quite a sophisticated and complicated matter, since one can read a lot of sociological or even geographical information in a name, if one is familiar with the Lhukonzo/Kinande language. This chapter focuses on the names given to the babies who are born after the sibling they follow has passed away. Mutaka and Kavutirwaki (2008: 405) give several examples of these names. These are: *Mútsuba* or *Nzúbâ* or *Músubáhô* ('the person who replaces, the one who comes back'), *Kyábu* ('garbage or rubbish heap/pit'), *Kyabíro* ('the "thing" that lasts some days only'), *Syághúswâ* ('he should not be thrown away') and *Kabuthirwaki* ('why is this child born again, not long after another child has died?'). There are other names that they do not mention. These include: *Bahwere* ('they are finished'), *Kibaya, Kithi* or *Kikoma* ('leaf') and the plural of these words (e.g., *Bibaya* or *Makoma*), *Kisika* or *Kasika* ('one layer of a banana stem') or the plural form *Bisika, Mughuswa* ('the one thrown away') and *Muthaka* ('soil'), among others. The objective of this chapter is to explain the rationale behind these death avoidance or prevention names that the Bakonzo people give to their children by delving into their figurative properties, and to examine the different ways in which the figures of speech deployed in each name work to reveal the cultural logic behind the naming.

2 Methodology

The study employs qualitative methods of data collection to enable an in-depth understanding of the different ways in which the death prevention or avoidance naming system among the Bakonzo people communicates at a figurative level. The focus on local names locates the study in the Bakonzo people's lived experiences; for this reason, the researcher ensures that the methods he uses to analyse the names are "driven by local knowledge, customs, and traditions and not (. . .) imposed from other contexts" (Linabary, Krishna and Connaughton 2017: 448).

The researcher collected data through three major methods: a close reading of the names and their nuances within the context of the culture of the Bakonzo people; a document review of important texts, such as Mutaka and Kavutirwaki's *Kinande/Konzo English dictionary: With an English-Kinande Index*; and in-depth interviews with two key informants purposively selected on the basis of their deep knowledge and understanding of Konzo culture. The first key informant is a musician who composes and sings in the Lhukonzo language; the other one is a researcher and writer of books on diverse aspects of Konzo history and culture.

The analysis of data is thematic and contextual. The researcher delineates the key ideas and themes that the selected names carry, and the context(s) in which these names are given and used. The emphasis on context is informed by Lisman's suggestion that in literary studies, studying a work of art – the researcher considers names as works of art writ small – "should include an attempt to understand the social context, especially the basic ideological rationalisations in which the works are rooted" (1988: 74). The analysis also engages Achebe's conviction that "every literature must seek the things that belong unto its peace, must, in other words, speak of a particular place, evolve out of the necessities of its history, past and current, and the aspirations and destiny of its people" (1975: 9–10).

3 Theoretical framework

The chapter engages with the theory of onomastics, which Gerdabi defines as "a branch of sociolinguistics that investigates the significance of naming things, people, and places" among a particular people or group of people (2017: 126). The researcher explores the significance of naming among the Bakonzo people in the context in which the names focused on here are given – death. This is important, for, as Ndlovu argues, a name can carry nuances that speak to particular histories or experiences, such as suffering and dying, in the case of the Zimbabwean city, Bulawayo, which is "Ndebele for one who is killed" (2018: 73). In exploring the significance of the names that are focused on in this chapter, the researcher draws on three theoretical concepts that he finds informative and insightful for this study, viz., the hidden transcript, the trickster, and the figurative use of language.

In his acclaimed book *Hidden Transcripts: Domination and the Arts of Resistance*, Scott (1990) makes a compelling argument that the researcher draws on to explain the name *Kyabu* 'garbage heap or rubbish pit', which the Bakonzo people may give to a child who follows a sibling who has passed away, as a way of tricking death into thinking that the child is worthless, and therefore not worth killing. Scott argues that:

> Every subordinate group creates, out of its ordeal, a 'hidden transcript' that represents a critique of power spoken behind the back of the dominant. The powerful, for their part, also develop a hidden transcript representing the practices and claims of their rule that cannot be openly avowed. A comparison of the hidden transcript of the weak with that of the powerful and of *both* hidden transcripts to the public transcript of power relations offers a substantially new way of understanding resistance to domination. (1990: xii; author's emphasis)

Drawing on the English novelists George Eliot and George Orwell, Scott demonstrates that "the process of domination generates a hegemonic public conduct and a backstage discourse consisting of what cannot be spoken in the face of power" (1990: xii). In his view, this backstage discourse necessitates novel ways of interpreting "the rumors, gossip, folktales, songs, gestures, jokes, and theater of the powerless as vehicles by which, among other things, they insinuate a critique of power while hiding behind anonymity or behind innocuous understandings of their conduct" (1990: xiii). In this chapter, the researcher considers some of the Konzo death prevention or avoidance names an example of Scottian backstage discourse, and examines how this discourse plays out as a figurative weapon that the resourceful Bakonzo deploy to challenge death and "his" authority.

The other theoretical concept deployed in this chapter is that of the trickster, drawn from oral literary studies. In numerous African folktales, there is great emphasis on animal tricksters:

> small, wily, and tricky animals who cheat and outdo the larger and more powerful beasts. They trick them in a pretended tug of war, cheat them in a race, deceive them into killing themselves or their own relations, gobble up their opponents' food in pretended innocence, divert the punishment for their own misdeeds on to innocent parties, and perform a host of other ingenious tricks. (Finnegan 2012: 335)

The above examples of the trickster's cunning show that he is quite obnoxious, as some of his wiles and tricks go against acceptable community norms and values. This is why Scheub observes that "it is difficult to see [the] Trickster in a moral framework" (2012: 6). Because of this, using him as an interpretive frame for the study can come with many ethical and moral problems. However, there are two aspects of his identity and trade that are critical for this study. The first one is his inexhaustible resourcefulness, which is evident in his quickness of thought in wriggling out of the difficult situations he lands himself in, particularly those involving much larger and stronger adversaries. The second one is his unwavering determination to ensure that his physical vulnerability does not stop him from achieving whatever he has set his eye on. It is these two aspects, the researcher suggests, that make Pinto observe that African trickster tales highlight "images of resistance, subversion, wisdom's delicate balance of caution and cunning and eventual triumph against great odds" (2009: 99), thereby engendering "culturally-relevant means of hope", since "[t]he less powerful members of societies have always had an incentive to invent tactics that would enable them to cope with some comfort with the more powerful" (2009: 100).

Indeed, in this study, the notion of the trickster is used to understand how the Bakonzo people resourcefully respond to death in a bid to stop him from killing their children, by giving them names that are meant to trick him into thinking that a child is worthless and that therefore there is no point in killing it. In this way, death is comparable to the mighty animals (elephants, hippos, buffaloes, pythons, etc.) that the usually diminutive trickster (a rabbit, spider, hare, etc.) triumphs over, thanks to his cunning and ingenuity. Of course, there are times when the trickster fails in his manouevres and gets outwitted and punished. This is similar to what happens to human beings in their encounter with death. Even a child given a name like *Kyabu* ('garbage heap or rubbish pit') can still die. This is why there is the name *Syághúswâ* (literally translated into English as 'he should not be thrown away'), which according to Mutaka and Kavutirwaki (2008: 405) is "given to a female or a male child born after several other dead children". In this name, we see human beings as naming tricksters outsmarted by their adversary, death.

Finally, the study also deploys the notion of the figurative use of language, drawn from literary stylistics. Wales (2014: 400) states that the goal of stylistics is not simply to describe the formal features of texts for their own sake, but to show their functional significance for the interpretation of texts, or to relate literary effects to linguistic "causes" where these are felt to be relevant. This view has guided the current researcher in explaining the different figures of speech used in the names, and how effective they are in communicating the meaning and the logic of the names.

4 Literature review

The subject of names and naming practices in Africa are well researched. For this reason, this section focuses on studies of death prevention names. In "Akan Death-prevention Names: A Pragmatic and Structural analysis", Obeng (1998) discusses different death-prevention names and the rationale behind their choice. His approach to the subject is ethnolinguistic, since he analyses death-prevention names according to the kinds of message(s) they carry, as well as sociolinguistics, since his study "shows how language provides information about the name-givers' and name-bearers' social networks and how sociocultural needs are reflected in the naming system" (1998: 171). This insightful article has two gaps that this chapter attempts to fill. First and foremost, Obeng's analysis hints at literary devices like the use of satire and irony, but he does not engage with them to show how they are put to work in the naming exercise. This is because – as already pointed out – he approaches his subject from an ethnolinguistic and sociolinguistic perspective, not from a literary one. Secondly, one of the article's findings is that some names "reveal death's ability to spare one's life, to show compassion or to pardon" (1998: 183). This observation is at variance with what this chapter tries to do – focusing on how name givers trick or defy death as the only way of ensuring that the newly born child lives, rather than making direct prayers to it for mercy and compassion.

Doyle's "'The Child of Death': Personal Names and Parental Attitudes towards Mortality in Bunyoro, Western Uganda, 1900–2005" (2008) discusses a range of death prevention names in colonial and post-independent Bunyoro from a historical perspective. Using church baptismal registers, the author "analyses the names given to over 22,000 babies baptized between 1900 and 2005 in the Roman Catholic parish of Bujumbura-Hoima" (2008: 362), in order to trace "trends in naming patterns, and [to] argue that changes in naming reflect both variations in perceptions of mortality, and a wider, if uneven, shift in consciousness" (2008: 363) brought about by Christianisation, Western education and advances in biomedicine. The article gives a wide range of names relating to death, including death prevention ones, and explains the contexts in which they are given and the rationale behind their usage. Although the subject is competently handled, it is approached from a historical and ethnolinguistic perspective. Consequently, Doyle does not engage with the literary devices at play in the naming practices that he discusses, and how these engender a deeper appreciation of the death prevention names he focuses on. It is this aspect that this chapter delves into with regard to the names of another western Ugandan ethnic group, the Bakonzo.

In "The Structure of Ibibio Death Prevention Names", Mensah and Offong (2013) provide a thick analysis of the morphological and syntactic structures of the names, which reveals insights into the logic behind Ibibio naming practices. In "Frog, Where Are You?: The Ethnopragmatics of Ibibio Death Prevention Names", Mensah (2015) builds on the above article to discuss dozens of Ibibio death prevention names and the different contexts in which they are given. He identifies six roles that the names play: "To deceive the spiritual forces that the child is worthless since it has been given a despicable name by the biological parents"; "To hide the identity of the name bearer from the underworld forces"; "To question the uncertainty and temporality of life"; "To recognize the existence of superior powers or forces that hold the key to life and death"; "To provide psychological relief to the name giver for the tension generated by past frustrating experiences"; and "To demonstrate the invincibility of death" (Mensah 2015: 129). Both studies do a wonderful job of providing ethnolinguistic and sociolinguistic insights into the death prevention names, but they do not engage with the literary properties of the names, such as the use of figurative language inherent in them. This chapter contributes to the debate on death prevention names by providing a literary stylistic perspective on them.

In "Why Are They Named After Death? Name Giving, Name Changing and Death Prevention Names in Gújjolaay Eegimaa (Banjal)", Sagna and Bassène "provide an analysis of the morphological structures and the meanings of proper names and investigate name changing practices among Eegimaa speakers", furthermore showing that "in addition to revealing aspects of individuals' lives, proper names also speak to important aspects of speakers' social organisation" (2016: 40). The article gives a detailed account of two categories of death prevention names – those given to spirit children who choose when to be born and when to die in a cycle that can go on for a long time if not broken, and those given to children who do not die because they want to return to their spirit parents, but because of the workings of witchcraft practised by the enemies of the parents. Despite its insightfulness with regard to explaining the motivations behind the choice of specific death prevention names, the article does not engage with the literary aspects of the names for the simple reason that it is written from an ethnographical perspective.

In "Daring Death among the Tumbuka: A Socio-Semantic Analysis of Death-Related Personal Names", Musonda, Ngalande and Simwinga (2019) reflect on the meanings of some death-related names among the Timbuka of Zambia, for instance *Chifwenge* ('let it die'), *Chakufwa* ('it is dead'), *Malalo* ('graveyard'), *Chiponde* ('funeral') and *Chakumanda* ('it belongs to the grave'), among others. These names, the authors observe, are an act of defiance in the face of death and a way of trivialising its power (2019: 118). But the article does not explain how the names perform this work of defiance and trivialisation of death. In fact, the discussion part of the paper is very short, constituting as it does just two and a half of the 13 pages; for this reason, it only provides an outline of the names and what they mean. Besides, the literary elements of the names are not included in the scope of the paper.

Finally, in "An Ethnopragmatic Analysis of Death-Prevention Names in the Karanga Society of Zimbabwe", Mamvura (2021) gives a detailed discussion of a wide range of death prevention names and the work they are believed to do in ensuring that newly born babies do not follow their siblings. Examples of these names are *Mahonye* ('maggots'), *Manyowa* ('manure'), *Guva* ('grave'), *Marinda* ('graves'), *Rufu* ('death') and *Marufu* ('deaths'), to mention but a few. A very rich article that benefits from previous scholarship on death prevention names, Manvura's work remains solely anchored in the ethnographical domain, and does not venture into the literary sphere to examine how the names he discusses work as forms of literary communication. It is this angle that this study brings to the discussion of the Konzo names focused on here, many of which are quite similar to what the scholars reviewed above have selected for their analyses, despite the fact that they come from different parts of Africa.

5 This baby's name is *Kibaya/Kithi* ('Leaf'): Naming as an Act of Trickery

In Uganda, infant and child mortality is a common problem that parents face. The Uganda Demographic and Health Survey of 2016 gives the information below about the prevalence of this problem:

> For the 5-year period before the survey, infant mortality was 43 deaths per 1,000 live births and under-5 mortality was 64 deaths per 1,000 live births. At these levels, 1 in 23 Ugandan children dies before reaching his or her first birthday, and 1 in 16 do not survive to his or her fifth birthday. Forty-two percent of under-5 mortality occurs during the neonatal period. Infant mortality declined from 88 deaths per 1,000 live births in 2000–01 to 43 deaths per 1,000 live births in 2016. Under-5 mortality declined from 151 deaths per 1,000 live births to 64 deaths per 1,000 live births over the same period. (2016: 133)

This revelation – that 1 in 23 Ugandan children dies before reaching his or her first birthday, and 1 in 16 does not survive to his or her fifth birthday – shows how serious the problem of both infant and child mortality is.

One of the ways through which the Bakonzo people deal with the loss of children is to ensure that the next time they give birth, they choose a name that will trick death into believing that the newborn is valueless/worthless, and therefore not worth being killed. There are at least four kinds of such names. The first one depicts the child as valueless or worthless; thus, the name *Bighasaki* ('of what value is this?') may be given to it. The second depicts the child as soil (*Muthaka*) – an obvious allusion to the grave in which lies the departed one that the infant follows. The third kind of name depicts the newly born infant as a leaf (*Kibaya, Kikoma, Kithi*) or leaves (*Bibaya, Bikoma, Bithi*); and the final one depicts the infant as a garbage heap or rubbish pit (*Kyabu, Kibiriryo*, or in the plural form *Byabu, Bibiriryo*). In this section of the chapter, the researcher discusses the practice of giving newly born babies the names *Kibaya, Kikoma, Kithi* ('leaf') or *Bibaya, Bikoma, Bithi* ('leaves').

There are at least four ways of explaining the pervasiveness of leaf-based death prevention names among the Bakonzo. The first one is that it is a way of fooling death that there is no child to snatch – all there is is a leaf. So, when he (death) comes for a child with a familiar name (*Baluku, Bwambale, Masika, Kabiira, Muhindo*, and so forth), "he" will find none, which could drive "him" away. Secondly, leaves are so abundant that they are never in scarcity, even during the dry season. For this reason, they are not a commodity that anybody would hunger for, since everybody has leaves in their garden or neighbourhood. Giving a child the name 'leaf' is therefore meant to remind death that the child is ordinary and not special at all, so there is no reason why he, death, should get interested in snatching it away. Thirdly, leaves are ephemeral and short-lived, since sooner or later they turn yellow and fall to the ground. In other words, they live in a state of near-death, so to speak, so there is no reason why death – mighty as he is – should attack them, since they are not worth the effort. In any case, there cannot be any sense of heroism in attacking a thing in such a state of weakness, so if death attacks a child named 'leaf', it is quite cowardly of him, if not out rightly wanton. Finally, the name could be a boast directed to death that however much he tries, he cannot succeed in exterminating human beings since they are as numerous as the leaves in the world. True, human life is quite ephemeral and short-lived, like that of leaves, but the sheer number of human beings, like that of leaves, makes it more or less impossible for death to triumph in his evil plan to finish off the people. In a way, therefore, death deserves to be ridiculed since he is a failure in this respect, for there will always be numerous human beings – far more than he kills – thanks to the work of regeneration that human reproduction makes possible.

The major figure of speech at stake here is personification, "in which either an inanimate object or an abstract concept is spoken of as though it were endowed with life or with human attributes or feelings" (Abrams and Harpham 2012: 132). In the leaf-based names above, the abstract concept of death is imagined as having human attributes (for instance, reasoning) and human weaknesses (for instance, vulnerability to being fooled). This insight is similar to Doyle's observation that the Banyoro "conceived of death not only as a state of being or something impersonal which happened to people, but also as an active agent, a character with a personality [that] could be fooled by the wily, who had learnt its ways" (2008: 371). This explains why the child who follows the one who passed away is given the name 'leaf' in order to confuse death into thinking that it is not worth snatching it away, even when the reality is the very opposite. That is to say, the child is so loved and wanted by the parents, the family and the community that it is their ultimate desire that it should live. This means that the name contains an in-built verbal irony in it, that is, "a statement in which the meaning that a speaker implies differs sharply from the meaning that is ostensibly expressed" (Abrams and Harpham 2012: 184). The irony shows the resourcefulness of the people in the face of disaster: bothered by the problem of child mortality, the philosophers in the Konzo community come up with a language-based solution to the problem. The irony also serves as a form of poetic justice. If poetic justice is "the distribution, at the end of a literary work, of earthly rewards and punishments in proportion to the virtue or vice of the various characters" (Abrams and Harpham 2012: 299–300), then the fooling that death suffers at the hands of the people who give the name 'leaf' to their children as a way of keeping him (death) away from them is an appropriate form of punishment, since he leaves them in tears every time he strikes. The problem is that it is a "punishment" only at an imaginative level, for in the real world of day-to-day living, death could and does strike whenever it wills, irrespective of the name given to the child. This reminds the reader of the limitations and complexities that come with the use of irony, since it is capable of being ambiguous, thereby leading "to misunderstanding, confusion, or simply lack of clarity in communication", as Hutcheon (1992: 222) observes. This lack of clarity in communication is especially true if we consider the fact that interpreting what the name 'leaf' means can be approached from a different perspective that emphasises the useful, rather than the ephemeral or short-lived, as some leaves serve as food that sustains the community, while others serve as medicine that heals myriad diseases.

If we ask ourselves who the primary audience of the name 'leaf' is – its addressee, so to speak – it becomes apparent that it is death. It is he who is imagined as listening to the name, and getting confused about its meaning; it is he who is to decide to leave the child named 'leaf' alone because a person with such a name is not worth killing. It therefore follows that the name 'leaf' employs a figure of speech called apostrophe, which Kennedy and Gioia define as "a way of addressing someone or something invisible or not ordinarily spoken to" – say an inanimate object, an abstract thing or a spirit – as "a means of giving life to the inanimate (. . .); a way of giving body to the intangible, a way of speaking to it person to person"

(1995: 687). In other words, the apostrophe is very close to personification, as both give human attributes to non-human entities. The use of apostrophe in the name 'leaf' makes death a familiar foe – one with a face, so to speak. It is this that makes it possible for human beings to fight him with the resources of language at their disposal, in a manner that reminds the reader of Donne's famous holy sonnet "Death, Be Not Proud", in which the poet "both personifies and apostrophizes death in the first step of a strategy that will lead to the humbling and finally the death of death" (Miller and Greenberg 1981: 75), when all the dead wake up on Resurrection Day. Similarly, the Bakonzo people personify and apostrophise death in order to establish a firm ground on which to fight him. Had he remained shadowy and mysterious, it would have been hard, if not impossible, for them to use the resources of their language to challenge his lethal authority. In the next section, the discussion turns to those names that imagine the newly born baby as a garbage heap or rubbish pit, for the same purpose as discussed above – tricking death into believing the child is too worthless to kill.

6 This baby's name is garbage heap or rubbish pit: On metaphor, paradox, oxymoron and hyperbole as powerful weapons of the weak

Of all the figures of speech available to a creative writer or thinker, metaphor is the most pervasive. Indeed, Badick calls it "the most important and widespread figure of speech" (2001: 153). According to Childs and Fowler (2006: 139),

> a metaphor ascribes to some thing or action X a property Y which it could not literally possess in that context. Responding to this anomaly, the hearer or reader infers that what is meant is that X is Z, where Z is some property suggested by Y, X or the interaction of the two, that can be literally true of X in some context.

Wolosky draws our attention to Aristotle's insight into the etymology of the term metaphor – transfer – that is, "the transferal of some quality, or attribute, or word associated with one thing to another", which is what implies the comparison (2008: 30).

The name 'garbage heap' or 'rubbish pit' is metaphorical: in it we have the qualities of the garbage heap or rubbish pit (disorder, filth, rot, stench, germs, chaos, danger, etc.) being transferred to the bearer of the name (the newly born child). This transference is certainly shocking in the context of the naming ceremony of a newborn baby because of the irony it carries. Every family and family member holds their newborn in very positive terms that evoke love, care and esteem; because of this, we expect that the parents will give the baby a name that affirms its value and place in the family, that is, a name that shows that the child is loved, cherished, adored, wanted. It is quite disheartening, if not outrightly astonishing, therefore, to hear such a child given the very opposite of the name we expect: a name that points to something as shunned as a garbage heap or rubbish pit, which is "removed as far as possible from our presence because it has become revolting or worthless" (Anderson 2010: 35). The place, that is, where undesired and undesirable waste like leftover food, clothes, plastics, furniture, broken class, broken clay utensils, diapers, menstrual cloths or pads, dead rats, to mention but a few, are disposed of.

In this section of the chapter, the researcher explains how this metaphor works in the context of death prevention or avoidance names among the Bakonzo people. He also discusses other figures of speech that reinforce this metaphor – paradox, oxymoron and hyperbole. His aim is to underline the irony at play in the name, and the uses that this irony is put to. It is hoped that, just as in the previous section, the discussion here will shed some light on the ingenuity of the Bakonzo people in their struggle against death – that mighty force with which they have a constant tussle.

In the burial architecture of the Bakonzo people, the dead are laid to rest in the banana grove, which is usually the same site as is used for the garbage heap or rubbish pit. This makes the rubbish heap "a metaphor for the grave, a point of contact with the world of the dead," as MacGaffey (cited in Stam 1997: 285) puts it. In a way, therefore, the name of the newborn baby places it in architectural proximity with the departed sibling. One of the respondents argued that this placement is meant to "confuse" death into thinking that the newborn and the departed child are one and the same, thereby giving the former a chance to live.

Besides, the fact that the departed child lies next to the rubbish pit makes this site not one of gloom and desolation, but "a place of buried memories and traces" (Stam 1997: 283) of the baby they once held in their hands, a baby who once brought happiness into their hearts and smiles onto their faces. This makes the garbage heap or rubbish pit an ambiguous sign since it is at the same time "the quintessence of the negative – expressed in such phrases as 'talking trash', 'rubbish!' and 'cesspool of contamination'" and "an archaeological treasure trove precisely because of its concentrated, synecdochic, compressed character" (Stam 1997: 283). This ambiguity is reinforced by the fact that the garbage heap or rubbish pit is "the ultimate resting place of all that society both produces and represses, secretes and makes secret" (Stam 1997: 283), that it is to say, it is the most intimate but at the same time the most revolting.

Perhaps there is no better example of this ambiguity than human beings' attitudes to their own excrement, which is – ironically – what repels them the most (Anderson 2010: 46). But there is a reverse ambiguity at play in the naming: the baby called 'garbage heap' or 'rubbish pit' has not been given this revolting name because the parents are distancing themselves from it by marking it for the trash dump; rather, the name has been given so that the child may not end up in the rubbish pit, which is next to where the departed sibling is buried, as already observed above. The figure of speech used here is irony – the "expression of an opposite sentiment or idea" (Colebrook 2004: 9) – since the contextual meaning of the name is the very opposite of the literal meaning. But there is also hyperbole – a figure of speech in which an artist uses exaggeration of overstatement for emphasis (Kennedy and Gioia 1995: 687; Miller and Greenberg 1981: 218) or for humour (Mock 1998: 47). The overstatement lies in the parents' decision to devalue their baby to the level of comparing it to such a lowly place, the rubbish pit or garbage heap; while the humour (of the grim type) lies in the fact that at face value the name sounds like a joke, but when you understand its context (the passing on of the sibling and the belief that this kind of name could give the newborn a chance to live), you appreciate the dynamics of the cultural work at play.

Given the fact that the name inevitably gestures to the passing away of its owner's sibling, it is an allusion, as well – a figure of speech that Miller and Greenberg define as the "reference to specific events, characters, or scenes of a religious, historical, scientific, or literary nature" (1981: 56). The figurativeness of this device lies in the fact that by speaking out the child's name, one inevitably includes the departed sibling in the frame of reference, since that is where the "story" of the onomastic marker started. The effectiveness of this device is to capture the interdependence between the two children in the sense that the shadow of the one who is no more follows the one who was born afterwards everywhere it goes. So does death, the tireless stalker, who needs to be fooled with a name that at the literal level refers to the child lying next to the rubbish heap.

Besides, the name contains a paradox – "a statement or situation that seems absurd or contradictory on the face of it and yet may well be true in essence" (Miller and Greenberg 1981: 217). Usually, rubbish or garbage is considered worthless, but in the name given to the child, it becomes so valuable that its survival hinges on it. The parents of the child are so desperate that they will do everything possible to make sure their child survives, even if it means giving it a name that denotes apparent worthlessness. The idea is to challenge death to be self-respectful. Coming for a child called 'garbage heap' or 'rubbish pit' would turn him (death) into a carrion creature, so to speak; he is thus challenged to leave the child alone as a way of maintaining his self-respect and dignity.

In a way, the name is also oxymoronic in the sense that it contains the idea of "our valuable worthless child", that is to say, at play in the meaning of the name 'garbage heap' or 'rubbish pit' is the use of oxymoron par excellence – "the joining of words with apparently opposing meanings to make a new union" (Miller and Greenberg 1981: 76). This figure of speech underlines the ambiguity of what the parents are doing (it contains both a negative and a positive), as well as the entanglement they are in: to save their child, they have to subject it to a humiliating name. It also underlines their resourcefulness, as already mentioned, and their bravery, in the sense that they take the courage to go for the most revolting name available to them. Finally, it highlights the love they have for their child, as shown by the great lengths they go to in order to save it from death. The chosen name is therefore their hidden transcript to defy death and to declare life for their child. Never again, they seem to tell death, will you snatch our child away as we look on; this time, we shall fight you using the weapon of our naming practice. In this defiance, we see the will of the minute trickster who fights much larger animals, usually with success. The defiance also brings to mind Foucault's view that "[w]here there is power, there is resistance" (1978: 95), for rather than receiving death's might with a sense of defeat, the name givers decide to fight this dreadful, malevolent force with the linguistic resources they have, as a way of liberating themselves from its tyranny.

7 Conclusion

This chapter has demonstrated that, among the Bakonzo people, death prevention or avoidance names are a puzzle that needs to be unraveled; a maze through which one walks to find the way out to elucidation. In solving the puzzle and navigating the maze, context is key, for the meanings of the names are found in situations that the listener must be familiar with if they are to appreciate the creativity at play. Naming is a clue to the Bakonzo people's understanding of death as a mighty force that they can dare challenge with the linguistic resources at their disposal, which they put to onomastic use in an ingenious way meant to remove the sting from death's teeth. This ingenuity turns leaves into pearls, garbage into gold and trash into treasures, in a fascinating manner that this chapter has hopefully succeeded in capturing and explaining.

Suffice it to note that this naming practice is under pressure because of the power that foreign religions (especially Christianity and Islam) hold in African countries, as well as the pervasiveness of Western education on the continent. Among the Yoruba people of Nigeria, for instance, Akinnaso observes that foreign religions are minimising "the relevance of home context, an important principle of Yoruba naming", while Western education downplays "the esoteric and sometimes derogatory connotations of ritually motivated names" (1983: 156). Among the Bakonzo, there is a similar development. It is rare these days to find young people bearing the names discussed in this chapter; instead, they bear those that reference their new religions, but using the Lhukonzo language. Examples of these names include *Lhukogho* ('God's grace'), *Nimubuya* ('God is good'), *Athwanzire* ('God loves us') and *Thumusikireko* ('let us be steadfast in our faith in God'). This is meant to indicate that in whatever situation they are in, including the death of a child, the parents believe in the saving power of the Christian or Islamic God. Besides, despite the statistics on child mortality given above, the mortality rate of children under five years has actually fallen, thanks to modern improvements in healthcare and nutrition (Doyle 2008: 381). This means that death prevention or avoidance names meant to protect newborn children are now rare.

Finally, the researcher wishes to mention that writing this chapter has been a very rewarding experience for him. Dancygier and Sweetser are right when they observe that in analysing how figurative language works in poetry (their focus is on metaphor), "[t]he successful reader of a good minimalist piece feels the heady pleasure of independent meaning construction" (2014: 200). As he closely read and analysed the selected names for their poetic and philosophical meaning in the context of a death prevention practice and ethic, the researcher felt that his efforts mattered because the creativity inherent in the naming system of the Bakonzo people had not been subjected to a similar scholarly investigation before. He is also happy that whoever reads this chapter in future will gain a deep insight into the way these people "solve [the] problems they face in their environment, including those relating to life and death" (Sagna and Bassène 2016: 47). At the same time, however, he experienced moments of dejection, given the fact that the names under discussion are getting lost, as observed above.

This study has some limitations. It is possible that the researcher has read either too much or too little into the names discussed here, by attributing either too much or too little value to the figures of speech at play in each name. Besides, he has worked with only a few names, about six or so, with the focus being on just two categories – those that reference leaves (*Kithi, Bithi, Kikoma, Makoma*) and those that reference garbage heaps or rubbish pits (*Kyabu, Byabu*). Had he looked at a bigger sample, it is possible that he would have revealed more aspects of the creativity surrounding the naming practice that was the subject of this chapter. Finally, he approached the subject from a sociological-stylistic-literary perspective. A different approach – say feminist or historicist – might have given interesting insights quite different from the ones gleaned here. Despite these limitations, however, the researcher is quite certain that his discussion has shed light on a fascinating cultural practice that tells us so much about a people's wrestling with mortality and its chief agent, death, through the linguistic and stylistic resources available to them. It is his hope that this chapter will be of use to scholars who are interested in the literariness and philosophical richness of African names.

References

Abrams, M. H. & Geoffrey Galt Harpham. 2012. *A glossary of literary terms*. Wadwsorth: Cengage Learning.

Achebe, Chinua. 1975. *Morning yet on creation day*. London: Heinemann.

Akinnaso, F. Niyi. 1983. Yoruba traditional names and the transmission of cultural knowledge. *Names* 31 (3). 139–158.

Anderson, Christopher Todd. 2010. Sacred waste: Ecology, spirit, and the American Garbage Poem. *Interdisciplinary Studies in Literature and Environment* 17 (1). 35–60.

Badick, Chris. 2001. *The Concise Oxford Dictionary of Literary Terms*. Oxford: Oxford University Press.

Balyage, Yona. 2000. Ethnicity and ethnic conflict in the Great Lakes Region. Presentation at the *Conference on Conflict and Peace-Making in the Great Lakes Region at Windsor Lake Victoria Hotel, Entebbe, Uganda, 10–12 July 2000.*

https://opendocs.ids.ac.uk/opendocs/bitstream/handle/20.500.12413/4968/Balyage-MAK-Res.pdf?sequence=1 (accessed 3 October 2022).

Childs, Peter & Roger Fowler. 2006. *The Routledge dictionary of literary terms*. London: Routledge.

Colebrook, Clair. 2004. *Irony*. London: Routledge.

Dancygier, Barbara & Eve Sweetser. 2014. *Figurative language*. Cambridge: Cambridge University Press.

Doyle, Shane. 2008. 'The child of death': Personal names and parental attitudes towards mortality in Bunyoro, Western Uganda, 1900–2005. *The Journal of African History* 49 (3). 361–382.

Facci, Serena. 2009. Dances across the boundary: Banande and Bakonzo in the twentieth century. *Journal of Eastern African Studies* 3 (2). 350–366.

Finnegan, Ruth. 2012. *Oral literature in Africa*. Cambridge: Open Book Publishers.

Foucault, Michel. 1978. *The history of sexuality. Volume I: An introduction*. Trans Robert Hurley. New York: Pantheon Books.

Gerdabi, Hiam. 2017. Characters' names in the shade of literary tendencies: An onomastic approach to characters' names in *The Mayor of Casterbridge, A Portrait of an Artist as a Young Man*, and *The City of Glass*. *Interdisciplinary Literary Studies* 19 (1). 125–141.

Hutcheon, Linda. 1992. The Complex functions of irony. *Revista Canadiense de Estudios Hispánicos* 16 (2). 219–234.

Kennedy, X. J. & Dana Gioia. 1995. *Literature: An introduction to fiction, poetry, and drama*. New York: Harper Collins College Division.

Linabary, Jasmine R., Arunima Krishna & Stacey L. Connaughton. 2017. The conflict family: Storytelling as an activity and a method for locally led community-based peace building. *Conflict Resolution Quarterly* 34 (4). 431–453.

Lisman, C. David. 1988. Marxist literary theory: A critique. *The Journal of Aesthetic Education* 22 (2). 73–85.

Mamvura, Zvinashe. 2021. An ethnopragmatic analysis of death-prevention names in the Karanga society of Zimbabwe. *African Studies* 80 (1). 111–124.

Matte, Daniel M. 2021. The impact of Adventism on Bakonzo culture. *Encyclopedia of Seventh-Day Adventists*. https://encyclopedia.adventist.org/article?id=EE20 (accessed 8 August 2022).

Mensah, Eyo Offiong. 2015. Frog, where are you?: The ethnopragmatics of Ibibio death prevention names. *Journal of African Cultural Studies* 27 (2). 115–132.

Mensah, Eyo & Imeobong Offong. 2013. The structure of Ibibio death prevention names. *Anthropological Notebooks* 19 (3). 41–59.

Miller, Ruth & Robert A. Greenberg. 1981. *Poetry: An introduction*. London: Bloomsbury Publishing.

Mock, Jeff. 1998. *You can write poetry*. Cincinnati: Writer's Digest Books.

Musonda, Chola, Sunday Ngalande & John Simwinga. 2019. Daring death among the Tumbuka: A socio-semantic analysis of death-related personal names. *International Journal of Humanities Social Sciences and Education* 6 (7). 109–120.

Mutaka, Ngessimo M. & Kambale Kavutirwaki. 2008. The personal names of the Nande. *Kinande/Konzo English dictionary: With an English-Kinande index*. Trenton: Africa World Press.

Ndlovu, Sambulo. 2018. A nomen omen: Nuances of the toponym Bulawayo in history. *Nomina Africana: Journal of African Onomastics* 32 (2). 73–81.

Obeng, Samuel Gyasi. 1998. Akan death-prevention names: A pragmatic and structural analysis. *Names* 46 (3). 163–187.

Peterson, Derek R. 2012. The work of time in Western Uganda. *Citizenship Studies* 16 (8). 961–977.

Pinto, Cristina Ferreira. 2009. The animal trickster – An essential character in african tales. In Kristiina Kumpulainen & Auli Toom (eds.), *The proceedings of the 19th annual conference of the European Teacher Education Network*, 99–109. Helsinki: University of Helsinki. http://www.eten-online.org/uploads/FINAL_ETEN_22_Proceedings_2012-1350833013.pdf (accessed 1 March 2023).

Sagna, Serge & Emmanuel Bassène. 2016. Why are they named after death? Name giving, name changing and death prevention names in Gújjolaay Eegimaa (Banjal). *Language Documentation and Conservation* 10. 40–70.

Scheub, Harold. 2012. *Trickster and hero: Two characters in the oral and written traditions of the world*. Wisconsin: University of Wisconsin Press.

Scott, James C. 1990. *Hidden transcripts: Domination and the arts of resistance*. Yale: Yale University Press.

Stam, Robert. 1997. From hybridity to the aesthetics of garbage. *Social Identities* 3(2). 275–290.

Uganda Bureau of Statistics (UBoS) & ICF. 2018. *Uganda Demographic and Health Survey 2016*. https://dhsprogram.com/pubs/pdf/FR333/FR333.pdf

Wales, Katie. 2014. *A dictionary of stylistics*. London: Routledge.

Wolosky, Shira. 2008. *The art of poetry: How to read a poem*. Oxford: Oxford University Press.

Duoduo Xu

Chapter 11
Tibetan elements in spirit names in Dongbaism and Dabaism

Abstract: Southwest China is a region where contacts between many cultures occur. One of the local ethnic communities are the Moso people. The Moso language belongs to a Tibeto-Burmese branch of the Sino-Tibetan language family living on the border between Yunnan and Sichuan Provinces. Moso people still practise their indigenous religions, Dongbaism in their western branch (Naxi) and Dabaism in their eastern branch (Na). Dongbaists and Dabaists believe in animism and share the same origin. The two ethnic branches have differentiated from each other over time. The divergence is attested by many cultural elements, including their systems of spirits (gods and ghosts) and the composition of their oral chants. Dongba and Daba spirit names show massive influences from Tibetan Buddhism, but with different historical layers and styles that may be remnants of the Bon religion, the indigenous belief that prevailed in the Himalayan plateau before Tibetan Buddhism. Through the analysis of morphological structures, the paper explains the assimilation of Tibetan linguistic elements in Dongba and Daba naming practices and reconstructs the transition from Dabaism to Dongbaism. This study highlights the influence of the Bon religion on Moso people's cults from an anthropological-linguistic perspective. This multi-disciplinary work unveils, for the first time, the origin of the figures of mythical gods – and of their names – believed by local people to be the first Dongba/Daba priests of the Bon religion and it suggests the possibility of a widespread set of beliefs in more remote times. The etymological interpretation of local spirits' names reconstructs the roots of local folklore beliefs, while displaying multiple cultural strata attested through these spirits' names, as well as analysing the role of priests in introducing new cultural elements to the local communities.

Keywords: Dongbaism, Dabaism, names of spirits, Bon religion, Tibetan Buddhism

1 Introduction

Dongbaism and Dabaism are the indigenous religions of the Moso people, who live on the border between Yunnan and Sichuan Provinces in China. Moso people

Duoduo Xu, Nanyang Technological University, e-mail: duoduo.xu@ntu.edu.sg

https://doi.org/10.1515/9783110759297-011

believe in animism. The Moso are also known in contemporary linguistic studies by their endonym *Naish*, which contains the syllable *na* that is homophonic with the word for 'black' (/nɑ˦/). Black is one of the sacred colours of the Moso people. Therefore, the syllable *na* in the endonyms is also interpreted as 'big, noble'. Moso, on the other hand, is the traditional designation found in ancient Chinese literary records.

There are two major varieties of Moso (/Naish) languages: Naxi (ISO 639–3: nxq) and Na (ISO 639–3: nru), with 348,000 and 57,000 native speakers, respectively (He and Jiang 1985: 104–107).[1] There are several other minor branches, such as Malimasa, Laze and Ruke.[2] The Dongba culture of Ruke shows features distinct from Naxi Dongbaism. The alternative endonym of Ruke is *Naru* (/nɑ˩ʐu˧/, 'Na-warm'), which means 'Na people living in the warm region'.

The western branch was named with the new designation, Naxi, during the nationwide census on nationalities in 1954 (He 1989: 3). The eastern branch, whose speakers live in Sichuan Province, was recognized as Mongolian, possibly due to the similarity of "Moso" to Mongolian in Mandarin (*ménggǔ zú* 'Mongolian nationality').[3] The eastern branch, whose speakers live in Yunnan Province, as well as in Ruke, has maintained the old designation Moso.[4]

The terms "Dongbaism" and "Dabaism" derive from the word 'priest' in Moso (or Naish languages), which is romanised as *Dongba* in Naxi and *Daba* in Na, according to their transliterations in Mandarin.[5] The words *Dongba* and *Daba*, fur-

1 The statistics on the population and demographics of Naxi and Na are quoted from the annually updated census of the JOSHUA Project. URL: https://joshuaproject.net/languages/nxq; https://joshuaproject.net/people_groups/18610/CH.)

2 Some work provides IPA transcriptions of these endonyms. For example, pronunciations of *Malimasa* include: /mɑ˧li˥mɑ˧sɑ˧/ (He and Jiang 1985: 127) and /ma^{33}sa^{33}/ (Guo and He 1994: 8). *Laze* is read as /la^{33}ze^{33}/ in local languages (Jacques and Michaud 2011). *Ruke* was transliterated as "Zhĕr-khin" in Rock (1937). Various pronunciations of the name of this branch include: /ʐur˧k'ɑ˧/ (Li et al. 1972: 125), /ʑɣ̩ər^{33}k'o^{33}/ (Guo and He 1994: 7–8), and /ʐɯ˧kʰʌr˧/ (from the author's fieldwork notes collected from Yomi Village, Labo Township, Ninglang County, Yunnan Province).

3 The meaning of the syllable *mo* remains unclear. One of the interpretations is 'yak' (Fang 1944). According to my fieldwork notes, *Moso* is read as /mɯ˧so˧/ in the Ruke Naxi language and originally meant 'the son of the heaven'. In this case, the first syllable means 'heaven' and the second means 'people, ethnic group'.

4 Details on the ethnic nationality of Moso can be found in many linguistic and cultural studies, including, but not limited to, McKhann (1995) and LaPolla (2001).

5 The IPA transcription of *Dongba* is /to˧mbɑ˩/ (Li et al. 1972: 143), and of *Daba*, /dɑ˩pɑ˧/ (from the author's fieldwork notes). There are variants for *Daba*, e.g., *Dopo* (/do˧po˧/, Laze branch of Moso; Guo 1983: 107) and *Dafu* (/dɑ˩fu˧/, Daba oral chants, from the author's fieldwork notes). In 2011, the author cooperated with the Dongba Research Institute (Li Dejing and A Hongsheng) to document Daba oral chants. The Daba priest helping, Cee'er, was from Lijiazui Village (/li˩tɕɑ˧tsɯ˩/; abbreviated to LJZ), Wujiao Township, Muli County, Sichuan Province. It is a widespread convention,

Map 11.1: Map of Moso hamlets.[6]

thermore, originate from the Tibetan word “སྟོན་པ” (*ston pa*), which means ‘Buddha, mentor’ (Chos kyi grags pa 1957: 356).

The Moso people live on a cultural border between the Han and Tibetan traditions. The two ethnic branches of Moso have differentiated from each other over time, for geographical and historical reasons (see Ṅag dbaṅ mkhyen rab 1735/1993). Lijiang and Yongning Townships are the two main inhabited centres for the western and the eastern branches of Moso, related to two plains among the mountains. Yanyuan County is located in this historical Sino-Tibetan border area.[7] Some of the villages are named as military bases, e.g., *Qiansuo* ‘front-camp’ and *Housuo* ‘back-camp’. As mentioned in Xu (2017), Qiansuo is a Chinese name, due to its military affiliation in Ming Dynasty, which literally means ‘camp in the front’

currently, to apply the Mandarin transliteration to the term “priest”. Following the orthography designed for Naxi, the terms should be *Ddomba* and *Ddabba* (/ *Ddopo* / *Ddafu*), with tonal markings omitted for the sake of simplicity. However, many other less commonly used terms are transcribed according to *Naxi pinyin* in this article.

6 The place names in red boxes belong to Naxi, the ones in green boxes belong to Na, and the one in the yellow box marks the surrounding region. The map is taken from “Zhongguo Ditu Wang” (“Website of Maps of China”). URL: www.chinamaps.info/images/Province/chinamap%20Yunnan.jpg. LINK NOT WORKING

7 Some more historical events from this border area can be found, among others, in Gros (2019).

(Zhang 1733/1999, vol. 19: 58–59); *Waru* /wɑ˧ʐu˧/ (village-warm) is the traditional Moso name.[8] Muli County, adjacent to Yanyuan County, was governed by Tibet.

The governorship of Tibet ruled through both political and religious powers. This dual system promoted the spread of various sects of Tibetan Buddhism in the border areas, even after the feudal dynasties had ended. Gelug is currently the prevalent school of Tibetan Buddhism in Yongning area. There are traces of Karma Kagyu in the area, as well. Lugu Lake Township (also known as *Zuosuo* 'left-camp'), where the main temple of Bonpo is located, was described as a predominantly Bonpo district (Rock 1952: 3). Karma Kagyu, on the other hand, remains the largest school of Tibetan Buddhism in the Lijiang area.

2 Language and cultural heritage

As revealed by some outstanding works in Linguistics, focusing on anthropological aspects, languages are shaped by the origins, distribution, and characteristics of ethnic groups (Hymes 1993; Harrell 2001; Blount 2009). The linguistic exploration of the Dongba and Daba spirit names not only clarifies religious facts, but also provides insights into the role of languages in cultural practices and societal structures (cf. Foley 1997). Among indigenous communities, orally transmitted texts construct cultural identity (Hansson 1997). Dongba and Daba oral chants, besides preserving cultural elements and the wisdom of their peoples, show important flexibility in their contents. The changes occurring over time in oral chants, in fact, are connected with analogous changes in the social contexts, involving, for example, the religious and political environments. Therefore, the oral chants can be read as the unwritten history of their peoples, along with the memory of events and the interpretation of the world by Dongba and Daba priests, the spiritual leaders of the Moso communities.

The divergence between Dongba and Daba, as two religious movements, can be documented through many cultural elements, including their systems of spirits (gods and ghosts) and the composition of their scriptures. For example, when mentioning the events following the timeline of the seasons, the order in Dongba scriptures is winter-spring-summer-autumn, according to the Han Chinese pattern, whereas in Daba and Ruke Dongba, the order is winter-summer-autumn-spring,

8 Qiansuo Village (QS, for brevity) was the administrative centre of Qiansuo Township, Yanyuan County, Sichuan Province. Qiansuo Township ceased to be the administrative centre and was replaced by Lugu Lake Township Lugu Lake Township, Yanyuan County, Sichuan Province, in 2020.

where autumn and spring seem to have been added to the two major seasons in the highlands, i.e., ‘rainy] season’ (/mu˧ʐe˧˥/ ‘weather-warm’) and ‘dry season’ (/mu˧tsʰɯ˧/ ‘weather-cold’).[9]

(1a.) From the Dongba scripture *Genesis*
(/ts‘o˩-mbur˧-t‘u˧/, ‘human-migrate-arrive’; Li et al. 1978: 30–31)[11]

ts‘ɯ˧-mo˧-ts‘ɯ˧-sɯ˥-hɛ˧, ts‘ɯ˧-mbɛ˧-p‘ur˩-nɯ˧-bu˩, bu˩-lɛ˧-t‘u˧-mʌ˧-ȵi˩.
winter-season-winter-three-month winter-snow-white-EMPH-hatch hatch-TELIC-arrive-NEG-succeed
‘In the three months of winter, the white snow in winter hatches (the egg), the hatch did not succeed.’

ȵo˩-mo˧-ȵo˩-sɯ˥-hɛ˧, ȵo˩-hæ˧-p‘ur˩-nɯ˧-bu˩, bu˩-lɛ˧-t‘u˧-mʌ˧-ȵi˩.
spring-season-spring-three-month spring-wind-white-EMPH-hatch hatch-TELIC-arrive-NEG- succeed
‘In the three months of spring, the white wind in spring hatches (the egg), the hatch did not succeed.’

ʐo˩-mo˧-ʐo˩-sɯ˥-hɛ˧, ʐo˩-hɯ˩-nɑ˥-nɯ˧-bu˩, bu˩- lɛ˧-t‘u˧-mʌ˧-ȵi˩.
summer-season-summer-three-month summer-rain-strong- EMPH-hatch hatch-TELIC-arrive-NEG-succeed
‘In the three months of summer, the heavy rain in summer hatches (the egg), the hatch did not succeed.’

tʂ‘u˥-mo˧-tʂ‘u˥-sɯ˥-hɛ˧, tʂu˥-mo˧-tʂɯ˥-nɯ˧-bu˩, bu˩-lɛ˧-t‘u˧-mʌ˧-ȵi˩.
autumn-season-autumn-threemonth autumn-season-soil-EMPH-hatch hatch-TELIC-arrive-NEG-succeed
‘In the three months of autumn, the soil of autumn hatches (the egg), the hatch did not succeed.’

9 Vocabulary notes collected from Qiansuo Village.

10 Glosses of particles are mostly quoted from Lidz (2010: xxxi-xxxii). The particle /nɯ˧/ is glossed as an ergative marker following Pinson (2012: 273). The prefix of non-static verbs, /lɛ˧/, is analysed as a telic marker by the author (cf. Garey 1957).

(1b.) From the Daba oral chant *Lighting Incense on the New Year's Arrival* (/kʰu˦-ʂɯ˧-so˧-kæ˩/, 'year-new-incense-to light'; author's fieldwork data)

tsʰɯ˧-so˧-ɬi˧, æ˧ ʑi˧ hæ˧ næ˩-hɯ˩-ko˧-dzɯ˩.
winter-three-month *Aiyihaina*-lake-LOC-sit
'In the three months of winter, (*Shu*) lives in Aiyihaina lake.'

ʐe˧-so˧-ɬi˧, ʐɯ˩ nɑ˧ ʐɯ˧ ʌr˧-dʑɯ˩-ʁo˧do˧-dzɯ˩.
summer-three-month big mountains-mountain-above-sit
'In the three months of summer, (*Shu*) lives in big mountains.'

tʂʰu˧-so˧-ɬi˧, pʰur˩ lɑ˧ æ˩ pʰur˩-æ˩-ʁo˧do˧-dzɯ˩.
autumn-three-month white cliff-cliff-above-sit
'In the three months of autumn, (*Shu*) lives on white cliffs.'

ni˧-so˧-ɬi˧, zɯ˦-ze˧-bɑ˧-pʰur˩-dzɯ˩-ʁo˧do˧-dzɯ˩.
spring-three-month grass-beautiful-flower-white-tree-above-sit
'In the three months of spring, (*Shu*) lives on blossoming trees.'

In another instance, the coordination of the four geographic directions is shown to be the opposite, if Dabaism and Ruke Dongbaism are compared to Dongbaism (Xu 2018). The divination figure in Dongbaism, *Bage* (/pɑ˧kʌ˩/, Li et al. 1978: 115), uses a frog to indicate the four directions: the head points to the South and the tail points to the North. In the centre of Lijiang area, the frog is positioned upside down, aligned to the convention of the Chinese orientation perspectives: the North is located in the upper part of the map, and the South in the lower part, e.g., the Bage Figure in He (1989: 144).[11] In other genres of Dongbaism, the frog is a "standing" figure (e.g., Figure 11.1).

In Dongba legends, the frog *Haishee Bamei* (/hæ˧ʂɯ˩pɑ˥mɛ˧/), who lived in the sacred lake *Meelee Ndajji* (/mɯ˧rɯ˥ndɑ˧dʑi˩/), brought to the world the knowledge of *Wuxing* ('the five primary elements'), using its body to indicate the five cardinal directions.[12] The "frog" is quoted from the Chinese translation of Dongba,

11 There are traces of systems with geographical coordinates in which the south is in the upper part of a map, in ancient Chinese culture. The map excavated from the Mawangdui 马王堆 Tombs (2nd century BC [Han Dynasty]), in Hunan Province, marked east on the left and west on the right (Mawangdui Hanmu Boshu Zhengli Xiaozu 1975: 101–102). The map unearthed from the Fangmatan 放马滩 Tombs (239 BC [Qin Dynasty]) marked east on the right and west on the left (He 1989). Li (2004: 243) pointed out that the current geographic orientation of the Han People possibly originated from the Qin Dynasty (221–206 BC).

12 Cf. "The Origin of Moso Divination" (/py˩p'ɑ˩kwɑ˥ʂo˩/, 'chant-divination-manner-to seek for'), in Li et al. (1978); "White Bat Seeking for Scriptures" (/^{1}tʂhʌ^{3}gu^{1}kɔ^{3}ʂo/; IPA: /tʂʰʌ˥gu˩kɔ˥ʂo˩/, 'dirt-to chase-scripture-to seek for'), in Fu (2012).

Haishee Bamei. The interpretation of the creature is subject to debate. For example, Ge (1999: 7) pointed out that the creature should be translated as 'turtle', since the syllable *Pa* is not identical to 'frog' in the Naxi vocabulary. Moreover, the worship of the frog is not indigenous to the Dongba culture.

The Naxi word for 'frog' (/pɑ˧/) has a Tibetan cognate, སྦལ (*sbal*). *Haishee Bamei* also has its Tibetan counterpart, [མ་ཧཱ་] གསེར་གྱི་རུས་སྦལ (*[ma hā] gser gyi rus sbal*; '[fabulous] golden tortoise'; Das 1902: 1189). In Tibetan, *rus sbal* means 'turtle', while *sbal* is used as a morpheme for amphibians, e.g., frog, crab, lizard (Chos kyi grags pa 1957: 613, 836; Hummel 1969: 144).

A more complete / enriched geomantic version of *Bage* was attested in Daba's collection. It is in a woodblock print of the Bon religion called *Dagua Tu* 打卦图 ('the divination figure'; see Figure 11.2). In this diagram, the animal for orientation is a mythical creature named *Cobbi Gguhun* (/tsʰo˧bi˩gu˩hũ˧/). According to Daba Awo, from Wujiao Village, this animal lives underground; his movements cause earthquakes.[13]

Figure 11.3 shows a combination of *Bagua* (the eight trigrams; སྤར་ཁ་བརྒྱད *spar kha brgyad*) and *Jiugong* (the nine halls diagram; སྨེ་བ་དགུ *sme ba dgu*). *Bagua* and *Jiugong* are believed to be *Hetu* and *Loshu*, the two omens given by nature to human beings in Chinese legends. According to Kong Anguo's ([156 BC–74 BC]) annotation of *Hongfan* 洪范 (a chapter in *Shang Shu* ['Classic of History']), *Bagua* arose from the Yellow River on the back of a dragon-horse, while the scroll of *Jiugong* arose from the Luo River on the back of a turtle. The mythical creature *Cobbi Gguhun*, shown in Figure 11.2, therefore also seems to be an association of a dragon-horse with a turtle.[14] The Tibetan word for 'dragon-horse' is *klung rta* ('river horse'), which literally means 'horse of the river' (Diény 1987: 116–117).

Dongba manuscripts are relatively well-documented: the *Annotated Collection of Naxi Dongba Manuscripts*, for instance, contains 100 volumes.[15] The main difference between the two branches is the adoption of Han Chinese cultural elements in Dongba culture, which shares a profound Tibetan background with Dabaism. These distinctive features provide clues to reconstruct the multiple layers of Dongba and Daba traditions from when exotic cultural elements were introduced.

The religious power identified with the government affects the life of common people. Moso People had their traditional manner of giving names. It was divined by Dongba and Daba priests based on the eight trigrams and the zodiac (as shown

13 Wujiao Village (/ʁɯ˩dʑo˧/; WJ, abbreviated) is the administrative centre of Wujiao Township, Muli County, Sichuan Province.

14 Some other variants of this figure can be found in the graphic collection compiled by Douglas (1978) on the Bon religion and Tibetan Buddhism.

15 This collection is often mentioned as *Quanji* 全集 ('complete collection') for short in Naxi studies.

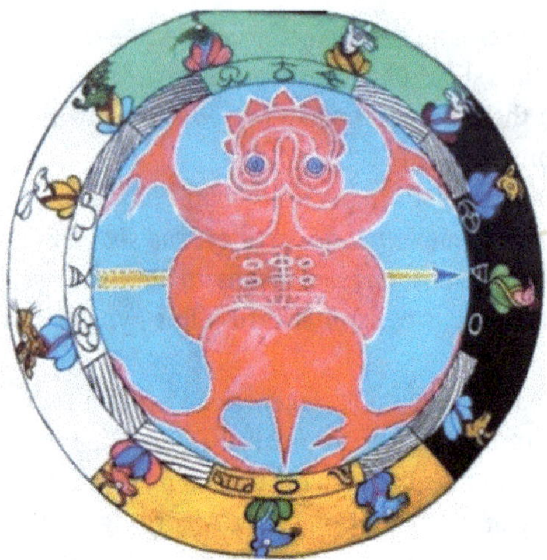

Figure 11.1: Fresco in the Dongba Culture School in Wumu Village, Baoshan Township, Yulong County, Yunnan Province (January 2011, photo by Xu Duoduo).

Figure 11.2: Divination figure of Bon religion in Wujiao village, Wujiao township, Muli County, Sichuan Province (woodblock print on linen cloth; July 2010, photo by Zhao Liming).

in the divination figures). Nowadays, in the eastern branch, it is more popular to invite a Lama priest to give a Tibetan name to a newly born family member. Lama priests, along with Daba priests, are often invited to serve in ritual ceremonies for the Moso community. Tibetan anthroponyms generally consist of two disyllabic words. The family name, not often mentioned, is generated through the use of Moso local terms and is placed before the given name. In the western branch, most people have a Han Chinese name: a family name plus a given name of one or two character(s). In the clusters located in between, it is sometimes also possible to spot "mixed" names: a Han Chinese family name plus a two-syllable Tibetan name.

This chapter aims at an in-depth analysis of Tibetan linguistic features in Dongba and Daba spirits' names, which will contribute to a better understanding of the diachronic hierarchy of the spirit system in Dongbaism and Dabaism. Moreover, the cultural exchange happened in this Sino-Tibetan borderland.

3 Spiritual world

Dongba scriptures and Daba oral chants are the encyclopaedia of the Moso people, who share a complex spiritual world. This spiritual world includes deities from animistic beliefs and spirits introduced from other cultures, mostly from Bon and Tibetan Buddhism. Ghosts, along with the gods, are addressed as spirits in the Dongba and Daba cultures.[16] Spirits are considered the "soul" of objects or matters. The profound Bon influence is broadly recognised in studies on Dongbaism and Dabaism.[17] The spirits of Tibetan origin are categorised as the latest acquired entities in Dongbaism, according to Bai (2012: 49), while the other two earlier categories include the old spirits (original indigenous spirits worshipped by the Moso community) and the new spirits (spirits created in Dongba scriptures).

According to current available resources and fieldwork interview notes, there are three realms in the spiritual world of Dongbaism and Dabaism: heaven, the human world and the underworld. In Daba culture, the gods of nature are the gods living in heaven. In Dongba culture, gods introduced from the Bon religion and ancestors live in heaven, while the gods of nature are neighbours or brothers of

16 Normally, "ghost" refers to a soul after the death of the body, but sometimes, the spirits that do damage or cause diseases are also considered "ghosts". "God" generally refers to a supernatural deity, immortal, dealing with specific aspects of the world and human life. According to the mindset of Dongba and Daba priests, spirits of certain objects, such as nymphs, are spirits with powers equivalent to the gods.

17 Including, but not limited to Bacot (1913), Rock (1952), and Yang (2012).

human beings. The underworld is the realm of ghosts. In Dongba culture, the mountain spirits, some of which are named after *Shu* (gods of nature), also belong to the ghost sphere (Xu 2021: 139). The three realms, where deities of heaven, human and ghost live, are located between the sky and the ground (Guo 2017).

Despite the distinctive features of the spirit system, Dongba and Daba spirits can be classified into five categories:

– gods in heaven;
– *dharmapalas*;
– gods of nature;
– ghosts;
– legendary priests.

Furthermore, five types of naming processes can be individuated among the various designations for spirits in Dongba and Daba cultures: categorical names, group noun-epithets, domain noun-epithets, feature noun-epithets and proper nouns (or anthroponyms) (Xu 2021: 141). In other words, the various cultural elements, independently of the categories of spirits, are named following specific patterns and incorporated into the local religious framework.

Tibetan elements have been attested in all these five categories. The generic designation for god is *Ggalha* (/gɑ˩ɬɑ˧/) in Dabaism, and *Hei* (/^{2}hä/; IPA: /he˧/) in Dongbaism. The term is translated as *Pusa* 菩萨 in Chinese, and *bodhisattva* in Sanskrit. It corresponds to ལྷ (*lha*) in Tibetan. *Ggala* (/^{2}ngaw-^{1}la/; IPA: /ŋgɑ˧lɑ˩/) derives from Tibetan དགྲ་ལྷ (*dgra-lha*), which means 'god of war' (Rock 1972: 85; Chos kyi grags pa 1957: 151).[18]

Among the generic designations of Dongbaism, *Pula* (/^{2}p'u-^{1}la/; IPA: /pʰu˧lɑ˩/) corresponds to ཕོ་ལྷ (*pho-lha*), in Tibetan (Rock 1972: 41).[19] Bai (2012: 62) translated it as *Zhizun Shen* 至尊神 ('the supreme gods'). The Tibetan term literally means 'the god of man', as a parallel of *mo-lha* ('the god of woman'; Stein 1972: 222). In Moso culture, the two major deities of the human sphere, in the spirit system, are *Ddo* (/ɖo˩/; 'the god of male / *yang*') and *Sei* (/se˧/, 'the god of female / *yin*'). *Ddo* is also called *Abaddo* (/ɑ˧pɑ˧ɖo˩/) in Daba oral chants and is believed to be the deity who created the world.

The eighth day of the second month in the lunar calendar is a popular festival celebrated by many ethnic groups in North-West Yunnan Province. Moso People also call it *Sanduo Festival* (三多/三朵) in Chinese. *Sanduo* is the god of war, as well

18 The IPA transcriptions for Rock's studies in this chapter are based on Michailovsky and Michaud (2006).

19 It literally means 'the god of man' (Stein 1972: 222).

as the *dharmapalas* of the Yulong Mountain (Ceinos Arcones 2012: 80–81). The name of the god *Sanduo*, pronounced as /^{2}ssan ^{2}ddo/ (IPA: /sæ˧do˧/), is the denomination for Lijiang in Tibetan (ས་ཐམ། *sa-tham*; Rock 1972: 42). It was transliterated as *Sandan* 三赕 in *Yuan Yitong Zhi* ('Atlas of the Great Yuan Dynasty').[20]

In most cases, spirit names with multi-syllabic structures are of Tibetan origins. These Tibetan loans were transliterated, with some adjustments, in order to match with the phonemic system of Naish languages. One of the distinctive features differentiating Tibetan and Naish languages is the syllabic structure: Naish languages do not have consonantal codas. Therefore, the consonantal coda in the Tibetan words is dropped, or merged to the vowel of the previous syllable, which results in a nasalised vowel, or attached to the following syllable and read as a pre-nasalised consonant (which exists among Naxi phonemes).[21] For example, the god of fire, *Ssanbbala* (/zɑ̃˩bɑ˧lɑ˩/), corresponds to the god of fortune, *Jambhala* (ཛམ་བྷ་ལ *dzam-bha-la*), in Tibetan Buddhism (Chandra 1999: 1500–1514). The Dongba god *Shela Oge* (/ʂʌ˥lɑ˧o˧kʌ˩/, No.2038 in Li et al. 1972) is a homonym of *Shenlha Wökar* (གཤེན་ལྷ་འོད་དཀར *gshen-lha-od-dkar*) in the Bon religion, and is possibly 'the god of priest' (Kværne 1995: 24–25).[22] His name is translated/interpreted as 'the Big God of the Center' according to Rock (1972: 216).

In these examples, the Tibetan spirits are generally introduced with their standard appellations, but with new "roles". As Jackson (1979: 101–102) noticed, the majority of deities occur only once or twice in Dongba scriptures, and knowledge of their origins is vague.

The Tibetan elements are sometimes scattered among the spirits names. Li et al. (1972: 148–149) documented 24 major *Shu* (gods of nature) in the five spatial directions, including the king and queen of each of the four categories of the *Shu* living in the centre. The four categories of *Shu* include *Shu, Nii, Diu* and *Sadda*. Their Dongba glyphs consist of the basic figure of *Shu* and other pictographs representing the syllables in their names (see Table 11.1).

20 The original text: "州治三赕，亦曰样渠头赕" ('the administrative center of Tong'an Perfecture, Lijiang Road', is Sandan, also called Yangtouqu Dan; Fang 1998: 95). In contemporary Mandarin Chinese, the place name *Yangtouqu* 样渠头 is written as 依古堆 (/i˧gɣ˧dy˨/; Fang and He 1979: 39). It is the local name for Lijiang in the Naxi language, and means 'the turn of the Jinsha River' (Li 2001: 1).

21 One example of this type is the name of the Dongba lunar mansion, 'star of the tail-peak' /nɑ˩ŋgv˧/. The equivalent Tibetan term is ནམ་གྲུ *nam gru* (cf. Xu 2016: 123–124).

22 Etymological reconstructions of *gShen* include: 'shaman' in Old Tibetan by Hoffmann (1944), 'butcher' in Old Tibetan by F.W. Thomas and J.V. Manen, and 'saviours' or 'teachers" by A.H. Francke (Hummel 1992).

Among the morphemes in the *Shu* designations, 'king' has been used in four *Shu Shu*, one *Nii Shu* and one *Diu Shu.*[23] The word is transcribed as /dʑʌ˩bv˧/ or /dʑi˧bv˧/ in the Naxi language, and it is a Tibetan loan, རྒྱལ་པོ (*rgyal po*; Chos kyi grags pa 1957: 176). The sub-joint letter ཡ leads to the palatalisation of the basic velar letter ག, which results in an alveolo-palatal consonant /dʑ/, as attested in some contemporary Tibetan varieties (Qu 1996: 142–143).

According to Rock (1972: 123), *iko Sozzee* (/^{2}yi-^{2}k'o-^{3}sso-^{3}dzǐ/; IPA: /i˧kʰo˧so˥dzɯ˥/), a *Shu* King (Nāga King, in Rock's terminology) guards the east (the eastern *lokapāla*), and it is identical to the Tibetan ཡུལ་འཁོར་སྐྱོང (*yul-hkhor-skyong*)[24], which means *dhṛtarāṣṭra* in Sanskrit. The phonetically similar segments in the designations of *Nii Shu*, such as *Sozee* (/so˧tsɯ˥/, /ʂo˩tsɯ˥/), *Keeso* (/kʻɯ˧so˧/) and *Keseizee* (/kʻɯ˧sɛ˩tsɯ˥/), are possible variants of *iko Sozzee* in the Dongba context.

Another word attested multiple times in *Shu*'s appellations is *Lvnrhua* (/rv˩-ndʐwɑ˧/). It has been spotted in the name of *Diu Shu*, 'King living in the centre' (No. 1983 in Li et al. 1972: 148), in the *Shu* King of Sumeru (/^{1}lv-^{2}ndzhwua ^{2}gyi-^{2}bbŭ/; IPA: /ndʐwɑ˧ dʑi˧bv˧/), and in the *Shu* King of the East (/^{1}ssu ^{2}gyi-^{2}bbŭ ^{1}lv-^{2}ndzh-wua/; IPA: /ʂu˩ dʑi˧bv˧ rv˩ndʐwɑ˧ /; Rock 1972: 108, 121). Rock (1963: 246) recorded *Lvnrhua*, which means 龙马 'dragon-horse' in Chinese, and 'wind horse' in Tibetan (རླུང་རྟ *rlung-rta*). It is believed to bring fortune and good luck.

There are other *Shu* Kings as well. For example, a green *Shu* King in the North is named *Mida* (/^{1}ssu ^{2}gyi-^{2}bbŭ ^{2}mi-^{3}dta/; IPA: /sɯ˩ dʑi˧bv˧ mi˧tɑ˥/; Rock 1972: 121, 157).[25] The denomination has Tibetan origins, མིག་བཀྲ (*mig-bkra*), consisting of 'eye' and 'bright' (Chos kyi grags pa 1957: 30, 636). In other words, the proper noun *Mida* actually describes the feature of the *Shu* spirit in Tibetan, while the meaning is taken for granted in the Dongba context.

Similar to other categories of spirits, there are ghost kings living in the five spatial directions attested in Dongba manuscripts (Li et al. 1972: 141). In Dabaism, some ghost symbols have been inscribed in the wooden bars with carved idols for making *tsampa* sacrifice in local rituals.[26] This kind of wooden bar is called *Jjirumu* (/dʑi˩ʐu˧mu˩/) in Na (the eastern branch of the Naish languages), which means

23 These translated terms consist of the categorical name of *Shu* (i.e., *Shu, Nii,* and *Diu*) as the first syllable and the generic name of the god of nature as the following syllable.

24 A segmental gloss could be "realm-followers-guard" (Chos kyi grags pa 1957: 800, 102, 57–58).

25 The "north" is a generic idea of cardinal direction, possibly referring to Mongolia. Yet it is not identified with real places in the Dongba and Daba oral chants. According to the geographic notions of Moso, Han people (/hä/) live in the east, Bai people (/lä-bbä/) live in the south, Ggvzzu people (/gv-dzu/, possibly Tibetan) live in the west, Ggolo people (/ggo-lo/, possibly Mongolian) live in the north, and Moso live in the centre (Jackson 1979: 283; He 1989: 85, 143).

26 *Tsampa* is the flour made from highland barley. Dongba and Daba priests use *Tsampa* dough to make idols for rites.

Table 11.1: The kings of *Shu* in the five directions.

Loc.	East	South	West	North	Center	
Cat.	1. /ʂv˩/, *Shu Shu*					
No.	1973	1974	1975	1976	1977	1978
Pic.						
IPA	dʑʌ˩bv˧ – t‘ɑ˥iʌ˧	dʑʌ˩bv˧ – ndʐwɑ˧pv˥	dʑʌ˩bv˧ – pɛ˧mɑ˧	dʑʌ˩bv˧ -to˧tɕo˥	tsɛ˧nɑ˧rɯ˩tʂ‘ɯ˥	ʂv˩ – mɛ˧ -nɑ˩pv˥
Gl.	King-Ta'ie	King-Nrhuabv	King-Beima	King-Dojo	Tsena Leechee	Shu-female-Nabv
Cat.	2. /ɳi˧/, *Nii Shu*					
No.	1991	1992	1993	1994	1995	1996
Pic.						
IPA	tʂ‘ʌr˧ɳi˧t‘o˧bɑ˩ -k‘ɯ˧so˧	p‘v˧ɳi˧dv˩ -k‘ɯ˧sɛ˩tsɯ˥	sɯ˧dʷɑ˧ -ʂo˩tsɯ˥	tɕi˧ndo˩ -so˧tsɯ˥	lo˩ – i˧ – dʑi˧bv˧	lo˩ – i˧ – dʑi˧mo˧
Gl.	Chenii Tobba-*dharmapalas*	Pvniidu-*dharmapalas*	Seeddua-*dharmapalas*	Jindo-*dharmapalas*	Valley-POSS-King	Valley-POSS-Queen
Cat.	3. /tʏ˧/, *Diu Shu*					
No.	1979	1980	1981	1982	1983	1984
Pic.						
IPA	ʂʌ˥tɑ˥dʑʌ˧o˩	i˥mbv˧ho˩mo˧	mɑ˩iʌ˥mɑ˩mbv˧	rwɑ˩pɑ˧dʑʌ˧o˩	rv˩ndʐwɑ˧ -dʑʌ˩bv˧	ɳi˥tʂɯ˧ko˩wɑ˧
Gl.	Sheda Jje'o	imbv Homo	Ma'ie Mambv	Luaba Jje'o	Lvnrhua-King	Niizhee Goua
Cat.	4. /sɑ˩dɑ˥/, *Sadda Shu*					
No.	1985	1986	1987	1988	1990	1989
Pic.						
IPA	sɑ˩dɑ˥ – tso˧kv˥	sɑ˩dɑ˥ – hɑ˧tɕ‘i˧	sɑ˩dɑ˥ – lɑ˩pɑ˥	sɑ˩dɑ˥ – lɑ˩ʔɑ˥	no˧mbɯ˩rɯ˧t‘o˧pɑ˧	sɑ˩ – rv˧ – ɕi˧mɑ˩no˥
Gl.	Sadda-Zogv	Sadda-Haqi	Sadda-Laba	Sadda-La'a	Nombeelee Toba	Sadda-Dragon (female)-Ximano

'model for worshipping the *bodhisattva* of water' (*Shu* in charge of water). In one of the wooden bars from Qiansuo Village, preserved by Daba Luzo, major ghosts are attested in four directions. On the same side of the bar, there are two similar signs dedicated to the left ghost and the right ghost. Considering the paradigm in Dongbaism, with two spirits in the centre representing each gender, the major ghosts of the left and the right in Dabaism could hypothetically correspond to the centre. Table 11.2 displays these major ghosts in the five directions and a possible morphological analysis.

The major ghosts in the east, south and north all contain the word 'King' (/dʑʌ˧bv˧/) in their designations. The last two syllables in the appellation of the major ghost in the west, *Seepv* (/sɯ˧p'v˧/), correspond to སྲིན་པོ (*srin po*), which means *rākṣasa* in Sanskrit (Rock 1972: 277; Chos kyi grags pa 1957: 921).

The designations of the ghost in the centre are named after the *Qiyao* ('the seven luminaries'): *Mima* (/mi˧mɑ˩/) means མིག་དམར (*mig dmar*; 'Mars') and *Gessa* (/kɯ˧zɑ˩/) means གཟའ (*gza*; 'planet'). The name of the ghost king in the centre, *Seiddei* (/sɛ˧dɛ˧/), possibly corresponds to སེ་བདུད (*se-bdud*; Rock 1972: 165) in Tibetan, which means 'demon'. The name of the ghost queen in the centre, *Namo* (/nɑ˩mo˧/), could mean 'goddess', according to its Tibetan counterpart གནམ་མོ (*gnam mo*).[27]

There is no morphological resemblance between the names of the major ghosts. However, the major ghosts in the east and in the south show onomastic connections between Dabaism and Dongbaism: 1) *Ddussa* (/du˧zɑ˧/) and *Derssa* (/ʈʌr˩zɑ˥/); 2) *Sheerhee* (/ʂɯ˧dʐɯ˧/) and *Sheenrhee* (/ʂɯ˩ndʐɯ˧/). Rock (1972: 301) pointed out the correspondence with the ghost king in the south with གཤིན་རྗེ་རྒྱལ་པོ (*gshin-rje rgyal-po*). The first two syllables, གཤིན་རྗེ, correspond to the Sanskrit term *yamarāja*. Therefore, the term literally means 'the king *yamarāja*', which is transliterated as *Yanluo Wang* 阎罗王 in Chinese.

In another instance, a ghost king is named *Naree Zonmbu* (/nɑ˩ʐɯ˧tso˥mbv˧/, No.1878 in Li et al. 1972). The first two morphemes in the designation can be analysed as 'black' and 'snake'. The word *Zonmbu* possibly corresponds to the Tibetan term for 'king': བཙན་པོ (*btsan po*; Chos kyi grags pa 1957: 674).

The proper nouns are often accompanied by the description of the figures. For example, *Dongba of Ggvzzee* is /gv˧dzɯ˩-p'ur˩-pʏ˧mbv˩, tʏ˧so˧tʂ'ɯ˥mbv˧/ (*Ggvzzee* People – *Pur* [specific term for Tibetan priest] – Bonpo, *Diuso Cheembv*; Li et al. 1972: 144). Since *Shu* is everywhere in nature, a priest is needed by all the spirits. The priest of *Sadda Shu* is *Satu Jjiwu* (/^{1}ssaw-^{3}ndaw ^{2}bpö-^{1}mbö ^{2}ssaw-^{2}t'u-^{1}gyi-^{3}wu/; IPA: /sɑ˩ndɑ˥ py˧mby˩ sɑ˧tʰu˧dʑi˩wu˥/; Rock 1972: 223). The priest of the god *He* is named *Labbv Tugo* (/^{2}hä ^{2}bpö-^{1}mbö ^{1}la-^{2}bbŭ-^{2}t'u-^{3}gko/; IPA: /he˧ py˧mby˩ lɑ˩b-

27 The Tibetan entries are quoted from Chos kyi grags pa (1957: 472, 649, 769).

Table 11.2: The major Daba ghosts in the five directions.

	Dongba	Daba	Daba Symbols
East	/ʈʌr˩zɑ˥-dʑʌ˧bv˧/ (No.1874) 'Derssa-King'	/ʂʌ˧-du˧zɑ˧/ 'She-Ddussa'	
South	/ʂɯ˩ndʐɯ˧-dʑʌ˧bv˧/ (No.1875) '*yamarāja*-King'	/ɬo˧-ʂɯ˧dʐɯ˧/ 'Lho-Sheerhee'	
West	/lɛ˥tɕʻi˧-sɯ˧pʻv˧/ (No.1876) 'Leiqi-rākṣasa'	/no˩mʌ˩mu˧/ 'Nomemu'	
North	/nv˩ndzɯ˧-dʑʌ˩bv˧/ (No.1877) 'Nunzee-King'	/dʐwɑ˩njɑ˩tɕo˧/ 'Rhua'niajo'	
Center	/mi˧mɑ˩-sɛ˧dɛ˧/ (No.1872) 'Mars-demon' /kɯ˧zɑ˩-nɑ˩mo˧/ (No.1873) 'planet-goddess'	/tsɑ˧/ 'Za' /wɑ˧pʰu˧-du˩-æ˩mi˧/ 'leftside-Ddu Ghost-Mother'	[29]

v˧tʰu˧ko˥/; Rock 1972: 209). Sometimes, spirits with the same name are differentiated through their titles, for example, '*Shu* King *Leesso*' (/^{1}ssu ^{2}gyi-^{2}bbŭ ^{3}llü-^{2}zo/; IPA: /sɯ˩ dʑi˧bv˧ ɭɯ˥zo˧/) and '*Shu* Lord *Leesso*' (/^{1}ssu ^{2}ggŏ ^{2}swue-^{2}p'ä ^{3}llü-^{2}zo/; IPA: /sɯ˩ sɯ˧pʰe˧ ɭɯ˥zo˧/; Rock 1972: 120, 138).

In the Moso context, the Tibetan terms are used as proper nouns (or anthroponyms), which are considered merely phonetic symbols without concrete meanings. Nevertheless, through such morphological re-analysis, the meanings of the spirits' denominations can be narrowed down. Moreover, there are certain rationales behind the onomastic "collage", which could be defined as "cultural translation" (cf. Poupard 2020: 89–90).

According to Dongba scriptures, there are three master priests (*Biumbv* /pɤ˧mbv˩/) of the three main ethnic groups: Ggvzzee (Tibetan), Moso and Minjia (Bai People; Li et al. 1972: 144). The '*Biumbv* of Ggvzzee' (/^{2}ddü-^{2}sso-^{3}ch'i-^{3}mbbŭ/; IPA: /tɤ˧so˧tʂʻɯ˥mbv˧/) is homonymic with the first Karmapa of Karma Kagyu (ཀརྨ་བཀའ་བརྒྱུད) in Tibetan Buddhism, whose name was དུས་གསུམ་མཁྱེན་པ (*dus gsum mkhyen pa*; Rock 1972: 202). The denomination can be glossed as 'generation-three-know-per-

28 The two symbols for the major ghosts on the left and the right could hypothetically correspond to the centre.

son' (Chos kyi grags pa 1957: 399). It literally means 'the person knowing three generations'.

The *Biumbv* of Moso, *Liushee Madda* (/lɤ˩ʂɯ˧ma˩da˥/), and the *Biumbv* of Minjia, *Seibbv Seirv* (/sɛ˩bv˧sɛ˥rv˧/), have metaphorically been assigned the roles of the second son and the third son of Dongba Shilo, the founder of Dongbaism. *Dongba Shilo* was the equivalent of the founder of Yung-Drung Bon, *Tonpa Shenrab* (སྟོན་པ་གཤེན་རབ), who was created to assimilate the Buddhist *bodhisattva* in Zhang-Zhung (ཞང་ཞུང) culture (Hummel 1992). Yung-Drung Bon is the second phase of the Bon religion in history, which emerged in the 10th and 11th centuries (Kværne 1972: 27–29; Keown 2003).

Dongba scriptures are considered ancient resources preserving the pre-Buddhist Bon tradition (cf. Rock 1955; Tucci 1976; Mathieu 2015). So far, the earliest date found in Dongba manuscripts is 1703 (Mueggler 2011: 91), while there are no explicit dates in the oral chants. The search for the historical paths of Bon and Dongba could be conducted in parallel. Yung-Drung Bon evolved from Old Bon after incorporating Buddhist doctorines, while the Tibetan Buddhism elements attested in Dabaism and Dongbaism could date back to an earlier stage. The analysis of Tibetan elements in Dongba and Daba spirit names also provides a lens through which to observe how Buddhism was introduced to the Bon religion.

4 Etymology of Tibetan elements

This section provides a list of repeatedly used Tibetan words in spirits' designations. The awareness of these elementary elements contributes to a better understanding of Dongba and Daba spirits' onomastics and to the detection of connections between spirits in distinct traditions. It opens a window through which to observe the introduction and localisation of exotic religions in the Moso context, the cross-cultural evolution of myths, as well as of language *strata* in the Sino-Tibetan family.

In the case of *Lvnrhua* (/rv˩ndʐwa˧/), the mythical creature 'wind-horse' apparently has two homophonic spellings: ཀླུང་རྟ (*klung-rta*; river-horse) and རླུང་རྟ (*rlung-rta*; wind-horse). Karmay (1997: 413) suggested that *klung-rta* derived from a Chinese myth about the 'dragon-horse', as interpreted in Kong Anguo's annotations (Early Han Dynasty). Stein (1972: 186) specifies that *rlung* is *prāṇa* ('breathe'). In Tibetan regions, 'wind-horse' refers to the five-coloured prayer flags and is depicted as a horse carrying a treasure (Beer 2003: 67–68). It is painted as a dragon bringing a manuscript on its back in the Dunhuang manuscript *Pelliot chinois 2683* (Drège and Moretti 2014).

The Chinese idiom, *feng ma niu bu xiangji* 风马牛不相及 ('wind-horse-OX-NEG-encounter', "completely unrelated entities/events"), was first spotted in *Zuo Zhuan* (*The Commentary of Zuo* on *Chunqiu*), compiled in the late 4th century BC. So far, this idiom is generically explained as a metaphor of two unrelated objects, while the character *feng* is explained as 'lost' or as 'induction between animals' (*Ci Hai*: 4006, 4012). If *feng-ma* in *Zuo Zhuan* meant 'wind-horse', the metaphor of this idiom is well-explained. This lexicon has been long-lost in the Han Chinese context. Nevertheless, if the idiom is used as a wordplay in pre-Qin texts, the term *rlung rta* existed in the Chinese vocabulary by that time.

Some other frequently used Tibetan terms in spirits' designations include *yung-drung, dorje, yeshe, bema, japo, gonpo, chenpo* and *napo*. They are also utilised for personal names, where they are transcribed with Chinese characters with similar pronunciations.

Yung-Drung (གཡུང་དྲུང; gyung-drung; 雍仲; symbol: 卍) means 'eternal / ever-lasting', in Bon (Karmay 1997: 105). It is equivalent to the Buddhist *dorje* (Chos kyi grags pa 1957: 808; Kværne 1995: 11). In Moso languages and dialects, it is read as /i˧ɖwɑ˧/ (Li et al. 1972: 131), /²ghügh-²ddo/ (IPA: /ɯ˧do˧/; Rock 1963: 117), or /i˩do˧/ (author's notes on interviewing Daba Awo). *Yung-Drung* is often attested at the beginning of the spirits' names. For example, in the appellative of the goddess *Yung-Drung Lamo* (/i˧ɖwɑ˧lɑ˧mo˧/, Li et al. 1972: 157). The Daba spirit in charge of exorcism is named *Yung-Drung Konddo Ssonbu* (/i˩do˧kõ˥do˧zõ˩pu˧/). *Konddo* means 'universal' in Tibetan (ཀུན་ཏུ; *kun-tu*; Chos kyi grags pa 1957: 9). *Samantabhadra*, which is *Puxian Pusa* (普贤菩萨) in Chinese, is called ཀུན་ཏུ་བཟང་པོ (*kun-tu bzang-po*) in Tibetan, which is translated as 'The All-Good' (Kværne 1995: 23). The *dharmapala iema* (/iʌ˧mɑ˩/, Li et al. 1972: 155), the Buddha headwear, also known as 'five-buddha headware', is named *Yung-Drung Ba'i Wu'erma* (/i˩do˧pɑ˧i˩wu˩ʌr˧mɑ˧/). This *dharmapala* guards the rituals of healing diseases called *Nati Bu* (/nɑ˥tʰi˧pu˩/). In this designation, the *dharmapala iema* maintained its Tibetan form: དབེར་མ (*wer-ma*).

Dorje (རྡོ་རྗེ), in Tibetan Buddhism, means 'indestructibility' (Chos kyi grags pa 1957: 444). It also refers to the ritual weapon *vajra*. It is pronounced *Ddvrhee* (/dv˩dʐɯ˧/) in Dongbaism, and *Ddujjee* (/du˩dʑɯ˧/) in Dabaism. The term is translated as *Jingang* 金刚 ('diamond ore'), in Chinese, transliterated as 都基 or 多吉 when used as person's name. Li et al. (1972: 156) documented a 'nine-headed god' named *Geeko Ddvrhee* (/kɯ˩k'o˥dv˩dʐɯ˧/). The designation has a variant, *Geeko*, in which the less semantically distinctive segment *Ddvrhee* is omitted.

Yeshe (ཡེ་ཤེས; *yeshes*) means 'perfect; absolute wisdom' (Rock 1972: 28). It is also a word often spotted at the beginning of epithets. The deity *Yeshe Heiddee* (/¹yi-³shi ²hä-¹ddü/; IPA: /i˩ʂʅ˥ he˧ɖɯ˩/), the sorceress *Yeshe Jjimee* (/¹yi-³shi ²gyi-²mun̲/; IPA: /i˩ʂʅ˥

dʑi˧mɯ˧/), and the *dharmapala iema Yeshe Songu Iema* (/¹yi-³shi-²sso-²ngu ²yu-¹ma/; IPA: /i˩ʂʅ˥ so˧ŋgu˧ jɤ˧mɑ˩/) are examples.[29]

Bema (བྱམས་མ; *byams ma*) means 'the Loving Lady' in Tibetan, *prajñāpāramitā* in Sanskrit, transliterated as 般若, in Chinese, which means 'wisdom' (Kværne 1995: 22, 28). It is attested in the proper nouns of the *Shu Shu* king of the west, *Jjebbv Bema* (/dʑʌ˩bv˧-pɛ˧mɑ˧/) and the mother of the *Tse* ghost *Ddvgo Bema* (/¹ddv-¹gko ²bpä-¹ma, ¹dsä ²ggŏ ¹ä-¹mä /; IPA: /dɣ˩ko˩ pe˧mɑ˩, tse˩ gɤ˩ e˩me˩/).

Japo (རྒྱལ་པོ; *rgyal po*), as mentioned above, means 'king, ruler' in Tibetan. The velar consonant is palatalised in the Naish languages. Therefore, it is pronounced as Jjebbv" or *Jjibbv* (/²gyi-²bbŭ/; IPA: /dʑi˧bv˧/), despite the Tibetan spelling. Its female counterpart, 'Queen' (རྒྱལ་མོ; *rgyal mo*; Chos kyi grags pa 1957: 177), is read as *Jjimee* (/²gyi-²mu͟n/; IPA: /dʑi˧mɯ˧/). Besides the *Shu Shu* monarch in the centre, another pair is recorded in Rock (1972: 210): *Kiu'i Japo* (/¹khü-²yi-²gyi-²bpŭ/; IPA: /kʰy˩i˧ dʑi˧bv˧/) and *Kiu'i Japo* (/¹khü-²yi-²gyi-²mu͟n/; IPA: /kʰy˩i˧ dʑi˧mɯ˧/). In another instance, *Nonjji Japo* (/nõ˧dʑi˩-dʑʌ̃˩bɣ˧/), in Dabaism, can be interpreted as 'the King of Treasure'. The Tibetan word for 'treasure' is ནོར་མཛེས (*nor dzes*; Chos kyi grags pa 1957: 471).

Gonpo (མགོན་པོ; *mgon po*; 依怙) means *nātha*, a subtype of *dharmapala*. When used as a proper noun, the term refers to *Śākyamuni*, *Avalokiteśvara* and *Mahākāla* (Chos kyi grags pa 1957: 157). The spirits named after *gonpo* include the spirit who assisted Tonpa Shilo to become a deity, the big god *Yeshe Gonpo* (/¹yi-³shi ²ngv-²mbbŭ ²hä-¹ddü/; IPA: /i˩ʂʅ˥ ŋgv˧mbu˧ he˧ɖɯ˩/), and the *dharmapala Iema Yeshe Gonpo* (/¹yi-³shi ²ngv-²mbbŭ ²yu-¹ma/; IPA: /i˩ʂʅ˥ ŋgv˧mbu˧ jɤ˧mɑ˩/) (see Rock 1972: 29, 194).

Chenpo (ཆེན་པོ; *chen po*) means 'the great one' (Rock 1963: 114; Chos kyi grags pa 1957: 269). One of the three major *dharmapala gonpo*, *Mahākāla*, is called ནག་པོ་ཆེན་པོ (*nag po chen po*) in Tibetan. The *Sadda Shu* living at the foot of Sumeru is named *Laba Chenpo* (Rock 1972: 163). The complete epithet is: /¹ssaw-³ndaw ¹la-²bpa ³ch'i-³mbbŭ/, IPA: /sɑ˩dɑ˥-lɑ˩pɑ˧-tʂʰɯ˥mbv˥/. In the Ruke scripture about the origins of the *Shu* family, the *Shu* ancestor in the east is called *Ta'ia Chenpo* (/tʰɑ˩iɑ˥tɕʰi˥mbu˧/), while the one in the west is named *Mare Chenpo* (/mɑ˩ɭe˧tɕʰi˥m-bu˧/).[30] The chief of Golo Tibetan (a historical figure) was also named after *Chenpo*: /¹ggŏ-³lo ¹ho-²bpö ³ch'i-³mbbŭ/ (IPA: /gɤ˩lo˥ ho˩py˧ tʂʰɯ˥mbv˥/), which means 'the great chief Hopy of Golo' (Rock 1963: 114).

29 Cf. Rock (1972: 28, 59, 194); Li et al. (1972: 156).

30 The title of the manuscript is /ʂu tʰu tɕɤ / (Shu - to arrive - to appear , which means „The Advent of *Shu*". This scripture was chanted and interpreted by Dongba Shi Maning in September 2011, with the assistance of Yang Baorong. Dongba Shi Maning and Yang Baorong were from Yomi Village, Labo Township, Ninglang County, Yunnan Province.

Napo (ནག་པོ; nag-po), the first segment of *Mahākāla* in Tibetan, means 'black' (Chos kyi grags pa 1957: 459). This term has been attested in the epithets of the *Ddu* ghost (/^{1}ddv- ^{2}mbu ^{1}na-^{3}bpŭ/; IPA: /dv˩mbu˧ nɑ˩pv˥/), *Nii Shu* of *Ddu* ghost (/^{2}nyi ^{1}ddv ^{1}na-^{3}bpŭ/; IPA: /n̥i˧dv˩ nɑ˩pv˥ /), *Shu Shu* of *Ddu* ghost (/^{2}ssu ^{1}ddv ^{1}na ^{3}bpŭ/; IPA: /sɯ˧dv˩ nɑ˩pv˥/), and Mother *Shu* (/^{2}ssu ^{2}mä ^{1}na ^{3}bpŭ/; IPA: /sɯ˧me˧ nɑ˩pv˥/).[31] According to Rock (1972: 165), the *Shu Shu* of *Ddu* ghost, living in the west, is the Moso equivalent to སེ་བདུད་ནག་པོ (*se-bdud nag-po*).

To sum up, many Tibetan words, with their Bon and Sanskrit etymology, can appear in the spirit epithets of various categories of spirits. For instance, *Yung-Drung* has been attested in the designations of the *dharmapala iema*, meaning 'goddess, great god'; *Dorje* has been found in the designations of the *dharmapala iema* and Tonpa Shilo; *Yeshe* has been spotted in the appellations of the great god, the shaman priest and the *dharmapala*; *Bema* has been spotted in the designations of *Shu* and ghosts; *Japo* is used for the epithets of gods, *Shu*, and ghosts; *Gonpo* is used for the epithets of great god, *dharmapala*, Tonpa Shilo, and ghost; *Chenpo* has been applied to the names of *Shu*, gods, and shaman priests; *Napo* is frequently utilised to name *Shu* and ghosts; and *Lvnrhua* is found in the names of several *Shu* kings.

The same term can be used to name different categories of spirits. In terms of word order, *Yung-Drung* and *Yeshe* are generally located at the beginning of the epithet; *Gonpo* comes after *Yeshe*; *Chenpo* and *Napo*, generally, are located at the end of the epithet. The meaning of these Tibetan terms, by crossing over the categories of spirits, became formularized for certain features of each spirit. There are some limits, though. *Yung-Drung* accompanies the epithets of gods and *dharmapalas*, while *Napo* accompanies the epithets of *Shu* and ghosts.

The spirit epithets with exotic origins are generally transliterated phonetically in Chinese studies. However, the analysis of the structure of spirit designations in Dongbaism and Dabaism, along with the understanding of the application of Tibetan terms, contributes to revealing the cultural evolution behind the anthroponyms of the spiritual system. While they are treated as proper nouns in Dongba and Daba onomastics, they contain descriptions of the features of the spirits. In some cases, a morphological analysis may lead to the reconstruction of a spirit's genealogy.

In the Dongba classics about the origin of Moso divination (see footnote 13), the Dongba scriptures were given by a goddess named *Perzzee Samei*, living on the top of the sacred mountain *Juna Rulo* ('mount-big-Rulo').[32] The onomastic variants

31 Cf. Rock (1972: 28, 59, 194); Li et al. (1972: 156).

32 IPA transcriptions: /ndʑo˩nɑ˧ʐwɑ˥rwɑ˧/ (Li et al. 1978: 33); /^{3}dʑy^{1}nɑ^{1}ʐɔ^{2}lɔ/ (dʑy˩ nɑ˥ ʐɔ˥ lɔ˧) (Fu 2012: 92).

of *Perzzee Samei* include /p'urɹndzɯ˧sɑ˧mɛ˧/ (Li et al. 1978: 95), /^{3}phʌɹ ^{2}ndzɯ ^{2}sɑ ^{2}me/ (IPA: /pʰʌrɹndzɯ˧sɑ˧me˧/; Fu 2012: 44), and /p'ər^{21}dzɿ^{33}sa^{33}me^{33}/ (Li 1997: 55). Li et al. (1972: 151) interpreted this spirit as 'the patriarch of divination, a goddess'. Fu (2012) glossed it as 'female Buddha' (*Nü Fo* 女佛). As stated in Li (1997: 55), she provided not only the Dongba manuscripts, but also the divination of many other ethnic groups, including Indians, the Yi people, Tibetans and the Bai people; as for her technical category, she is a sorceress. This ancient goddess, who existed before Dongbaism, is categorised as one of the latest gods according to Bai (2012: 65). This means that the name *Perzzee Samei* was introduced from Bon.

The designation of *Perzzee Samei* consists of '*Pur* god' (/p'urɹ/; the Tibetan sorceress), 'master' (/ndzɯ˧/), and 'female; great' (/mɛ˧/). Therefore, this proper noun contains the spirit's role (domain noun-epithet). It literally means '*Same*, the master of sorceress(/sorcerer)'.

There are two major types of priests in Dongba culture: *Biu* (/pɤɹ/), in charge of chanting (exorcism, prayer), and *Pa* (/p'ɑɹ/), in charge of divination. In Dongba pictographs, *Biu* is written as a Dongba priest with the five-buddha headwear: (No.1902); *Pa* is written as a female sorcerer: (No.1908), sometimes with hair open: (No.1909).

Perzzee Samei is written as a sitting woman, with 'beard' (the symbolic sign of power) and the pictograph 'air' to mark her name: (No. 2018).[33] In contemporary Dongbaism, Dongba priests may specialise in either or both of these duties, although the glyphs indicate the gender distinction between sorcerers with different expertise. In Chinese context, the female sorcerer was called *Wu* 巫, and the male sorcerer was *Xi* 觋, while the female term is also used as a generic word for sorcerer. In other words, a female sorcerer was the norm.

Samei could be a content word, like the other Tibetan terms used for personal names. Indeed, it seems to be one of the many cognates for 'Shaman'. It is *samân* in Tungus, *samâne* in Tocharian B, *śramaṇa* in Sanskrit ('monk') and གསལ་མོ (*gsal mo*) in Tibetan ('sorceress'; Kværne 2009: 19; Chos kyi grags pa 1957: 933). Scholars reconstructed some etymologies for this word through modern languages. In Sibe, the word for 'Shaman' is *samen*, which means 'omniscient perso'. It consists of *sar* ('to know') and *mame* ('honorific title for female'; Tong 1989: 204). In Manchu, *saman* consists of the root *sam* ('see') and the suffix *an*, which means 'the person knowing' (Zhao 2002). *Perzzee Samei*, with its Bon origin, traces back the Dongba culture to the time when Shamanism was a popular primitive belief in Eurasia (Ermakov 2008).

The first Daba, according to Daba Awo, was *Yung-drung Mebu Zzeeru* (/iɹdo˧ mʌ˧pu˧ dzɯ˧ʐu˧/; '*yung drung*-sky-chant-*Zzeeru*'). He is among the five figures on

33 The glyphs and glosses are quoted from Li et al. (1972).

the Buddhist headwear of Daba priests (*Erna* /ʌr˩ŋʌ˧/). Daba and Dongba priests wear the headwear for exorcism rituals.

The five images in Figure 11.3 are collected from Daba Awo's *Za'ali* (/tsɑ˧ɑ˧li˩/), a sort of religious painting used in rituals worshiping *Shu*. Figure 11.3a, as seen above, represents a kind of *dharmapala* in charge of protecting people from diseases, which is called ཝེར་མ (*wer-ma*) in Tibetan, and *iema* (/iʌ˧mɑ˩/) in Naxi. Figure 11.3c, as explained by the Daba priest, represents the greatest god of the world, *Śākyamuni* in Buddhism. Figure 11.3d shows a *garuda* different from the one usually seen in the Dongba context: showing its profile, holding a snake with both hands, and with completely open-winged. In the *thangka* 'Welsé Ngampa' documented in Kværne (1995: 96–97), five *garudas* can be found, among which "the great *garuda* of Immutable Body" is in a similar model. The spirit in Figure 11.3e, according to the Daba priest, is also in charge of protecting people from diseases, like the *dharmapala* in Figure 11.3a. The designation literally means 'eternal black *dorje*'. The appearance and duty of this spirit make it possible for it to be a *Mahākāla*, one of the major *gonbo* (མགོན་པོ) in Tibetan culture.

Figure 11.3a: *Yung-drung Ba'i dharma-pala Wu'erma* (/i˩do˧pɑ˧i˩wu ˩ʌr˧mɑ˧/)

Figure 11.3b: *Yung-drung Mebu Zzeeru* (/i˩do˧mʌ˧pu˧ dzɯ˧ʐu˧/)

Figure 11.3c: *Laqi Dibishe* (/lɑ˧tɕʰi˩ti˧p i˩ʂʌ˩/)

Figure 11.3d: *Ru'er Zzeiqi Gai'er* (/ʐu˩ʌr˧dze˩t ɕʰi˩kæ˧ʌr˩/)

Figure 11.3e: *Yung-drung Chuana Dorje* (/i˩do˧tʂʰwɑ ˧nɑ˧do˩dʑi˧/)

Figure 11.3: The five figures in a Daba painting, by Daba Awo from Wujiao Village, Wujiao Township, Muli County, Sichuan Province (Dongba paper; July 2011, photo by Li Wenshan).

Besides the "prefix" and the honorific term *yung-drung* ('eternal') shared by Figures 11.3a, 11.3b and 11.3c, the following segment of *Mebu Zzeeru* has a homophonic counterpart in Dongbaism: *Mebiu Zzeeru* (/mə˧py˨dzɿ˧ʐv˨/, *Quanji*, vol 10: 208). Rock (1972: 215) explained this figure as "an ancient celestial Dongba" (/^{2}muàn̲ ^{1}bpö ^{2}dzī ^{1}szŭ/; IPA: /mɯ˧py˩dzɿ˧zɯ˩/). Li et al. (1972: 153) classified it as a major deity in rituals for dispelling rumours (/mʌ˧pɤ˩zɯ˧ʐo˩/). Bai (2012: 71) described it as a god of war, belonging to the time of the latest gods.

The multiple explanations of this spirit reveal a diachronic process of the localisation of a Tibetan deity. Dabaism introduced this spirit, powerful in supressing demons, and worshipped it as the patriarch of the indegenous religion. It reflected the basic responsibilities of a Daba priest. Dongbaism, on the other hand, traced back its origin to Tonpa Sharab, the founder of the Bon Religion. *Mebu Zzeeru*, then, was interpreted as a legendary priest from heaven. Later on, his role changed, along with the evolving Dongba spirit system, and he became a god of war.

On the other hand, the deity in Figure 11.3c could be Tonpa Shenrab. The first segment of the designation, *Laqi*, could derive from *lha-chen* ('god-great') in Tibetan. The second segment, *Dibi-she*, could be *Tonpa Shenrab* in the local pronunciation, or an earlier variation in the Moso language. Rock (1937: 174) recorded the three variants of *Tonpa Shenrab* in Dongba (Na-khi), Ruke Dongba (Zhěr-khin) and Daba (hli-khin): *dto-mba shi-lo*, *to-mba shera* / *to-mba zhěr-la*, and *ti-mba shera*, respectively. Fang (1981: 351) has documented the pronunciation *Dibba Shilo* (/ti˧bɑ˩ʂʅ˥lo˧/). Therefore, the epithet reveals this deity as a descendant of *lha-chen sTon-pa Shenrab* (ལྷ་ཆེན་སྟོན་པ་གཤེན་རབ་མི་བོ), literally meaning 'the great god – *bodhisattva* – Shenrab'. As mentioned above, Tonpa Shenrab in Bon was assimilated with Buddha. Like in the legend of Gautama, Tonpa Shenrab was a prince (of Tazig [rTag-gzigs]) before founding the Bon doctrine (Skorupski 1986: 39–40).[34] The fact that the Daba priest recognises *Laqi Dibishe* as a great god like *Śākyamuni*, instead of the preceptor of Dabaism, indicates a stage of the Bon transmission when Tonpa Shenrab was not yet completely "organic" to the indigenous beliefs of Moso.

5 Conclusion

This case study, developed with an anthropological-linguistic approach, analyses significant elements of the cultural heritage still preserved in the Sino-Tibetan borderland. The names of the Tibetan spirits in Dongbaism and Dabaism are generally transliterated in Mandarin contexts. However, through an in-depth etymological analysis, it is possible to narrow down their cultural origin, rather than assigning them to the generic context of Tibetan Buddhism. The etymology of the spirits'

---

34 According to Van Driem (2001: 33), "Tazig" refers to Bactria and Sogdiana. Scholars noticed the multiple sources of Bon (Tucci 1976: 304). The doctrines were brought to Zhang-Zhung by the disciples of Ton-pa Shen-rab, then transferred into Tibet. In Zhang-Zhung, Shen-rab is addressed as *dMu-ra*, and Bon is *gyer* (Snellgrove 1967).

names indicates that Dongba and Daba inherited their religious foundations from the Yung-Drung Bon doctrine, following a pattern similar to the making of Tibetan personal names. The designations of Buddhist deities were adapted into Tibetan languages through Zhang-Zhung, the extinct lingua franca spoken in Tibet (Hummel 2000: xiv; Matisoff 2001). The multi-syllabic designations are generally considered proper nouns (/anthroponyms). An etymological analysis of the segments reveals their descriptive features.

Zhang-Zhung belongs to the western Bodish/Tibetic language branch (Bradley 2002). The ancient Zhang-Zhung civilization originated as early as 3,900 years ago (Norbu 2013: 19), with archaeological discoveries dating roughly from 500 BC (Aldenderfer 2007). This kingdom of Bon "vanished" with the rise of Tibet in the mid-7th century, during the reign of Srongtsen Gampo (སྲོང་བཙན་སྒམ་པོ; Beckwith 1987: 20), just like the indigenous cultures gradually faded from Han Chinese contexts, possibly ever since the first Empire's Qin Dynasty. However, these "marginalised" cultures survived at the frontier between cultural borders. Dongbaism and Dabaism, accompanying the daily lives of the Moso People, turn out to be the echoes of the Bon religion through history.

Dongbaism and Dabaism were influenced, to different extents, by the Bon religion. When introduced to Dongbaism and Dabaism, the Tibetan cultural elements were adapted to the local languages. The dialectal differences could have generated distinctive pronunciations of the same deity names, or the same cultural terminology. The correspondences, sometimes, can be subtle in being recognised.

At the same time, Dongba and Daba priests may have developed distinctive interpretations of the role of the spirits. As a consequence, the same deity could have been assigned different roles in these two cultural contexts (e.g., *Mebu Zzeeru* [Daba] / *Mebiu Zzeeru* [Dongba], *Dibishe* [Daba] / *Dongba Shilo* [Dongba]). Indeed, the phonetic counterparts in the two religious branches do not correspond to the spirits' roles. Dongbaism has developed a more complex spiritual system compared to Dabaism, and has absorbed more Han Chinese notions.

Through an anthroponymic lens, it is possible to figure out the multi-layered knowledge structure described above and to analyse a spiritual world that, presumably, dates back to a remote era characterised by shamanic beliefs and reconstructable by following the linguistic traces of its path of transmission. Moreover, the stratified name system of the Dongba and Daba spirits contributes to the reconstruction of the cultural identity of the Moso community, which is an indispensable epistemological element in understanding the Chinese people as a population with diverse and multi-faceted origins (Fei 1989).

References

Aldenderfer, Mark. 2007. Defining Zhang Zhung ethnicity: An archaeological perspective from far western Tibet. In Amy Heller & Giacomella Orofino (eds.), *Discoveries in Western Tibet and the Western Himalayas: Essays on history, literature, archaeology and art. Tibetan Studies*, 1–22. Leiden: Brill.

Bacot, Jacques. 1913. *Les Mo-so. Ethnographie des Mo-so, leurs religions, leur langue et leur écriture.* Leiden: Brill.

Bai, Gengsheng. 2012. *Dongba Shenhua Yanjiu* [A study on Dongba mythology]. Kunming: Yunnan University Press.

Beckwith, Christopher. 1987. *The Tibetan empire in central Asia.* Princeton: Princeton University Press.

Beer, Robert. 2003. *The handbook of Tibetan Buddhist symbols.* Boulder: Shambhala.

Blount, Ben. 2009. *Handbook of pragmatics.* Athens: University of Georgia.

Bradley, David. 2002. The subgrouping of Tibeto-Burman. In Chris Beckwith & Henk Blezer (eds.), *Medieval Tibeto-Burman languages*, 73–112. Leiden: Brill.

Ceinos Arcones, Pedro. 2012. *Sons of heaven, brothers of nature: The Naxi of Southwest China.* Kunming: Papers of the White Dragon.

Chandra, Lokesh. 1999. *Dictionary of Buddhist iconography* (vol. 5). New Delhi: International Academy of Indian Culture and Aditya Prakashan.

Chos kyi grags pa. 1957. *Zangwen Cidian* [Mi rigs dpe skrun khaṅ gis Pe-cin du bskrun pa'o]. Beijing: Minzu Chubanshe.

Cihai Bianji Weiyuanhui [Editorial Committee of Cihai]. 1989. *Ci Hai* [Word ocean]. Shanghai: Shanghai Cishu Chubanshe.

Das, Sarat Chandra. 1902. *A Tibetan-English dictionary, with Sanskrit synonyms.* Calcutta: Bengal Secretariat Book Depot.

Diény, Jean-Pierre. 1987. *Le symbolisme du dragon dans la Chine antique.* Paris: L'Institut des Hautes Etudes Chinoises.

Dongba Culture Research Institute. 1999. *Naxi Dongba Guji Yizhu Quanji* [Complete collection of annotated Naxi Dongba manuscripts]. Kunming: Yunnan Remin Chubanshe.

Douglas, Nik. 1978. *Tibetan Tantric charms and amulets.* New York: Dover Publications.

Drège, Jean-Pierre & Costantino Moretti. 2014. *La fabrique du lisible. La mise en texte des manuscrits de la Chine ancienne et médiévale.* Paris: Collège de France, L'Institut des hautes études chinoises.

Ermakov, Dmitry. 2008. *Bø and Bön: Ancient Shamanic traditions of Siberia and Tibet in their relation to the teachings of a Central Asian Buddha.* Kathmandu: Vajra Publications.

Fang, Guoyu. 1944/2001. Mosuo Minzu Kao [A study of the Moso ethnic group]. In Chaomin Lin (ed.), *Fang Guoyu Wenji – Disi Ji* [Collected works of Fang Guoyu (IV)], 20–98. Kunming: Yunnan Jiaoyu Chubanshe.

Fang, Guoyu & Zhiwu He. 1979. Naxizu de Yuanyuan, Qianxi, he Fenbu [The Origin, Migration, and Distribution of Naxi People]. *Minzu Yanjiu* 1. 33–41.

Fang, Guoyu. 1981. *Naxi Xiangxing Wenzi Pu* [A dictionary of the Naxi pictographic writing]. Kunming: Yunnan Renmin Chubanshe.

Fang, Guoyu (ed.). 1998. *Yunnan Shiliao Congkan* [Historical series of Yunnan] (Vol. 3). Kunming: Yunnan Daxue Chubanshe.

Fei, Xiaotong. 1989. *Zhonghua Minzu Duoyuan Yiti Geju* [The Chinese people with multiple origins]. Beijing: Zhongyang Minzu Xueyuan Chubanshe.

Foley, William. 1997. *Anthropological linguistics: An introduction.* Oxford: Blackwell.

Fu, Maoji. 2012. *Naxizu Tuhua Wenzi "Baibianfu Qujing Ji Yanjiu"* [A study of a Naxi pictographic manuscript "white bat's search for sacred books"]. Beijing: Commercial Press.

Garey, Howard. 1957. Verbal aspects in French. *Language* 33. 91–110.

Ge, Agan. 1999. You Naxi Xiangxingwen Baocun de Hetu Luoshu [Hetu and Loshu preserved in Naxi pictographs]. *Minzu Yishu Yanjiu* (4). 3–22.

Gros, Stéphane. 2019. *Frontier Tibet: Patterns of change in the Sino-Tibetan borderlands*. Amsterdam: Amsterdam University Press.

Guo, Dalie. 1983. Muli Zangzu Zizhi Xian Xiangjiao Gongshe 'Nari' he 'Laze' Ren de Wenhua Xisu [The cultures and customs of Nari people and Laze people living in Xiangjiao Commune, Muli Tibetan Autonomous County]. In Shaoming Li & Tong Enzheng (eds.), *Yalong Jiang Xiayou Kaocha Baogao* [A report on the lower streams of the Yalong River], 106–126. Kunming: Zhongguo Xi'nan Minzu Xuehui.

Guo, Dalie & Zhiwu He. 1994. *Naxi Zu Shi* [History of Naxi People]. Chengdu: Sichuan Renmin Chubanshe.

Guo, Ying. 2017. Ren zai "Tiandi zhi Jian": Naren de Daba Wenhua yu Richang Shenghuo [Daba culture and daily life of Na People]. *Wenhua Yichan Yanjiu* (1). 25–37.

Hansson, Inga-Lill. 1997. Orally transmitted texts of the minorities in East and Southeast Asia: Suggestions for research across borders. *Asia Pacific Viewpoint* 38 (2). 145–154.

Harrell, Stevan. 2001. *Ways of being ethnic in Southwest China*. Seattle: University of Washington Press

He, Jiren & Zhuyi Jiang. 1985. *Naxi Yu Jianzhi* [A brief description of the Naxi language]. Beijing: Minzu Chubanshe.

He, Shuangquan. 1989. Tianshui Fangmatan Qinmu Chutu Ditu Chutan [A preliminary study on the map excavated from Qin tombs in Fangmatan (Tianshui)]. *Wenwu* 2. 12–22.

He, Zhiwu. 1989. *Naxi Dongba Wenhua* [Dongba culture of Naxi people]. Jilin: Jilin Jiaoyu Chubanshe.

Hoffmann, Helmut. 1944. Gsen. Eine lexikographisch-religionswissenschaftliche Untersuchung. *ZDMG* 98. 340–358.

Hummel, Siegbert. 1969. The sMe-ba-dgu, the magic square of the Tibetans. *East and West* 19 (1). 139–146.

Hummel, Siegbert. 1992. gShen. *Bulletin of Tibetology* 28 (3). 5–8.

Hummel, Siegbert. 2000. *On Zhang-Zhung*, trans. Guido Vogliotti. Dharamsala: Library of Tibetan works and archives.

Hymes, Dell. 1993. "Anthropological linguistics": A retrospective. *Anthropological Linguistics* 35 (1). 9–14.

Jackson, Anthony. 1979. *Na-khi Religion: An analytical appraisal of the Na-khi ritual texts*. Hague: De Gruyter.

Jacques, Guillaume & Alexis Michaud. 2011. Approaching the historical phonology of three highly eroded Sino-Tibetan languages: Naxi, Na, and Laze. *Diachronica* 28 (4). 468–498.

Karmay, Samten. 1997. *The arrow and the spindle: Studies in history, myths, rituals and beliefs in Tibet*. Kathmandu: Mandala Book Point.

Keown, Damien. 2003. *A dictionary of Buddhism*. Oxford: Oxford University Press.

Kværne, Per. 1972. Aspects of the origin of the Buddhist tradition in Tibet. *Numen* 19. 22–40.

Kværne, Per. 1995. *The Bon religion of Tibet: The iconography of a living tradition*. London: Serindia Publications.

Kværne, Per. 2009. Bon and Shamanism. *East and West* 59 (1). 19–24.

LaPolla, Randy. 2001. The role of migration and language contact in the development of Sino-Tibetan language family. In Robert Dixon & Alexandra Aikhenvald (eds.), *Areal diffusion and genetic inheritance: Case studies in language change*, 225–254. Oxford: Oxford University Press.

Li, Guowen. 1997. *Dongba Wenhua Cidian* [Dictionary of Dongba culture]. Kunming: Yunnan Jiaoyu Chubanshe.

Li, Lincan, Kun Zhang & Cai He. 1972. *A dictionary of Mo-So hieroglyphics*. Taipei: Wenshizhe Publishing House.

Li, Lincan, Kun Zhang & Cai He. 1978. *Mosuo jingdian yizhu jiuzhong* [Translations and annotations of Mo-So scriptures]. Taipei: National Institute for Compilation and Translation.

Li, Qunyu. 2001. *Xinbian Lijiang Fengwu Zhi* [New compilation of sceneries of Lijiang]. Kunming: Yunnan Renmin Chubanshe.

Li, Xueqin. 2004. *Zhongguo Gudai Wenming yu Guojia Xingcheng Yanjiu* [A study on the ancient Chinese civilization and the formation of nations]. Taipei: Zhishufang Chubanshe.

Lidz, Liberty. 2010. *A descriptive grammar of Yongning Na (Mosuo)*. Austin: University of Texas at Austin dissertation.

Mathieu, Christine. 2015. The story of Bon in the Naxi Dongba religion. In Andrea Di Castro & David Templeman (eds.), *Asian horizons: Giuseppe Tucci's Buddhist, Indian, Himalayan and Central Asian Studies*, 348–408. Melbourne: Monash University Publishing.

Matisoff, James. 2001. The interest of Zhangzhung for comparative Tibeto-Burman. In Yasuhiko Nagano & Randy LaPolla (eds.), *New research on Zhangzhung and related Himalayan languages*, 155–180. Osaka: National Museum of Ethnology.

Mawangdui Hanmu Boshu Zhengli Xiaozu [The repair team of silk manuscripts from Mawangdui Han tomb]. 1975. Changsha Mawangdui Sanhao Hanmu Chutu Ditu de Zhengli [The repair of the map excavated from the No. 3 Han Tomb in Mawangdui (Changsha)]. *Wenwu* 2. 35–42+97+101–102.

McKhann, Charles. 1995. The Naxi and the nationalities question. In Stevan Harrell (ed.), *Cultural encounters on China's ethnic frontiers*, 39–62. Seattle: University of Washington Press.

Michailovsky, Boyd & Alexis Michaud. 2006. Syllabic inventory of a Western Naxi dialect, and correspondence with Joseph F. Rock's transcriptions. *Cahiers de linguistique – Asie Orientale* 35 (1). 3–21.

Mueggler, Erik. 2011. *The paper road: Archive and experience in the botanical exploration of West China and Tibet*. Berkeley: University of California Press.

Ṅag dbaṅ mkhyen rab. 1735/1993. *Muli Zhengjiao Shi* [Mu-li chos 'byuṅ], trans. Lurong Geding. Chengdu: Sichuan Minzu Chubanshe.

Norbu, Namkhai. 2013. *The light of Kailash: A history of Zhang Zhung and Tibet, Volume 1: The early period*, trans. Donatella Rossi. Berkeley: North Atlantic Books.

Pinson, Thomas. 2012. *A Naxi-Chinese-English Dictionary*. Kunming: Yunnan Minzu Chubanshe.

Poupard, Duncan. 2020. With the power of their forefathers: Kinship between early Tibetan ritualists and the Naxi Dongba of South-West China. *Revue d'Etudes Tibétaines* 56. 89–124.

Qu, Aitang. 1999. *Zangzu de Yuyan he Wenzi* [The language and writing of Tibetan]. Beijing: Zhongguo Zangxue Chubanshe.

Rock, Joseph. 1937. The Zher-khin tribe and their religious literature. *Monumenta Serica* 3. 171–188.

Rock, Joseph. 1952. *The Na-khi Nāga cult and related ceremonies*. Rome: Instituto Italiano per II Medio ed Estremo Oriente.

Rock, Joseph. 1955. The Zhi-ma funeral ceremony of the Na-khi of Southwest China. *Anthropos* 9. i–xvi, 1–230.

Rock, Joseph. 1963. *A ^{1}Na-^{2}khi-English encyclopedic dictionary (Part I)*. Rome: Istituto Italiano per il Medio ed Estremo Oriente.

Rock, Joseph. 1972. *A ^{1}Na-^{2}khi-English encyclopedic dictionary (Part II)*. Rome: Istituto Italiano per il Medio ed Estremo Oriente.

Skorupski, Tadeusz. 1986. Tibetan G-Yung-Drung Bon monastery in India. *The Tibet Journal* 11 (2). 36–49.

Snellgrove, David. 1967. *The nine ways of Bon: Excerpts from gZi-brjid*. London: Oxford University Press.

Stein, Rolf. 1972. *Tibetan civilization*, trans. Stapleton Driver. Stanford: Stanford University Press.

Tong, Keli. 1989. *Xibozu Lishi yu Wenhua* [History and culture of the Sibe people]. Urumchi: Xinjiang Renmin Chubanshe.

Tucci, Giuseppe. 1976. *Le religioni del Tibet*. Rome: Edizioni Mediterranee.

Van Driem, George. 2001. Zhangzhung and its next of kin in the Himalayas. *Senri Ethnological Reports* 19. 31–44.

Xu, Duoduo. 2016. Lunar mansion names in South-West China: An etymological reconstruction of ancestral astronomical designations in Moso, Pumi, and Yi cultures compared with Chinese and Tibetan contexts. *Onoma* 51. 101–129.

Xu, Duoduo. 2017. Five newly documented village names of Moso people: A frontier toponoymic system. *Review of Historical Geography and Toponomastics* 12: 37–44.

Xu, Duoduo. 2018. The five-color theme in Dongba scriptures. *Asian Highlands Perspectives* 51. 33–65.

Xu, Duoduo. 2021. Noun-epithets of Dongba and Daba oral traditions. *Linguistics of Tibeto-Burman Area* 44. 133–156.

Yang, Fuquan. 2012. *Dongbajiao Tonglun* [A general introduction to Dongbaism]. Beijing: Zhonghua Shuju.

Zhang, Jinsheng. 1733/1999. *Sichuan Tongzhi* [Annals of Sichuan] (vol. 2). In Yun Ji, Xixiong Lu and Shiyi Sun. (eds.) *Siku Quanshu – Shibu 11 Dili* [Complete books of the four repositories, history XI, geography]. Hong Kong: Digital Heritage Publishing Limited.

Zhao, Zhizhong. 2002. "Saman" Cikao [The etymology of "Saman"]. *Zhongyang Minzu Daxue Xuebao* 3. 139–141.

Eyo O. Mensah

Chapter 12 The appropriation of animal names as personal names in Ibibio and Tiv onomastic traditions in Nigeria: An ethnopragmatic study

Abstract: This chapter explores the motivations for the adoption of animal names as personal names among the Ibibio and Tiv people of Nigeria from an ethnopragmatic conceptual framework. The study examines the physical connection between animals and humans, and the cultural practices or beliefs that influence the choice of animal names as personal names. Data were collected through participant observations, semi-structured interviews and informal conversations with participants in Uyo and Makurdi, where the Ibibio and Tiv people are predominantly found. The study discovered that the two cultures exhibit functional similarities in which animals have a profound social and cultural relationship with humans and the natural environment, playing significant roles as religious totems for worship and as objects of sacrifice for ritual purposes. Parents, therefore, give the names of certain animals to their children to project their social, cultural and religious leanings and ideologies. Others admire certain specific characteristics of these animals, such as courage/bravery (lion), strength (tiger), resilience (eagle), invincibility (frog), aggression (crocodile) and large size (elephant and hippopotamus). Ethnopragmatically, it is the locally constitutive meaning ascribed to the desirable features, character or behaviour of these animals in addition to their actual physical attributes that gives rise to personal names bestowed on children. The study aims to highlight the permeating social influence of animals in the larger

Acknowledgements: The research leading to these results has received funding from the European Union's Horizon 2020 research and innovation programme under the Marie Sklodowska-Curie grant agreement No.754340, awarded to the author; I owe a debt of gratitude for this funding. I also wish to thank the Freiburg Institute for Advanced Studies (FRIAS), University of Freiburg for the award of the Marie S. Curie FCFP Senior Fellowship, during which stay this research was carried out. I am grateful to the anonymous reviewers of this article. They contributed insights and perspectives that greatly improved the quality of this chapter. I thank all the participants who participated in this study, especially Jighjigh Ishima (Benue State University, Nigeria) and Iniobong Ekpo (University of KwaZulu-Natal, South Africa). I thank Evelyn Effiong for referencing assistance. The remaining errors are mine.

Eyo O. Mensah, University of Calabar and University of Ghana, e-mail: eyoomensah@unical.edu.ng

https://doi.org/10.1515/9783110759297-012

cultural framework of the Nigeria society and to illuminate how animals can be re-inserted into the structure of indigenous knowledge systems through naming.

Keywords: animals, personal names, identity, ethnopragmatics, Ibibio, Tiv

1 Introduction

The Ibibio people are found predominantly in Akwa Ibom State, south-eastern Nigeria. They speak the Ibibio language, a Lower-Cross language of the Benue-Congo sub-family of the larger Niger-Congo family of languages (Faraclas 1989). The Tiv people occupy north-central areas of Nigeria in Benue, Taraba, Nasarawa and Plateau states. They speak Tiv, a member of the Tivoid family of languages of the Benue-Congo family of the Niger-Congo phylum (Mensah and Ishima 2020). The Ibibio and Tiv cultural traditions share a common concern in bestowing animal-related names on children. This practice is rooted in the pervading social influence, economic significance, agricultural importance and nutritional value of animals in these societies. The relationship between humans and animals in every cultural tradition has informed perceptions and laid the foundations for the representation of animals based on locally constitutive connotations. This is reflected in the way humans have adopted animal names as personal names for their children in the Ibibio and Tiv cultural contexts.

Personal names are linguistic universals that convey important social and cultural information about the name giver and bearer. Every society uses personal names in some form (Bramwell 2016). They are primary modes of identification and means of individuating or distinguishing members of the society. Among the Ibibio and Tiv people of Nigeria, animal-inspired names form an important source of personal names. They are an important means of integrating newly-born children into their societies. This justifies the claim by Geerts (1973), who argues that naming is the act of converting anybody into somebody; Haviland et al. (2013) put it more succinctly when they state that the practice of naming an infant in any society marks its social transmission from a state of nature to a state of culture. This evidence points to the fact that the naming tradition of every culture signals the beginning of the name bearer's recognition as an authentic social being. Blount (2015) maintains that personal names carry different social significances, and represent their bearers' cultural, social and legal identity. This state of affairs implies that names are interesting aspects of human lives and societies with their unique cultural references and connotations. They are full of significant resonances, linking their bearers to family history, cultural traditions and other social aspects of life (Eckert and McConnell-Ginet 2013).

Among Nigerian onomastic traditions, naming means different things to different people; the general consensus, however, is that naming is a reflection of the values, norms, philosophy and worldviews of the people. Agyekum (2006) describes the functional correlation between culture and naming. He maintains that (African) names are not arbitrary labels but are very much based on socio-cultural and ethnopragmatic contexts of their bestowal and use. The main point of his argument was that while Western names are predictable, African names are generally not predictable, but are defined by the social and cultural contexts that identify their bearers. They are also embedded with enormous cultural scripts that give access to the interpretation of cultural experiences. Blount (2015) corroborates this position further when he states that personal names can link individuals into social histories, both locally within the family and more broadly within society, both reflective of an underlying system of knowledge. This evidence also buttresses the claim that personal names are essential aspects of the cultural and historical systems in which the society is embedded. In every culture, there is a physical connection between humans and animals with varying degrees of interaction. Animals have a profound relationship with humans and the environment and one way of sustaining this interface, for the Ibibio and Tiv people of Nigeria, is the adoption of animal names as personal names.

This chapter interrogates the choice of animal-related names as personal names among the Ibibio and Tiv people of Nigeria from an ethnopragmatic approach (Goddard 2006; Goddard and Ye 2015), with a view to deepening understanding of how the anthropocentric order can be deconstructed. Ethnopragmatic insights will enable understanding of the motivations for and perception of the adoption of animal-related names as personal names. The study unveils the sociocultural values that are hidden in animal-related personal names, and highlights the flow of knowledge between humans and animals that is useful in protecting and preserving aspects of traditional names. The study is a significant entry point into the anthropology of naming, as it illuminates the place of animals in our social reality.

2 Personal names and naming in the African cultural context

Personal names are the foremost means of constructing social identities. They are used to individuate, reference and address their bearers as unique personalities within a particular society or community of practice. Naming is a form of cultural communication that often resonates with the historical experience and social reality of the name giver (Ansu-Kyeremeh 2000; Mensah, Alexander and Ayeni 2022). This form of communication is often created within a multiplicity of contexts. Alford (1988) argues that names are effectively used to categorise individuals as males and females. In this way, naming strengthens gender identification and socialisation. Parents also use names to communicate their beliefs and expectations. One such belief is their religious identity and orientation. Mensah (2020) maintains that personal naming is a productive site for the performance of religious identity and for situating religious beliefs in their external spiritual world. The study identifies religious identity as a form of social capital which simultaneously reinforces community solidarity and cohesion. Such religion-related names relate the name giver's transcendental experiences and religious virtues, which are embodied in the name bearer as a means of coping with life's challenges. In certain cultures, names provide insights into communal or family occupations. Among the Ibibio and Tiv people of Nigeria, for instance, occupational names are bestowed on children to sustain a family's line of business or to showcase opportunities for entrepreneurship (Mensah et al. 2019; Mensah 2015). Such names are also used to reinforce family identity, and to create avenues for empowerment and social support.

Names and naming can also be used to communicate different shades of emotion and state of mind. According to Mensah, Dzokoto and Rowan (2021), some African traditional names have emotional information encoded in them, especially the expression of negative and positive emotional states which define the psychological development of the name-bearer. In some African contexts, particularly where name avoidance taboos persist, calling certain people by their names could be seen as impolite behaviour. In Cameroon, for instance, Anchimbe (2011) demonstrates how alternative nomenclatures and pseudonyms are used in the place of personal names in order to be polite and show deference to the addressee. According to this thinking, reinforcing name avoidance can enable one to benefit from the addressee's in-group social acceptance and maintain societal order and communion.

The phenomenon of death-prevention names is pervasive in the literature of African anthroponyms (see Akung and Abang 2019; Doyle 2008; Obeng 1998; Mamvura 2021; Mensah 2015; Mensah and Offong 2013; Sagna and Bassène 2016). These studies concur in their recognition of the tension between underworld forces and humans. This mainly results in the bestowal of despicable names on children in order to hide their identities from the underworld spiritual forces and to ensure their survival. Names in this regard serve as a form of communication between the living and the dead. They demonstrate the inevitability of death and recognise the existence of a superior power that holds the key to life and death (Mensah 2015; Mamvura 2021). Names and naming can also be used as tools for power, control and dominance. The adoption of English names by many of the world's cultures and traditions is not only evidence of growing globalisation but a tacit acceptance of English as a global brand and identity. Mensah (2022) argues that the *Englishisation* of Africa's indigenous names is strongly related to favourableness towards western culture and influence, and is a style that affiliates name bearers with modernity, prestige and power. The English language has reinforced its domination in many cultural contexts across the world and this hegemony has suppressed lesser indigenous languages and cultures and compromised their cultural integrity. Since names are part of the lexicon that constitutes language, they are not immune to such influence. This evidence reveals that names are not rigid markers of identity, but rather, are fluid and dynamic.

Names and naming in Africa can also be sources of social dialogues and cultural narratives with the physical environment. These mainly include the topography, floral and faunal resources. These natural resources are useful in providing food, shelter, occupation and protection to mankind and are incorporated into the onomastic system, which speaks to their usefulness within the ecosystem. They also enhance the economic and social well-being of the people. Iloh (2021) recounts that natural resource-related names are bestowed on children as a way of appreciating the value they have added to human existence, health and general well-being. Mensah et al. (2019), however, argue that such names (among the Tiv people of Nigeria) are ways of recreating and maintaining natural resources and promoting the prosperity of the community. The present study further extends scholarship on the relationship between naming and the natural environment with a particular focus on the appropriation of animal names as personal names, which reinforces interdependence and harmony and strengthens social relations between higher and lower animals.

3 The connection between animals and humans

Animals are important biological resources that have contributed to the preservation of a healthy natural environment all over the world. An evaluation of the relationship between humans and animals has been informed by historical, social, religious, biological and philosophical factors (Lohani 2010; Maehle 1994). This relationship is often defined in terms of mutual dependability and continuity. Humans rely on animals for their subsistence, economy, security, medicine and even leisure, as animals are sources of meat and protein, with immense commercial value and with a significant role in sports and entertainment. In the Ibibio and Tiv cultural contexts, where there are rich faunal assemblages, animals are valuable resources in their bio-cultural diversity, and are of central concern to the anthropocentric imaginary and contemporary social life of their societies. Animals depend on humans for their welfare, domestication and conservation. They are of high value to the society. Animals are rich sources of protein and energy through meat, fish, milk, honey and eggs, which are absorbable micronutrients that are highly nutritious. Animal-based foods contribute to a healthy diet. According to Roesel (2019), animal-sourced foods contribute towards food and nutrient security in terms of caloric (energy) intake and also in terms of the nutrients that are essential for the healthy functioning of the human body.

Animals also serve draught purposes (e.g. bull, ass etc.) and others function in transporting agricultural products from one location to another (e.g. donkey, camel etc.). Netam and Jaiswal (2018) state that draught animals are used for agricultural operations like tillage, seedbed preparation, sowing, weeding, threshing and post-harvest operations. The use of these animals has reduced the need for human labour in cultivation, weeding and harvesting. In this way, animals increase human productivity, improve efficiency, enhance the quality of products and encourage large-scale farming and production (Reynolds et al. 2015). Employing these animals in the field has also reduced stress and injuries, thus improving the health quality and well-being of humans. Animals are also used in sport, leisure activities and amusement, especially in racing and organised fighting. There are growing global concerns from animal rights defenders, who campaign to ban the use of animals in entertainment, competitive games and spectacle or recreational activities to safeguard the lives of the animals involved, which may be subjected to confinement and deprivation. Scanes (2018) supports such a move in order to end the high rate of cruelty towards animals: a lifetime in chains and cages and the barbaric pumping of animals full of steroids and pain killers. The portrayal of animals in these activities is demeaning and distressful, and is an example of animals suffering in human care.

Animals also provide avenues for generating economic resources for individuals, companies and even countries. Leather industries around the world depend on hides and skin as their primary raw materials. Manufactured goods such as footwear, bags, sofas, garments and belts are leather products which provide employment opportunities to many people and help some countries like China, Brazil, Russia and India to gain foreign exchange from exports. Animal skins from sheep, goats and cows are also used in the production of musical instruments like drums and traditional bagpipes (Garaj 2011). The gut strings that are used in stringing guitars and violins also come from animals. Piano keys can be made from a variety of animal bones. Animal horns, mainly from ram, cow and elephant tusks, are used to make local trumpets and pipes for traditional music and other purposes. Cox (2012) believes that manufacturers have preferred domestic animal skins over synthetic plastic (in the past) for musical instruments because of their durability and the beautiful melodies they produce. He contends that such instruments give music a sense of feeling.

Significantly, animals also have socio-religious values. Teeter (2000) identifies animal worship rituals and animal sacrifice as two ways in which animals are related to humans spiritually. Animal worship involves the veneration of a god by means of a representative animal, for example, in certain places, like in Idemili, Anambra State, eastern Nigeria, sacred snakes are worshipped as religious totems. Snakes are believed to be household spirits that contain the souls of deceased ancestors (Ekeopara 2011). Animal sacrifice, on the other hand, entails killing and offering an animal for a ritual purpose. This practice hinges on the belief that in the history of religious ideas the earliest gods were animals or plants (Jones 2005). The purpose of animal worship and/or sacrifice is the glorification of sacred animal deities to seek guidance or protection or to appease them for a past wrongdoing. It is widely believed that in places where this practice is prevalent, animals are not worshipped for their own sake; instead, the sacred power of a deity was believed to be manifested in an appropriate animal that was regarded as a representation or incarnation of the deity (Britannica 2021). This evidence reveals that animals are part of the religious culture in some societies, and they give meaning and expression to the divine order.

Another crucial usefulness of animals to humanity has been in the area of medical science, particularly in orthodox and traditional medicine, a phenomenon that has come to be known as “zootherapy” (Alves and Alves 2011). Animal-based remedies are believed to be cheap, effective and accessible, especially in traditional medicine, where they have rich therapeutic and medical properties. The animals that provide the raw materials for these remedies are usually found in the wild (Soewu and Adekanola 2011). Animal-based remedies offer protection against fatal infections and provide antibacterial and antibiotic medications to improve people’s health and well-being as complementary medicine.

Humans also keep animals as pets for companionship and security. Such animals include dogs, cats and birds. Studies have found that, in comparison with people without pets, those with pets have some relative advantages, which include health and mood-boosting. Acher (1997) reports that ownership of pets reduces stress and anxiety, and creates opportunities for socialisation, as it helps pet owners to meet new people, overcome loneliness and add value to their daily routine. From the afore-mentioned review, it is evident that there exists a strong bond between animals and humans, and the relationship between them is symbiotic; while humans derive enormous benefits from their association with animals, they are also disposed to care for animals by providing for their welfare and keeping them in clean and hygienic environments. Midgely (1988: 36) aptly captures this relationship thus: “animal characteristic properties can be used to supply a foil, a dramatic contrast lighting up the human image”.

4 Ethnopragmatics and the study of personal names

This study adopts the ethnopragmatic model as the analytical framework to drive the interpretation of data and discussion of the findings. Ethnopragmatics is an approach to the study of meaning in language in terms of locally constitutive beliefs or insiders' perspectives. It investigates the cultural logic that reinforces verbal interactions by using semantic explications and cultural scripts. Goddard (2006) emphasises that ethnopragmatics deals with how the speech practices of a particular speech community can be understood from a culture-internal perspective in terms of values, norms and beliefs. Taken as a whole, it is concerned with understanding discourse in a cultural context. Goddard and Ye (2015) identify semantic explications and cultural scripts as the primary methodological tools of ethnopragmatics. They contend that semantic explications are based on decomposing cultural notions in terms of simple meanings that appear to be shared between all languages, using Natural Semantic Metalanguage (NSM), which avoids implicit Anglo-centrism and standardises the terms of description. The notion of cultural scripts, on the other hand, is "a powerful new technique for articulating cultural norms, values, and practices which are clear, precise and accessible to cultural insiders and to cultural outsiders alike" (Goddard and Wierzbicka 2004: 153). Cultural scripts, therefore, activate core values, ideals and background norms that enable people to understand and interpret cultural experiences.

The ethnopragmatic model has been applied in a wide range of studies involving local speech practices. Gladkova and Romero-Trillo (2014) conduct an ethnopragmatic analysis of the concept of beauty in English, Russian and Spanish, and conclude that the distribution of meaning across different lexical domains suggests the presence of different models of cultural, contextual and cognitive patterns in the three languages. Similarly, Ameka (2009) examines access rituals with a particular emphasis on greetings and libation rituals in some Ghanaian languages and cultures, and observes that there are constraints on these communicative interactions in terms of their enactment, ideologies and values they embody. Levisen (2018) applies the ethnopragmatic framework to the analysis of black humour, which is commonly constructed as a local catalogue for socially recognised laughing. He compares Danish, French and English conceptualisations of blackness in humour performances, which vary considerably. He concludes that the main function of Danish black humour is to enhance the feeling of group solidarity. Mensah, Silva and Inyabri (2020) have utilised the ethnopragmatic framework to explicate the practice of libation rituals among the Kiong-speaking Okoyong people in Odukpani, south-eastern Nigeria. The study interrogates libation rituals as locally coherent and meaningful performances that offer a renewed sense of security to the living. The practice is vital in sustaining the transition, mobility and sacredness that connect the living with the ancestors, who are the sources of tribal tradition and its stability. Based on a review of these studies, ethnopragmatics highlights semantic repertoire and cultural scripts in local speech situations. It attempts to increase understanding of speech practices in terms of what makes sense to the people concerned. We must be able to understand the meaning of the relevant culturally important labels and words for local values, social categories, speech acts, and so on (Goddard and Wierzbicka 2004).

Naming is a culture-specific speech practice, and many studies have adopted the ethnopragmatic framework to investigate and shape conversations on names and naming. Mensah (2015) uses the ethnopragmatic approach to investigate the phenomenon of death-prevention names among the Ibibio. He opines that such names are used to generate and maintain some level of assurance and security that is vital for a name bearer's survival, given the implicit assumption that spiritual forces are at work. Similarly, Mamvura (2021) also investigates death-prevention names among the Karanga people in Zimbabwe through the ethnopragmatic framework. He submits that such names counter the power of supernatural forces, which are believed to be responsible for the death of children. The author concludes that death-prevention names are not mere arbitrary labels but are expressions with larger sociocultural meanings. In a related study, Ehiheni (2019b) uses ethnopragmatic theory to explicate how Yoruba personal names are formed and their socio-onomastic functions in the Yoruba ethnolinguistic ecology. The study describes Yoruba names as linguistic categories with a deep indexical relationship to sociocultural significations. The ethnopragmatic approach has also been adopted by Boluwaduro (2019) to analyse ideological and identity processes in Ibibio personal names. The study argues that Ibibio names are intrinsically localised to enable name bearers to transfer the cultural conceptualisation of their names into their lived experiences. This study is closely linked to Mensah et al. (2021), which uses the ethnopragmatic approach to investigate emotion-referencing names among the Ibibio. They maintain that Ibibio names are used to express emotion and construct the personhood and identity of the name bearer. The names have both positive and negative valance, which may impact psychologically on the name bearer's perception of self. These studies reveal that personal names are significant linguistic symbols which are culturally conceptualised and contextualised. Names are words and expressions that exist in the lexicon of a language; their interpretation is not based on semantic stereotypes but on another level of meaning that takes cognisance of the local culture and its interpretive force.

5 Methodology

This qualitative ethnographic research involved a ten-month process of field data collection in Uyo (Akwa Ibom State, south-eastern Nigeria) and Makurdi (Benue State, north-central Nigeria). The choice of these research sites was facilitated by an already established community of practice where the use of animal names as personal names is a prevalent cultural practice. The researcher employed the services of two language assistants in each study area (fluent speakers of the Ibibio and Tiv languages), who liaised between participants and the researcher. Fifteen participants were selected in each area using the purposive sampling technique. Participants were selected by the field assistants based on their willingness to participate in the research, and on being bearers, givers or users of animal-related personal names. In addition, they demonstrated a vast knowledge of names and naming as cultural practices. The socio-demographic characteristics of each participant, including name, age, gender, marital status, education, occupation and religion, were recorded. All participants' names have been anonymised. The age range of participants falls between 15 and 77 years. Some of these variables were useful in terms of the cultural contexts in which personal names were given and used, and they also shaped and influenced the choice of names. All participants gave informed consent for interviews and recordings. For those who could not read or write, the consent statements were read and interpreted for them to sign.

Three ethnographic approaches were employed in the data collection process: participant observations, semi-structured interviews and informal conversations. Participant observation is an approach that afforded the researcher a first-hand opportunity for interaction with name bearers, givers and users, including parents, community members, elders, chiefs and peer group members. In this regard, the researcher had twenty encounters in each research area in meeting halls, households, farms, playgrounds and streets. Semi-structured interviews enabled the researcher to work around the participants' schedules and convenience, and to elicit more personal information about the motivations for and meanings of names. This approach also helped the researcher to adjust questions and incorporate new information that acted as an impetus for further questioning. Participants in each area were interviewed to understand their opinions and perceptions towards animal names adopted as personal names. There was informal conversation with participants about the motivations for the names and their sources. Open-ended questions were asked concerning choices of names and their subjective interpretations. In this regard, participants talked about the kinds of situations they faced that prompted the bestowal of animal names. The researcher sought to understand the mechanisms of this naming regime through local history, in addition to these field observations, and why these mechanisms are more prevalent among the Ibibio and Tiv people than other indigenous people in Nigeria. The researcher also sought to understand the perceptions of community members and their inner thoughts regarding the use of animal names as personal names.

A digital audio recorder and field notes were used as tools for data collection for the study. A corpus of 50 animal-related names was obtained from the field across the two areas, given the rich history of this category of personal names in the Ibibio and Tiv cultures. There was a total of three hours of audio recordings of interviews in each area with name bearers, givers and users. Data were coded into relevant social categories, transcribed and translated. The conceptual framework has therefore limited the scope of the relevant data to only animal-related personal names. The descriptive method has been adopted in the analysis, interpretation and discussion. This method highlights the main features of the data and accentuates the views, opinions and perspectives of participants in their own words.

6 Data analysis

In the analysis that follows, I categorise animal-related names in the Ibibio and Tiv onomastic systems into the relevant cultural scripts or thematic tropes. The representation of power is a salient motivation, followed by their use as death-prevention labels, in addition to other peculiar traits and symbolisms which are admired in animals.

6.1 Animal names that symbolise power

The Ibibio and Tiv are highly patriarchal societies where the bestowal of names on children is a gendered practice. Male and female children are named and socialised based on the existing gender binary and traditional gender division of labour. Men are socially expected to act in their prescribed roles as bread winners in their families and assume privileged positions in the society, and women are expected to be in charge of home management and the rearing of children. This pattern of distribution often results in unequal power relations. In these traditions, male children are given animal-related names as a representation of power. The animals in Tables 12.1 and 12.2 have physical characteristics such as power, strength, courage and fierceness. The adoption of their names as personal names is representative of a prototype of masculinity. For instance, a participant was asked to explain why he named his son *Ɓeghà* 'Lion' (Tiv) and his response was as follows:

> The lion has many positive attributes in Tiv mythology: first, it is a very courageous animal; it is also widely regarded as the king of jungle, that is a mark of royalty, and significantly, lions are very social animals. They live in groups, work together to defend the territory and hunt. These are the salient features I wish to see him imbibe in the future. They will guide his life as a man. (Alagh 43)

This participant has shown from this account that it is the attributes which an animal has that are identified and communicated through names, thus making naming a socially situated discursive practice (Mensah et al. 2021). The same ideology lies behind the names *Ékpè* 'Leopard/Lion' and *Énìn* 'Elephant' among the Ibibio. In essence, these attributes shape name bearers' psycho-social development, and speak more to their aspirations in life. From the perspective of ethnopragmatics, an ideal man deserves to be powerful in terms of working hard to provide for his family. The man has to show the impulse to love his wife and children, and assert his influence on his family and beyond. He needs to be courageous to protect and care for his family. Part of this protection is the provision of a safe, healthy and happy environment for his family. Significantly, he has to value people and promote communal living, where one person's challenge is everybody's challenge. Royalty symbolises wealth, which is a parental expectation for an enduring social status for their children. According to one participant, the Tiv community is an inclusive society where people are valued and appreciated. Interdependent relationships define the organisational structure of the society, and communality and co-operation with one another are the basis for harmonious social relationships (Mensah and Eni 2019).

Table 12.1: Ibibio male names that index power.

Ibibio name	**Gloss**
Ékpè	Leopard/Lion
Òfiòm [Èfiòm]	Crocodile
Ńtrúpóm	Eagle
Ásábọ́	Python
Énàñ	Bull

The crocodile was also portrayed as a very powerful reptile in the two cultures, and is equally part of their onomastic traditions. Crocodiles occupy a wide variety of aquatic habitats, and co-exist with a great diversity of human cultures in a variety of social and economic contexts (Pooley 2016). This implies that crocodiles are an essential part of the Ibibio and Tiv social existence. In both cultures, crocodiles are perceived as monsters which "loom large in people's imagination" (Fijn 2013: 1).

Table 12.2: Tiv male names that reflect power.

Tiv name	Gloss
Bèghá	Lion
Ámbè	Crocodile
Gáfá	Eagle
Kùsùgh	Electric Eel
Ńyínyá	Horse

Among the Ibibio, crocodiles play a role in their earliest spiritual lives. The crocodile is considered a sacred animal and a revered creature. One participant believed that it was used to embody ancestors in the Ibibio cosmology. However, its contemporary symbolism is that it represents toughness and aggression, which are attributes that align with masculine ideals. These are notable features which are within the dimension of power. Names like *Èfiòm* (Ibibio) and *Ámbè* (Tiv) are used to promote the qualities embodied in the crocodile.

The eagle also has a rich cultural history among the Ibibio and Tiv people. It represents strength, bravery and wisdom in the two cultures. Additionally, the Ibibio portray the eagle as a symbol of freedom. According to this portrayal, the eagle has limitless creativity and imagination, and is not restrained by space or time. A participant maintained that the eagle is a powerful and intelligent bird because it can fly to an altitude beyond the reach of other birds and see the world from a higher perspective than human beings. The bestowal of names from this category is tied to the personhood and authentic social selves of the name bearers so that these attributes can define their psychological growth and future developmental trajectories.

Bulls and horses are important social animals among the Ibibio and Tiv people respectively. For the Ibibio, *Énàñ* 'Bull' is portrayed as a symbol of great stamina, strength, determination and stubbornness. These are essential traits of masculinity which parents desire their male children to have in order to motivate their behaviour and guide their life courses more broadly. A participant justified the choice of his name, *Énàñ* 'Bull' as follows:

> The bull is a very muscular animal with extraordinary courage and strength. It displays strong will and what I may call positive stubbornness because you cannot coerce it to do your bidding all the time. These are the qualities I value in the animal, and they have driven my personality and given meaning to my life. (Felix 49).

Significantly, this participant also alluded to the unique attributes embedded in his name as the motivation for the bestowal of the name, and he tended to be guided by the socially-conceived attributes of this name in directing his life course.

The Tiv participants argued that horses are highly valuable animals in the Tiv cultural context. They are mainly projected as symbols of endurance, strength, courage and freedom. A participant further reiterated the importance of horses by saying that apart from their masculine attributes, horses are beautiful animals with valour and integrity. He stated that these are also essential values of life one could imbibe to improve positive attitudes and co-operation. The electric eel (fish) among the Tiv is also regarded as a symbol of strength and masculinity, given its ability to shock and its use of electricity to navigate its world. A participant explained the choice of his son's name *Kùsùgh* 'Electric Eel' in this way:

> The electric eel is a celebrated creature among our people. It is one fish that is respected for its bravery and strong character because it knows how to teach its enemies the lessons of their lives. These are the noble qualities and ideals l expect to see my son embodying as he grows up. (Caleb 52)

This account details the fact that a seemingly simple creature like electric eel can have a deeper meaning embedded in the cultural semantics of the Tiv, which can inform a person's life's course, destiny and emotional well-being. On the whole, it has been established that the appropriation of animal names as personal names by the Ibibio and Tiv people is largely based on perceptions of qualities or power semantics that are unique to these animals. By giving this category of names to children, participants are reinscribing and recreating the social, cultural and religious significance of animals in their anthropomorphic existence.

6.2 Animal names as death-prevention labels

In both Ibibio and Tiv cultures, there is a strong belief in reincarnation, which defines a cycle of birth-death-rebirth of children to the same family. Children are valued as reincarnated ancestors in these traditions, and one way of continually renewing the relationship between the living and the dead is through naming. Names are used to rejuvenate and enliven the memory of dead ancestors. Such names are believed to strengthen paternal bonds and establish stronger connection between name bearers and their living or dead relatives (Close 2012; Mensah, Silva and Inyabri 2020). However, the problem of infant mortality has greatly disrupted the reconciliation of the past (represented by the ancestors) with the present (represented by living beings). To bridge this gap, certain names are carefully selected and bestowed on children to fight infant mortality. Animal-related names form an important regime of such names.

Among the Ibibio and Tiv, animal-related names, which are represented in Tables 12.3 and 12.4, are bestowed on children in circumstances involving infant mortality and reincarnation. The Ibibio regard the animals in Table 12.3 as worthless; they do not have any economic, nutritious or intrinsic cultural value. They are merely used as strategies to deceive underworld spiritual forces that a child is not valued or wanted so that its life can be spared. A participant explained the subtle psychology behind the choice of these names as follows:

Table 12.3: Ibibio animal names as death-prevention labels.

Ibibio name	Gloss
Íkúọ́d	Frog
Ékpọ́k	Lizard
Ékpú	Rat
Ùtèrè	Vulture
Ídíáñ	Cricket

Table 12.4: Tiv animal names as death-prevention labels.

Tiv name	Gloss
Ígyō	Pig
Íkyègh	Fowl
Bágù	Monkey
Alōm	Hare
Ìkyángè	Guinea Fowl

> These names are generally given to children in order to assuage the wrath of the spirits against them. In Ibibio cosmology, such children were asked by their spiritual parents to come to earth and inflict pain and agony on their earthly parents; when they fail to discharge this responsibility, they are recalled to the spiritual world. So these names serve to counteract such destructive influences to enable the child to live. (Efiong 67)

This account acknowledges the existence of forces which are in a higher realm of existence than humans, and which can also influence the course of human activities and events. The animal names appropriated as personal names in this context are portents of evil. They are viewed with highly negative feelings. Some of them, like vulture, have a strong connection to supernatural activities. They represent bad luck and potential danger. Others, like lizard and rat, are associated with inhospitable events, which are believed to be used in magic. Taken together, animals which do not have strong social connections with the Ibibio are often used as death-prevention strategies.

The Tiv, on the other hand, share the same beliefs and ideologies as the Ibibio on infant mortality and the bestowal of death-prevention names, but instead use animals which can be domesticated as death-prevention names. They believe that these animals have deep symbolisms in their cultural history and are thus to be projected in the lives of the name bearers. According to one participant, *Ígyō* 'Pig', is a symbol of wealth and good luck, *Íkyègh* 'Fowl' represents the virtue of parental care and love, *Bágù* 'Monkey' stands for joyfulness and intelligence, *Alōm* 'Hare' signifies rebirth or the renewal of life, and *Ìkyángè* 'Guinea fowl' stands for industriousness and an enterprising spirit. Generally, this regime of names is widely used as reverse psychology, a form of manipulation that involves giving a name that does not seem to be desired on the surface, with the aim of expecting an opposite effect.

6.3 Other attributes embedded in animal names

There are cultural depictions of other animals by the Ibibio and Tiv which led to their names being adopted as personal names. Such animals play essential roles in their societies. Tables 12.5 and 12.6 demonstrate names in this category. *Éwá* 'Dog' among the Ibibio is portrayed as a symbol of loyalty, protection and love. It is the closest animal to humans in terms of bonding, friendliness and social presence. According to one participant, children are named after these dog-specific attributes to enable them to appreciate these values as the foundation upon which to model their character traits. Chimpanzees are also valued among the Ibibio for their curiosity, creativity and playfulness.

Table 12.5: Ibibio animal names with other significations.

Ibibio name	Gloss
Éwá	Dog
Ọ́mọ́n	Chimpanzee
Íním	Parrot
Énìn	Elephant
Ékwọ̀ñ	Snail

Parents draw references from these attributes into their children's lives through naming. In this respect, animal names are generally components of cultural identity formation and define the way in which people make sense of their social worlds. *Íním* 'Parrot' is a bird highly valued by the Ibibio people because of its beauty and

Table 12.6: Tiv animal names with other significations.

Tiv name	Gloss
Bùá	Bullock
Àzèmbè	Black Kite
Gbèr	Nightjar
Nōr	Elephant
Gbíndè	Adder

bright colours. It is believed to be a source of good fortune and represents beauty and intelligence. It has a reputation as a 'talking bird' and features prominently in Ibibio folk culture, including stories, songs and oratory. On why children are named after parrots in Ibibioland, a participant explained as follows:

> *Íním* 'Parrot' is a name that is given to a very beautiful, intelligent and loquacious child. It does not celebrate loquaciousness per se but guides the name bearer to be mindful of what he or she says because there is real power behind words. The power to create and destroy is on the lips. (Nsikak 60)

Based on this account, the ethnopragmatic reading of the name is to guide people to be circumspect in their verbal behaviour; to evaluate the use of their tongue in a way that will not land them in trouble, especially in a culture that values free speech. Therefore, the essence of a name like *Íním* 'Parrot' among the Ibibio is for people to keep their words healthy and become more introspective about them.

The elephant is another important social animal in Ibibio cultural history. It is valued for its large size, stamina and fertility. This cultural depiction also gives the elephant a deep representation in Ibibio folk and social life. For instance, one of the local government areas inhabited by the Ibibio in Akwa Ibom State is *Ḿkpát Énìn* 'Elephant feet'. A participant informed me that the name *Énìn* 'Elephant' is often given to extremely fat children at birth. This example shows that while all other animals in this category depict internal features and attributes, the elephant is used to characterise both internal and external physical features. Another ethnopragmatic implication of this name, according to this participant, is that the elephant is also a source of longevity given its high life expectancy.

The snail is associated with the rich cuisine culture of the Ibibio but also has a deeper and more significant social meaning. It symbolises the virtues of tolerance and perseverance, and may also depict fertility. Children are named *Ékwọ̀ñ* 'Snail' not as a celebration of the creature but in annexing the unique traits associated with snails into the personhood of their children.

Among the Tiv, *Àzèmbè* 'Black kite' and *Gbèr* 'Nightjar' are important birds that evoke layers of signification. The black kite is an amazing bird of prey that feeds mainly on dead animals, and it represents vision, freedom and expansiveness, according to one participant. A nightjar is a fun-loving bird that actively flourishes by night while the dew forms. It is said to evoke feelings of honour, efficiency and flexibility. Children are named after these birds as a form of emotional attachment to the exceptional attributes which they portray. The same ideology is equally pervasive in the names *Nōr* 'Elephant' and *Gbíndè* 'Adder'. While the elephant is a symbol of fertility, protection and empathy, the adder is associated with wisdom and the "renewal of mankind" given the special way it sheds its skin, as explained by a participant. In all instances, animals are the signifiers because they represent the physical objects or concrete images of names; their peculiar attributes are the signified because they represent the meaning that is ultimately expressed by the names. In other words, there is a complete metaphorical transfer of meaning in the conceptual system (Halupka-Resetar and Radic 2003). From the perspective of ethnopragmatics, these names are said to be speech practices or communicative acts whose meanings can only be fleshed out on account of the locally constitutive values and norms that make sense to the Ibibio and Tiv cultural insiders.

7 Conclusion

In this study, the reconstruction and appropriation of animal names as personal names in the Ibibio and Tiv onomastic traditions in Nigeria has been explored using the ethnopragmatic analytical framework which evaluates the study of speech practices based on the values and norms that make sense to the people concerned. The study has examined the relationship between humans and animals and established a symbiotic link between these two elements of the natural environment. This relationship is influenced by biological, religious, socio-cultural and philosophical factors. Animals are essential components of the ecosystem and biodiversity, and contribute faunal resources to promote a healthy natural environment. They are worshipped as religious totems and sacrificed to appease the gods for wrongdoings. They serve enormous social functions to humanity in terms of food production, agriculture, sports and entertainment, medicine and in the production of musical instruments. They are also domesticated to serve security and stress-relieving purposes to man. The Ibibio and Tiv natural environments are homes to rich faunal assemblages, in addition to a long cultural history with animals. In these cultures, animals have also been reinscribed into the indigenous knowledge systems. In this study, the motivations for the adoption of animal names as personal names have been provided and ethnopragmatic insights into the essence of animal names adopted as personal names offered. The ideology behind the appropriation of animal names as human names is deeply ingrained in the values and attributes which each animal embodies and symbolises. The traits identified are expected to be transferred into name bearers' lived experiences, to guide their life course and to be reinforced throughout their life trajectories (Mensah and Iloh 2021). I also discovered that animal-related names among the Ibibio and Tiv may be significant death-prevention labels to safeguard the lives of bearers and ensure their survival of the wrath of malevolent underworld forces. Infant mortality was a complex life situation for parents in these societies; they resorted to the use of "profane and despicable" animal names as a counterforce to ensure the survival of their children. Beyond the scope of this belief, I maintain that infant mortality is mainly caused by low maternal education, birth defects and pregnancy complications, and that improvement in maternal healthcare services and education will reduce incidences of infant mortality in these cultural traditions. The study concludes that animal-related personal names may seemingly have little or no connection with the objects they reference but that they have deeper meanings based on Ibibio and Tiv cultural scripts. The study aims to deepen the social relationship between humans and animals, taking into account the permeating social influence of animals in the larger cultural fabrics of the Nigerian society. It is an attempt to decentre human beings in the classificatory structure of naming and to put animals at the centre of our social reality.

References

Acher, John. 1997. Why do people love their pets? *Evolution and Human Behaviour* 18. 237–259.

Agyekum, Kofi. 2006. The sociolinguistics of Akan names. *Nordic Journal of African Studies* 15 (2). 206–235.

Akung, Jonas & Oshiga Abang. 2019. I cannot baptize Satan: The communicative import of Mbube death-prevention names. *Sociolinguistic Studies* 13 (2–4). 295–311.

Alford, Richard. 1988. *New Haven*, CT: HRAF Press.

Alves, Romulo & Humberto Alves. 2011. The faunal drugstore: Animal-based remedies used in traditional medicines in Latin America. *Journal Ethnobiology and Ethnomedicine* (9). DOI:10.1186/1746-4269-7-9.

Ameka, Felix K. 2009. Access rituals in West African communities: An ethnopragmatic perspective. In Gunter Senft & Ellen Basso (eds.), *Ritual Communication*, 127–151. New York: Routledge.

Anchimbe, Eric. 2011. On not calling people by their names: Pragmatic undertones of sociocultural relationships in a postcolony. *Journal of Pragmatics* 43. 1472–1483.

Ansu-Kyeremeh, Kwasi. 2000. Communicating Nominatim: Some social aspects of Bono personal names. *Research Review* 16 (2). 19–33.

Blount, Benjamin. 2015. Personal Names. In John Taylor (ed.), *Oxford Handbooks Online*. 616–633. Oxford: Oxford University Press.

Boluwaduro, Eniola. 2019. Ideology and identity construction in Ibibio personal names. *Sociolinguistic Studies* 13 (2–4). 231–250.
Bramwell, Ellen. 2016. Personal names and anthropology. In Carole Hough (ed.), *The Oxford* handbook of names and naming 263–278. Oxford: Oxford University Press.
Britannica. 2021 Animal worship. *Encyclopedia Britannica.* https://www.britannica.com/topic/animal-worship (accessed 25 September 2021).
Close, Haley. 2012. Hello, I love you, won't you tell me your name?: An anthropological investigation of naming. Wooster, OH: College of Wooster senior undergraduate thesis.
Cox, Carole. 2012. *Literature-based teaching in the content areas*. Thousand Oaks, CA: SAGE.
Doyle, Shane. 2008. The child of death: Personal names and parental attitudes towards mortality in Bunyoro, Western Uganda. *Journal of African History* 49 (3). 361–382.
Eckert, Penelope & Sarah McConnell-Ginet. 2013. *Language and gender*. Cambridge: Cambridge University Press.
Ehineni, Taiwo Oluwaseun. 2019a. A morphophonological, morphosyntactic and ethnopragmatic study of Yoruba personal names. Bloomington, Indiana: Indiana University PhD thesis.
Ehineni, Taiwo Oluwaseun. 2019b. The ethnopragmatics of Yoruba personal names: Language in the context of culture. *Studies in African Languages and Culture* 53 (1). 69–90.
Ekeopara, Chike. 2011. *Ethical order and stability in traditional Igbo society*. Calabar: University of Calabar Press.
Faraclas, Nicholas G. 1989. The Cross River languages. In John Bendor-Samuel (ed.), *The Niger-Congo languages*, 277–394. Lauhaum: University Press of America.
Fijn, Natasha. 2013. Living with crocodiles: Engagement with a powerful reptilian being. *Animal Studies Journal* 2 (2). 1–27.
Garaj, Bernard. 2011. Rural musical instruments at the turn of two centuries. The case of bagpipes in Slovakia. In Gisa Jahnichen (ed.), *Studia Instrumentorum Musicae Popularis*, 105–115.
Geertz, Clifford. 1973 *The interpretation of cultures: Selected essays*. New York: Basic Books.
Gladkova, Anna & Jesus Romero-Trillo. 2014. Ain't it beautiful? The conceptualisation of beauty from an ethnopragmatic perspective. *Journal of Pragmatics* 60. 140–159.
Goddard, Cliff. 2006 Ethnopragmatics: A new paradigm. In Cliff Goddard (ed.), *Ethnopragmatics: Understanding discourse in cultural context*, 1–30. Berlin: De Gruyter Mouton.
Goddard, Cliff & Anna Wierzbicka. 2004. Cultural scripts: What are they and what are they good for? *Intercultural Pragmatics* 1–2. 153–166.
Goddard, Cliff & Zhengdao Ye. 2015. Ethnopragmatics. In Farzad Sharifian (ed.), *The Routledge handbook of language and culture*, 66–85. London: Routledge.
Halupka-Resetar, Sabina & Biljana Radic. 2003. Animal names used in addressing people in Serbian. *Journal of Pragmatics* 35. 1891–1902.
Haviland, William A., Harald E. Prins & Bunny McBride. 2013. *Cultural anthropology: The human challenge*. Stanford, CA: Cengage Learning.
Iloh, Queendaline. 2021. A study of Igbo and English personal names: An ethnopragmatic analysis. Port Harcourt: Ignatius Ajuru University of Education dissertation.
Jones, Robert. 2005. *Secret of the totem: Religion and society from McLennan to Freud*. New York: Columba University Press.
Levisen, Carsten. 2018. Dark, but Danish: Ethnopragmatic perspectives on black humour. *Intercultural Pragmatics* 15 (4). 515–531.
Lohani, Usha. 2010. Man-animal relationships in Central Nepal. *Journal of Ethnobiology and Ethnomedicine* 6 (31). 1–11.

Maehle, Andreas-Holger. 1994. Cruelty and kindness to the brute creation: Stability and change in the ethics of the man-animal relationship, 1600–1850. In Aubrey Manning & James Serpell (eds.), *Animals and human society*, 81–105. London: Routledge.
Mamvura, Zvinashe. 2021. The ethnopragmatic analysis of death-prevention names in the Karanga society of Zimbabwe. *African Studies* 80 (1). 111–124.
Mensah, Eyo. 2015. Frog, where are you?: The ethnopragmatics of Ibibio death prevention names. *Journal of African Cultural Studies* 27 (2). 115–132.
Mensah, Eyo. 2020. Name this child: Religious identity and ideology in Tiv personal names. *Names: A Journal of Onomastics* 68 (1). 1–15.
Mensah, Eyo. 2022. The Englishisation of personal names in Nigeria. *English Today* 37 (3). 152–164.
Mensah, Eyo & Jighjigh Ishima. 2020. Sentential names in Tiv. *Studia Linguistica* 74 (3). 645–664.
Mensah, Eyo, Ekawan Silva & Idom Inyabri. 2020. An ethnopragmatic study of libation rituals among the Kiong-speaking Okoyong people in Southeastern Nigeria. *Journal of Anthropological Research* 76 (3). 347–366.
Mensah, Eyo, Josephine Alexander & Queen Ayeni. 2022. The ethnopragmatic functions of Owe and Tiv personal names. *Language Sciences* 91. 1–12.
Mensah, Eyo & Rosemary Eni. 2019. What's in the stomach is used to carry what's on the head: An ethnographic exploration of food metaphors in Efik proverbs. *Journal of Black Studies* 50 (2). 178–201.
Mensah, Eyo & Imeobong Offong. 2013. The structure of Ibibio death prevention names. *Anthropological Notebooks* 19 (3). 41–59.
Mensah, Eyo & Queendaline Iloh. 2021. Wealth is king: The conceptualization of wealth in Igbo personal naming practices. *Anthropological Quarterly* 94 (4). 699–723.
Mensah, Eyo, Vivian Dzokoto & Kirsty Rowan. 2021. The functions of emotion-referencing names in Ibibio. *International Journal of Language and Culture* 8 (2). 218–244.
Mensah, Eyo, Kirsty Rowan, Akase Tiav & Jighjigh Ishima. 2019. Aspects of traditional Tiv naming practices: A sociocultural account. *Sociolinguistic Studies* 13 (2–4). 209–231.
Midgely, Mary. 1988. Beasts, Brutes and Monsters. In Tim Ingold (ed.), *What is an animal?*, 35–46. London: Routledge.
Netam, Ashulala & Payal Jaiswal. 2018. Role of animal power in the field of agriculture. *International Journal of Avian and Wildlife Biology* 3 (1). 62–63.
Obeng, Samuel. 1998. Akan death-prevention names: A pragmatic and structural analysis. *Name: A Journal of Onomastics* 46 (3). 163–187.
Pooley, Simon. 2016. A cultural herpetology of Nile crocodiles in Africa. *Conservation and Society* 14 (4). 391–405.
Reynolds, Lawrence, Meghan C. Wulster-Radcliffe & Debra K. Aaron. 2015. Importance of animals in agricultural sustainability and food security. *Journal of Nutrition* 145 (7). 1377–1379.
Roesel, Kristina. 2019. Smallholder pork: Contributions to food and nutrition security. In Pasquale Ferranti, Elliot M. Berry & Jock R. Anderson (eds.), *Encyclopaedia of food security and sustainability*, 3, 299–309: Elservier
Sagna, Serge & Emmanuel Bassène. 2016. Why are they named after death? Name giving, name changing and death-prevention names in Gújjolaay Eegimaa (Bangul). *Language Documentation and Conservation* 10 (1). 40–70.
Scanes, Colin. 2018. Animals in entertainment. In Colin Scanes & Samia Toukhsati (eds.), Animals and human society, 225–255. London: Elsevier.
Shahabi, Mitra & Maria T. Roberto. 2015. Metaphorical application and interpretation of animal terms: A contrastive study of English and Persian. *Languages in Contrast* 15 (2). 280–293.

Soewu, Durojaye & Temilolu Adekanola. 2011. Traditional-medical knowledge and perception of pangolins (*Manis sps*) among the Awori people, Southwestern Nigeria. *Journal of Ethnobiology and Ethnomedicine* (25). DOI:10.1186/1746-4269-7-25

Teeter, Emily. 2000. Animals in Egyptian religion. In Billie J. Collins (ed.), *A history of the animal world in the Ancient Near East*, 251–270. Boston: Brill.

Philip Manda Imoh

Chapter 13
A structural study of Basà death prevention names

Abstract: This paper investigates personal naming practices as a strategy for preventing death among the Basà people of North-Central Nigeria from a structural perspective; that is, it seeks to identify and analyse certain names and naming patterns given as a way of preventing infant mortality. In the Basà society and culture, death prevention names can generate and maintain some level of assurance and security that is vital for the survival of a child, given the belief that certain spiritual forces are responsible for incessant child mortality. These names are believed to link the bearers with their past ancestors and deities. The qualitative approach was used with the study population and it is a descriptive theory free approach. The primary data were obtained from 50 respondents comprising name bearers, name givers, teachers and elders whose ages ranged from 20–75 in the Bassa and Toto local government areas of Kogi and Nasarawa states, and the Federal Capital Territory, Abuja, Nigeria, as well as from introspection supplemented by school registers in the study areas. The secondary data were obtained via the onomastic literature. Different factors are responsible for the bestowal of the first name, but this study focuses only on names influenced by death, particularly those used to appeal to ancestors and deities and used to taunt, dare death and appeal to deities and ancestors as a way of lamenting the death of children and averting further mortality. This study discovered that personal naming among the Basà people goes beyond mere personal labels to telling stories that index various social and psychological factors and circumstances surrounding the family and the birth of the name bearer. Sometimes, these names serve as appellations and as a means of communication to the addressees, who are usually ancestors or deities whose main aim is to forestall the mortality of the named infants. Death prevention names range from simple lexemes to complex words, compound words and sentences.

Keywords: Anthroponym, anthroponomastics, Basà, death prevention, ethno-pragmatics, morphological processes, personal names

Philip Manda Imoh, Nasarawa State University, Keffi, Nigeria, e-mail: philipmanda@nsuk.edu.ng, philipimoh@gmail.com

https://doi.org/10.1515/9783110759297-013

1 Introduction

The Basà language is spoken in various locations in North-Central Nigeria, including the six area councils of the Federal Capital Territory; Kokona, Nasarawa, Toto and Doma Local Government Councils of Nasarawa State; Bassa, Dekina, Ankpa and Kotonkarfe Local Government Areas of Kogi State; Kontagora Local Government of Niger State; and Agatu and Markurdi Local Government Areas of Benue State. Some of these locations are characterised by different dialectal variants, each of which is identified by its name, but all varieties are mutually intelligible. The Basà language is classified as a member of the Western Kainji branch of Kainji language family also referred to as Rubasa (Basa Benue) (Crozier and Blench 1992: 32).

Anthroponomastics is a sub-field of onomastics that studies proper names, especially personal names, also called anthroponyms. Naming practices, although universal among human societies, are remarkably idiosyncratic in style and custom. This work focuses on death prevention names as attested in the Basà ethnic group. Death prevention names are bestowed on the children of families who have suffered cycles of mortality and rebirth. To forestall this happening, the people have strategised a way of overcoming it by bestowing weird or strange names on children that are sometimes very unusual. These names are believed to protect the name bearers from the spirit of death and other underworld forces which are believed to control the spirits of the affected infants and their right to live, in order to forestall further child mortality. This subtle strategy is a socio-cultural method of daring or appealing to the spiritual or underworld forces to free the affected children from the cycle of death and reincarnation and allow them to live. Though this approach is quite common among Africans, there are some idiosyncrasies in the Basà socio-cultural practice in combating child mortality. The focus of this study is not just the ethno-pragmatic implications of these names but their grammatical structures. The study intends to investigate the structure of death prevention names in the Basà language from the simplest to the most complex ones in order to consider whether or not they differ in structure from other conventional personal names in the language.

2 Literature review

Names exist as part of the socio-cultural setting of every society. Being part of the society that gives them, they act as a window through which the world is understood and appreciated (Mutunda 2011). They are used as conduits of information, especially on society's attitudes or observations towards the named (Mapara et al. 2009: 9). Musonda, Ngalande and Simwinga (2019) state that it is important for one to have a good knowledge of the imagery and metaphors of the language under consideration in order to appreciate its names.

Studies of personal names have been carried out in the onomastic literature in different disciplines, such as linguistics (Akinnaso1980; Ubahakwe 1981; Oduoyoye 1982; Essien 1986; Aceto 2002; Agyekum 2006; Mensah 2013, 2015, 2017; Mensah and Ishima 2020), psychology (Steele 1988; Steele and Smithwick 1989), anthropology (Bean 1990; Obeng 1998; Ukpong 2007) and sociology (Ngade 2011; Suzman 1994). There are also sociological, historical, philosophical, cultural and literary studies on personal names. Personal names are pivotal to the socio-cultural fibres of every society as there is no known society in the world which does not give names to every child. This fact justifies the academic interest in studying personal names as they are not just indices of identification, but rather, are underlain by different forms of communication. Anderson (2004: 435) presents a syntactic and morphological comparison of French, English and Greek names where he proposes the universality of names as belonging to the category of determinatives, such as pronouns and determiners; however, names are inherently neither definite nor indefinite, as their functions differ from those of regular arguments of the predicator. Conclusively, he argues that each language varies. His argument reveals that the grammatical structure of personal names usually synchronises with the grammar of the language. Mensah and Ishima (2020) argue otherwise, suggesting that this may not always be true for all languages. They prove this with contemporary German names, where Plank (2011: 269) shows that family names in this language have "subtle but comprehensively severed ties with their ancestral word classes in their morphology upon attaining name status in spite of their origin in nouns and adjectives and in spite of retaining the phonology and syntax of their origin". He (Plank) further argues that this manifests in inflection and derivation, and thus results in the traditional word class categorisation of family names as a type of noun in languages, especially in languages like German, where both the lexicon and grammar can be affected. In virtually all African naming systems, names have meaning based on their semantic and pragmatic contents. Though this claim is contested and may not be applicable to all African names, it is true for most. This assertion is contrary to the findings of researchers like Searle (1958), Dixon (1964) and Lyons (1977), whose opinion is that personal names do not have sense or meaning but that what they represent is only unique and individuating. In the Basà language and culture, all names have meanings based on semantic and pragmatic contents and contain the story of the bearer, the family, etc.

Mensah and Ishima (2020) argue that in the African context, little attention has been paid to the grammatical description of personal names. They report that Mwangi (2015: 259) undertook a linguistic study of Kikuyu grammar and observed that the coding of information into names is basically characterised by its lexical, syntactic and pragmatic roles in the language. He (Mwangi) demonstrates in his investigation that Kikuyu grammar is largely contained in its personal names. His investigation was based on certain morphosyntactic phenomena like compounding, affixation and reflexivisation, which show how the feminine names in the language are grammaticalised. This plausible fact reveals that names are words that are attested in the lexicon and that have semantic structure and exhibit morphosyntactic characteristics, which thus constitute abstract properties of grammar (Mensah and Ishima 2020).

Hussein (1997: 25) submits that personal names are ambiguous properties of every linguistic community, given that names are words (with expressions of character) that exist in a language which are an essential part of the linguistic repertoire of their bearers, users and givers and are valuable carriers of identity that reflect the dominant attitudes and socio-cultural values of a community. Names are founded on people's cultural heritage and therefore reflect major currents in their history and worldview. For this reason, they are deeply attached to indigenous traditions and embed significant psychological and pragmatic attributes. It is also believed that names in Africa have deep spiritual contexts and cosmology (Obeng 1988; Mensah 2015). Mapara (2013: 15) opines that personal naming in Shona culture practice is seen as a rite of passage marking the transition from the womb into the community. This opinion is supported by Mensah and Ishima's claim that personal naming practices, especially in Africa, "act as narrative discourses where stories that provide insights to lived experience are told" (2020: 4). Haviland et al. define naming "as a social transition from a state of nature to a state of culture" (2013: 130).

In the Basà naming tradition, personal names are given based on certain social and cultural parameters which require reflecting on the situation or circumstances surrounding the conception and birth of the child and the situation surrounding the parents, family, community, etc. Imoh (2019) studies the structure of Basà personal names, outlining the various structures of Basà personal names, namely words, phrases, clauses and sentences. Imoh and Dansabo (2020a) study the ethnopragmatics of Basà personal names, with a general investigation into the language and socio-culture of Basà naming practices; Imoh and Dansabo (2020b) examine Basà sentential names, focusing on those names that are composed in sentences and undergo complex morphological and morphosyntactic operations to derive their surface forms; Imoh (2020) surveys onomastics and names as indirect communication in Basà, with a study of anthroponyms, toponyms and zoonyms as a strategy of indirect communication in the Basà language. This work differs from the former in that it seeks to investigate the structure of death prevention names and their ethno-pragmatic sense by lamenting infant mortality and expressing wishes and prayers which are targeted at forestalling further infant mortality.

In the onomastic literature on African naming practices, especially the aspect of grammatical description, there are a number of related studies in linguistic onomastics such as Mensah and Ishima (2020), who investigate sentential names in Tiv and categorise Tiv names into several types of sentences, examining their semantic, pragmatic, social and spiritual meanings. Their investigation shows that Tiv names reflect the grammatical structure of the Tiv language. Mandende (2009) discovered that in Tshivenda, names have referential and cultural meanings composed from nouns, verbs, adjectives and larger units like phrases, compounds and relative clauses. He claims that in this language, naming forms an indispensable part of the grammar. Linguistically, Mapara argues that names are part of language and constitute phrasal, clausal and sentential categories. He further argues that they may be syntactically characterised as complete statements, questions or commands, which are appropriately situated in the realm of language study. Jauro, Ngamsa and Wappa (2013) undertook a structural study where they categorised names based on their morpho-semantic attributes, namely word classes, and studied their semantic and pragmatic meanings.

A linguistic study of personal naming practices reveals that these names can be found in different linguistic categories, including lexemes, phrases, clauses and sentences of various types and functions. These possibilities have not been explored extensively to explicate the various grammatical structures, especially in the Basà situation, which is productive in this way. Hence, this study aims to explore the different linguistic categories of death prevention names to fill the existing gap in the grammar of Basà names, especially those that are ethno-pragmatic in meaning, as a way of contributing to the linguistic onomastic or onomastic literature in general.

Concerning the meaning of names, Olawale (2005: 9) argues that "in Africa, there is so much meaning in a name. If you are given the right name, you start off with certain indefinable but very real advantages".

In Bantu languages, according to Moyo (1996), and especially in the Ngoni-Tumbuka ethnic group in Malawi, there is a preference for names with historical undertones such as *Mopara* ('wilderness', a name given after the deaths of several infants) and *Tafwachi* ('what is wrong with us'). They are based on the family or society's history.

Koopman (1990) undertook a study of names in Zulu society, reaching a conclusion that name givers and bearers are aware of the names but that the ability to read between the lines depends on the cultural continuity in which language is embedded, which is not applicable or known to all. It is argued, therefore, that pragmatics comes into play, complimented by semantics.

Epstein and Kole (1998: 26) maintain that "every utterance occurs in a culturally determined context or situation". Hence, the meaning of a name can only be understood in relation to the knowledge of the context in which the naming is based. This contextual information is therefore important as the meanings of names are based on "complex social negotiations, learned and interpreted through socialization" (ibid.). Thus, this implies that only those who are members of the society and participate fully in its activities can construe the deep meaning embedded in the names and related communicative interactions (Beattie 1957: 37).

Finnegan (1976: 173), considering names whose meanings cannot be deciphered from their surface forms, suggests that "the colourful, often figurative quality of many of these names should be brought out. There are, of course, many names which are relatively straightforward with little overt meaning. Others, however, are richly allusive".

Musonda, Ngalande and Simwinga (2019) maintain that one should have adequate knowledge of the language's imagery and metaphors to fully appreciate the aspect of naming. Mutunda (2011) asserts that a name is like a document where one can read the history, culture and heritage of the individual or of the family in time and space. This view is related to the current investigation as a name is used to unveil the bearer's cultural identity, the family's wish and prayer. He further states that in addition to the psychological role of a name in establishing a person's identity, names convey to those who know their origin and meaning the social and cultural experiences of the people who created them. These names also show how members of the community regard themselves because they reflect values, traditions and events. Similarly, Mashiri et al. (2013) assert that naming in African societies always reflects the socio-cultural and ideological realities of the societies that give or bear the names. This, according to Musonda, Ngalande and Simwinga (2019), shows how sociocultural factors play a major role in the selection and bestowal of names.

Akung and Abang (2019) contend that, in Mbube and in Africa as a whole, naming practices serve as a form of cultural communication that depicts the beliefs, values and worldviews of the people. Names also contain descriptive information about the circumstances of birth, order of birth, lived experience of the namegiver and important historical events that have heralded children's births (ibid.: 296). This is in consonance with Diala (2012: 79–80), who argues that reincarnation names are strong weapons of ritual invocation in some African cultures. Akung and Abang (2019) believe that, among the Yoruba in south-western Nigeria, death prevention names (DPN) are mostly direct pleas to name bearers or indirect communication with spiritual forces. They are deliberate intervention strategies to guarantee the survival of their bearers. Examples include such names as *Ikúdáyìsí* 'death relieved this one', *Dúrótìmí* 'stay with me', *Kòkúmò* 'S/he is dying again', etc.

Akung and Abang also recorded a typology of DPN, which they generally define as being applied to "children who are believed to be at risk of dying in their infancy, to ensure their survival" (2019: 54). The two categories are:

i. Children who are believed to have supernatural powers and a strong link with the supernatural world of spirits and ancestors to which they belong. They are believed to have the ability to choose to return to the supernatural world by dying shortly after birth. They differ from normal children in that they have the power to be born from the same mother, only to die when they choose. As soon as the supernatural power is diminished through a ritual, the link with the supernatural world is broken and the child is expected to survive. Thus, the death prevention name is part of the strategy to break the cycle of birth and death and ensure their long-term survival.

ii. The second category of children considered at risk is those who are victims of external forces, especially witchcraft. The children are not believed to have any supernatural power. They are also given death prevention names as a strategy to avert death and protect them from malevolent forces.

Sagna and Bassène (2016: 46) opine that the study of death prevention names in Gújjolaay Eegemaa (Senegal), among other things, improve the understanding of not only the meaning of names but also the belief system, including the conceptualisation of the different supernatural forces that can affect the life of a newborn and those who can protect it.

They (Sagna and Bassèene) also found that symbolic ritual names are given to infants to prevent them from dying. They assert that these names are given to children who are believed to have supernatural power, which enables them to come to life and die again and again from the same mother. In this language, they are called *Úññil* 'flying children' or 'spirit babies'. The children, they add, are identified through their unusual behaviour, for instance, producing very strange screams regularly at night. If they are old enough to speak, the way they talk about their imminent death to join "their real parents" from another world can also be an indication that they need special attention. They further submit that babies who need special names are those whose mothers have had many unsuccessful pregnancies or have had children who died very early in their infancy. Another category they reported with death prevention names are those who are victims of external malefic forces like witches; this, they exemplify thus:

(1) *Gu-yyah*
CL8-grave
'grave'

(2) *Ju-sotten*
2PL-deceive
'you deceive' (Sagna and Bassène 2016: 54)

Concerning this category of names, Sagna and Bassène say, "Although it may not be relevant whether a person can be wholly indifferent to a given name, it is important to note that an extensive range of reactions can be evoked" (2016: 52). This is in agreement with what Maenetsha (2014: 1) says about death prevention names being forms of devaluation which name givers employ to protect children from ancestors who want to take them away. This she (Maenetsha) exemplifies with her own death prevention name, *Mathakala* 'Rubbish', because she was born following a still birth. The name was a way of protecting her from the spiritual forces of death. She reports that this strategy was intended to devalue her essence and render her unattractive to the killer forces. Death prevention names are therefore traditional identifying resources to connect with ancestral spirits as they offer namegivers a sense of protection and security (Akung and Abang 2019: 301). Names like *Ebèbè* 'Nothing', *Egbùdù* 'Toilet' and *Bùlèm* 'satan', according to them, are death prevention names in Mbube which deeply reflect the anxieties of the people and their grief. Names such as *Adè* 'Grandfather', *Ené* 'Grandmother', etc., they argue, reflect the belief in reincarnation. They state that the names are given when the newborn has striking features that are similar or have a true resemblance to a dead relative (Akung and Abang 2019: 305).

In Mensah and Offong's (2013) study, they investigated the morphological and syntactic structures of Ibibio death prevention names. They discovered that these names range from simple lexical items (words) to complex sentences and provide a window onto the Ibibio grammatical structure. They say that this category of names does not have any formal properties in common, as distinct from ordinary names. They submit that, at the level of the lexicon, these names are primarily nouns and a few adjectives, e.g. *Sémé* 'laments', *wá* 'sacrifice', *Kari* 'tricky', *Táhá* 'spirit', etc. Some are complex words with affixes (prefixes) attached. E.g., *í-sàñ* 'journey', *í-muk* short', etc. Another productive morphological process they discovered is compounding; this, they exemplified with *Uruk-ikot* 'rope-bush' (i.e. snake), *Òkpòrò-ìsìp* 'nut-kernel' (palm kernel), etc. Others are larger linguistic structures such as sentences. This category, they report, has the following sentence types: affirmative statements, negative statements, imperative sentences, interrogative sentences, cleft constructions, serial verb constructions and complex sentences.

3 Research methodology

3.1 Data generation/elicitation and research participants

The study was conducted using a qualitative research approach and employed a descriptive linguistics framework, that is, it is theory free. The primary sources of data elicitation included oral interviews, participant observation and focus group discussions with the sample population. The data elicited were verified by the researcher, given his native intuitions of the Basà language. In some instances, the data were gathered through discussions and these discussions aided the researcher in verifying the authenticity of the data gathered. These procedures were also supplemented by introspection, based on the fact that the researcher is a native speaker. The field work was carried out in Basà speaking areas of Kogi and Nasarawa states and Abuja (Federal Capital Territory), North-Central Nigeria. The data were analysed in four tiers, namely, the raw data, followed by the Leipzig Glossing Rules, then the semantic meaning and finally the pragmatic meaning (where applicable).

Selection of participants was done randomly, taking into account that all participants are native speakers with native intuitions, who were between 20 and 75 years of age and willing to participate in the investigation. These randomly selected participants were both literate and non-literate native speakers of the Basà language. The selection was also based on their experience and good knowledge of Basà naming conventions and also their vast knowledge of culture, both as name givers and bearers/users. Information on sociobiographical variables was collected, namely, gender, occupation, religion and educational background. 25 men and 25 women participated in the investigation, and their levels of education, religions and occupation vary. Eight participants were graduates from accredited higher institutions, nine were A-Level holders, 20 were secondary and primary school leavers and 13 were uneducated. Oral interviews, focus group discussions and participant observation were the instruments deployed to elicit the primary data. A non-structured interview method was adopted in which open or flexible questions were asked to elicit the targeted data on various categories of Basà death prevention names. We also asked questions on the factors motivating the use of death prevention names, as well as their semantic and deep (pragmatic) meanings and symbolism in the Basà culture. Responses were compared to validate their authenticity. A multimedia recorder and field notes were used to record the information obtained. Out of 75 names obtained, the most relevant ones to the study (39) were selected and analysed. The data were coded, transcribed, translated and tone-marked.

4 Data presentation and analysis

Death prevention names can be studied from morphological, morphosyntactic and syntactic perspectives. The approaches adopted in this work are both morphological and morphosyntactic because both morphological and morphosyntactic operations apply. These names, like other categories of Basà anthroponomastics, range from simple lexemes to complex sentences, which provide a window onto the Basà grammatical structure. This category of names in Basà is predominantly nouns at the lexical level; there are few adjectives and fewer verbs. These names are characterised by some complex morphological processes to derive personal names, such as nominalisation, deadjectivisation, conversion and the adjectivisation of verbs. In what follows, simple words are presented and analysed.

Table 13.1: Nouns as names.

	Underlying noun		Derived names	Meaning
i.	*ùdukwo*	'market'	*Dukwo*	market
ii.	*tù'wo*	'death'	*Tù'wó*	death
iii.	*Ùdàkwọ̀*	'ant hill'	*Dàkwọ̀*	ant hill
iv.	*ọ̀dáję*	'grave instrument'	*Dáję*	instrument for citing a grave site
v.	*cẹ̀nję*	'land'	*Cènję*	land
vi.	*Ùtwotwo*	'gravel'	*Twotwo*	gravel
vii.	*Àgàzama*	'herbaceous'	*Gàzama*	herbaceous
viii.	*Àwara*	'giant grass'	*Wara*	giant grass

The data in Table 13.1 are noun stems which undergo the process of elision of the initial sound of the basic word or syllable to derive personal names. This process applies to the derivation of proper nouns for every noun that begins with a vowel. This is because Basà personal names rarely begin with a vowel sound; hence, those that begin with an initial consonant sound are not affected by this rule (process). For instance, see the data in Table 13.1 (ii) and (v), where *Cènje* 'land' maintains its basic form because it begins with a voiceless affricate sound (/tʃ/). In (ii), the rule of elision does not apply, but in the derived word, the tone of second syllable is modified from its basic mid tone to high in the derived proper noun. In (v), *Cènje* 'land' maintains its original form without any morphological or phonological process or adjustment.

Few names composed of verbs were found in the corpus of data. There were two categories of this name type, namely those that make commands and those that are inflected. Those that make commands, although they could be regarded as imperative sentences, are composed of one or more verbs in their present infinitive form; those that are inflected verbs are formed based on the appropriate method of inflecting such verb stems. The category of single verbs as names is exemplified in Table 13.2. The other category will be discussed in examples (21) to (23). These names appeal indirectly to death spirits or deities to forestall further deaths.

In Table 13.2 (i), the verb base of the derived name *Gûre*, both syllables of which are characterised by [HH] tones, is modified in the derived name with a falling tone on the initial syllable and a mid-tone on the second or last syllable. The implication of the name is 'the deceased child has returned/reincarnated'. The given name is a wish to prevent another cycle of death and rebirth.

Table 13.2: Verbs as names.

	Underlying verbs	Derived names	Meaning
i.	*Gúré*	*Gûre*	'returned'
ii.	*Námá*	*Námá*	'to stay'
iii.	*Fwósò*	*Fwósò*	'get rotten'
iv.	*Nwǫ́ma*	*Nwǫma-nẹ*	'misfortune'
	Misfortune	misfortune-APPL	

The people believe in reincarnation and consider that the deceased child is the same one that returns through the process of rebirth or reincarnation. They prove this by making a cut the body of a deceased child in a particular place before burial and mysteriously, in the next rebirth, the child is born with a mark in the position where the deceased child was cut. This incision is also another mysterious strategy of forestalling further child mortality.

Námá and *Fwósò* maintain their basic (present infinitive) forms. Meaning wise, *Námá* means 'to stay'; it appeals to the spirit of death to spare the named child. *Fwósò* means 'get rotten'. It dares the spirit of death by telling it through the named child that it can go ahead and kill the child as usual and the child will get rotten. This is a strategy to ensure the survival of the named child. Pragmatically, the name giver(s) present their wish or prayer to deities through the name. It is a reverse way of appealing to the killer forces to spare the named child.

The verb in (iv) is derived from a basic verb *nwóma* which means 'misfortune'. The derived verb is suffixed with the suffix-*ne*, an applicative marker whose additional meaning is 'misfortune for either the name bearer or the name givers or both'. The meaning derives from the misfortune, particularly infant mortality, which the family has suffered. The name bestowed on the child is an expression of lamentation, fear and prayer to their ancestors or deities to show mercy on the child and on subsequent children and to spare them.

The next category of names is those composed of adjectives. The majority of names in this category are derived from verbs by certain morphological processes. This category, like the verbal category, is not as productive as the nominal category; it was very difficult eliciting this category of names during the fieldwork. These names are presented in Table 13.3 below.

Fwéshí is derived from the verb stem fwósò, that is, it is a process of adjectivisation where the adjective name *Fwéshí* is derived from a verb base *fwósò*. The meaning of the derived name is related to the meaning of the underlying verb. The morphological behaviour of this name is characterised by internal modification: the vowel of the first syllable (i.e., a back high vowel) is replaced by a high-mid front vowel; the consonant of the second syllable (i.e., an alveolar fricative) is replaced

Table 13.3: Names as adjectives.

	Underlying verbs		Derived names	Meaning
i.	*Fwósò*	'get rotten'	*Fwéshí*	Rotten
ii.	*Shíngò*	'fed up'	*Shinji*	fed up.PST

by a palato-alveolar (post-alveolar) fricative; and the vowel of the second syllable (a back low vowel) is replaced with a front high vowel. The socio-cultural meaning of *Fwéshí* is, 'the child will die and get rotten like other infants' (who preceded her). It is noteworthy that the modification in the first syllable is a progressive assimilation because it is engendered by the post-alveolar fricative following the high-mid tone. The name is a lamenting appeal to the deities to forestall further infant mortality; that is, it is a negative name that gives an impression that the named child is already dead, so that malevolent spirits will not be determined to kill it for the second time.

Shinji in Table 13.3 (ii) derives from the verb *shíngò* 'fed up', which expresses the lamenting and frustration of the name giver(s) over the frequent child mortality. The morphological processes underlying its derivation involve the tones of the two syllables being modified, with the HL tones of the basic verb being replaced by MM tones; the velar stop is replaced by the voiced affricate.

During the fieldwork, a few examples were elicited where nouns are derived from verbs by various morphological processes. Table 13.4 below presents data for this category.

Table 13.4: Nominalisation.

	Underlying verb	Gloss	Derived name	Gloss
i.	*Nyíngátángà*	'console'	*Ànyìngàtọ̀*	'consolation'
ii.	*Lásọ̀*	'win'	*Tọ̀lasọ*	'victory'
iii.	*Nwọ́ma*	'misfortune'	*Tọ̀nwọ̀mà*	'misfortune'

The morphological processes deriving the names in Table 13.4 are as follows. In (i), *nyíngátángà* 'console' is the basic verb which derives *Ànyìngàtọ̀* 'consolation'. The noun is derived by prefixing the verb stem with *a-* and eliding the last syllable *-gá*. In (ii), *Tọ̀lasọ*is derived by affixing the verb stem with the nominalising prefix *-tó* and modifying the tones of the basic verb from [LL] to [MM]. In (iii), the name is derived by affixing the verb stem with a productive nominalising prefix *-tó* and modifying of the basic tones from High Low to Low Low. Socioculturally, *Ànyingàtọ̀* means 'consolation', that is, trusting God that the named child will survive. *Tọ̀lasọ* in (ii) is also an expression of faith or optimism that the named child will have victory over the spirit of death.(iii) contrasts with (i) and (ii) in that, in retrospect, it expresses a lamentation over the death(s) of the earlier infants and assumes that the named child will bring more misfortune as it is expected to die. The surface meaning is not what is implied by the name giver; the underlying meaning is a prayer to the ancestors and /or deities to spare the named children and allow them survive.

The study also discovered a very small set of verb phrases headed by a negative verb stem to express a lack of what is specified in the object position. This is exemplified in examples (3) to (5).

(3) *zá* *utumwa* → *Zátumwa*
NEG.has.PERF message
'Has no message'

(4) *zá* *ùwè* *ìbìye* → *Zábìye*
NEG.has.PERF thing good
'Have nothing good'

(5) *zá* *ilimwẹ̀* → *Zálimwẹ̀*
NEG.has.PERF usefulness
'Have no value'

The verb phrases in (3) to (5) all begin with a negative verb, followed by a direct object, the lack of which is expressed in each example. The initial vowel of the direct object is elided to derive the surface form. In (3), the surface meaning of *Zátumwa* is that the named child 'has no message', i.e. the child will not be useful for messaging as it may die like others. The name givers lament the uselessness of the named child. The initial vowels of each part of the compound *ùwẹ̀ ìbìye* gets elided, deriving *Wẹ̀bìye*, which means nothing good is expected from the name bearer. The name giver expresses their fear from their previous experience. (5), *Zálimwẹ̀* means the named child has no value because it is a candidate of death. The name cautions whoever is rejoicing over the named child to be cautious and take a cue from past experience. The names are lamenting expressions and prayers to deities to reverse the cycle of death and rebirth in the family through the named child.

At the sentential level, Basà death prevention names are very productive and demonstrate a number of structural types. In this language, sentential names are basically declarative or imperative, with a very few interrogatives and riddles. This category of names is characterised by complex morphological processes that derive nouns from larger linguistic units. In what follows, the data for this category are presented and analysed, unveiling their structures and intricate morphological processes and meanings.

The structure of names in this category comprises subject, verb and complement or object, which is the basic word order. This is the most productive source of names in the language. Examples include:

(6) *Bọ̀* *máa* *nyisa* → *Mânyísá*
3SG 1SG.HAB entice/deceive
'S/he is enticing me'

(7) *Ń* *ta* *hânsà* → *Tâsà*
1SG PROG think
'I am still thinking'

(8) *Bọ̀* *zhananẹ* → *Zhananẹ*
3SG go-HAB
'S/he will go again'

(9) *Ń* *tà* *'wanẹ*
1SG PROG hold
'I am still holding'

Examples (6) to (9) are statements of facts. They give information to the interlocutor. Anybody familiar with the Basà socio-cultural tradition, upon hearing these names, can infer the motivations for their bestowal, because they summarise the story of the name bearers and givers. This implies that, preceding the birth of the name bearers, the name givers had suffered the loss of a child; hence, the names bestowed on the bearers area way of offering prayer to the gods to forestall further child mortality and spare the named children.

Structurally, the constituent of the name in (6) includes the subject and predicate. The subject, the dominant noun phrase, serves as the head of the sentence. The predicate is headed by the verb *nyísá*, which acts the object *máa* '1SG'. It implies that the named child only entices or deceives the name giver as it is expected not to survive like others; that is why the habitual marking morpheme *máa* is attached to the verb stem.

Basà is basically Subject Verb Object (SVO), as earlier stated, but where the patient is in the first person (singular or plural) the object occurs before the verb. In (7), the verb is intransitive. The sentence is characterised thus: it is headed by a first person singular subject, followed by a progressive marker and the verb phrase-made up of the verb only. The name giver, regardless of the arrival of the child, still ponders on the mishaps that have befallen him/her, on a concern that threatens his/her faith about the survival of the named child. In (8), the structure is headed by a third person singular pronoun and followed by a verb phrase composed of a complex verb stem: the verb *zḥe* and the bound morpheme (suffix) *-nanẹ*, which is a habitual marker. The construction implies that the name bearer, based on their (name givers) established fact, will die. (9) is characterised by the first person singular subject *Ń*, the future marker *tá* and the VP *'wanẹ*, a sentence whose derived/surface form requires the deletion of the subject and the merging of the progressive marker *tà* and the verb. This implies that the name giver is keeping the infant pending while the ancestors decide what happens to it. It is a lamentation and prayer to the ancestors, pleading for the survival of the named child.

The study also discovered a set of sentences that are negative statements as death prevention names. This set of names is characterised by a negative operator (affix) attached to the verb stem which negates the whole proposition. This category is exemplified in (10) to (12) below.

(10) *Ń* *lane-shẹ* → *Láshẹ*
1SG worthy-NEG
'I am not worthy'

(11) *Ń* *jérí-shi* → *Jéríshi*
1SG want-NEG
'I don't want'

(12) *Ń* *zá* *iyi* *mẹ̀* *hiẹñ* → *Zệmẹ̀hiẹñ*
1SG NEG thing to say
'I don't have anything to say'

In (10), *Láshẹ* is structurally characterised thus: the subject *Ń* occurs before the VP which deletes in the derived form. The VP is made up of only the verb stem because it is intransitive. The verb is suffixed with a negative operator which negates the entire proposition. The implication is that it is a lamentation of the name givers' desperation as a result of their past experience (infant mortality); the name givers are not worthy of the blessing of the child. (11) is structurally characterised thus: the sentence is headed by first person singular subject and followed by a verb phrase (deleted in the surface form), which comprises the verb stem suffixed with a negative operator which implies that the name givers are fed up with the disappointments occasioned by incessant death and rebirth cycles and express their displeasure and lamentation that they are no longer interested, death should carry the child off as usual. (12) Comprises the subject, a negative verb 'to have', an object and an independent clause. The derived form undergoes the derivative processes of clipping the subject; the negative operator is retained but its tone is modified from a high to a falling tone, the direct object of the negative verb clips. The implication of the name is that the name giver is speechless, as a result of their past experience. One common thing in each of the cases in the above data (i.e., 10 to 12) is that the subject, in each case, is a (first person singular) nominative pronoun. For (10) and (11), the name givers outright reject the offer of the named child, whereas in (12), there is a condition that is based on the antecedent; the name giver will only make their remark if the named child survives. The negative marker in (10) and (11) differs from that in (12). In (10) and (11), it is morphologically marked, that is *-shẹ*, whereas in (12), it is syntactically marked, that is *zá*.

4.1 Names as commands

This study uncovered death prevention names that consist of imperative constructions. Names in this category semantically function as commands or constitute orders (Crystal 2007).Typically, this sentence type has no overt subject and it is made up of the verb in the imperative mood and a direct object as a complement. This category can be exemplified in (13) to (15) below.

(13) *Zhága nà ambẹ̀* → *Zhánǎmbẹ̀*
go.IMP to bush
'Go to the bush/woods'

(14) *Ñdá mó 'wo* → *Ndómó'wo*
leave.1SG AGR die
'Leave me, let me die'

(15) *Gó ì shilo ba* → *Shilóba*
let.3SG 3SG lay there
'Leave it there'

(13) is characterised by clipping the second syllable of the verb base *zhága* and merging it with the preposition and the object of the preposition. The initial sound of the complement elides and leaves its mid tone on the remaining vowel of the preposition before they are compounded. Hence, the vowel of the preposition is characterised by rising tone. In (14), the verb, the agreement marker and the verb stem compound to derive the surface form. (15) is derived by clipping the initial verb and the third person impersonal pronoun and merging the second verb and the adverb of place *ba*. The meaning of (13) is a command to the named child to go to the woods where it is believed the spirits of the dead repose. This is born from

the frustration and desperation at the cycles of death and rebirth the name givers have suffered. The name in (14) is also an expression of lamentation and desperation by the name givers, speaking as if on behalf of the named child that 'he should be allowed to die'. In (15), *Shílóba* is a death prevention name given to a male child, commanding or advising the people concerned to be careful about making merry for the named child; it is better they watch and see if he will survive first rather than make merry and mourn him at last. This is also based on their past experience. These commands, pragmatically, are prayers offered in a reverse way to malevolent spirits to withdraw their determination to kill the named children.

There is another subset of imperative names found during the course of the fieldwork which make negative commands. Structurally, they are not different from the set in (8), but are preceded by a negative operator which, in this case, is not an affix but an independent morpheme, but also negates the whole proposition. This subset of imperatives can be presented and analysed in (16) to (18) below.

(16) *Tà mà họngá* →*Tàhọngá*
NEG 2SG.OBJ laugh
'Don't laughat me'

(17) *Tà ínà* →*Tà'ínà*
NEG lost
'Don't get lost'

(18) *Tò 'wó* →*Tò'wo*
NEG die
'Don't die'

Example (16) is derived by eliding the object of the sentence, which occurs sentence medially, and combining the negative operator and the verb stem. It is a command by the name giver to his/her addressee or antagonists, instructing them to stop their mockery as the name givers are hopeful for a better family future. (17) is derived by a simple process of merging the two lexemes, commanding the named child not to get lost (die) like the other children who suffered infant mortality. (18) is like (16) in its derivational process, and is an instruction to the name bearer (a male child) not to die. This instruction is borne from the anticipation that the named child is likely to die like those born before it, hence the command 'don't die'. This set is characterised by faith or optimism regardless of the unfavourable past. It is akin to the belief system in Christianity.

Another subcategory of names is those that are in question form but that are not conventional questions, like Wh-questions or polar questions, but riddles.

Riddles are questions that describe things or people in extremely difficult and confusing ways, which are answered in a clever and amusing manner, and are considered a clever way of teaching. They usually require an answer as their meaning, followed by a deeper or pragmatic meaning (Imoh 2019). They are also used as personal names and zoonyms (animal names) in the Basà language. These humorous puzzles are related to the meanings of these names by virtue of the circumstances surrounding the birth of a child. They are not sentences but they trigger a response or an answer in a sentence form. This subtype is exemplified in (19) and (20) below.

(19) Riddle: *Tègèri*

Bù-jwê	*bọ̀*	*ọna*	*yẹ́-she*	*ògú*	*ìbẹ-ò*
N.PRE-inventor	of	city	eat-NEG	inheritance	it-EMPH

'The founder of a city doesn't enjoy the inheritance of it'

(20) Riddle: *Mêjida*

È	*bene-ni-shi*	*tu'wo*	*isẹbwẹ-o*
3SG	out-APPL-NEG	death	anger-EMPH

'Getting offended with death is only futile'

This category of death prevention names in Basà is quite productive but those that are death biased are quite scanty. Only a few were found in this research.

In (19), *Tègèri*, the founder of a city does not enjoy its inheritance. It is given to a male child and it means that the fact that a child is born does not guarantee its survival. This name is given to a child whose birth is preceded by a series of infant losses. *Mêjida* in (20) is interpreted as 'Getting offended with death is only futile'. It implies that death is so powerful that one cannot face it in a fight or physical confrontation, no matter how frustrated or hurt one may be, i.e. no matter the number of infant deaths recorded in the family, one is handicapped as there is nothing one can do to combat death. The name is bestowed on a male child as a way of demonstrating the superiority of death in relation to human beings and of appealing to the ancestors, recognising their power to kill or spare infants.

Another category of death prevention names in Basà are those consisting of serial verb constructions. During the fieldwork, very few of this category were elicited which were clearly verb serialisations, where a name comprises two or more verbs in a simple sentence. They are exemplified in (21) to (23) below.

(21)

Nâ	*ndá*	*zhaga*	→ *Ndâzhaga*
2SG.IMP.PRO	do	go.PROG	

'Continue doing what you are going'

(22) *Ńmâ nyísá* → *Mânyísá*
take deceive/mock
'deception /mockery '

(23) *Ǹ ndá mó 'wo* → *Ndámó'wo*
1SG leave.1SG let.1SG.AGR die
'Leave me, let me die'

This category of Basà names is quite productive but those that are death preventive are quite scanty. In this search, only a few were found.

Example (21) is derived by clipping the second person singular imperative marker and merging the serial verbs. It is a name bestowed on a male child to guarantee its survival after a series of deaths and rebirths. The derived name comprises two verbs of equal grammatical value.

Ndâzhaga (22) implies that the addressee should do what they can within the little period available to the child before it goes (dies). (22) is composed of two verbs *mâ* 'take' and *nyísá* 'mock/deceive' bestowed on a male child. It implies that the named child only came to mock or deceive the beneficiaries. (23) is derived by merging all the lexical items to form a compound. *ndá*is a verb that means 'leave' (in the first person singular), *mó* means 'let' and agrees with first person singular number and *'wo* means 'die'. The derived form is characterised by eliding the sentence subject, i.e. the syllabic nasal *Ǹ*'1SG', and merging the three verbs to derive the surface form. On the surface it means that the name giver, through the name bearer, dares death and demands that the named child should be allowed to die; ethno-pragmatically, it makes a desperate appeal to the deities or ancestors to allow the named child to survive. These names sound very derogative but are derogatory-protective names that deceive the forces responsible for the deaths of children, making them believe that the named children are worthless. This is deployed as a strategy to ensure the survival of the name bearing child because it is believed that the malevolent spirits allow the bearers of such names to survive due to their negative appeal.

5 Conclusion

This study investigated the structure of death prevention personal names in the Basà language, whose communicative tendencies can deepen our linguistic and cultural knowledge of Basà. This investigation shows that this category of names is characterised by important linguistic properties which can provide more empirical insights and facts into linguistic onomastics. We have attempted a systemic investigation of formal grammatical information on the Basà naming practices, which has unveiled the phonology, morphosyntax, semantics and pragmatics and also brought out other aspects of information beyond the domains of linguistics (extra-linguistics) that underlie personal naming. The study has unearthed facts about the intricacies of sentential names in Basà, through which names are derived by complex phonological, morphological and morphophonological processes such as elision, clipping, replacement, modification, compounding, affixation and desententialisation (that is, larger grammatical units such as clauses and sentences shrunk into smaller grammatical units such as lexemes, complex words and compounds to derive personal names).

The study discovered that this category of names does not have any properties that are uncommon among ordinary names. They are made up of nouns, adjectives, complex words where affixes are attached to bases, compounds, noun phrases, and sentences such as statements, imperatives, interrogatives and riddles. The study shows that only death prevention names consist of interrogative sentences and very productive negative declarative structures. Imperative sentences are also productively used. Ethno-pragmatically, these names tell the bitter stories behind their bestowal that are understood by those who are familiar with the socio-cultural traditions of the ethnic group.

In conclusion, this study aligns with Chomsky (1986), who argues that grammar constitutes a tacit knowledge of what the native speakers know about their language, a fact that is also applicable to the grammar of names.

Abbreviations

1SG	first person singular
2SG	second person singular
3PL	third person plural
3SG	third person singular
AGR	agreement
AGR-O	object agreement
AGR-S	subject agreement
APPL	applicative
AUX	auxiliary
EMPH	emphasis
FUT	future
HAB	habitual
IMP	imperative
NEG	negative/negation

N-PRE	noun prefix
OBJ	object
POSS	possessive
PREP	preposition
PRO	pronoun
PROG	progressive
PST	past
REFL	reflexive

References

Aceto, Michael. 2002. Ethnic personal names and multiple identities in Anglophone Caribbean speech communities in Latin America. *Language in Society* 31. 577–608.

Agyekum, Kofi. 2006. The sociolinguistic of Akan personal names. *Nordic Journal of African Studies* 15 (2). 206–235.

Akinnaso, Niyi F. 1980. The sociolinguistic basis of Yoruba personal names. *Anthropological Linguistics.* 22 (7). 275–304.

Akung, Jonas & Oshega Abang. 2019. I cannot baptize Satan: The communicative import of Mbube death-prevention names. *Sociolinguistic Studies* 13 (2–4). 295–311.

Anderson, John. 2004. On the grammatical status of names. *Language* 80. 435–474.

Bean, Susan. 1990. Ethnology and the study of proper names. *Anthropological Linguistics* 22 (7). 305–316.

Beattie, John M. 1957. Nyoro personal names. *Uganda Journal* 21. 99–106.

Chomsky, N. 1986. *Barriers.* Cambridge: MIT Press.

Crozier, David H. & Roger M. Blench. 1992. *An index of Nigerian languages* (2nd edition). Dallas: SIL.

Crystal, D (2007. *A dictionary of linguistics and phonetics.* London: Blackwell.

Diala, Isidore. 2012. Colonial mimicry and postcolonial re-membering in Isidore Okpewho's Call me by my rightful name. *Journal of Modern Literature* 36 (4). 77–95.

Dixon, R. M. W. 1964. On formal and contextual meaning. *ActaLinguistica* 14. 23–46.

Epstein, Edmund & Robert Kole. 1998. *The language of african literature.* Trenton, NJ: African World Press.

Essien, Okon. 1986. *Ibibio names: Their structure and their meanings.* Ibadan: Day Star Press.

Finnegan, Ruth. 1976. *Oral literature in Africa.* Oxford: Oxford University Press.

Haviland, William, Harald Prins & Bunny McBride. 2013. *Cultural anthropology: The human challenge.* Stanford, CA: Cengage Learning.

Hussein, Riyad. 1997. A sociolinguistic study of family names in Jordan. *Grazer linguistiches studien* 4. 25–41.

Imoh, Philip Manda. 2019. An onomastic study of the structure of Basà personal names. *ANSU Journal of Language and Literary Studies (AJLLS)* 1 (5). 56–72.

Imoh, Philip Manda. 2020. Onomastics: An indirect communicative strategy among the Basà people. *Journal of the Linguistics Association of Nigeria* Supplement IV. 214–232.

Imoh, Philip Manda & Dansabo Friday. 2020. Basà personal names: An ethno-pragmatic survey. *The Griot, Journal of West African Association for Commonwealth Literature and Language Studies* 3. 182–202.

Imoh Philip Manda. 2020. The sentential names in Basà. *Nigerian languages' studies (NILAS)* 4 (2). 85–98.

Jauro, Barnabas John Ngamsa & John Peter Wappa. 2013. A morphosemantic analysis of the Kamue personal names. *International Journal of English Language and Linguistics* 1. 1–12.

Koopman, Adrian. 1990. Some notes on the morphology of Zulu clan names. *South African Journal of African Languages* 4 (1). 333–337.

Lyons, John. 1977. *Semantics.* Cambridge: Cambridge University Press.

Maenetsha, Kholofelo. 2014. *To the black woman we all knew.* Cape Town: Modjaji Books.

Mandende, Itani Peter. 2009. *A study of Tshivenda personal names.* Pretoria: University of South Africa dissertation.

Mapara, Jacob. 2009. The indigenous knowledge system in Zimbabwe: Juxtaposing post-colonial theory. *The Journal of Pan African Studies* 3. 139–155.

Mapara, Jacob. 2013. *Shona sentential names: A brief overview.* Mankon, Bamenda: Langaa Research and Publishing.

Mashiri, Pedzisai, Emmanuel Chabata & Ezra Chitando. 2013. A sociocultural and sociolinguistic analysis of postcolonial naming practices in Zimbabwe. *Journal for Studies in Humanities and Social Sciences* 2. 163–173.

Mensah, Eyo. 2013. The structure of Ibibio death prevention names. *Anthropological Notebooks* 19. 41–59.

Mensah, Eyo & Imeobong Offong. 2013. The structure of Ibibio death prevention names. *Anthropological Notebook* 19 (3). 41–59.

Mensah, Eyo. 2015. Frog, where are you?: The ethnopragmatics of Ibibio death prevention names. *Journal of African Cultural Studies* 27. 115–132.

Mensah, Eyo. 2017. Proverbial nicknames among rural youth in Nigeria. *Anthropological Linguistics* 59. 414–439.

Mensah, Eyo & Ishima J. 2020. Name this child: Religious identity and ideology in Tiv personal names. *A Journal of Onomastics* 68 (1). 1–15.

Musonda, Chola, Sunday Ngalande & John Simwinga. 2019. Daring death among the Tumbuka: a socio-semantic analysis of death-related personal names. *International Journal of Humanities Science and Education (IJHSSE)* 6 (7). 109–120.

Mutunda, Sylvesta. 2011. Personal names in Lunda culture milieu. *International Journal of Innovative Interdisciplinary Research* 1 (1). 14–22.

Moyo, Thema. 1996. Personal names and naming practices in Northern Malawi. *Nomina African* 10 (1–2). 10–19.

Mwangi, Kinyanjui Peter. 2015. What's in a name?: An exploration of Gìkuyu grammar though personal names. *International Journal of Humanities and Social Science* 5. 259–267.

Ngade, Ivo. 2011. Bakossi names, naming culture and identity, *Journal of Africa Cultural Studies* 23 (2). 111–120.

Obeng, Samuel G. 1998. Akan death-prevention names: A pragmatic and structural analysis. *Names* 46 (3). 163–187.

Oduyoye, Modukpe. 1982. *Yoruba names: their structures and naming.* London: Karnak House.

Olawale, F. 2005. *News journal community advisory board.* Ibadan: Heinemann.

Plank, Frans. 2011. Differential time stability in categorial change: Family names from nouns and adjectives, illustrated from German. *Journal of Historical Linguistics* 1 (2). 269–292.

Sagna, Serge & Emmanuel Bassène. 2016. Why are they named after death? Name giving, name changing and death prevention names in Gújjolaay Eegimaa (Bangul). *Language Documentation and Conservation* 10. 40–70.

Searle, John. 1958. Proper names. *Mind* 67. 166–173.

Steele, Claude M.1988. The psychology of self-affirmation: Sustaining the integrity of the self. *Advances in experimental social psychology* 21. 261–301.

Steele, Kenneth &Laura Smithwick. 1989. First names and first impressions: *A fragile relationship*. 21. 517–523.

Suzman, Susan M. 1994. Names as pointers: Zulu personal naming practices. *Language in society* 23. 253–272.

Ubahakwe, Ebo. 1981. *Igbo names: their structure and their meanings.* Ibadan: Day Star Press.

Ukpong, Edet. 2007. *An inquiry into culture: Ibibio names*. Uyo: Dorand Publishers.

Section Four: **Cultural implications in anthroponym typology**

Reyhan Habibli

Chapter 14 Typology and motivations for Azerbaijani personal names

Abstract: Personal names are considered important language units from actual, cognitive and emotional standpoints. As in any language, in the Azerbaijani language personal names are responsive to changes in fashion and other popular trends in society. Choices and usage of personal names are constantly at the centre of public attention. Therefore, this study is significant not only for the theory of proper names but also for other related domains, such as applied onomastics, sociolinguistics, cultural studies, psycholinguistics, etc. The object of the research is Azerbaijani personal names, with a focus on Turkic personal names and naming. These are borrowed names which have been used in the Azerbaijani language for a long time and have been adapted to the language. The main purpose of this study is to consider the traditions and motives behind name giving in Azerbaijan, and to determine the principles of nomination therein. The chapter also engages with ways of forming personal names, and further analyses the interlinguistic and extralinguistic factors influencing the development of the naming system. The research uses both descriptive and comparative methods within general linguistic and onomastics. Data sources include reference books on personal names, personal name dictionaries, and statistical bulletins. The chapter demonstrates that the formation and development of name systems take place under the influence of different factors.

Keywords: anthroponyms, name giving, Azerbaijani personal names, mentality, extralinguistic factors, linguacultural, traditions

1 Introduction

Names, their meanings, and motives for name giving have always interested people. Anthroponyms are part of the linguistic, social, and ethnocultural experience of a people. Human factors and personalities play important roles in the development of personal naming systems. Any person is both a carrier of a name and a name

Reyhan Habibli, Baku State University, Azerbaijan, e-mail: rhabibli@bsu.edu.az

https://doi.org/10.1515/9783110759297-014

creator. A personal name differentiates a person from others in the society, and as a result a person becomes an object and subject of civil-law. The anthroponymicon, which meets the needs of nomination, communication and the exchange of information, is a complex system of connections and relations of the onymic facts. These are different from the dynamic, etymological and structural standpoints. The study of the anthroponymic system reveals the dynamics and development processes of a given country's anthroponymicon. All people have their own traditions of name giving. The formation of anthroponyms is connected to people's worldviews, customs, traditions, lifestyle, everyday life and history. Their study identifies facts related not only to the name bearer but also to the whole society.

Azerbaijani anthroponomy is enriched by the various lexical units, especially appellative nouns. Plenty of abstract notions that are common nouns are used as personal names in the Azerbaijani language, including the following examples: a) boys' names: *Uğur* 'luck', *Ümid* 'hope', *Qüdrət* 'power', *Xəyal* 'dream', *İntiqam* 'revenge', *Zaman* 'time', *Tale* 'fate', etc.; b) girls' names: *Həqiqət* 'truth', *Həyat* 'life', *Xatirə* 'memory', *Təranə* 'melody', *Röya* 'dream', *Sevinc, Fərəh* 'joy', *İntizar* 'expectation', etc. (see Abdullayev 1985; Aydın Abi Aydın 2002; Azərbaycan dilinin böyük izahlı onomastik lüğəti 2007; Xudiyev 2014; Qurbanov 2004, 2019; Qurbanova 2019; Məmmədli 1995; Mirzə 1993; Paşayev and Bəşirova 2011). Eternal human dreams, aspirations and hopes for the child are also motivations for some Azerbaijani names; for example: a) boys' names: *Alim* 'scientist', *Sahib* 'owner', *Ilkin* 'firstborn', *Mubariz* 'fighter', *Nadir* 'rare', *Zafar* 'victory', *Jasarat* 'courage', etc.; b) girls' names: *Gozel* 'beauty', *Sadagat* 'fidelity', *Irade* 'will', *Metanet* 'tenacity', *Nazli* 'coquette', etc. Although most names are gender specific in Azerbaijani, there are exceptions that are gender neutral, such as *Arzu* 'wish', *Mahabbat* 'love', and *Yadigar* 'memory'.

Some Azerbaijani names are formed on the basis of geographical terms, natural phenomena, times of day, seasons, etc. These names include girls' names such as *Chemen* 'meadow', *Shelale* 'waterfall', *Seher* 'morning', *Shebnem* 'dew', *Bahar* 'spring', while typical boys' names are *Bulud* 'cloud', *Ildırım* 'lightning', *Tufan* 'storm', *Sahil* 'shore' and, *Gunduz* 'in the afternoon'. To derive most personal names, morpho-semantic derivations are prevalent in Azerbaijani. For example, deverbatives include the girl's names *Guler* 'she will laugh', *Sevar* 'she will love' and *Solmaz* 'she will never wither', and the boys' names *Anar* 'he will remember', *Yanar* 'he will glow' and *Vurgun* 'enamored'. Some names are derived from adjectives such as *Gullu* 'flowery', *Telli* 'curly', *Antiga* 'excellent', *Aziz* 'dear' and *Aydin* 'clear'.

2 Background to Azerbaijani naming

The history of name giving traditions has been reflected in a number of studies. These works provide information about various customs, sources and principles of name giving (Paşa 1977; Həsənov 2002; Hüseynova 1986; Ağayeva 1986; Rəhimbəyli 1993; Firidunlu 1993; Xalıqova 1993; Şahbazlı 1995; Xalıqov 1995). According to these authors, the influence of people's traditions and customs on personal names is undeniable. In Azerbaijan a personal name determines the life path of a person; therefore, name giving is an important ceremony in their life. Each name is social and historical in nature, since it does not only reflects not only public tastes in a particular period but also characterises the people's worldview, social relations, ideology and traditions. According to Успенский (1996), "The name reflects the tradition of name giving adopted in a certain social environment. In this regard, the name acts as a social sign and social characteristic of a person". This is the general law of onomastics: each proper name is the result of history and the property of society. While methods of forming anthroponyms are individual and unique, along with this individuality there is a certain commonality inherent in all peoples. Naming conventions are created within a culture and, in turn, become part of the culture, as Xudiyev (2014: 5) suggests:

> Antroponimlər sistemi xalqın dünyagörüşünə uyğun formalaşıb inkişaf etdiyi üçün meydana gəlmiş antroponimik mədəniyyət xalqın ümummənəvi mədəniyyətinin başlıca bir sahəsini təşkil edir
>
> [A system of anthroponyms is formed and develops according to the people's worldview and the emergent anthroponymic culture forms the people's main sphere of the general spiritual culture].

The modern Turkic anthroponymic systems, including the Azerbaijani name system, preserve the pre-Islamic pra-Turkic model in their composition. The Turkic people gave names on the basis of certain features, events and conditions. Names were given by the head of the family or the tribal leader. Concerning the semantics of Albanian (Turkic) anthroponyms, Qeybullayev (1992: 22) wrote:

> (. . .) qədim türklərdə (demək, o cümlədən qədim albanlarda) oğlan uşağına ad qoyduqda böyüyəndən sonra onun ağıllı, xoşbəxt igid, yaxşı el başçısı, sərrast atıcı, sağlam bədənli olması arzusu əsas yer tuturdu
>
> [(. . .) When the ancient Turki (i.e. including the ancient Albanians) gave names to boys, the meanings they considered were that the boy must grow up clever, happy, brave, healthy; he must be a good leader, and a good citizen].

There were also symbolic names in the ancient Turkic peoples' anthroponymy, derived from their orature. The heroes' names in the 11th century poetic "*Kutadgu bilig*" are symbolic. These include *Gundogdu* 'the sun has risen', *Aydoldu* 'full moon',

Oydulmush 'praised' and *Odgurmush* 'awakened'. The personal names in the epic "*Kitabi-Dede Gorgud*" reflect the ancient Turkic names: *Gorgud, Bayandur, Salur Gazan son of Ulash, Deli Dondar son of Uruz Seljuk, Aruz Goja, Bamsi Beyrek, Yeynek, Garaja Choban, Elek, Basat, Bugaj son of Dirse khan, Bekil and Ekrek.*

From Turkic history, we can decipher early names as being derived from terrestrial and geomorphological features. Later on, the names tended to be derived from social activities and organisation. Abulgazi khan Khiveli, in his work "*Ancestry of the Turkmen*" (1958), noted that *Oghuz khan* had six sons: *Gun khan* (*Gün* – 'sun'), *Yulduz (Ulduz) khan* (*Ulduz* 'star'), *Gok khan* (*Gök* – 'sky'), *Tag khan* (*Dağ* – 'mountain') and *Tenggiz (Deniz) khan* (*Dəniz* – 'sea'). His 24 grandchildren were not named for natural features but for social ones and their names were: *Kayi*– 'strong', *Bayat* – 'rich', *Alka-Oyli* – 'appropriate', *Kara-Oyli* – 'where he would stand', *Yasir* – 'rejecting all', *Yazir* – 'acquiring', *Dudurgap* – 'retaining, ruling the country occupied by him', *Duker* – 'circle', *Avshar* – 'hardworking', *Kizik* – 'hero, brave man', *Bekdeli* – 'a brilliant orator', *Kar-kin* – 'hospitable', *Bayindir* – 'peaceful, peace-loving', *Bechana* – 'workable', *Chavuldur* – 'honest, decent', *Chepni* – 'hero, brave man', *Salor* – 'armed with a sword', *Imir* – 'rich, wealthy', *Alayontli* – 'one who has a skewbald horse', *Bukduz* – 'pliable', *Uregir* – 'kindly, good', *Igdir* – 'great, big', *Ava* – 'with high rank' and *Kinik* – 'respectable'.

The ancient Turks gave different names to their children depending on age. There were different names given in childhood, in adolescence and in adulthood. If a person demonstrated courage, they attracted more names. As a rule, people, especially men, were known by the name given to them after showing courage. That is to say, the ancient Turkic names were connected to the person's activity, service, and social position. The child's physical development, behaviour, appearance, parents' beliefs, wishes, personality, age and interests were reflected in the Azerbaijani names in the pre-Islamic period. Azerbaijani personal names mostly consisted of Turkic words in the Middle Ages. The changes in the social life also influenced names. The number of native Azerbaijani names decreased during subsequent cultural transitions. Some of the ancient Turkic names found in medieval sources include *Kokche* 'blue; pretty', *Aslantekin* 'looks like a lion', *Aytekin* 'looks like the moon', *Yeltekin* 'looks like a wind', *Tagtekin* 'looks like a mountain', *Tashtekin* 'looks like a stone', *Bilkin* 'knowing, aware', *Guntogdu* 'the sun has risen' and *Aglamish* 'tearstained'. However, after the adoption of Islam by Turks, Arabic names gradually pushed the Turkic names into the background. That does not mean, however, that the Turkic names totally disappeared. The ancient Turkic names were always widely used in the oral and written literature.

In ancient times, there was a perception among Azerbaijani people that choosing a lucky name for a child could put them in danger and shorten their life. Bad names were preferred for children in order to mislead evil forces. Qurbanov (2019: 11) asserts that:

> Bəzi xalqlar ad vasitəsilə şər qüvvələri aldatmağa çalışmışlar. Bu məqsədlə uşağa *"İlənmiş", "Yaramaz", "İtquyruğu", "İtyeməz"* kimi pis ad verib onu ölümdən xilas etməyə səy göstərmişlər. Belə adlar türk xalqlarında çoxdur. Bir sıra xalqlar Əzrayılı çaşdırmaq üçün uşaq xəstələnəndə adını da dəyişmişlər. Bütün bunların hamısı ada son dərəcə yüksək qiymət verməyin, onun insan üçün əvəzsiz əlamət hesab edilməsinin nəticəsidir
>
> [Some people tried to deceive evil forces with names. It is for this purpose that children were given such bad names as *Ilenmish* ('smelly'), *Yaramaz* ('no good'), *Itguyrugu* 'dog's tail', *Ityemez* 'even a dog will not eat him/her', in order to save children from death. There are a lot of such names among the Turkic people. Some people even changed a child's name when he/she was ill in order to mislead Azrayil (Azrayil is the angel of death). All this demonstrates the value Turkic people put in personal names].

Paşayev (2015: 30) opines that such names are regarded as 'amulets', 'deceptive', or 'misleading'. He further states, "Bunlar insanların dini inamları və müvafiq adət-ənənələrlə əlaqədar olur. Qoruyucu adlar müəyyən zərurət nəticəsində yaranır" [They are connected with peoples' beliefs and relevant customs and traditions. Amulet names emerge by necessity].

The desire for boy children has always been a factor in Azerbaijani naming conventions. In ancient times the birth of a boy made the family much happier. Parents would expect to have a son. They looked on him as a successor to the head of the family, an assistant to the father, and the future owner of the household. A daughter, on the other hand, was not considered to be of equal importance. It was common to find names denoting negative emotions bestowed on daughters. Tanriverdiyev (1996: 133) states that:

> Mənfi emosiyalı qadın adlarının yaranması əski inamla, konkret desək, "qız uşağı dalbadal doğulan ailələrdə axırıncı qıza Qızqayıt, Oğlangərək və s. adlar verilərsə, bir daha qız uşağı deyil, oğlan doğular" inamı ilə bağlıdır. Türk estetikasının zənginliyindəndir ki, bəzən belə şəraitdə də mənfi emosiya müsbət motivli adla ifadə olunmuşdur (məsələn, Gülbəs, Gülyetər, Bəslər və s.)
>
> [The creation of girls' names with negative emotions is associated with ancient beliefs, and more specifically, with the belief that – "if in families where girls are born in a row such names as *Gyzgayit* 'girl, go away', *Oglangerek* 'we need a boy', etc., are given then in this case not a girl, but a boy will be born". Sometimes, even in such cases, a negative emotion is expressed by a name with a positive motivation, which is explained by the richness of Turkic aesthetics (for example: *Gulbes, Gulyeter* 'enough flowers', *Besler* 'enough', etc.)].

The use of negative names for girls, motivated by the desire to have male children, was prevalent in ancient times, but is less prevalent today.

3 Gender in Azerbaijani personal names and naming

In Azerbaijani the main participants in name giving are the father and the mother. However, the role of the elders in this regard is also great. Observations show that boys are mainly given names by the father and grandfather while the mother and the grandmother are more active when it comes to giving a name to a girl. As the status of a woman in society rises, her influence on name giving also increases (Xəlilli 2021; Şenel 2017; Calp 2014; Herdağdelen 2016; Gülensoy 2012; Şişman 2018; Gerhards and Tuppat 2020). Calp (2014) analysed the names of girls and boys widely used in Turkey, in particular in the province of Agri. The purpose of his study was to determine etymological similarities and differences between the most commonly used personal names in the province of Agri and across the country. Şenel (2017), in his study, speaks about the role of men and women in name giving in the family. In his opinion, although the role of a man (father and grandfather) in name giving is greater, the role of a woman (mother and grandmother) increases when they become influential in society.

Herdağdelen (2016), in his research, demonstrates that girls' names have a greater diversity than boys'(e.g., the top 15 male names cover 25% of the male population, whereas the top 28 female names cover 25% of the female population). Şişman (2018) also researched personal names in the Ulupamir district and she came to the conclusion that in this district, the most common girl's name is *Fatma*, and the most common boy's name is *Mehmet*. In her opinion, the most preferred and fashionable names in society are religious names and these are liked by the elders in families. Xəlilli (2021) studied the process of name giving in the Turkic epics and she notes that in the Turkic heroic epics, along with the naming of heroes, there are also cases of naming heroines too. Gülensoy (2012) considers the personal names that are given to boys and girls in Turkey at the present time. He notes that, at present, religious names (which are names used in the Koran), historical Turkic names and names of animals, plants, places, etc. are widely used in name giving. He further notes that in families with many daughters, such names as *Yeter* 'enough', *Dyondu* 'returned' are given to girls, while in families where a son has died, such names as *Satilmish* 'sold', *Dursun* 'let him stay', *Durdu* 'stopped' and *Allahverdi* 'God gave' are given to boys.

Gerhards and Tuppat (2020) analysed gender differences in immigrants' ethnic boundary making, using the example of name giving. They drew on the well-established finding that immigrants are more likely to choose a name that is common in the host country (a boundary crossing strategy) for female than formale children. Their analysis shows that immigrants' name giving practices are gendered. Girls more often receive names that are common in the host society than boys. They find that this gender difference can be explained both by features of the country of origin and by the level of integration into the host society.

4 The Azerbaijani anthroponymic system

The personal name, patronym, surname, nickname, and pseudonym constitute the national anthroponymic system in Azerbaijan. All these serve as individual designations of a person. Although was a common feature in the past to have many names, a person is now given one official name. However, people still have many names even though they are not documented. In the modern Azerbaijani language, the formula for the official name of a person consists of three components: the personal name, the patronymic and the surname. The use of this formula is legalized; the formula personal name + patronymic + surname is fixed in the passport and other official documents. The rules for giving such names are expressed in legislative documents, and this legal force regulates name giving. The fixing of the three-component formula as an authoritative norm for the official name of a person by legislation contributes to the transformation of its components into stable elements that form the anthroponymic system. This norm remains unchanged to this day, since the requirements of social life determine its expediency.

5 Methodology

This research engages general linguistic and onomastic methods. It is a descriptive approach which combines the methods of observation, classification, interpretation, generalization, and etymology. It further employs interpretative, component, and contextual analyses. These methods and approaches make it possible to reveal the common and specific linguistic peculiarities of the personal names considered. The study is an interdisciplinary approach to the analysis of personal names and it considers linguistic facts together with culture, sociolinguistics, and ethnolinguistics. Undoubtedly, the study of proper names requires extensive extralinguistic and, historical-etymological information. The data was collected through document analysis, which included journals and books, dictionaries of personal names, reference books, and onomastics literature. Some of the data were collected on internet web pages. Observations, interviews and intuitive knowledge were also sources for the data.

6 Motives for naming new-borns in Azerbaijan

There are key motivations in naming new-born children in Azerbaijan and these are gender, kinship and the parents' wishes. Key social events and misfortune also play a key role in the name giving conventions.

6.1 Gender

In most societies, men are accorded higher social status than women and these dominant positions are also reflected in the content of their names. In Azerbaijan it is no accident that such qualities as firm will, leadership, courage, fearlessness, heroism, valour, prowess, nobility, power, resilience, dignity, loyalty, fairness, humanism, endurance, militancy, fighting spirit, steadfastness, invincibility, generosity and, diligence are reflected in the names of boys. The following are boys' names based on words meaning heroism, pride and greatness: *Alov* 'flame', *Atlikhan* 'rider khan', *Boyukaga* 'great aga', *Budag* 'bough', *Gaya* 'rock', *Gilinj* 'sword', *Garabey* 'great bey' (*bey* – is a title for a chieftain), *Garakhan* 'great khan' (*khan* – is a title for a chieftain), *Igid* 'brave', *Orkhan, Ordukhan* 'army-khan', *Gachay* 'striving forward, running', *Gochar* 'brave man', *Erkin* 'matured, masculine', *Geray* 'steadfast, resilient'. Some boys' names are formed from words meaning courage, heroism and bravery, such as: *Bahadir* 'hero', *Galib* 'winner', *Gahraman* 'hero', *Mubariz* 'fighter', *Rashadat* 'bravery', *Pehlivan* 'wrestler', *Metin* 'steadfast' and, *Dayanat* 'perseverance, steadfastness'.

Since there is no linguistic category of gender in the Azerbaijani language, the gender of personal names is determined on the basis of their semantics. Beauty and tenderness are associated with girls' names and the concepts used to name them include: beauty, tenderness, purity, attractiveness, generosity, simplicity, sincerity, politeness, decency, honesty, fidelity, gentleness, politeness, courtesy, delicate taste and, loveliness, etc.; for example, *Nazaket* 'politeness', *Afet* 'nice, pretty', *Guler* 'smiling, merry, joyful', *Heyran* 'to be in love, admired, charmed', *Hagigat* 'truth, verity', *Halima* 'sweet disposition, patient (woman)', *Irada* 'willpower', *Latafet* 'beauty, tenderness', *Mehriban* 'gentle, good-hearted', *Melek* 'angel', *Merhemet* 'mercy, kindness', *Malahat* 'nice, charming', *Metanet* 'tenacity, endurance', *Merifet* 'courtesy, good breeding', *Zarifa* 'gentle, slim', etc.

Girls' names can also be derived from boys' names using the formant *a/ə* which indicates gender. This affix derives girl's names from boy's names, as in the following examples: *Adil* 'fair' – *Adila, Arif* 'understanding, knowledgeable' – *Arifa, Azad* 'free, independent' – *Azada, Vahid* 'one, single' – *Vahida, Vusal* 'meeting, rendezvous, achieved desire' – *Vusala, Habib* 'friend, beloved' – *Habiba, Jamal* 'a nice face;

beauty' – *Jamala, Zahid* 'ascetic' – *Zahida, Kamil* 'perfect' – *Kamila, Mahir* 'skillful, capable' – *Mahira, Naib* 'deputy, lawyer' – *Naiba, Nahid* 'teenager; planet Venus' – *Nahida, Rafig* – *Rafiga, Nail* 'achieving the fulfillment of his/ her desire' – *Naila, Nasib* 'friend; share, fate' – *Nasiba, Ramil* 'divination on earth' – *Ramila, Rashid* 'hero, brave' – *Rashida, Said* 'happy' – *Saida, Farid* 'incomparable, rare' – *Farida, Salim* 'healthy, without blemish' – *Salima, Rasim* 'painter' – *Rasima, Khalid* 'eternal, permanent' – *Khalida, Elmir* 'leader of the people' – *Elmira.* Most such names sound like new names: they enrich the vocabulary, and sometimes there is a difference in their meanings.

Some of the Azerbaijani personal names are androgynous; this means that they can be given to both girls and boys. These names include the following: *Dursun* 'let him stand', *Sadagat* 'fidelity', *Saadat* 'happiness', *Tarlan* 'falcon', *Shirin* 'sweat', *Khaver* 'sunrise', *Ismet* 'purity', *Izzet* 'honour', *Shafag* 'dawn', *Hayat* 'life', *Khurshud/Khurshid* 'sun', *Ulduz* 'star', *Sahavat* 'generosity', *Ulfet* 'friendship', *Yagut* 'ruby', *Yadigar* 'memory', *Gudret* 'power', *Javahir* 'jewel', *Ziver* 'adornment', *Arzu* 'wish', *Almaz* 'diamond', *Vefa* 'fidelity', *Gunesh* 'sun', *Hanifa* 'real', *Vilayat* 'region', *Gunduz* 'afternoon', *Mahabbat* 'love', *Intizar* 'suspense', *Parvin* 'Pleiades', *Sultan* 'sovereign', *Turan* 'the place where the Turks live', *Cherkez* 'rider, the name of one of the Caucasian peoples', *Adalet* 'justice', *Dayanat* 'steadfastness', *Zafar* 'triumph', *Mubarak* 'congratulations!', *Tebessum* 'smile', *Metleb* 'desire', *Seher* 'morning', *Sharaf* 'honour', *Merifet* 'civility', *Lachin* 'falcon', *Sayad* 'hunter', *Yaver* 'helper', *Ruzgar* 'breeze', *Afet* 'beauty', *Bahar* 'spring', *Bulbul* 'nightingale', *Barat* 'money document', *Dilaver* 'brave', *Gismet* 'share', *Gemer* 'moon', *Ziyafet* 'feast', *Iffet* 'morality', *Gulshad* 'joyful flower', *Kifayat* 'enough', *Iltifat* 'mercy', *Inayat* 'mercy', *Mahnur* 'moonlight', *Seyran* 'a place for walking', *Sharafat* 'honour, glory', *Khoshbakt* 'happy'. Such names make it difficult to determine the gender of the bearer. There are more than 100 such names in Azerbaijani anthroponymy.

Androgynous names are also connected to the conditions in which a baby was born and to the status of the family. For example, long-awaited babies are given names that express the happiness of the parents, regardless of their gender. Hüseynzadə (1990: 45) links the emergence of androgynous names to the lack of a gender category in the Turkic languages:

> Azərbaycan dilində cins kateqoriyasının olmaması müştərək şəxs adlarının – həm qadınlara, həm də kişilərə verilə bilən adların geniş yayılmasına imkan yaratmışdır. Aslan, Arzu, İzzət, Məhəbbət, Tərlan, Xavər, Şəfayət, Şirin, Şövkət və onlarca bu qəbildən olan şəxs adlarının referentləri eyni dərəcədə qadınlar da, kişilər də ola bilər. Müştərək şəxs adlarında onların alınma və ya türk mənşəli olmasından asılı olmayaraq cinsi göstərici rolu oynayan heç bir morfoloji əlamət özünü göstərmir
>
> [The lack of a gender category in the Azerbaijani language caused the emergence and wide dissemination of androgynous names. The referents of such names as Aslan, Arzu, Izzet,

Mahabbat, Tarlan, Khaver, Shafayat, Shirin, Shovket and many others can be used for both women and men. There is no morphological feature indicating gender in these androgynous personal names, be they of Turkic or foreign origin].

6.2 Kinship

There are some names that are connected to the Azerbaijani kinship system and terms. These names are used for both sexes. Words for family relations such as *dede, ata* 'father', *baba* 'grandfather', *gardash, dadash* 'brother', *emi, dayi* 'uncle' and *bala* 'baby' are widely used to form boys' names in the Azerbaijani language; for example, *Dedekhan, Dedejan, Agababa, Khanbaba, Hajibaba, Atabala, Atakhan, Atakishi, Bal(a)oglan, Balagardash, Agadadash, Dadashbala, Agaemi, Baladayi.*

There are three applications of kinship terms to derive boys' names in the Azerbaijani anthroponymic system. There are names based on the words that mean family relationships, such as *Ata, Atalar, Atam, Atash, Atababa, Baba, Babalar, Babash, Bala, Balaemi (bala – emi), Dadash,* and *Dede.* Of these, only the word *bala* 'baby, child' from the appellatives in this anthroponymic subgroup is related both to girls and boys, the rest are related only to men. The word *dede,* which is the appellative of the anthroponym *Dede* does not reference just 'father' but also 'master', as in 'Master Ashug' (Ashug – a folk singer and storyteller among the Azerbayjanis). The people called the talented Ashug "Dede". Thus, the association of the word *dede* with such meanings as 'wisdom', 'generosity' and, 'foresight' prompted its use as an anthroponym. Masculine kinship terms are also used as boys' names, as in *Atakishi, Atamoglan, Babakishi, Dedekishi, Emikishi,* etc. (*kishi* 'man', *oglan* 'boy'). Some kinship terms are combined with loanwords to derive hybrid boys' names, as in the examples, *Alibaba, Alibala, Aligardash, Huseynbala.*

Feminine kinship terms are also used to derive girls' names; terms such as *nene* 'grandmother', *ana* 'mother', *baji* 'sister', *bala* 'baby' and, *giz* 'daughter' derive the following feminine names: *Nenegiz, Nenekhanim, Anakhanim, Gulbaji, Khanbaji, Balagiz, Anagiz.* These can be used as plain kinship terms, as in *Anabala, Anabaji, Anagelin, Nene, Nenesh, Nenebaji.* The kinship terms can also be combined with titles, as in the following examples: *Agabaji, Agadostu* (a hybrid name), *Aganene, Anakhanim, Balakhanim, Bibikhanim, Khanbaji, Khanimbaji, Shahbaji* (a hybrid name: *shah* is a Persian title), *Shahnene.*

Azerbaijani people also use the system of rhymed names and they have been doing so since ancient times. Children are given names that rhyme with those of their parents or older kin. There are a lot of rhymed names in the Azerbaijani people's history. For example, father and son have rhymed names such as *Mehrab – Sohrab, Natig – Namig, Fikret – Hikmet, Shahin – Ramin* and, *Mubariz – Hafiz.* The father's name can also rhyme with the daughter's, as in *Eldar – Nubar, Eldar – Nigar, Chingiz – Nurangiz, Elkhan – Turkan* and, *Yashar – Bahar.*

6.3 Parents' desires

There are some personal names that are connected to the parents' wishes, dreams, desires, and attitudes. Such names serve different purposes. There are names that express parents' feelings, anxietiesy, and attitudes to a child; these include the girl's name *Aziza* 'dear', the boys' names *Ugur* 'luck', *Sevindik* 'we were glad', *Hasrat* 'desire' and, *Umid* 'hope', and the androgynous names *Intizar* 'expectation' and, *Shirin* 'sweat'. Some names express parents' wishes, such as the androgynous name *Khoshbakt* 'happy', and the boy's name *Shadman* 'happy man'. Some also express the joy of the parents, such as the girls' names *Farah* 'joy, delight', *Saadat* 'happiness', *Sevdim* 'I loved', *Sevimli* 'lovely', *Sevinj* 'joy'; the boy's name *Tapdig* 'we have found'; and the androgynous name *Nahayat* 'at last, finally'.

There are some Azerbaijani names that are motivated by the parents' desire to have a son. They are given only to girls, with the common idea and wish of having a son; these include *Tamam, Yeter, Basti* 'enough', *Giztamam, Gizyeter, Gizbes* 'girls enough', *Oglangerek* 'we need a son'. Suffice it to state that these names are no longer common. However, some girls' names, based on disappointment, protest or discontent caused by the birth of a daughter instead of a son, are still prevalent. Examples include *Basti, Tamam, Yeter, Kifayat* 'enough', *Gizyeter, Giztamam, Gizbes, Gizgayit* (*giz* – girl) 'girl enough', 'girl, go away', *Gulbes, Gultamam* (*gul* – flower) 'flower enough', *Istemez* 'does not want'. However, the attitudes towards sons and daughters were not the same in all families. There were some parents who desired a daughter who created the name *Khoshgadam* 'a good step'.

Names based on parents' desire for their children to be pretty, handsome or beautiful are also prevalent. Girls' names such as *Aybeniz* 'moon face', *Gulbeniz* 'flower face' and *Yarashig* 'charm' are examples. For boys, the main desires are for the son to be clever, educated, and a good speaker, not to be beautiful as for girls; the names include *Natig* 'speaker', *Vagif* 'knowing everything', *Agil* 'clever, wise', *Kamil* 'perfect', *Maarif* 'education', *Kamal* 'mind', *Yuksel, Ujal* 'rise up!'. Parents also wish their boys to be skillful, resourceful and brave, through names such as *Shujaet, Jasarat* 'courage', *Jahangir* 'conquering, occupying the world, conqueror, famous'. Some names of boys also indicate that parents wish their sons to be rich and successful; for example, *Sarvat* 'wealth', *Jalal* 'splendour, magnificence', *Dovlet* 'state, power, wealth', *Bakhtiyar* 'happy'. There are also names based on parents' desire for their children to live long, such as the boys' names *Minyashar* 'thousand lives', *Yashar* 'living', *Sonmez* 'does not go out' and the androgynous name *Dursun* 'let him/her stand'.

6.4 Other social motivations

There are some socio-religious motivations for name giving in Azerbaijan. For example, a long-awaited child is given such names as *Arzu* 'wish', *Arzuman* 'desirable', *Istek* 'desire', *Yegane* 'the only', *Vahid* 'single'. Certain events influenced and continue to influence name giving; for example, if a woman dies in childbirth, the baby is given such names as *Sakit* 'quiet', *Solgun* 'withered', *Intizar* 'suspense', *Yadigar* 'memory'. If another child is born to the family after a deceased baby, he/she is given such names as *Evez* 'instead', *Aziz* 'dear', *Otkem* 'overproud', *Nail* (male) /*Naile* (female) – 'achieved', *Hadiye*, *Tohfe* 'present, gift'. The birth order of children is also taken into account during name giving; for example, *Ilkin* 'firstborn', *Nubar* 'first gift', *Sani* 'the second', *Ezel* 'beginning', *Birjegul* 'a single flower', *Birgul* 'one flower', *Rabiyya* 'the fourth daughter'.

7 The structure of Azerbaijani personal names

Azerbaijani personal names take different structures; some are derived from appellative nouns, some from verbs and adjectives. Some of the names are compound nouns while others are sentential.

7.1 General nouns

Azerbaijani personal names are formed in different ways; some are drawn from common nouns such as the girls' names *Almaz* 'diamond', *Bahar* 'spring', *Hagigat* 'truth', *Savad* 'literacy', *Yagut* 'ruby', *Maral* 'deer', *Sadaf* 'mother-of-pearl', *Susan* 'lily', *Jeyran* 'gazelle', *Shamama* 'a small inedible melon', *Inji* 'pearl', *Saltanat* 'realm'; the boys' names *Taleh* 'fate', *Ilham* 'inspiration', *Intigam* 'revenge', *Etibar* 'trust', *Adil* 'fair man'. Some are derived from common administrative-territorial units such as the boys' names *Olke* 'country', *Diyar* 'region', *Merkez* 'centre'; and the androgynous names *Memleket* 'country', *Mahal* 'district'. Some of the names are formed from common nouns for natural phenomena, such as the girls' names *Shafag* 'dawn', *Hava* 'weather', *Ayaz* 'cold weather', *Bulud* 'cloud', *Ildirim* 'lightning', *Gurshad* 'driving rain', *Leysan* 'heavy rain'; the boys' names *Tufan* 'storm, blizzard', *Gursel* 'tempestuous stream', *Boran* 'snowstorm'; and androgynous name *Yagmur* 'rain'.

Some Azerbaijani names are formed from common nouns for respect, homage and spiritual values. Girls' names in this category are *Nazaket* 'courtesy, politeness' and *Najiba* 'nobility'. Boys' names include *Hormet*, *Ehtiram* 'respect', *Giymet* 'rate' and *Aziz* 'dear'; and androgynous names are *Izzet* 'honour, respect' and *Merifet* 'enlightenment, civility'. Some names are derived from terms for art, artistic words and literary genres, such as the girls' names *Novella, Hekaya, Hekayat* 'story', *Ravayat* 'legend'; and the boys' names *Ashug* 'a folk singer', *Shair* 'poet', *Adib* 'writer', *Alim* 'scientist', *Nasir* 'prosaist, prose-writer', *Dastan* 'saga'.

Names connected with bodies of water bodies are also common, as in the girls' names *Daryanur, Nurdarya, Ummangul* from the words *darya* 'sea', *umman* 'ocean'. Geographical notions such as earth and sky, and other common geographical features in the Azerbaijani language, are used to derive names such as the girls' names *Menzere* 'view, scenery', *Shelale* 'waterfall'; and the boys' names *Sarhad* 'boundary', *Sahra* 'desert', *Zirva* 'peak, top', *Muhit* 'environment', *Iglim* 'climate'.

Azerbaijani social and material culture also contributes to the formation of personal names. Some names are formed from elements in the material culture; for example, *Ayna* 'mirror', *Gumash* 'dense texture', *Gelem* 'pen, pencil' (girls' names). Some boys' names are formed from the military ranks and military units. For example, *Asker* 'soldier', *Zabit* 'officer', *Sarkar* 'military leader', *Sardar* 'governor', *Goshun* 'troops', *Alay* 'regiment'. There are also a number of names connected with social events; for example, *Ingilab* 'revolution', *Doyush* 'battle', *Tarikh* 'history'. However, most such names are given to boys. There are also some girls' names, such as *Sulhiya, Sulhsever, Sulhnur, Sulhnura, Sulhzar*, formed from the word *sulh* 'peace', created with the desire for peace.

7.2 Personal names formed from adjectives

There are also names formed from adjectives, depicting features and qualities such as colours. These names include the girls' names *Gozel* 'beautiful', *Agja* 'white girl', *Gesheng* 'nice', *Goychek* 'pretty', *Alagoz* 'grey-eyed', *Garagoz* 'black-eyed', *Saritel* 'yellow curl', *Yaxshi* 'good', *Telli* 'curly', Garatel 'black curl', *Gulandam* 'beautiful tender girl', *Zarif* 'elegant, delicate', *Zarifa* 'tender', *Inje* 'subtle, delicate', *Antiga* 'ancient, rare, excellent', *Khirda* 'small'; and the boys' names *Gara* 'face', *Garakhan* 'big khan', *Garaja* 'blacktop', *Sari* 'yellow', *Javan* 'young', *Goja* 'old man, great', *Meykhosh* 'sweet and sour'. Other adjectives used are *zar* 'gilding', *shad* 'glad', *shan* 'merry'; they derive the girls' names *Zargalam, Zarbuta, Gulmaya, Gulshan*; and the boys' names *Ershad, Elshad*. There are also names based on words referring to human qualities. The following names are formed from these notions in the Azerbaijani language: *Etibar* 'trust', *Etimad* 'confidence', *Etigad* 'faith, belief', *Motabar* 'reliable', *Amin* 'sure'. The girl's name *Amina* is formed from the boy's name *Amin*. Some of the names are formed from numerals; they are connected to the quantity and order of the qualities described. Such names include the girls' names *Birja*,

Birjakhanim (*bir* 'one'), *Ifrat* 'abundance, galore', *Yegana* 'one, single', *Minnur* (*min* 'thousand'), the boys' names *Vahid* 'single', *Ilkin* 'the first', *Sani* 'the second'; and the androgynous name *Ilknur* (*ilk* 'first').

7.3 Deverbatives through affixation

Some Azerbaijani personal names are formed from verbs by means of affixes. Some examples are the girls' names *Guler* 'smiling, merry, joyful, she will laugh', *Gulush* 'smile, laugh', *Sever* 'will love', *Sevinj* 'joy', *Solmaz* 'she will never fade, unfading', and the boys' names *Baxish* 'glance, view', *Donmaz* 'irreversible', *Donush* 'turn, crucial', *Dashgin* 'overflow'.

7.4 Compound personal names

Some names are formed in the analytical way; such names are compound names in the form of combinations of words. Some are actually sentences. For example, *Aygun* 'moon+day', *Aysu* 'moon+water', *Gulyaz* 'flower+spring', *Tezegul* 'new flower' (girls' names); and for boys, *Adigozel* 'wonderful name', *Dashdemir* 'stone+iron', *Javanshir* 'young lion', *Eldost* 'people+friend'. Some of the combinations result in sentences, as in *Elsevar* 'he loves his people', *Sevindik* 'we were glad', *Garyagdi* 'it snowed', *Tapdig* 'we have found', *Dayandur* 'stop and stand', *Allahverdi* 'God has given' (boys' names), and *Gulgez* 'go and look for flowers', *Bagdagul* 'a flower is in the garden' (girls' names). Feminine kin terms such as *xanım* 'mistress', *ana* 'mother', *nənə* 'grandmother', *bacı* 'sister', *qız* 'girl' are also components of compound anthroponyms like *Boyukhanim* 'great mistress', *Nenegiz* 'grandmother-girl', *Anakhanim* 'mother-mistress', *Gizbala* 'girl-baby', *Khanbaji* 'khan-sister'. Masculine kin terms are also used to derive compound boy names like *Khanoglan* 'khan-boy', *Babakishi* 'grandfather-man', *Atakishi* 'father-man', *Atakhan* 'father-khan', *Balagardash* 'baby-brother', *Ataemi* 'father-uncle'.

It is also common to combine two common nouns to derive compound personal names. The examples include girls' names such as *Anabala* 'mother+baby', *Gulbahar* 'flower+spring', *Gulbadam* 'flower+almond', *Gulsabah* 'flower+morning', *Zargalam* 'gilding+pen', *Gulchohra* 'flower+face', *Nargelem* 'pomegranate+pen', *Gulchichek* 'flower+blossom', *Lalechichek* 'poppy+flower'. The typical boy names in this category are *Dashdemir* 'stone+iron', *Eldeniz* 'people+sea', *Dunyamali* 'world's heritage', *Shiraslan* 'lion+lion' (a hybrid word which consists of the Persian word *shir* 'lion' and the Turkic word *aslan* 'lion'), *Dedekishi* 'father+man', *Emikishi* 'uncle+man'.

Compounding in personal names can also combine two personal names, as in *Mammadjafar* (boy's name), *Fatmanisa* (girl's name). The combination can also be of a common noun and proper name, as in the boys' names *Ertogrul* (*er* 'hero'+ *togrul* 'falcon'), *Huseyngulu* (*gul* 'slave'), *Aligardash* (*gardash* 'brother'), *Alibaba* (*baba* 'grandfather'). Some names are compounded because they express religious belief and the names of deities form part of the names, as in *Ojaggulu* 'slave of hearth', *Tanrikhan* 'God+khan', *Allahveren* 'God-given', etc. (boys' names). Some of the names consist of kinship terms, as in *Atababa* "father+grandfather", *Ataemi* 'father+uncle', *Baladadash* 'baby+brother', *Dadashbala* (boys' names); and *Anabala* 'mother+baby', *Anabaji* 'mother+sister', *Anagelin* 'mother+bride' (girls' names).

There are cases whereby the first component is an adjective; for example, *gara* 'black', as in *Garakhan, Garabey, Garakishi, Garaoglan*; *khas* 'genuine, pure, special', as in *Khaspolad* 'genuine steel, special steel'(boys' names). Other names contain the adjective *ag* 'white': *Aggul, Aggun, Aggiz, Agjagiz, Agjabeniz, Agjagul, Agkhanim*; *boyuk* 'great': *Boyukgelin* 'great bride, daughter-in-law'; *gara* 'black': *Garagoz* 'black eye', *Garagile*; *inje* 'tender': *Injegul, Injechichek, Injegiz*; *yakhshi* 'good': *Yakhshigul, Yakhshichichek, Yakhshikhanim*; *teze* 'new': '*Tezegul* 'new flower'; *goychek, gozel* 'pretty, nice': *Goychekgul, Goychekgelin, Gozelgul*; *sari* 'yellow, blonde': *Sarigul, Saritel* (girls' names). Such girls' names as *Aggul, Agjagul, Garagile, Injegul, Yakhshigul, Goychekgul, Gozelgul* and *Sarigul* are hybrid as some of their parts are Persian. In some cases, the first component is a numeral *bir* 'one' as in *Birgul, Birjegul, Birjegiz* (girls' names). Sometimes, as a result of rearranging the components in compound personal names, new names are formed; for example, *Agakhanim – Khanimaga, Anakhanim – Khanimana, Zargalam – Galamzar, Gunay – Aygun* (girls' names), *Agamir – Miraga, Beymirza – Mirzabey, Agahuseyn – Huseynaga, Balabey – Beybala, Samedaga – Agasamed, Alimammad – Mammadali* (boys' names).

7.5 From titles

There are several personal names based on the titles *Aga, Agalar, Agasi, Khagan, Khanlar, Beyler* (boys' names), and *Khanim, Beyim, Khatin* (girls' names). These titles are also common in the formation of Turkic anthroponyms, where they are combined with the suffix "*tekin*". The titles can be combined to derive personal names, as in the following examples: *Agabey, Agakhan, Khanaga, Agasultan* (boys' names), and *Agabeyim, Agabanu* (the hybrid name *banu* is a Persian word for 'mistress'), *Agakhanim, Khanimaga, Khanimsoltan, Bikekhanim, Beyimkhanim* (girls' names).

Titles also combine with other word categories to form personal names; for example, they combine with common nouns, as in *Bayramkhatun* 'holiday+*khatun*', *Gulbanu* 'flower+*banu*', *Gonchabeyim* 'bud+*beyim*' (girls' names); and *Beydemir* '*bey*+iron', *Elkhan* 'people+*khan*', *Gelemshah* 'pen+*shah*' (boys' names). Azerbaijani titles also combine with Arabic-Persian appellatives to form a number of hybrid personal girls' names; for example, *Zarkhanim, Gulkhanim, Narkhanim, Nurtekin, Nurkhanim, Khanimzar, Khanimgul, Khangul.* There are also compound personal names which consist of a title and kinship term and vice versa, as in *Agababa, Agagardash, Agadayi, Agadadash, Agaemi/Agami, Atabey, Atakhan, Babakhan, Bababey, Agabala, Balaga (bala+aga), Balakhan, Balabey, Beybala, Beydadash, Khanbala, Khanbaba, Gardashkhan, Dedekhan, Khanemi* (boys' names). The girls' names in this category include *Khanimbaji, Khanimana, Agabaji, Aganene, Anakhanim, Balakhanim, Bibikhanim, Khanbaji.* The respect function of titles motivates these combinations. Other compound names consist of a title and a personal name and vice versa; for example, *Agabeshir, Agagurban, Agazeynal, Agazeki, Agayusif, Agakazim, Agakerim, Azizaga, Azizbey, Azizkhan, Ahmedaga, Khanali, Khanahmed, Bedirkhan, Mammadkhan, Chingizkhan* (boys' names).

7.6 Sentential Azerbaijani personal names

There are personal names formed on the basis of a simple (narrative) sentence; for example, *Agaverdi* 'Lord gave', *Garyagdi* 'It snowed', *Beyverdi* '*Bey* gave' (*bey* – is a title for a chieftain), *Beygeldi* '*Bey* has come', *Babaverdi* 'a grandfather gave', *Khudaverdi/Tanriverdi/Tariverdi* 'God gave', *Khangeldi* 'Khan has come', *Ojaqverdi* 'hearth gave', *Allahverdi* 'Allah ('God', an Arabic word)+*verdi* ('gave', a Turkic word), *Imamverdi* ('Imam', an Arabic word)+*verdi* ('gave', a Turkic word), *Allahshukur* 'thank God', *Khanverdi* 'Khan gave' (boys' names); and *Besler* (*bes+olar*) 'that is enough' (girl's name). It should be noted that while the word *Khuda* 'God' is explained as a Persian word in dictionaries, Məhərrəmli (2016: 115) relates it to the Turkic theonym '*gut*'. There are also personal names that take the form of an imperative sentence, like *Agadur* (*Aga, dur!* 'Master, stand!'), *Gizgayit* (*Giz gayit!* 'Girl, go away'), *Gizyeter* (*Giz yeter!* 'Girls are enough'), *Oglangerek* (*Oglan gerek!* 'We need a boy'; *Dayandur* (*Dayan! Dur!* 'Stop! Stand!'); *Erol* (*Er ol!* 'Be a man/hero'), *Yuksel, Ujal* ('Rise up!'). Although the above-mentioned personal names are completely lexicalised units, clearly, their predicate is expressed by the imperative form of a verb in the second person singular.

8 Conclusion

Azerbaijani personal names are rooted in the Turkic tradition and they have been influenced by Arabic and Persian cultures. While the ancient tradition was that one had many names, the advent of registration has limited the number of official names. The Azerbaijani anthroponymic system has three components which are the forename, the patronym and the surname. Personal names are derived from nouns, adjectives, enumerators and verbs. These can combine to form compound names or even sentential ones. The key motivations for name giving are gender, kinship, parents' desires for their children and events around a child's birth. Boys are associated with strength and courage while girls are associated with beauty and tenderness. There is evidence from the naming conventions that sons are the preferred children over daughters, although this is not as rampant as in the ancient Turkic times.

References

Abdullayev, Bəhruz. 1985. *Azərbaycan şəxs adlarının izahlı lüğəti* [Explanatory dictionary of Azerbaijani personal names]. Baku: Azerneshr.

Ağayeva, Firəngiz. 1986. Addəyişmə adətləri haqqında [About the customs of name change]. In Afat Qurbanov (ed.), *Problems of Azerbaijani onomastics* 1. 16–18. Baku: API.

Aydın Abi Aydın. 2002. *Şəxs adları lüğəti* [Dictionary of personal names]. Baku: Chirag.

Azərbaycan dilinin böyük izahlı onomastik lüğəti. I kitab. Antroponimlər. 2007. [Large explanatory onomastic dictionary of the Azerbaijani language]. Book I. Anthroponyms. Baku: Nafta-Press.

Calp, Mehrali. 2014. Kişi adları üzerine dilbilimselbir çalışma (Ağrı ili örneği) [A linguistic study on person names (an example of Agrı province)]. *Journal of Turkish Research Institute (Ataturk University)* 52. 27–49.

Firidunlu, Firidun. 1993. Gürcüstanda yaşayan Azərbaycan türklərinin adqoyma ənənəsi [Tradition of name giving of Azerbaijani Turks living in Georgia]. In Afat Qurbanov (ed.), *Problems of Azerbaijani onomastics* iv. 235–237. Baku: ASPU.

Gerhards, Jurgen & Julia Tuppat. 2020. Gendered pathways to integration: why immigrants' naming practices differ by the child's gender. *KZfSS Kölner Zeitschrift für Soziologie und Sozialpsychologie* 72. 597–625.

Gülensoy, Tuncer. 2012. XXI. yüzyılda Türkiye kişi adlarına bir bakış [An approach for personal names in Turkey in 21st century]. *İDİL* 1 (5).

Herdağdelen, Amaç. 2016. Modern Türkiye'de kişi adları [Personal names in modern Turkey]. *Dilbilim Araştırmaları Dergisi.* 16–32. https://arxiv.org/ftp/arxiv/papers/1801/1801.00049.pdf (accessed 28 February 2023)

Həsənov, Həsrət. 2002. *Adlar tarixin, xalqın milli nişanəsi kimi* [Names as a national sign of history, people]. Baku: Nurlan.

Hüseynova, S. 1986. Azərbaycan antroponimiyasında adət-ənənələr haqqında [About the customs and traditions in Azerbaijani anthroponymy]. In Afat Qurbanov (ed.), *Problems of Azerbaijani onomastics* 1. 52–53. Baku: API.

Hüseynzadə, Çingiz. 1990. Azərbaycan şəxs adlarında cinsi əlamət haqqında [The gender feature in Azerbaijani personal names]. In Afat Qurbanov (ed.), *Problems of Azerbaijani onomastics* iii. 44–45. Baku: API.

Кононов, Андрей. 1958. *Родословная туркмен. Сочинение Абу-л-Гази хана Хивинского* [Ancestry of the Turkmens. Works of Abu-l-Ghazi Khiva Khan]. Moscow-Leningrad: Publishing House of Academy of Sciences of the USSR.

Məhərrəmli, Baba. 2016. *Dünya dillərində homogen sözlər* [The homogeneous words in the world languages]. Baku: Khazar University.

Məmmədli, Nadir. 1995. *Adını mən verdim – yaşını Allah versin* [I gave the name – God will give the age]. Baku: Maarif.

Mirzə, Osman. 1993. *Adlarımız. Məlumat kitabı* [Our names. Reference book]. Baku: Azerbaijan Encyclopedia.

Paşa, Aydın. 1997. *Azərbaycan antroponimiyasının leksik problemləri* [Lexical problems of Azerbaijani anthroponymy]. Baku: Maarif.

Paşayev, Aydın. 2015. *Azərbaycan antroponimikası* [Azerbaijani anthroponymy] Baku: Elm ve tehsil.

Paşayev, Aydın &, Alimə Bəşirova. 2011. *Azərbaycan şəxs adlarının izahlı lüğəti* [Explanatory dictionary of Azerbaijani personal names]. Baku: Mutarjim.

Qeybullayev, Qiyasəddin. 1992. *Qədim türklər və Ermənistan* [The ancient Turki and Armenia]. Baku: Azerneshr.

Quliyev, Əbülfəz. 1999. *Əski türk onomastik sözlüyü* [The ancient Turkic onomastic vocabulary]. Baku: Elm.

Qurbanova, Fidan. 2019. *Azərbaycan şəxs adları. İzahlı lüğət* [Azerbaijani personal names. Explanatory dictionary]. Baku.

Qurbanov, Afad. 2004. *Azərbaycan onomalogiyasının əsasları* [Foundations of Azerbaijani onomology], vol. 2. Baku: Nurlan.

Qurbanov, Afad. 2019. *Azərbaycanlı şəxs adları ensiklopediyası* [Encyclopedia of Azerbaijani personal names]. Baku: Azerbaijan National Academy of Sciences.

Rəhimbəyli, Fəridə. 1993. Adın etnoqrafiyası [Ethnography of names]. In Afat Qurbanov (ed.), *Problems of Azerbaijani onomastics 4*, 41–43. Baku: ASPU.

Şahbazlı, Faiq. 1995. Türk adqoyma mədəniyyəti [Turkic culture of name giving]. In Afat Qurbanov (ed.), *Problems of Azerbaijani onomastics 5*, 156–159. Baku: ASPU.

Şenel, Mustafa. 2017. Gençliğin adıyla imtihanı [Shenel, M. The test of the young by their names]. *International Journal of Turkic Dialects Research*, 1 (1). 72–84

Şişman, Rabia. 2018. Kişi adları üzerine dilbilimsel çalışma [Linguistic research on personal names]. *Turkish Studies*. https://atif.sobiad.com/index.jsp?modul=makale-detay&Alan=sosyal&Id=AXC_OaycyZgeuuwfWDhm (accessed 28 February 2023).

Tanrıverdiyev, Əzizxan. 1996. *Türk mənşəli Azərbaycan antroponimləri* [Azerbaijani anthroponyms of Turkic origin]. Baku: ASPU.

Успенский, Борис. 1996. Мена имен в России в исторической и семиотической перспективе [Uspensky, B. Change of name in Russia in historical and semiotic perspective]. In *Uspensky, B. Selected Works. Volume. Language and culture*, 187–202. Moscow: School "Languages of Russian culture".

Xalıqova, Rəna. 1993. Adqoymada tarixi-ənənəvi prinsip [The historical-traditional principle in name giving]. In Afat Qurbanov (ed.), *Problems of Azerbaijani onomastics* 4. 211–212. Baku: ASPU.

Xalıqov, Fikrət. 1995. Folklorda adalma motivləri [Motives of name giving in folklore]. In Afat Qurbanov (ed.), *Problems of Azerbaijani onomastics 5*, 33–35. Baku: ASPU.

Xəlilli, Jalə. 2021. Türk xalq qəhrəmanlıq dastanlarında alp qadın və advermə motivi [Alp woman and naming motivation in Turkic national heroic epics]. *Ipek Yolu* 2. 169–173 (Azerbaijan University).

Xudiyev, Nizami. 2014. Azərbaycan antroponimlərinin təşəkkülü və inkişafı [Formation and development of Azerbaijani anthroponyms]. In N. Khudiyev (ed.), *Selected works*, vol. IX, 1–149. Baku: Elm ve tehsil.

Chia-Jung Pan

Chapter 15
The grammar of personal names in Saaroa

Abstract: This chapter presents an in-depth exploration of Saaroa personal names in Taiwan and their culture, reflecting their expressions of cultural beliefs and practices. Special attention has been paid to the structures and characteristics of personal names and their corresponding vocative forms, senior names and teknonymy. In Saaroa, personal names may reflect teknonymy when names' bearers acquire a son or daughter, and exhibit morphophonemic alternations. Saaroa personal names can co-occur with a case marker when exhibiting grammatical alignment, a definite marker when conveying the categorical meaning or the emotive meaning, and a number word when emphasising pluralisation and countablity. Syntactically, they can occur in structures such as topicalisation, modification and coordination.

Keywords: personal name, kinship, teknonymy, Austronesian, Saaroa

1 Introduction

As Bramwell (2016) explains, names reflect cultural diversity, may change at different stages of life or stay the same, and show connections with the community.[1] Based on the literature on 47 naming practices in 60 societies from 1871 to 1980, Alford (1988) analyses cultural variability, revealing that names are universal in societies, but that name practices show great differences with regard to the address, nicknames, changes of name, patronymy and many other aspects of naming.

Van Langendonck and Van de Velde (2016: 33) mention that the study of names has not received much attention from the perspective of grammar. Names are the most prototypical nominal categories since they are morphologically unmarked. Among all types of names, personal names are the most typical ones, since they bear no descriptive meaning and are commonly used to designate individuals.

1 The study was supported by a Major Project of the National Social Science Foundation of China (grant number 18ZDA298).

Chia-Jung Pan, Center for Linguistic Sciences, the Institute of Advanced Studies of Humanities and Social Sciences, Beijing Normal University, e-mail: chiajung.pan216@gmail.com

https://doi.org/10.1515/9783110759297-015

One of the features of the naming system of the indigenous peoples of Taiwan is the maintenance of traditional naming lists (Wei and Liu 1962). Each ethnic group has a set of names inherited from ancestors, and these ancestors' names are given to their descendants. A salient feature of name giving is that brothers, father and son, sisters, and mother and daughter cannot bear the same name.

No special attention has been paid to the study of personal names in Saaroa, an Austronesian language of Taiwan.[2] This chapter examines personal names in Saaroa from the anthropological and linguistic perspective. The major questions posed in this chapter are:

(A) What are the characteristics of personal names and vocative forms, senior names and teknonymy in Saaroa?

(B) What are the grammatical features of personal names in Saaroa?

In this study, "plain form" and "vocative" are used when people are described and addressed, respectively. "Seniuor names" and "teknonymy" are used when people become old and have babies, respectively. Teknonymy is a naming practice used to address adults according to the names of their children, normally being treated as an ethnological or anthropological issue but not being examined as a linguistic subject.

This chapter is organised as follows. Section 2 gives an anthropological linguistic profile of Saaroa, providing background information useful to the subsequent discussions. Personal names and vocative forms, personal names and senior names and teknonymy are discussed in Sections 3, 4 and 5, respectively. Section 6 describes the salient grammatical feature pertaining to Saaroa personal names. Section 7 concludes this chapter.

2 Anthropological linguistic profiles of Saaroa

Prominent anthropological linguistic information is provided in this section, including location, population and speakers, the language and its present state, kinship and marriage, and birth-giving and related taboos.

2 Austronesian languages of Taiwan are labeled Formosan languages. Those who use these languages are indigenous peoples. At present, 16 ethnic groups are officially recognised by the Taiwan government, including Amis, Atayal, Bunun, Kanakanavu, Kavalan, Paiwan, Truku, Puyuma, Rukai, Saaroa, Saisiyat, Sakizaya, Seediq, Thao, Tsou and Yami. Each group has its own language or several dialects, which have the same name as the group name.

(A) Location

A small number of Saaroa people live in Maya Village, Namaxia District, while the majority of Saaroa people live in Taoyuan Village and Gaozhong Village, Taoyuan District, Kaohsiung City, Taiwan. There are four major Saaroa communities, Lhilhala, Paiciana, Talicia and Vilanganʉ. Lhilhala, consisting of two minor communities, Tangulha and Karavun, is located in Taoyuan Village. Among the four communities, it is the northernmost one. Paiciana is situated in Gaozhong Village, including three minor communities, Rʉlhʉcʉ, Paapanara and Sʉlhʉnganʉ. Rʉlhʉcʉ is the place where most Saaroa people live. The fourth community, Talicia, lay to the north of Taluoliu River in Gaozhong Village and vanished in the middle twentieth century. Since then, Saaroa people of this community have relocated to Paiciana. Vilanganʉ, encompassing the area called Suaci, lies to the east of Laonong River and on the opposite side of the mouth of the Taluoliu River in Gaozhong Village. The location of Saaroa is shown in Map 15.1.

(B) Population and speakers

According to the population census conducted by the Council of Indigenous Peoples in January 2021, the population of Saaroa is 419. At the time of Chiu's (2008) ethnological study, 38 people, accounting for 14.29 percent of the population, were able to speak the language. However, based on our fieldwork in the villages, only a limited number of Saaroa people are genuine native and fluent speakers.[3] At the time of writing (2022), fewer than ten people can speak the language fluently. Most speakers live in Gaozhong Village and one speaker live in Taoyuan Village. In recent years, the government and the Saaroa communities have been striving to offer Saaroa language learning courses for young people and children in the elementary school and in communities, in order to regain language vitality and to conserve the Saaroa language. Due to the limited number of qualified language teachers, lack of learning motivation and lack of practical utility in daily life, these efforts have nevertheless had only a limited impact.

(C) The present state of the language

No dialectal variations have been observed in different Saaroa communities. Due to the multiracial state of the area where Saaroa people live, a number of Saaroa people are multilingual speakers, and capable of understanding and speaking the languages of other neighbouring ethnic groups. For example, in addition to the

3 The fieldwork was primarily conducted in Kaohsiung, Taiwan, during 2008–9, augmented by elicitation and discussion with native speakers during three subsequent three trips: one from August 2008 to July 2009, another from February 2011 to May 2011 and the other in May 2020.

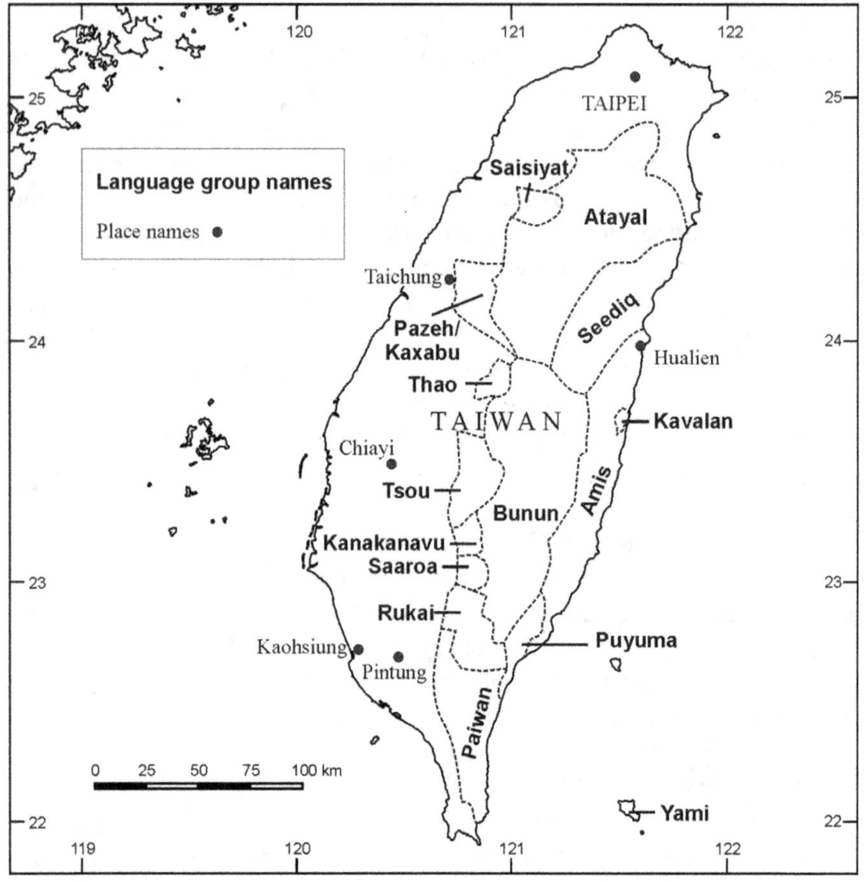

Map 15.1: Location of Saaroa (Pan 2018: 658).

national language, Mandarin Chinese, many people can understand and speak Taiwanese Southern Min, another dominant language in Taiwan. Moreover, a large number of old people can speak Bunun fluently, a dominant language of indigenous people in the area. For historical reasons, old people who were born during the period of Japanese colonisation before World War II are able to speak Japanese. In terms of its writing system, the Roman script was employed in previous materials in Saaroa. On December 15, 2005, a standard orthography system for Formosan languages was officially stipulated by the Council of Indigenous People and the Ministry of Education of Executive Yuan, Taiwan. At the moment, a number of Saaroa people can write their own language with this standard orthography system.

(D) Kinship and marriage

Liu (1969) shows that the social structure of the Saaroa is patrilineal. Similarly, in our fieldwork, the Saaroa kinship system was found to be classificatory; marriage is patrilineal and mostly patrilocal. Saaroa marriage is now established under the consent of the bridegroom, the bride and their parents, while Saaroa people had a strict system of monogamy, based on women marrying into men's families. Although polygamy and another type of marriage, i.e., accepting or adopting a son-in-law who would live in the wife's territory and assume the role of a son, did not exist in the Saaroa tradition, under the influence of Bunun and Han people, these two types of marriage, which were not prevalent in the Saaroa tradition, have been adopted by a few Saaroa people in recent decades. Saaroa people generally hold the view that the ideal husband or wife should possess the virtues of assiduity, cleverness, obedience, strength and hunting skills, and should not have the vices of lying, theft, sloth and lust.

(E) Birth-giving and related taboos

Due to the limited number of Saaroa people, the birth of children is always welcomed by Saaroa people. They are not particularly fond of boys, although marriage is patrilineal and mostly patrilocal. What they consider as ideal or best is that the families should include boys and girls in equal numbers. Despite the fact that they cherish children, they think it inauspicious for mothers-to-be to conceive twins, genetic freaks or deformed foetuses. In addition, they consider it disgraceful to have illegitimate children. Saaroa people believe that the pregnant woman's husband should abide by certain taboos related to drinking and eating during gestation, e.g., avoid eating animal lungs, scorched food, the meat of pregnant animals and twin fruits. Apart from these, the husband should not eat monkeys; otherwise, after the birth, the baby will look like a monkey. The husband should avoid drinking deer's blood; otherwise the expectant mother will bleed a lot during delivery. The husband should not keep interchanging sitting with standing while eating, and should put chairs in order immediately after eating; otherwise the fetus will stay in his wife's womb and she may have a difficult delivery. Also, after food has been cooked, the husband should be cautious in putting pots or pans down after lifting them up. The pregnant woman herself should not eat reheated rice, taken back home by her husband after going hunting. In addition, there are some taboos beyond of drinking and eating during pregnancy that are still adhered to by the Saaroa people. The pregnant woman's husband is prevented from chopping wood with branches, tying things together and attending ceremonies and important activities. For example, in the past he was not allowed to go head-hunting during his wife's pregnancy. The husband is required to get up when he hears the rooster's crow; otherwise the fetus will stay in his wife' womb and she may have a difficult delivery.

3 Personal names and vocative forms

Vocative is a nominal label for addressing people. Special attention has been paid to vocatives with overt markings. The definitions of vocatives tend to emphasise only one aspect, either a formal structure or a functional component. The reason for this is explained by Lambrecht (1996: 267) in terms of the deictic nature of vocatives and their grammatical status as non-arguments. Lambrecht (1996: 267) regards vocatives as sentence constituents, maintaining a relationship between a discourse referent and proposition. Some definitions of vocatives tend to be syntactic. Zwicky (1974: 787) defines the vocative in English as an element with a special intonation which does not serve as an argument of a verb in a sentence. Another definition from a syntactic perspective is given by Levinson (1983: 71), emphasising the non-integrated nature of vocatives as noun phrases that refer to the addressee, which are syntactically, semantically and prosodically independent of sentences. Sonnenhauser and Hanna (2013) hold the view that vocatives are important in perceiving the sentence pragmatically.

In Saaroa, morphological alternation is the most important means to mark the vocative. 36 Saaroa personal names were collected in our fieldwork. Whether these names have corresponding specific meanings or connotations remains unclear. Even if they did have, they are no longer remembered by current Saaroa people. Saaroa personal names must correlate with specific genders (sexual classification), and the correlation is culturally conventionalised.[4] Among these personal names, 12 names are used for females and 24 names for males. Some of the names have corresponding vocative forms. Tables 15.1 and 15.2 show these Saaroa female and male names with their corresponding vocative forms.[5]

Table 15.1: Female names and their vocative forms.

Names	Vocatives	Names	Vocatives
'Uusu	Uusuu	Lhaa'u	Lha'uu
Apʉʉ	Apʉʉ	Lhatingai	Tingaii
ʉlʉkʉ	ʉʉkʉʉ	Na'apu	Na'apuu
Inguruu	Iinguu	Pi'i	Pi'ii
Kuatʉ	Kuatʉʉ	Vanau	Naau
Langui	Languii		

4 Unlike well-known Indo-European languages that have linguistic gender, Saaroa does not have it.

5 Orthography follows IPA, with the following exceptions: ' = glottal stop, c = unaspirated voiceless alveolar affricate, ng = velar nasal, l = alveolar flap, lh = alveolar lateral fricative, r = trill and ʉ = high central unrounded vowel.

Table 15.2: Male names and their vocative forms.

Names	Vocatives	Names	Vocatives
'Aavi	'Avii	Pali	Palii
Amalhʉ	Maʉʉi	Pauli	Paulii
ʉlʉngaanʉ	Ngaanʉʉ	Takanau	Takanauu
Kilhakilhau	Kilhakilhauu	Tamaulhu	Maulhuu

There are some morphophonemic alternations, including vowel lengthening, vowel shortening, consonant deletion, syllable deletion and suppletion. Vowel lengthening is applied to the word-initial, word-medial or word-final vowel. Vowel shortening is applied to a long vowel of a personal name in the word-medial position. Consonant deletion is applied to the initial consonant of a personal name. Syllable deletion is applied to a personal name in which a syllable in word-initial, word-medial or word-final position is deleted, or two syllables in word-initial position are deleted. Suppletion is found if the personal name and its vocative form are not fully related to each other. Each morphophonemic alternation is shown in boldface.

(1) a. vowel lengthening: word-initial: *Ing**ur**uu* → ***Ii**ng**uu***; word-medial: *Van**a**u* → *N**aa**u*; word-final: *Pauli* → *Paul**ii***
   b. vowel shortening: e.g., *'**Aa**vi* → *'**A**vii*
   c. consonant deletion: e.g., *'Uusu* → *Uusuu*
   d. syllable deletion: one syllable: word-initial: ***Ta**maulhu* → *Maulhuu*; word-medial: *ʉ**lʉ**kʉ* → *ʉʉkʉʉ!*; word-final: *Ing**uru**u* → *Iinguu*; two syllables: ***ʉlʉ**ngaanʉ* → *Ngaanʉʉ*
   e. suppletion: *Amalhʉ* → *Maʉʉi*

Some personal names apply more than one morphophonemic rule. For example, in (2a), a long vowel in word-initial position is shortened and a short vowel in word-final position is lengthened. In (2b), a word-initial consonant is deleted and a short vowel in word-final position is lengthened. In (2c), one or two word-initial syllables are deleted and a short vowel in word-final position is lengthened. Each morphophonemic alternation is illustrated in boldface.

(2) a. vowel shortening + vowel lengthening: e.g. *'**Aa**v**i*** → *'**A**v**ii***
   b. consonant deletion + vowel lengthening: e.g. *'Uus**u*** → *Uus**uu***
   c. syllable deletion + vowel lengthening: e.g. ***Ta**maulh**u*** → *Maulh**uu***; ***ʉlʉ**ngaan**ʉ*** → *Ngaan**ʉʉ***

4 Personal names and their corresponding senior names

Saaroa personal names vary when Saaroa people are senior or become old. This variation is attested in both female and male names. The Proto-Austronesian form **t-ama* refers to ‘father’ and ‘uncle’. In Saaroa, senior people are expected to be above the age of 60. When addressing senior people, *tama-*, a shortened form of *tamalʉngalʉ* ‘uncle’, is added to the nominal root of an adult name, as shown in the following examples. It is interesting and important to note that the use of *tama-* for both female and male names is a linguistic reflection that Saaroa is patrilineal.

Some Saaroa female and male names and their corresponding senior names are provided in Tables 15.3 and 15.4.

Table 15.3: Female names and corresponding senior names.

Female names	Senior names	Female names	Senior names
’Uusu	Tam’uusu	Langui	Tamalangui
Apʉʉ	Tanakʉapʉ	Lhaa’u	Tamlhaa’u
Aruai	Tamaaruai	Lhatingai	Tamlhatingai
ʉlʉkʉ	Talhivʉrʉkʉ	Na’apu	Tamna’apu
Inguruu	Tamainguruu	Pi’i	Tampi’i
Kuatʉ	Tamakuatʉ	Vanau	Taavanau

Table 15.4: Male names and corresponding senior names.

Male names	Senior names	Male names	Senior names
’Aavi	Tama’aavi	Palii	Tamapalii
’Angai	Tama’angai	Pauli	Tamapaulii
’Angu’u	Tama’angu’u	Piacʉ	Tamapiacʉ
’Atai	Tama’atai	Piauli	Tamapiauli
Amalhʉ	Tamalingalʉ	Sʉʉkʉ	Tamasʉʉkʉ
Caʉpʉ	Tamacaʉpʉ	Takanau	Tamatakanau
ʉlʉngaanʉ	Tavʉtavʉrʉnga	Tamaulhu	Tamatamaulhu
Kilhakilhau	Tamakilhakilhau	Tautau	Tamatautau
Paani	Tamapaani		

Two elements to which morphophonemic rules may be applied are *tama-* (cf. *tamalʉngalʉ* ‘uncle’) and the nominal root of the personal name. *Tama-* (cf. *tamalʉngalʉ* ‘uncle’) has four variants: *tama-*, *tam-*, *tana-*, *ta-*, and *taa-*. *tama-* may undergo vowel deletion and becomes *tam-*. Alternatively, *tama-* may undergo syllable deletion and then becomes *ta-*, which may then undergo vowel lengthening, becoming *taa*-. Morphophonemic alternations of *tama*- and their corresponding examples are demonstrated below.

(3) a. vowel deletion: e.g., *'Uusu* → ***Tam**-'uusu*; *Lhaa'u* → ***Tam**-lhaa'u*
b. syllable deletion: e.g., *Apʉʉ* → ***Ta**-nakʉapʉ*; *ʉlʉkʉ* → ***Ta**-lhivʉrʉkʉ*; *Amalhʉ* → ***Ta**-malingalʉ*; *ʉlʉngaanʉ* → ***Ta**-vʉtavʉrʉnga*
c. vowel lengthening: e.g., *Vanau* → ***Taa**-vanau*

Some nominal roots of personal names do not alter when they are used to address people.

(4) a. ***Aruai*** → *Tama-**aruai***
b. ***Inguruu*** → *Tama-**inguruu***
c. ***Langui*** → *Tama-**langui***
d. ***'Aavi*** → *Tama-**'aavi***

Some nominal roots can undergo (morpho-) phonological rules, including vowel shortening, syllable insertion, syllable deletion, *ʉlʉ* → *vʉrʉ* and suppletion. Vowel shortening refers to a long vowel in word-final position becoming a short one. Syllable insertion indicates that one or two syllables are inserted before the nominal root form. Syllable deletion is applied when the word-final syllable is omitted. *ʉlʉ* → *vʉrʉ* indicates that *ʉlʉ* in the first two syllables of the nominal root form becomes *vʉrʉ*. Suppletion indicates that the nominal root form does not correspond to any (morpho-)phonological rule. These morphophonemic alternations are demonstrated below.

(5) a. vowel shortening: *Ap**ʉʉ*** → *Ta-nakʉ-ap**ʉ***
b. syllable insertion: one syllable: *ʉlʉkʉ* → *Ta-**lhi**-vʉrʉkʉ*; two syllables: *'Apʉʉ* → *Ta-**nakʉ**-apʉ*; *ʉlʉngaanʉ* → *Ta-**vʉta**-vʉrʉnga*
c. syllable deletion: *ʉlʉngaanʉ* → *Ta-vʉta-vʉrʉnga*
d. *ʉlʉ* → *vʉrʉ*: ***ʉlʉ**ngaanʉ* → *Ta-vʉta-**vʉrʉ**nga*; ***ʉlʉ**kʉ* → *Ta-lhi-**vʉrʉ**kʉ*
e. suppletion: ***Amalhʉ*** → *Tama-**lingalʉ***

There is a correlation between these (morpho-)phonological alternations and *tama*-. As shown in (5a-d), when these (morpho-)phonological changes take place, *tama*- undergoes syllable deletion and becomes *ta*-.

5 Teknonymy

A representative study of teknonymy in Austronesian languages is H. Geertz and C. Geertz (1964). The study examines teknonymy in Bali and shows its vital impact on village organisation, kinship formation, age grades and genealogical amnesia. Geertz (1973: 369) describes the personal names of Balinese as arbitrarily coined nonsense syllables which avoid duplication in the community, and which cannot reflect family connections. The birth order names and teknonymy can indicate the classification of the referential system in Bali.

There is a paucity of research on teknonymy in Formosan languages. A representative study is found in Wei and Liu (1962), which mentions that it is common for indigenous people of Taiwan to give personal names linked with clan or lineage naming systems, patronymic or matronymic linkage naming systems, or with both, as in Amis.[6] In Yami, a person will obtain another name when he or she has a child.

In Saaroa, personal names may reflect teknonymy when name bearers acquire a son or daughter, and have morphophonemic alternations. The birth order names and teknonymy can indicate the classification of the referential system in Saaroa. A couple is in relationship by affinity before the birth of the child; this transforms into consanguinity through teknonymy since they share the name of the same child.

Ting (1987: 383–384) briefly describes seven names reflecting teknonymy. In this study, it is noteworthy that while most personal names remain unchanged, only a small number of Saaroa personal names are altered.[7] Teknonymy is reflected in the first-born child's gender. These male and female personal names undergo morphophonemic alternations to reflect their variations in social status. Saaroa male and female personal names reflecting teknonymy that we found in our fieldwork are illustrated in Tables 15.5 and 15.6.

Table 15.5: Female names reflecting teknonymy.

Female names	Male first-born child	Female first-born child
Apʉʉ	Inalaanapʉ	Inalukapʉ
Aruai	Inalaanaruai	Inalukaruai
ʉlʉkʉ	Inalaanʉlʉkʉ	Inaapʉlʉkʉ
Inguruu	Inalaaninguru	Inalikinguru
Vanau	Inalaavanau	Inalukuvanau

6 For the kinship terminology of Amis, readers are referred to Liu (1961).

7 It is unclear why some names remain unchanged.

Table 15.6: Male names reflecting teknonymy.

Male names	Male first-born child	Female first-born child
Amalhʉ	Amalaanamalhʉ	Aakamalhʉ
ʉlʉngaanʉ	Amaamalhʉlʉngaanʉ	Amaamalhʉlʉngaanʉ
Palii	Amalaapalii	Amalaapalii

Based on these personal names reflecting teknonymy, some descriptions and analyses, in line with Ting's (1987) observations, are summarised below.

(6) a. all vowel-initial names are prefixed by *n-* (for a son) or *k-* (for a daughter) to address the person who has had a child;
b. *ina* is a shortened form of *ina'a* 'mother'; *ama* is a shortened form of *ama'a* 'father';
c. *ina-laa* is an honorific form indicating 'mother having a son'; *ina-lu* is an honorific form meaning 'mother having a son'; *ama-ama* is an honorific form indicating 'father having a son'; *aa* is an honorific form meaning 'father having a daughter';
d. *-li* in *ina-li* is derived from the base *-lu*, assimilated by the vowel of the following syllable *k-inguru*;
e. the *u* of *ku-* in *ina-lu ku-vanau* is added because Saaroa does not allow consonant clusters;
f. the male form *ama-laa* is a change similar to the female form *ina-laa*.

6 Grammatical features of personal names

Saaroa is an agglutinative language. Morphological units include affixes, roots, stems and clitics. The three most productive morphological processes are affixation, reduplication and compounding. Most affixes are prefixes, while the number of infixes, circumfixes and suffixes is relatively small. The basic constituent order is VAO, if transitive, and VS, if intransitive.

There are some special grammatical features of personal names, including definiteness, case, number and countablity; besides, personal names can occur in syntactic structures such as topicalisation, modification and coordination.

6.1 Definiteness

Whether proper names are inherently definite has been argued repeatedly (e.g., Dalberg 1985: 129; Pamp 1985: 113; Wotjak 1985: 7, 13; Abbott 2002; Allerton 1987; Lyons 1999; Anderson 2003: 351, 394; and Anderson 2004). Saaroa personal names, which have a fixed extension, exhibiting a presupposition of uniqueness and existence in discourse, are bound to have this grammatical meaning. However, in Saaroa, the feature "definite" can be overtly marked by the enclitic *na*, as shown in (7) and (8), and has two functions, a classificatory (categorical) and emotive function. These functions relate to the categorical meaning and to the emotive meaning, respectively. The definite marker takes on a classificatory role with personal names. The emotive function is of an augmentative nature. The definite enclitic *na* is attached to men's and women's names to express familiarity with respect to the name bearer. Furthermore, Saaroa shows an overt distinction between arguments and vocatives, using the definite marker only with arguments, i.e., in the referential use of names, rather than in vocatives or name giving contexts.

(7)	*m-ari-a-pici*	*a*	***Langui=na***	*kiu'u*	*maataata.*
	AV-hand.motion-IRR-split	NOM	female.name=DEF	wood	tomorrow

'Langui will chop so as to make wood split tomorrow.'

(8)	*tam*	*m-a-lhatʉra*	***Caʉpʉ=na.***
	very	AV-STAT-strong	male.name=DEF

'Caʉpʉ is very strong.'

6.2 Case

In Saaroa, personal names as well as other nouns take case markings. These markings do not differ for proper names and other nouns. In Pan's (in press) analysis, there are three types of case: nominative, genitive and oblique. Nominative case marks actor-like arguments in the actor voice construction, patient-like arguments in the patient voice construction, and location arguments and transported themes in the locative voice construction. Oblique case marks patient-like, location, instrument and beneficiary arguments in the actor voice construction. Genitive case marks possessor and actor-like arguments in non-actor voice constructions, including patient voice and locative voice constructions. Nominative and genitive are morphologically identical, but syntactically different.

Table 15.7: Case marking system. (Pan in press)

Nominative	Genitive	Oblique
(k)a	(k)a	n(a)

Example (9) shows that the agent *Tautau* is marked by the nominative case marker *a* in the actor voice construction. Example (10) illustrates that the agent *Langui* is marked by the genitive case marker *a* in the patient voice construction. The genitive case marker *ka* marks the possessor *Langui*, as shown in example (11). Example (12) illustrates that the peripheral argument *Vanau* is marked by the oblique case marker *na*.

(9) *lhi-m-ari-tamaku* ***a*** ***Tautau.***
PFV-AV-hand.motion-cigarette NOM male.name
'Tautau has smoked.'

(10) *lhi-pu'a=*isa ***a*** ***Langui*** *kani'i* *ʉtʉvʉ=na.*
PFV-buy(PV)=3.GEN GEN female.name this sugar.cane=DEF
'Langui has bought the sugar cane.'

(11) *karʉkʉlhʉ* *a* *Pi'i* *m-u-a-saa-sala*
often NOM female.name AV-motion.on.foot-IRR-RED-road
m-alhukua ***salia=isa*** ***ka*** ***Langui.***
AV-get.to house=3.GEN GEN female.name
'Pi'i often goes to Langui's house.'

(12) *saa-pala<va>vililh-a=ami* *ka* *kana* *cucu*
3.GEN-<RED>stealthily.follow=REP.EVID NOM PF person
salia=isa *k<um>ita* *m-uritalhivaʉ* ***na*** ***Vanau.***
house=3.GEN <AV>see AV-have.a.love.affair OBL female.name
'It is said that he stealthily followed the person to his house and saw him having a love affair with Vanau.'

6.3 Number and countability

Personal pronouns appear in the singular and in the plural, e.g., *ilhaku* 'I' and *ilhal-hamu* 'we'. Due to their fixed denotation, personal names occur only in the singular. When the speaker wants to stress the pluralisation and countability status of personal names, a numeral is used, as in (13).

(13) *m-ali-lʉpʉngʉ* *a* *'Aavi* *nua* *Pauli=na*
AV-verbal.action-finish NOM male.name CONJ.COOR male.name=DEF
m-ari-sangilhi *t<um>u-sa-**sua**=cu* *t<um>angi.*
AV-verbal.action-BR <AV>cry-RED-two=COS <AV>cry
'After 'Aavi and Pauli quarreled, both of them cried.'

6.4 Syntactic structures

In addition to typical clause types, e.g., intransitive, transitive, declarative, negative, interrogative and imperative clauses (Pan 2012), Saaroa personal names occur in syntactic structures such as topicalisation, modification and coordination. Example (14) illustrates that the female name *Langui* is followed by the marker *ia* and established as an expression of the sentence topic by being relocated to the front of the sentence, as opposed to the canonical position that core arguments occupy further to the right.

(14) ***Langui*** ***ia,*** *m-a-aru=cu* *n* *kani'i*
female.name TOP AV-STAT-exist=COS OBL this
saa-sarʉʉ-ana.
RED-soil/dirt-LOC.NMLZ
'Langui used to live in this place.'

Example (15) shows a syntactic construction in which the personal name *Timusunga* is modified by the verb phrase *maaru a cucu'u* 'there is a person'. In Saaroa, personal names can be the head of a noun phrase (like English *a hard-working **John***), as in (15), and the modifier (like English ***John's** book chapter*), as in (11), in which the personal name acts as the possessor modifying the possessee (***Langui's** house*).

(15) *m-a-aru* *a* *cucu'u* *pi-ngalha* ***Timusunga***
AV-STAT-exist NOM person have-name male.name
m-a-aru-aru *isana* *m-iaʉrʉkʉlhʉ.*
AV-STAT-RED-exist 3.OBL AV-settle.in
'There is a person called Timusunga settling in this place.'

It is commonly held that coordination occurs when two linguistic units are adjoined but are not grammatically dependent on each other. The conjunctive coordinators *lha* 'and' and *nua* 'and' are used to link two constituents, which can be clauses, phrases or individual words, and usually these elements can be transposed with one another.[8] Similar to other constituents, male and female names can be linked and transposed.

(16) *lhi-c<um>apa* ***Amalhʉ*** ***nua*** ***Langui*** *na* *papa'a.*
PFV-<AV>broil male.name CONJ.COOR female.name OBL meat
'Amalhʉ and Langui have broiled meat.'

(17) *m-aa-lhuulhungu* *a* ***Tautau*** ***lha*** ***Vanau***
AV-BE:LOC-stream NOM male.name CONJ.COOR female.name
pasa-ula-ulaula'ʉ.
play-RED-BOUND.ROOT
'Tautau and Vanau are playing at a stream.'

7 Concluding remarks

This study has shown that Saaroa personal names are gender-specific and chosen from grandparents or generations above. A baby cannot be given a name which is exactly the same as its parent's name. Saaroa personal names may have corresponding vocative forms and senior forms, which are reflected in some morphophonemic alternations, e.g., vowel lengthening, vowel shortening, consonant deletion, syllable deletion and suppletion. Another interesting phenomenon of Saaroa personal names is teknonymy, reflected in the first-born child's gender. These male and female personal names undergo morphophonemic alternation to display their change in social status. The grammatical features of personal names in Saaroa include definiteness, case, number and countablity, and they occur in grammatical structures such as topicalisation, modification and coordination.

Abbreviations

1, 2, 3	first person etc.
ASP	aspect
AV	actor voice
BR	bound root
CONJ	conjunction
COOR	coordinator

8 The distinction between *lha* and *nua* is not clear, and needs to be studied further.

COS change-of-state
DEF definite
EVID evidential
EXCL exclusive
GEN genitive
INCL inclusive
IRR irrealis
LOC location
LV locative voice
NMLZ nominalisation
NOM nominative
OBL oblique
PF pause filler
PFV perfective aspect
PV patient voice
RED reduplication
REP reported
STAT stative
TEMP temporal
TOP topic

References

Abbott, Barbara. 2002. Definiteness and proper names: Some bad news for the description theory. *Journal of Semantics* 19 (2). 191–201.

Alford, Richard D. 1988. *Naming and identity. A cross-cultural study of personal naming practices*. New Haven, CT: Human Relations Area Files, Inc.

Allerton, David J. 1987. The linguistic and sociolinguistic status of proper names. *Journal of Pragmatics* 11 (1). 61–92.

Anderson, John M. 2003. On the structure of names. *Folia Linguistica* 37. 347–398.

Anderson, John M. 2004. On the grammatical status of names. *Language* 80. 435–474.

Bramwell, Ellen S. 2016. Personal names and anthropology. In Carole Hough (ed.), *The Oxford Handbook of Names and Naming*, 263–278. Oxford: Oxford University Press.

Chiu, Ying Jer 邱英哲. 2008. Yuyan liushi yu fuzhen—yi Gaozhong cun Hla'alua ren weili 語言流失與復振:以高中村 Hla'alua 人為例 [Language shift and revitalization: a case study of Hla'alua in Gao Jhong Village]. Taidong: Guoli Taidong daxue shuoshi lunwen 臺東:國立臺東大學碩士論文 [Taitung: National Taitung University MA thesis].

Dalberg, Vibeke. 1985. On homonymy between proper name and appellative. *Names* 33 (3). 127-135.

Geertz, Clifford. 1973. Person, Time and Conduct in Bali. In *The Interpretation of Cultures: Selected Essays*, 360–411. New York: Basic Books.

Geertz, Hildred & Clifford Geertz. 1964. Teknonymy in Bali: Parenthood, Age-Grading and Genealogical Amnesia. *The Journal of the Royal Anthropological Institute of Great Britain and Ireland* 94 (2). 94–108.

Lambrecht, Knud. 1996. On the formal and functional relationship between topics and vocatives. Evidence from French. In Adele Goldberg (ed.), *Conceptual Structure, Discourse and Language*, 267–288. Stanford: CSLI Publications.
Levinson, Stephen. 1983. *Pragmatics.* Cambridge: Cambridge University Press.
Liu, Pin-hsiung. 1961. Xiuguluan ameizu de qinshu chengwei zhi 秀姑巒阿美族的親屬稱謂制 [Kinship Terminology of the Siukuluan Ami], *Zhongyangyanjiuyuan minzuxue yanjiusuo jikan* 中央研究院民族学研究所集刊 [Bulletin of the Institute of Ethnology, Academia Sinica] 11. 125–155.
Liu, Pin-hsiung. 1969. Shaaluazu de shehui zuzhi 沙阿魯阿族的社會組織 [Social Structure of the Saalua], *Zhongyangyanjiuyuan minzuxue yanjiusuo jikan* 中央研究院民族学研究所集刊 [Bulletin of the Institute of Ethnology, Academia Sinica] 28. 67–158.
Lyons, Christopher. 1999. *Definiteness*. Cambridge: Cambridge University Press.
Nicolaisen, Wilhelm F.H. (ed.). 1985. Special issue on theory about names. Special issue, *Names* 33 (3).
Pamp, Bengt. 1985. Ten theses on proper names. *Names* 33 (3). 111–118.
Pan, Chia-jung. 2012. A grammar of Lha'alua: an Austronesian language of Taiwan. Cairns: James Cook University PhD dissertation.
Pan, Chia-Jung. 2018. Evidentiality in Formosan Languages. In: Aikhenvald, Alexandra Y., and Dixon, R.M.W., (eds.) *The Oxford Handbook of Evidentiality*. Oxford University Press, Oxford, pp. 657–673.
Pan, Chia-Jung. (in press). Saaroa. In: Li, Jen-Kuei, Zeitoun, Elizabeth and Rik De Busser. (eds.) *Handbook on Formosan Languages*. Amsterdam: Brill.
Predelli, Stefano. 2008. Vocatives. *Analysis* 68 (2). 97–105.
Sonnenhauser, Barbara & Patrizia Noel Aziz Hanna. 2013. *Vocative! Addressing between System and Performance*. Berlin: De Gruyter Mouton.
Ting, Pang-hsin. 1987. Morphological change of personal names in Saaroa reflecting changes in social status. In Agatha Bramkamp, Yi-chin Fu, Arnold Sprenger & Peter Venne (eds.), *Chinese-Western Encounter: Studies in Linguistics and Literature*, 383–384. Taipei: The Crane Publishing Co., Ltd.
Van Langendonck, Willy &Mark Van de Velde. 2016. Names and grammar. In Carole Hough (ed.), *The Oxford Handbook of Names and Naming*, 17–38. Oxford: Oxford University Press.
Wei, Hui-lin & Pin-hsiung Liu. 1962. *Lanyu Yameizu de shehui zuzhi* 蘭嶼雅美族的社會組織 [*Social Structure of the Yami, Botel Tobago*], Zhongyangyanjiuyuan minzuxue yanjiusuo zhuankan 中央研究院民族学研究所專刊之 1 [The Institute of Ethnology, Academia Sinica Monograph 1].
Wotjak, Gerd. 1985. Zur Semantik der Eigennamen. *Namenkundliche Informationen* 48. 1–17.
Zwicky, Arnold. 1974. Hey, Whatsyourname. In Michael La Galy, Robert A. Fox & Anthony Bruck (eds.), *Papers from the Tenth Regional Meeting, Chicago Linguistic Society, April 19-21, 1974*, 787–801. Chicago: Chicago Linguistic Society.

Online resources and open data

Council of Indigenous Peoples. 2021. Yuanzhumin renkou tongji ziliao 原住民人口數統計資料 [Population census of indigenous peoples]. Retrieved from https://www.cip.gov.tw/en/search-result/index.html?q=population (accessed 28 February 2023).

Svenja Völkel

Chapter 16
Personal names and naming in Tongan language and culture

Abstract: Anthroponyms referring to individuals in Tongan society are a topic that has received little attention in anthropological-linguistic research so far. This paper addresses types of personal names and their historical development, naming practices and grammatical aspects of *hingoa* 'name', including alienable and inalienable possessive constructions, syntactic word class frames and honorific registers. All these aspects will show that personal names and the linguistic behaviour of *hingoa* is deeply embedded in the cultural context of this Polynesian society. Social concepts such as hierarchical order and the powerful position of the *mehekitanga* (father's sister) are crucial for naming practices, a component in the process of integrating a newborn into its social *kāinga* network (extended family). Furthermore, these cultural parameters are conceptualised in grammar, i.e., they reveal the meaning encoded in linguistic features.

Keywords: personal names & titles, social stratification, name giving, name avoidance, cultural conceptualisations in grammar

1 Introduction

Although the existence of personal names (or anthroponyms) is a cross-cultural/-linguistic universal, personal names, naming practices and the meaning of names show a great range of variation across languages and cultures (see Hockett 1963; Alford 1988). Anthropological-linguistic studies shed light on linguistic aspects of names and their embeddedness in the cultural context, including the cultural meaning of names and social practices of naming (see Bruck and Bodenhorn 2006; Bramwell 2016). Anthroponyms are not only lexemes referring to specific individuals, but the culture-specific meanings of names and naming reflect a larger understanding of social relationships, hierarchical structures and interpersonal practices. Often these culture-specific contexts offer a deeper understanding of or even an explanation for linguistic peculiarities.

Svenja Völkel, University of Mainz/Germany, e-mail: svenja.voelkel@uni-mainz.de

https://doi.org/10.1515/9783110759297-016

This paper will provide insights into the personal names and naming practices in Tongan, a Polynesian language and society. More precisely, it addresses types of names, social structures and naming practices, and the cultural idea and function of anthroponyms and *hingoa* 'name' in grammatical constructions. Altogether, it will become apparent that the linguistic aspects of names reflect culture-specific concepts and that naming practices are embedded in a broader cultural context of social togetherness.

These insights are based on linguistic as well as anthropological field research between 2002 and 2014, including participant observation and multiple kinds of survey. The majority of data is from Niutoua, a village in the eastern part of Tongatapu, the main island of Tonga.

Tonga is a Polynesian island state in the South Pacific, north-east of New Zealand. It consists of about 150 islands, of which 36 are inhabited. Due to very little immigration since the first settlement of Tonga by Austronesians around 1000 BC, the current population of about 103,000 inhabitants consists mainly of Tongans (96.5 per cent). The remaining 3.5 per cent are part-Tongans, Asians (mainly Chinese), Europeans and other Pacific Islanders (Lynch 1998: 51–57; Tongan Government 2011: 31). In contrast, emigration to the large surrounding states, namely New Zealand, Australia and the United States, is very substantial. As a consequence, there is significant contact and travel among the Tongans staying on the islands and those living abroad (Morton Lee 2003). In the course of history, the Polynesian population of Tonga was in contact with other Polynesian societies (e.g., during the times of the Tongan Empire), and later with the European explorers, followed by the missionaries, traders, etc. In contrast to the other Pacific Island States, Tonga was never formally colonised. However, it was a British protectorate from 1900 to 1970 (Campbell 2001: 133–134).

In contrast to the predominantly ego-centric concept of the person in modern Western societies, the Tongan society can be regarded as primarily socio-centric. This means that a person is perceived less as an individual autonomous subject but more as being defined by that person's particular position within a social group (Foley 1997: 264–269). In Tongan society, personhood and belonging are closely associated with ideas of hierarchy and kinship. As is characteristic for Polynesia, it is a chiefly society with a strongly stratified social structure. First, there are three classes of societal rank, namely the *tu'i* (king/queen, traditionally a paramount chief), *hou'eiki/nōpele* (chiefs, including officially appointed "nobles" in modern times) and *kakai/kau tu'a* (people/commoners). Second, there are status differences among members of the *kāinga*, i.e., the extended family, which encompasses all bilateral kin to whom ego traces a consanguineal relationship. The social status of ego is relative or relational, i.e., it is dependent on the kin relationship with another person (see Section 3). Societal rank, instead, is absolute, as it is ascribed by birth (Kaeppler 1971; Bott 1981) but titles are passed on at a later stage in life (see Section 2). The hereditary order is patrilineal, more precisely from the father to the eldest son upon the father's death (Völkel 2010: 46–47).

The indigenous language spoken on the islands is Tongan, a Polynesian language belonging to the Oceanic subgroup of the Austronesian language family. As is characteristic of Polynesian languages, it has a quite small phoneme inventory (with a phonemic distinction between long and short vowels), an open syllable structure ((C)V), a stem isolating character (no inflection but derivational affixes and reduplication), pronouns which are marked for number (singular, plural and dual) and person (with an inclusive-exclusive distinction in first person non-singular) but not for gender, and it distinguishes between alienable and inalienable possession. Furthermore, Tongan is a split ergative language (in which nominal NPs show an ergative/absolutive and pronominal NPs an accusative/nominative pattern) with prepositions and verb-initial word order, and it has honorific registers (three lexical levels) (Churchward 1953; Krupa 1982; Lynch 1998: 100–165). The second official language in Tonga is English. It plays a central role in administration, government and education, but as in most Polynesian countries, only a small percentage of the population speaks English as a first language. Most Tongans have learnt English in school, but there are also a number of Tongans, especially less-educated ones and those of the older generations, who only have rudimentary or even hardly any knowledge of English. Most educated people use English at work; however, this happens less than might be expected from its official status (Lynch and Mugler 1999: 1, 17–19). Generally, occupation and level of education determine the amount of English being used.

After this introductory background information on Tongan language and culture, Section 2 gives insights into Tongan personal names, including both traditional and current types, which have been severely influenced by Western contact. The practice of naming is then addressed in Section 3. Bestowing a name is regarded as an act of integrating a newborn into its family network, the privilege of patrilineal kin with higher status. Section 4 deals with *hingoa* 'name' in possessive constructions (4.1), syntactic word class frames (4.2) and honorific registers (4.3), demonstrating that cultural ideas of social relationships, the roles of giving and getting names, names representing a person and a form of chiefly/kingly name avoidance are conceptualised in these grammatical constructions. Finally, the article is concluded in Section 5, showing that names are a linguistic phenomenon deeply rooted in its culture-specific social context.

2 Personal names – traditional and current types

The Tongan word for 'name' is *hingoa*. This denotes any kind of name, including names for persons, places, animals and boats, but in particular it relates to personal names. The following types of anthroponyms are distinguished: given names (including Christian names or baptismal names, called *hingoa papi*), family names (*hingoa fakafāmili*), nicknames (*hingoa fakatenetene*, lit. 'called by a pet name or a friendly nickname', or *hingoa pau'u*, lit. 'an ill-mannered/naughty/mischievous name') and titles (*hingoa fakanofo*, lit. 'an appointed name') (Gifford 1929: 232–233; Churchward 1959: 225). The idea of given and family names has changed significantly over time due to European contact in the 19th century, as the loanwords *fakafāmili* (*fāmili* denoting the Western concept of "core family", while the traditional term *kāinga* describes the "extended family") and *papi* (or *papitaiso* 'baptise', an idea introduced by Christian missionaries) illustrate. This historical change concerns not only the system of names (a single given name → binominal system consisting of two parts: given name(s) plus hereditary family name) but also the names themselves (semantically transparent names, i.e., Tongan names with a lexical meaning → introduction of Christian names).

In traditional Polynesian societies, people were known by a single name. This name can be considered as a semantically transparent given name. Generally, it described a person in some way, or facts associated with the person, such as special circumstances at the time of birth, the birthplace or some other characteristic. Since the name could be changed or a component added (as a nickname) over the course of a person's life, it could also describe special abilities or the person's role in important situations. Remarkable events or actions would trigger such a change or addition to the name.

In (1), there is a list of such Tongan names with their lexical meanings. It is a selection of names of the people I met during my research. A more comprehensive list of names, as used in the 1920s, is given in Gifford (1929: 237–276).[1] Despite the time span of nearly 80 years, almost all of the names in (1) are also listed in Gifford. The examples show that these lexemes denote items (primarily plants or fish species), events (often natural phenomena or incidents at the time of birth),

1 Several of these names listed in Gifford are not only personal names but they also occur as place names or as the names of ships or streets, e.g., *Afā* ('hurricane'; a village on Tongatapu), *Haamoa* (Samoa), *Ha'apai* (an island group of the Tongan archipelago), *Niufo'ou* ('new coconut'; an island in the far north of Tonga), *Niutoua* ('two coconuts planted together'; a village on Tongatapu), *Pulupaki* ('the name of a fragrant garland of flowers'; the name of an interisland ferry), *Taufa'ahau* ('the shark god'; the name of the main road on Tongatapu).

Sometimes place names are also used to identify and describe a person by their place of residence.

properties (such as pride, desire or love), etc. which are associated in some way with the name bearer or the circumstances of their birth. One person told me that he was named *Kilikiti* ('cricket') after his grandfather, who was an excellent cricket player. Another person explained that her name was *Munilaite* ('moonlight'), because the full moon shone brightly on the night of her birth. Furthermore, these two examples also demonstrate that it is not only Tongan lexemes (e.g., *Mahina* 'month, moon') that are used as given names but also loanwords (e.g., *Munilaite*, the Tongan version of the English loanword 'moonlight'[2]). Due to their descriptive character, numerous of these semantically transparent names are actually gender-neutral. *'Ofa* ('love') and *Falema'ama* ('house for us two'), for instance, can be male as well as female names. Of course, there were also abilities and properties which were generally attributed only to a specific gender. Names of flowers, for instance, are mainly given to girls.

(1) Tongan names:
Afitu ('to scatter fire'), *Alisi* ('of noble kind'), *Angahiki* ('pride'), *Apakasi* (loanword: 'abacus'), *Ata* ('twilight, early dawn'), *Atamāhina* ('rising of the moon'), *Ate* ('shrub'), *Fakalelei* ('make peace'), *Fakaolakifanga* ('light on the beach'), *Faleola* ('a house of success'), *Fanguani* ('awaken'), *Fatafehi* ('hardwood platform'), *Fatai* ('creeping grass'), *Fehoko* ('joined, wish to succeed'), *Fekeila* ('spotted octopus'), *Fekita* (hon. 'to kiss'), *Fekau* ('order, message'), *Fetu'u* ('star'), *Fieiloeua* ('twilight light, dawn light'), *Fielea* ('wish to speak'), *Fifita* ('the cutting of the plaited leaves put round a tree for a *tapu*'), *Finau* (the name of a chief), *Fohe* ('a paddle, an oar'), *Fonofehi* ('the pieces of *fehi* wood'), *Heuifanga* ('to decoy at the anchorage'), *Ika* ('fish'), *Ikatonga* ('fish from Tonga'), *Kailopa* ('to eat *lopa* plant'), *Kalo* ('to move the head'), *Kaufo'ou* ('the new ones'), *Kelei* ('muddy'), *Kilikiti* (loanword: 'cricket'), *Koloa* ('wealth'), *Laiseni* (loanword: 'licence'), *Lata* ('to be at home'), *Laumanu* ('flock of birds'), *Loseli* (name of plant), *Luani* ('to be equal'), *Lupe* ('the fruit pigeon'), *Mahina* ('month, moon'), *Maile* ('the myrtle shrub'), *Malakai* ('to eat *mala* shark'), *Manako* ('like, desire'), *Manu* ('bird, animal'), *Matafeo* ('coral edge'), *Ma'ama* ('for us two'), *Moala* ('kind of yam'), *Mohenoa* ('to sleep when there is no need'), *Moli* ('orange, to move'), *Muli* ('a foreigner, a stranger'), *Munilaite* (loanword: 'moonlight'), *Naule'o* ('the good watcher'), *Ngalongalo* ('forgetful'; 'to sink slowly out of sight'), *Niuila* ('a coconut tree with a mark on it'), *Okalani* (loanword: 'Auckland'), *Pōhiva* ('a night of songs'), *Siale* ('flowering bush: gardenia'), *Siutaka* (of

2 Information regarding adaptations of loanwords to the Tongan phonology follows below (see also Note 3).

birds: 'fly hither and hither in search of food'), Tai ('to strike, beat'), *Tanaki* ('to count something, to collect'), *Tangitau* ('to cry and hold on to s.o.'), *Tapukitea* ('the evening star'), *Teuila* ('to try to be awake'), *Toa* ('courage, brave'; the *toa* tree), *Tuna* ('eel'), *'Ungatea* ('the fair *Unga*'), *Vea* (name of a chief), *Vai* ('water, liquid'), *'Ākolo* ('a town fence'), *'Amanaki* ('expectation'), *'Anau* ('a bunch'), *'Efitahi* ('carry it to the sea'), *'Evaipōmana* ('walk in thundering night'), *'Ofa* ('love, affection'), . . .

Numerous names are composed of multiple lexemes, such as *Manusiale* (*manu* 'bird, animal', *siale* 'flowering gardenia bush') 'the bird in the gardenia' and *Ikatonga* (*ika* 'fish', *Tonga* 'Tongan') 'Tongan fish'. *Kolokihakaufisi* (*kolo-ki-hakau-fisi* 'village-ALL-reef-Fiji') 'the village towards Fiji reef' and *Angaaetau* (*anga-'a-e-tau* 'way/form-POSS-ART-war') 'the ways of war' are contracted phrases even including grammatical elements.

The times of Western contact, primarily with missionaries, brought about major changes in the personal naming system: (a) Western names were adopted as given names, and (b) the binominal name system, consisting of given name(s) plus family name (or surname), was introduced and later, in the 1950s, officially implemented for census reasons (Neill 1955: 141).

Regarding (a), a selection of examples as I encountered them during my research is provided in (2). These are particularly given names of Christian Biblical origins, which became popular in the context of missionary work. They exist alongside the traditional Tongan names from (1), and some Tongans even have a traditional as well as a Western name. The adopted names, however, were phonologically adapted to the phoneme inventory and the syllable structure of the Polynesian language. Tongan, for instance, distinguishes between long and short vowels /a, a:, e, e:, i, i:, o, o:, u, u:/ (long vowels are written with a macron, e.g., *ā*, *ō*), has the consonants /f, h, k, l, m, n, ŋ, p, s, t, v, ʔ/ (the grapheme for /ŋ/ is *ng* and for /ʔ/ it is ') and has only open syllables of the form (C)V.[3] Hence the Tongan version of the names in (2), with the English version in brackets after it. In contrast to the traditional Tongan names, these Christian names are all gender-specific, as are their English counterparts. An interesting case is the male name *Paula*, which formally corresponds to the English female name 'Paula' due to the adaptation of the male name 'Paul' to the Tongan syllabic structure.

3 Typical phonemic adaptations are the replacement of /r/ by /l/, /d/ by /t/, /g/ by /k/ and /b/ by /p/, while /i/ is the default in vowel epenthesis (i.e., the insertion of vowels to produce open syllables without consonant clusters) if the vowel of a previous syllable is not repeated.

(2) Names of Christian origin:
Alipate (Albert), *Alisi* (Alice), *Fane* (Fanny), *Feleti* (Fred), *Isileli* (Israel), *Kalolaine* (Caroline), *Katalina* (Catherine), *Lavinia* (Lavinia), *Lēsieli* (Rachel), *Lisiate* (Richard), *Lopeti* (Robert), *Luseane* (Lucy Anne), *Maata* (Martha), *Makeleta* (Margret), *Malia* (Maria), *Melenaite* (Mary Knight), *Meliame* (Miriam), *Mosese* (Moses), *Paula* (Paul), *Pita* (Peter), *Sālote* (Charlotte), *Sāpate* (Sabbath), *Seini* (Jane), *Siaoso* (George), *Sione* (John), *Siosefa* or *Siosifa* (Joseph), *Siosiua* (Joshua), *Sosefina* (Josephine), *Suliana* (Juliane), *Taniela* (Daniel), *Teleisia* (Theresa), *Tēvita* (David), *Tomasi* (Thomas), *Viliami* (William), *'Aisea* (Isaiah), *'Inoke* (Enoch), . . .

Regarding (b), the binominal name system required family names. For this purpose, the traditional single names became surnames. More precisely, people were known by their own given name plus the given name of their father. This system then became frozen and the patronyms became hereditary surnames – a cross-linguistically widespread development (cf. Hanks 2006: 299). As a general rule, the children now receive the family name of their parents, and at marriage women take the names of their husbands. Morton (1996: 55–56) mentions that this is not the case, however, for illegitimate children. They get the mother's family name and the father's name does not even appear on the birth certificate, even if the father is known and of social importance. A selection of family names which I collected during my research is given in (3). The fact that surnames are originally given names explains why the names in (3) are similar to those in (1) and could also be listed there. *Fefita*, for instance, is a given name for *Fefita Langoia* and a surname for *Naule'o Fefita*. The given names of Christian origin (as in (2)), however, were only adopted when family names were introduced so they were not patronyms at the time and thus do not function as surnames. However, there are also surnames of Western origin such as *Simiti* (English: Smith) and *Saafi* (German: Schaaf), which became Tongan family names through the marriage of Tongan women to Western men.

(3) Family names:
Fe'ao ('where is the cloud'), *Fielakepa* (name of a chief; 'wishing to be a Fijian'), *Fifita* ('the cutting of the platted leaves put round a tree for a tapu'), *Filiai* ('to choose amongst many things'), *Folau* ('travel, voyage'), *Foliaki* ('to encircle, surround'), *Fonua* ('dry land, country'), *Fukofuka* (name of a tree), *Fungavai* ('the surface of the water'), *Helu* ('a comb'), *Hingano* (name of a tree), *Kata* ('laugh'), *Langi* ('sky'), *Langoia* ('to be covered with flies'), *Latu* ('sail unfurled'), *Laulā* ('a fleet of vessels'), *Liku* ('the weather shore, cliff-bound coast'), *Lolomanaia* ('handsome'; 'most excellent oil'), *Mafi* ('a conqueror'), *Mahina* ('month, moon'), *Maka* ('stone, rock'), *Moimoi* ('to send a present to s.o.'), *Niuila* ('a coconut tree with a mark on it'), *Pohahau* ('night moisture, dew'),

Taufatofua ('the shark of *Tofua* island'), *Taumoefolau* ('a good voyage'), *Tuputupu* ('clouds that have a landlike appearance from the sea'), *Tu'ineau* ('king of *Neau*'), . . .

The majority of the names in (1) to (3) are also listed in Gifford (1929: 237–276). Thus, the major changes had already taken place prior to his research. Nevertheless, the popularity of names may have changed since then. Very popular given names today are, for instance, *Mele, 'Ana, 'Ofa, Sione* and *Sālote*. Some of them have a traditional Tongan as well as Christian meaning, e.g., *'Ana* ('cave'; Anna), *Mele* ('a defect, a blemish'; Mary). Unfortunately, Gifford (1929: 234–237) does not provide information about the frequency of names, but he does point out that the names occurring differ to a considerable extent across the Tongan island groups.

Given names are often used in a shortened version, such as *Noke* instead of *'Inoke, Nako* instead of *Manako, Kiti* instead of *Kilikiti, Le'o* instead of *Naule'o, Lia* instead of *Amelia*, or *Sifa* instead of *Siosifa*. As these examples show, the shortened version usually consists of the final two syllables. Alternatively, it can consist of the first two syllables, e.g., *Mela* instead of *Melaia, Suli* instead of *Suliana, Peni* instead of *Penisoni, Tape* instead of *Tapenisi*, or *Muni* instead of *Munilaite*. The shortened version is generally used to call people, especially members of the extended family and other closely related persons.

Apart from the shortened version of the given name, people may be called and known by a nickname. Thus, a person's official name as indicated in the passport may not be the name by which they are known in the village or in school. The name used can also be a nickname and the official family name may in practice be replaced by the place of residence or the father's first name (see Note 1; Morton 1996: 51).

My own name, *Svenja*, was also Tonganised. Transformed according to Tongan phonetics, it became *Suvenia*, which is also the English loanword 'souvenir'. The shortened form of it was *Nia*. By people who did not know my name, I was called by the ethnonym *pālangi* ('European, white skinned person'). My family name never played a role except for administrative purposes (e.g., on my visa, research permit or flight tickets).

Persons of higher rank (i.e., chiefs, the king or queen and members of the royal family) were and are known by a second kind of name, their titles. Like any Tongan, they get a given name after their birth, but after the death of the previous title holder, they inherit the title – generally the eldest son will become the new title holder, but it can also be the eldest daughter if there are no male heirs. Since the major changes in the societal order at the end of the 18th century, there is the King/Queen (*Tupou I* to currently *Tupou VI*), with the title *Tu'i Kanokupolu*, and a group of officially appointed chiefs with *nōpele* titles (given in (4)) and hereditary estate, plus a number of other traditional chiefly titles and *matāpule* titles, who are chiefs' attendants (Bott 1981; Campbell 2001: 99). *Tāmale*, for instance, is the chief of Niutoua and his *matāpule* are *Fainga'a* and *Tofavaha*. While title holders are addressed and referred to by their titles on official occasions, their birth names are used in private contexts. During my stays in Niuoua in 2002–2004, *Malū Lolomana'ia* was the current *Fainga'a* and, while he was called by his *matāpule* title, *Fainga'a*, on official occasions such as *fono* (village meetings), close family members called him by his civil name *Malū* in private contexts (Völkel 2010: 19, 47).

(4) *Nōpele* titles:
Ata ('twilight, early dawn'), *Fakafanua* ('to give land'), *Fakatulolo* ('to humble'), *Fielakepa* ('wishing to be a Fijian'), *Fohe* ('a paddle, an oar'), *Fotofili* ('to choose the stingray tail for making a spear'), *Fulivai* ('to change water'), *Fusitu'a* ('to pull from the back'), *Kalaniuvalu* ('climbed eight coconuts'), *Lasike* ('a rolled up sail'), *Lavaka* ('the sail of the vessel'), *Luani* ('to be equal'), *Malupō* ('a calm night'), *Ma'afu* ('ammunition, to burn'), *Ma'atu* ('to chew and give'), *Niukapu* ('a coconut shell used as a cup'), *Nuku* (an island name), *Tangipā* ('a bursting cry'), *Tuita* ('the fighting ruler'), *Tungī* ('the cry of the *tu* bird'), *Tupouto'a* ('*Tupou* the brave'), *Tu'iha'angana* ('the ruler of the *Ngana* lineage'), *Tu'iha'ateiho* ('king of the lineage of *Teiho*'), *Tu'ilakepa* ('the king of *Lakepa*'), *Tu'ipelehake* ('the favourite king'), *Tu'ivakanō* (a Fijian word), *Tu'i'āfitu* ('king of the seven fences'), *Vaea* ('the canoe to be broken away from the outrigger'), *Vaha'i* ('to separate by getting between the parties'), *Veikune* ('a good chief'), *Ve'ehala* ('the side of the road'), *'Ahome'e* ('the day of feasting'), *'Ulukālala* ('a good and brave chief')

The *nōpele* titles, listed with their lexical meanings in (4), are descriptive and semantically transparent, as are the traditional Tongan names in (1) and (3). Most of them have a meaning that has to do with seafaring, battle or political/spiritual power. These names are also listed in Gifford (1929: 237–276) and numerous of them also occur as given or family names. The difference is that *Ata*, *Luani* or *Fielakepa*, for instance, as given names, are received at birth and chosen by family members (see Section 3), while family names are received at birth and hereditarily determined, and titles are received upon the death of the former title holder and hereditarily determined. While every Tongan had or has a civil name (formerly a single given name; today given name(s) plus family name), titles are or were reserved only for a few.

Altogether, personal names are regularly used to address and refer to people, and it is also an important aspect of the socialisation process to associate people with their names (Morton 1996: 162–165). People are usually supposed to react if they hear their name, e.g., by saying *'io* ('yes') or *ko au* ('It's me.'). Calling the name in front of a person's *'api* (allotment), for instance, is a common practice when approaching that person. Furthermore, people address each other in greetings and farewells such as *NAME ē* ('Bye, NAME') when they meet on the way and at social events, speeches are started with introductory enumerations of the people present, in the order of their titles or duties (so called speech preludes; Churchward 1953: 303; Völkel 2010: 51–54). These practices clearly demonstrate that addressing each other by names has an important interpersonal function.

3 Naming practices

Birth, weddings and funerals are occasions on which the family is restructured in some way: At births newborns are integrated in the family, at weddings two families get connected, and at funerals the deceased physically leaves the family. All these occasions generally go hand in hand with naming or renaming practices or naming taboos.

The birth of a child is one of the crucial events in Tongan life. Other important occasions in the private life cycle are special birthdays (particularly the first, to celebrate that the child has survived the first critical year, the 21st to celebrate adulthood, and the 70th to celebrate and honour old age), weddings and funerals. Naming (*fakahingoa*), i.e., choosing the given name of a newborn, is one of the symbolic acts to welcome and incorporate the child into its *kāinga* (extended family network). Other symbolic practices to affirm the child's embeddedness in the social network include the exchange of gifts (Morton 1996: 50). Actually, the privilege of bestowing a name came be regarded as part of this complex exchange process, including physical gifts (*koloa*, i.e., valuable goods such as mats and bark cloth), tasks and privileges, which all reflect the social status among the family members. Tonga has a highly stratified chiefly society with relative status differences among relatives. This status is based on the following basic principles (Kaeppler 1971: 176; van der Grijp 1993: 164–165):

1 Within ego's generation, sisters have higher status than their brothers.
2 Among same-sex siblings, older ones have higher status than younger ones.
3. In the first ascending generation, patrilateral kin have higher status than ego and matrilateral kin have lower status than ego.

From these principles, it results that the father's sisters (*mehekitanga*), especially the eldest, have a particularly high status. The mother's brothers (*tu'asina*), conversely, are extremely low in status. These status inequalities become apparent in interpersonal behaviour. The relationship vis-à-vis the *mehekitanga* is characterised by restraint and obedience; she is treated with great honour and she controls the relationship. On special occasions such as births, weddings and funerals she receives the most valuable gifts, she sits in a prominent position and she fulfils privileged tasks. She is ascribed even the power (*mana*) to provoke the death of a newly born child of her brother (*'ilamutu*) or to influence its birth in a positive way (Douaire-Marsaudon 1996: 147–151). In most cases, she is the one who has the privilege of naming the newborn, or this will at least be a patrilateral kin member, such as the father's mother or the father's father (Morton 1996: 51).

In a small survey conducted in the village of Niutoua in 2002/2003, the *mehekitanga* was by far the most frequent name giver (11/27). Altogether, kin of higher status vis-à-vis the child, i.e., the *mehekitanga* (11/27) and other patrilateral kin (7/27), had this privilege in 18/27 cases. With siblings it became clear that the first-born was generally given a name by the *mehekitanga* and younger siblings then by other patrilateral kin. Other name givers were the parents (5/27), particularly the father, and close non-relatives (3/27). Relatives of lower status vis-à-vis the newborn, i.e., matrilateral kin, generally do not get the naming privilege. Such an exception occurred only once. Furthermore, the different age groups in the survey have shown that no fundamental changes to this practice seem to have occurred over time (see Table 16.1).

Table 16.1: Name givers – the privilege of naming (*fakahingoa*).

No. of participants named by:	**age: 16–30**	**age: 31–50**	**age: 51–85**	**Total**
– the (eldest) father's sister (*mehekitanga*)	5	3	3	11
– other patrilateral kin: the father's mother or the father's father	4	1	2	7
– parents: father or mother	2	2	1	5
– close non-kin: a priest, the father's friend, an American soldier	0	2	1	3
– maternal kin	0	1	0	1

Douaire-Marsaudon (1996: 147–149) describes the symbolic gift exchange process around birth in more detail. At the birth of a child, the child itself can be regarded as a gift from the mother's side to the paternal kin. In return, the father's *mehekitanga* and the child's *mehekitanga*, i.e., the father's side, bring a gift of *koloa* (valuable goods such as mats and bark cloth) to the maternal kin and the child's *mehekitanga* or another relative on the father's side gives a name to the child and thus affirms its embeddedness in the *kāinga*. Finally, the best *koloa* is again given to the child's *mehekitanga*.

In numerous cases, people are named after a relative of their patrilineage. These are generally kin of former generations, such as the father's parents or the father's grandparents. In my Niutouan survey, 20 out of 27 participants were named after a patrilateral relative. However, Tongans hardly ever get the same name as their father or mother. In the survey, only 3 out of 27 people had the same given name as their birth parents. In some cases, especially if the person after whom one is named is still alive, 'Junior' or *si'i* ('little') is appended to the name in order to avoid confusion (see also Morton 1996: 51). The remaining survey participants were named after friends of the family, priests or their kin, or circumstances at their birth (e.g., *Okalani*, the loanword 'Auckland', because the father's best friend just went there; *Munilaiti*, the loanword 'moonlight', because the moon was shining bright on the night of the birth).

4 The cultural meaning behind the grammar of *hingoa* 'name'

The Tongan lexeme *hingoa* means 'name' (Churchward 1959: 225). It is used in different grammatical constructions that reveal various aspects of cultural concepts linked to personal names. In this section, we will look at how the lexeme *hingoa* occurs in possessive constructions (4.1), syntactic word class frames (4.2), and honorific registers (4.3), and the cultural meaning that they conceptualise.

The culturally important idea of giving and getting a name and the associated concept of social relationships and power within the *kāinga* becomes apparent in Sections 4.1 and 4.2. A person may have two kinds of possessive relationships with a name: first, the name that is given to them (*hoku hingoa* – 'my name'), and second, the name that they give to someone (*'eku hingoa* – 'my name'). Furthermore, *hingoa* means 'name' or 'to be named', while *fakahingoa* (lit. 'to cause a name') describes the act of naming someone. In Section 4.3, we will then see that a name is regarded as representing a person. People of higher rank are *tapu* ('sacred, forbidden'), i.e., physical contact with them and their personal belongings needs to be avoided, and verbally, these items (including their 'name', *hingoa*) are described by indirect, metaphorical or Samoan honorific vocabulary (*huafa*, the equivalent of *suafa*, the Samoan term for a chiefly name).

Thus, a culture-specific understanding of names and naming is even conceptualised in grammatical constructions.

4.1 *Hingoa* 'name' in possessive constructions

As is characteristic of the Polynesian languages, Tongan makes a distinction between two possessive categories, namely alienable and inalienable possession.[4] Alienable or "acquired" possession is also called A-possession and inalienable or "inherent" possession is also called O-possession, named after the distinctive vowels (e.g., the possessive prepositions: *'a* – 'of (A)' as in (5b); *'o* – 'of (O)' as in (5a)).[5]

(5) a. *Ko e fale* ***'o*** *e 'eiki.*
PRES ART house POSS(O) ART chief[5]
'It is the chief's house.'

b. *Ko e me'alele* ***'a*** *Ikatonga.*
PRES ART vehicle POSS(A) Ikatonga
'It is Ikatonga's vehicle.' (Völkel 2010: 158)

Early descriptions treated A- and O-possession as a noun class system in which the possessee (i.e., the possessed items, such as the house in (5a) or the vehicle in (5b)) were categorised as either A- or O-possessed. This categorisation was regarded purely as a lexical conventionalisation, whereby certain items could be categorised into semantic groups of items (such as clothes, food, body parts, etc.) that are either A- or O-possessed. The idea of categorising possessees into two classes (A- versus O-possessed items) implies that the use of A- or O-possession is solely determined by the nature of the possessee. However, this is not the case.

Instead, there are numerous (if not all[6]) lexical items that can occur in A- as well as in O-constructions (e.g., *taki* in (6a) and (6b), or *fakatātā* in (7a) and (7b)).

4 In linguistic terms, a possessive construction expresses a relationship between two entities, a "possessor" and a "possessee", in which the possessee belongs to the possessor. This includes not only possession in the sense of ownership but many different kinds of relationships, such as kinship relations and part-whole relations.

5 The abbreviations used in the interlinear glosses can be found in the Leipzig glossing rules: https://www.eva.mpg.de/lingua/pdf/Glossing-Rules.pdf. The additional abbreviation PRES means 'presentative' and describes the Tongan preposition *ko* ('this/it is').

6 Taumoefolau (1996) argues that the semantic rules are most productive, and all nouns can be A- as well as O-possessed. Although we find examples in which even prototypical inalienable items such as body parts can be A-possessed, there seem to be exceptional cases that do not allow for both possessive constructions and /or are hardly explicable by the semantic rules, such as the control theories mentioned in Note 7 (see Lichtenberk 1983: 166; Völkel 2010: 174, 182).

(6) *'Oku ou taki ia.*
PRS 1SG lead 3SG
'I lead him.'
 a. *'eku taki*
 POSS:1SG(A) leading
 'my-A leading (i.e., the leading which is done by me)'
 b. *hono taki*
 POSS:3SG(O) leading
 'his-O leading/being led (i.e., the leading which is done to him)'
(Churchward 1953: 78)

(7) a. *'eku fakatātā*
 POSS:1SG(A) picture
 'my-A picture (i.e., a picture that I have painted/taken)'
 b. *hoku fakatātā*
 POSS:1SG(O) picture
 'my-O picture (i.e., a picture that is painted/taken of me)'
(Völkel 2010: 179)

These so-called minimal pairs demonstrate that the choice of A versus O is not dependent on the nature of the possessee but rather on the relationship between possessor and possessee. A- and O-possession classify the relationship in terms of "control". A-possession expresses that the possessive relationship, or more precisely its initiation, is controlled by the possessor, while such control is absent or remains unspecified in O-possessed constructions.[7] In (6a) and (7a), the possessor (ego) has control over the possessee (the leading) or the initiation of the possessive relationship (the creation of a picture which would not exist without the agency of the possessor, who takes or paints it). Such control on the part of the possessor is absent in the O-possessed constructions (6b) and (7b), because somebody else controls or creates the possessees.

Just like other possessees, *hingoa* 'name' also occurs in both A- and O-possessed constructions with the difference in meaning described. In (8a), the A-possessive indicates that the possessor has control over the 'name' or more precisely the

7 Wilson (1982: 15–16) distinguishes two control theories explaining the differences in semantics between A- and O-possession in Polynesian languages: the simple control theory (A: possessor has control over the possessee; O: default, i.e., such control is absent or unspecified) and the initial control theory (A: possessor has control over the initiation of the possessive relationship; O: default, i.e., such control is absent or unspecified), whereby the initial control theory is preferable to the simple control theory. For a more detailed discussion on Tongan see Völkel (2010: 167–194).

initiation of the possessive relationship. He/she is the one who creates it, i.e., it is the name that he/she gives to someone else. As we have seen in Section 3, in this case the possessor is the *mehekitanga* (father's sister) or another relative of the father's side. In (8b), instead, the O-possessive indicates that the possessor has no such control over the initiation of the possessive relationship, as the name is bestowed on him/her.

(8) a. *'eku* *hingoa*
POSS:1SG(A) name
'my-A name (i.e., the name that I give to s.o.)'
b. *hoku* *hingoa*
POSS:1SG(O) name
'my-O name (i.e., the name that is given to me)' (Völkel 2010: 177)

Thus, the different possessive constructions conceptualise the perspectives of giving and getting a name. This symbolises the power, right and control of integrating a newborn into its *kāinga*, the most central social network. From the name giver's perspective (i.e., a relative with higher *'eiki* status vis-à-vis the newborn), the A-possessive expresses this control (4a), whereas from the name receiver's perspective (who has lower *tu'a* status vis-à-vis the name giver), there is no such control, as expressed by the O-possessive (4b).

4.2 *Hingoa* 'name' in syntactic word class frames

Tongan and Oceanic languages in general are well-known for their lexical flexibility (Broschart 1997; Vonen 2000; van Lier 2017).[8] This means that lexical items can occur in multiple functions, namely predicative, referential and/or modificatory, without any morphological modification. *Faka'ofo'ofa* 'beautiful', for instance, can be used nominally, i.e., referentially as the head of an argument phrase (ART X), as in (9d); verbally, i.e., predicatively as the head of a TAM predicate (TAM X) as in (9c); adjectivally, i.e., as the modifier of an argument phrase (in postnominal position) as in (9a); and adverbially, i.e., as the modifier of a TAM predicate (in postverbal position) as in (9b).

8 Lexical flexibility includes multicategoriality, which is lexical flexibility in a narrow sense, and multifunctionality, which is also called grammatical flexibility (van Lier 2017: 242–243; François 2017: 294). As Völkel (2017) shows, Tongan is primarily flexible in terms of multifunctionality, i.e., flexibility as a property of entire word classes in the grammar rather than as a property of individual lexemes. However, this distinction is nor relevant for the argumentation in this section.

(9) a.

ha	*fefine*	*faka'ofo'ofa*
ART	woman	beautiful

'a beautiful woman'

b.

'Oku	*hiva*	*faka'ofo'ofa*	*'a*	*e*	*kui*	*fefine.*
PRS	sing	beautiful	ABS	ART	grandparent	female

'The grandmother sings beautifully.'

c.

'Oku	*faka'ofo'ofa*	*'a*	*e*	*fefine.*
PRS	beautiful	ABS	ART	woman

'The woman is beautiful.'

d.

hono	*faka'ofo'ofa*
POSS:3SG(O)	beautiful/beauty

'his/her/its beauty' (Völkel 2017: 453)

However, not all lexemes allow this extreme kind of flexibility to occur in all four functions. While property-denoting terms such as *faka'ofo'ofa* are highly flexible, object-denoting terms such as *hingoa* 'name' are much less flexible. While some of them may only be used nominally, i.e., in referential function (Völkel 2017: 465–472), *hingoa* can actually be used nominally (10a) and verbally (10b), but not in modificatory function (Völkel 2017: 488).

(10) a.

Ko	hai	ho	hingoa?
PRES	who	POSS:2SG(O)	name

'What is your name (i.e., the name given to you?' (see Section 4.2)

b.

'Oku	*'i*	*ai*	*ha*	*tamasi'i*	*heni*	*'oku*	*hingoa*
PRS	LOC	there	ART: unspec	boy	here	PRS	name

ko	*Sione?*
PRES	John

'Is there a lad here named John?'

(Churchward 1959: 225, glossing added by SV)

In (10b), *hingoa* is an intransitive verb with the meaning 'to be named'. This is comparable to the O-possessed construction described in Section 4.1, which also refers to the name that is given to someone. *Fakahingo* in (11), instead, is a transitive verb with the meaning 'to name s.o./s.th.'. It is composed of the causative prefix *faka-* and *hingoa* 'name'. Thus, the causative expresses that the agent is responsible for the existence of the name, which is comparable to the control over the name's creation expressed in the A-possessed constructions described in Section 4.1.

(11) Na'á ma faka-hingoa ia ko Pita.
PST 1DLexcl CAUS-name 3SG PRES Peter
'We named him Peter.'
(Churchward 1959: 44, glossing & translation added by SV)

4.3 *Hingoa* 'name' in honorific registers

Tongan and a few other Polynesian languages, such as Samoan, Uvean and Futunan, have honorific registers (Krupa 1982: 165; Lynch 1998: 257–258), called a language of respect by Churchward (1953). These are two limited sets of lexemes (in addition to the common lexicon of Tongan, *kakai* language): one set used to refer to people of chiefly rank (*hou'eiki* vocabulary), and another set to people of kingly rank (*tu'i* vocabulary). Some examples are given in (12). The head of a chief, for instance, is not called *'ulu* but *fofonga* (12a) and the king's bed is called *tōfā'anga* instead of *mehenga* (12b).

(12) a. head: *'ulu* (kakai) – *fofonga* (hou'eiki) – *langi* (tu'i)
b. bed: *mohenga/mohe'anga* (kakai) – *toka'anga* (hou'eiki) – *tōfā'anga* (tu'i)
to sleep: *mohe* (kakai) – *toka* (hou'eiki) – *tōfā* (tu'i)
c. food: *me'akai* (kakai) – *(me'a) 'ilo* (hou'eiki) – *(me'a) taumafa* (tu'i)
to eat: *me'a* (kakai) – *'ilo* (hou'eiki) – *taumafa* (tu'i)
d. to go: *'alu* (kakai) – *me'a* (hou'eiki) – *hā'ele* (tu'i)

As the example in (13) shows, the Tongan honorific registers are restricted to the lexicon and do not concern grammatical markers such as the tempus marker *na'e* (past) or the preposition *'a* (ablative) and *ki* (allative). In reference to Chief Tāmale's going, the *hou'eiki* term *me'a* is used instead of *'alu*, which would refer to the going of a commoner (12d). Furthermore, the honorific vocabulary are limited sets, i.e., not all lexemes have honorific equivalents. There is, for instance, no special *hou'eiki* or *tu'i* lexeme for *'aneafi* ('yesterday') or *kolo* ('village, town'). A more extensive list of honorific vocabulary that I created in collaboration with Hon. Fanetupouvava'u Tuita, the granddaughter of King Tāufa'āhau Tupou IV in 2002–03, is published in Völkel (2010: 210–213).

(13) A commoner (S) talking about Chief Tāmale (R) to another commoner (A):
Na'e me'a 'a Tamāle ki kolo 'aneafi.
PST **HOU'EIKI**:go ABS Tamāle ALL town yesterday
'Tamāle went to town yesterday.'

The language of respect serves to honour people of higher rank and thus to respect the societal stratification (see Section 1). Furthermore, anthropological-linguistic research has shown that these honorifics can also be regarded as a verbal taboo (Völkel 2022). The Polynesian concept of *tapu* (source of the loanword 'taboo') means that entities with more *mana* ('supernatural power of life'), such as persons of higher rank, their bodies, personal belongings, characteristics, actions and so forth, are "sacred" and it is "forbidden to get in touch with them". In addition to taboos prohibiting physical contact with them, the honorifics are a kind of verbal taboo. The respectful terminology (*hou'eiki* and *tu'i* lexemes) is limited to *tapu* entities, and its indirect (paraphrasing, metaphorical or generalising) character shows that direct verbal contact with the common signifier (the *kakai* lexeme) is avoided, just like physical contact with its signified (Völkel 2022). It is, for instance, not only taboo to touch the king's/queen's head, but his/her head is also not referred to by the *kakai* word *'ulu*. The metaphorical *tu'i* equivalent *langi* (meaning 'sky' in common language) is used instead (12a).[9] Furthermore, it is taboo to eat the king's/queen's leftover food or to sleep in his/her bed, just as these items are also not referred to by the *kakai* words but by the honorific equivalents *taumafa* (12c) and *tōfā'anga* (12b). Another typical strategy in avoidance styles is the borrowing of lexemes from neighbouring languages or varieties (Storch 2017: 312). Neither of the *tu'i* lexemes *taumafa* and *tōfā'anga* have a *kakai* meaning, but they are identical with the Samoan terms for the high chiefs' food or bed (Milner 1961: 300). Similar physical and verbal taboos apply to people of chiefly rank.

As (14) shows, *hingoa* 'name' is also one of the terms with honorific equivalents.

(14) name: *hingoa* (kakai) – *hingoa* (hou'eiki) – *huafa* (tu'i)

This means that the name is regarded as representing a person and thus, it is not only taboo to physically touch a chief or the king/queen but verbal contact is also avoided. *Hingoa* is a lexically ambiguous term (like multiple other Tongan honorifics[10]), referring to a commoner's name as well as to a chief's name. The king's/

9 *Langi* ('sky') as a respectful term for the king's head is a metaphorical description of the uppermost body part. The chief's food/eating is called *'ilo* (12c), which has the *kakai* meaning 'to know', and thus, the food of a chief is regarded as mental intake. An example of the generalising character of honorifics is *me'a*, the *hou'eiki* term for 'to go' (12d) and other movement verbs, which means 'thing' in the *kakai* language (Völkel 2010: 214–215).

10 Not all honorifics have three distinct lexemes, i.e., one *kakai* term, another term for *hou'eiki* and a third one for *tu'i*. Lexical ambiguity is characteristic of Tongan honorifics. There are cases in which the *kakai* and *hou'eiki* terms are the same (e.g., *hingoa*) and other cases in which *hou'eiki* and *tu'i* terms are the same. Moreover, multiple *hou'eiki* and *tu'i* terms are *kakai* lexemes with another meaning, such as we have seen in the example of *langi* (meaning 'sky' as well as 'king's/queen's head') and the examples given in Note 9.

queen's name is referred to as *huafa*, which is the Tongan equivalent of the Samoan honorific lexeme *suafa* for the name of high chiefs (Milner 1961: 300).

Altogether, the lexeme for names of higher ranked people is substituted by an honorific equivalent to avoid direct verbal contact. It is not only impolite but even taboo to use the *kakai* word *hingoa* to refer to the king's name. Likewise, individual names of people with chiefly or kingly rank are substituted by their titles, particularly in official settings (see Section 2). These are both kinds of name avoidance vis-à-vis people of higher rank.

5 Conclusion

The existence of anthroponyms is a cultural and linguistic universal. Personal names, naming practices and the meaning of names, however, differ cross-linguistically and cross-culturally. This is not surprising, since anthroponyms name social beings and reflect interpersonal concepts that are very different across societies. Therefore, names are a linguistic phenomenon that must be seen as embedded in its cultural context. An understanding of names and naming from a linguistic and from an anthropological perspective leads to connecting insights.

The example of Tongan has shown that culture-specific ideas of social togetherness and personhood, as well as situations of culture and language contact, have shaped the existing types of personal names and practices of naming; they are even conceptualised in grammatical constructions of *hingoa* ('name').

Formerly, Tongans had a semantically transparent single given name which described the person in some way, e.g., special circumstances at the time of birth, the birthplace or some other characteristic. Through Western contact in the 19th century, particularly with European missionaries, the types of names changed significantly. Given names of Christian Biblical origin were adopted in addition to the Tongan names and the binominal name system consisting of given name(s) plus family name was introduced. Thereafter, the father's given name was used as the family name and then these patronymics became frozen hereditary surnames. Newborns get their parents' family name and at marriage women take the family name of their husbands. The given name is generally given to the child by the *mehekitanga* (the father's sister) or other patrilateral kin. These are persons of higher social status who have the privilege and power of naming and thus integrating the child into their *kāinga* (the extended family network). This crucial idea of giving vs. getting a name is linguistically expressed in possessive constructions (*'eku hingoa* – 'my-A name, i.e., the name that I give to someone' vs. *hoku hingoa* – 'my-O name, i.e., the name given to me'), as well as in syntactic word class frames (*hingoa* as a noun or verb meaning 'name' or 'to be named' vs. *faka-hingoa* as a verb meaning 'to name someone').

People of chiefly and kingly rank in Tonga have names but they inherit titles upon the death of the previous title holder according to patrilineal primogeniture succession. Title holders are then addressed and referred to by the title on official occasions, while their birth name is only used in private contexts. Likewise, the common word *hingoa* 'name' is substituted by honorific equivalents in reference to people of higher rank, e.g., *huafa*, meaning 'name of a *tu'i* person'. These are both kinds of name avoidance relating to societal rank.

References

Alford, Richard D. 1988. *Naming and identity. A cross-cultural study of personal naming practices*. New Haven: HRAF Press.

Bott, Elizabeth. 1981. Power and rank in the Kingdom of Tonga. *Journal of the Polynesian Society* 90 (1). 7–81.

Bramwell, Ellen. 2016. Personal names and anthropology. In Carole Hough (ed.), *The Oxford handbook of names and naming*, 263–278. Oxford University Press.

Broschart, Jürgen. 1997. Why Tongan does it differently. Categorial distinctions in a language without nouns and verbs. *Linguistic Typology* 1. 123–165.

Bruck, Gabriele vom & Barbara Bodenhorn. 2006. *An anthropology of names and naming*. Cambridge: Cambridge University Press.

Campbell, Ian. 2001. *Island kingdom. Tonga ancient and modern*. Christchurch: Canterbury University Press.

Churchward, Clerk. 1953. *Tongan grammar*. Oxford: Oxford University Press.

Churchward, Clerk. 1959. *Dictionary Tongan – English, English – Tongan*. Nuku'alofa: Government of Tonga Printing Press.

Douaire-Marsaudon, Françoise. 1996. Neither black nor white. The father's sister in Tonga. *Journal of the Polynesian Society* 105 (2). 139–164.

Foley, William. 1997. *Anthropological linguistics. An introduction*. Oxford: Blackwell.

François, Alexandre. 2017. The economy of word classes in Hiw, Vanuatu. Grammatically flexible, lexically rigid. *Studies in Language* 41 (2). 294–357.

Gifford, Edward. 1929. *Tongan society*. Honolulu: Bernice P. Bishop Museum.

Hanks, Patrick. 2006. Personal names. In Keith Brown (ed.), *Encyclopedia of language and linguistics*, 2nd ed., vol. 9, 299–311. Amsterdam: Elsevier.

Hockett, Charles. 1963. The problem of universals in language. In Joseph Greenberg (ed.), *Universals of language*, 1–22. Cambridge, MA: MIT Press.

Kaeppler, Adrienne. 1971. Rank in Tonga. *Ethnology* 10 (2). 174–193.

Krupa, Victor. 1982. *The Polynesian languages. A guide*. London: Routledge.

Lichtenberk, Frantisek. 1983. Relational classifiers. *Lingua* 60. 147–176.

Lynch, John. 1998. *Pacific languages. An introduction*. Honolulu: University of Hawaii Press.

Lynch, John & France Mugler. 1999. *English in the South Pacific*. http://www.vanuatu.usp.ac.fj/paclangunit/English_South_Pacific.htm (accessed 30 May 2017).

Milner, G. B. 1961. The Samoan vocabulary of respect. *Journal of the Royal Anthropological Institute* 91. 296–317.

Morton, Helen. 1996. *Becoming Tongan. An ethnography of childhood.* Honolulu: University of Hawaii Press.

Morton Lee, Helen. 2003. *Tongans overseas. Between two shores.* Honolulu: University of Hawaii Press.

Neill, James Scott. 1955. *Ten years in Tonga.* London: Hutchinson.

Storch, Anne. 2017. Typology of secret languages and linguistic taboos. In Alexandra Y. Aikhenvald & Robert M. W. Dixon (eds.), *The Cambridge handbook of linguistic typology*, 287–321. Cambridge: Cambridge University Press.

Taumoefolau, Melenaite. 1996. Nominal possessive classification in Tonga. In John Lynch & Faʻafo Pat (eds.), *Oceanic studies. Proceedings of the first international conference on Oceanic linguistics.* Canberra: Pacific Linguistics, ANU.

Tongan Government. 2011. *Tonga 2011. Census of population and housing*, vol. 1. Nukuʻalofa: Statistics Department Tonga.

Van der Grijp, Paul. 1993. *Islanders of the South. Production, kinship and ideology in the Polynesian Kingdom of Tonga.* Leiden: KITLV Press.

Van Lier, Eva. 2017. Introduction. Lexical flexibility in Oceanic languages. *Studies in Language* 41 (2). 241–254.

Völkel, Svenja. 2010. *Social structure, space and possession in Tongan culture and language.* Amsterdam: Benjamins.

Völkel, Svenja. 2017. Word classes and the scope of lexical flexibility in Tongan. *Studies in Language* 41 (2). 445–495.

Völkel, Svenja. 2022. Tongan honorifics and their underlying concepts of *mana* and *tapu*. A verbal taboo in its emic sense. *Pragmatics & Cognition* 28 (1). 26–57.

Vonen, Arnfinn Muruvik. 2000. Polynesian multifunctionality and the ambitions of linguistic description. In Petra Vogel & Bernard Comrie (eds.), *Approaches to the typology of word classes*, 479–487. Berlin: de Gruyter.

Wilson, William. 1982. *Proto-Polynesian possessive marking.* Canberra: Pacific Linguistics, ANU.

Miguel Reyes Contreras

Chapter 17
A descriptive account of the modern Mazahuan onomastic system

Abstract: During pre-Columbian times in Mexico, onomastic systems were rich and varied. There are few written sources from which this can be proved, except from the documents left by the hegemonic groups in those days, like the Aztecs and Mayans. The onomastic systems of minor languages like Otomi and Mazahua virtually disappeared during the Mexican conquest, being replaced by the Spanish one. Gutierre Tibón (1961) and Villegas and Brambilla (2020) have made an account of some Otomi onomastic relics; they can be found up until the eighteenth century and there are a few references to names among the Mazahuas in Najera Yanguas (Knapp 2013). In the modern days, owing to the creation of Intercultural Universities, an interest in the revitalisation and strengthening of national languages and the grammar and phonetics of these languages has risen. They have been documented, to a large extent, by creating vocabulary records. In these records certain names appear but their structure seems to consist of adaptations of hypocoristics and word truncations (among other formation processes such as syncopation, shortening, apheresis, etc.) from Spanish (Reyes Contreras 2019b). In this paper, the modern way of nominating in modern Mazahua is explored, following the research around a corpus created in 2019. The objective is then to analyse this data from the lexicological and phonetic-phonological points of view, with the aim of providing a descriptive account of how the Spanish and Mazahuan systems together created a hybrid nomination pattern which is currently used and spread throughout the modern Mazahuan area in the centre of Mexico.

Keywords: Mazahuan, anthroponomy, hypocoristics, onomastic system, morphophonology

Miguel Reyes Contreras, Universidad Autónoma del Estado de México, Universidad de Ixtlahuaca CUI, e-mail: reyescontramiguel@gmail.com

https://doi.org/10.1515/9783110759297-017

1 Introduction

Naming is a universal phenomenon in language. The first interest about names and the object they name was philosophical, but it has also gained interest in Anthropology, Sociology and Linguistics. For most societies, and I would dare to say *all of them,* it is necessary to have a name to exist and to have a place in society. Be it a modern or an ancient group, naming is there to remind group members of their belonging to a community. Commonly, we attach a personal name to a new-born to make them unique; we also give them surnames, to make them part of a certain group, a family. Through lifetime they can acquire more than one kind of name; bynames, nicknames or pseudonyms may be acquired. Within the families there are some other forms of intimate reference, the family names, also called hypocoristics. All of these terms constitute an onomastic system.

When there is a clash of cultures, as happened during the Spanish conquest in Mexico, the dominant culture ends up changing or erasing the dominated culture, including its language, traditions and, as in this case, onomastic systems.

The main aim of this text, then, is to present an overview of the anthroponomical system of the modern Mazahuan language, spoken by about 200,000 people in the centre of Mexico. The core assumption is that the current anthroponymic system in the Mazahuan language is the result of a blending with Spanish because of language contact. Through a selection of Spanish names from a widespread calendar used in Mexico and interviews to record native speakers naming their correspondent equivalents into Mazahua, a corpus of about 200 names was developed. The corpus was analysed according to morpho-phonological features, including stress and truncation. The results reveal an interesting hybrid between Mazahuan phonology and morphology and the Spanish names, turning them into hypocoristics adapted to the disyllabic structure of Mazahuan lexis due to the vowel harmony of the language.

In the following pages I introduce the reader to the Mazahuas and the Mazahuan language and present a review of nationwide and worldwide studies on indigenous anthroponymic systems. I end up with a classification of names according to the different morphophonological processes they undergo.

2 Some notes about the Mazahuas

The Mazahuan people are also known as *jñatrjo*, a word which is composed of *jñaa* 'to talk' and *trjo* 'from' (a delimitative morpheme), which means 'from the word', 'from the talk' or, loosely speaking, 'we talk'. The Mazahuans are a people whose history is completely opaqued by the dominant groups that prevailed in the area, like the Chichimecs, the Aztecs and the Purepecha. The Mazahuans belong to one of the seven tribes who migrated from *Chicomoztoc* 'the place of the seven caves' (located in a place which has not been clearly identified) to the Valley of Mexico, the current location of the megalopolis of Mexico City. The word *Mazahua* derives from *Mazáhuatl*, which was the name of the chiefs of the tribes in the migration (CDI 2006).

The Mazahuas inhabit 14 municipalities in the northeastern part of the State of México (Map 17.1)[1] and two municipalities (Crescencio Morales and Zitácuaro) in the eastern part of Michoacán. The 14 municipalities in the State of Mexico cover 920 villages; 716 (77%) have Mazahuan speakers (Ramírez 2008: 3).

Map 17.1: State of Mexico and location of the Mazahuan people in the state of Mexico (source: edomex.gob and CEDIPIEM, open access).

1 Ixtlahuaca, Temascalcingo, Atlacomulco, Donato Guerra, El Oro, Villa Victoria, Villa de Allende, Jocotitlán, Almoloya de Juárez, Valle de Bravo, Ixtapan del Oro, San Felipe del Progreso and San José del Rincón.

Almost all Mazahuan speakers are bilingual and have kept many of their traditions alive through the years. In pre-Columbian times their land was between the empire of the Aztecs, who ruled the central part of Mexico, and the Purepecha, who ruled the state of Michoacán. When the Spanish arrived, they were freed from the Aztecs and then they lived under the rule of the Spanish invaders. Their language was influenced by the invader's one. We'll go back to this in the results section.

Jñatrjo or Mazahua (spoken by around 200,000 people) is a Mesoamerican language belonging to the Otopamean branch of the Otomanguean family. The branch is divided into Otomian and Pamean. The former contains the Central Otomian languages (including Mazahua, *Jñatrjo*, and Otomí, *hñähñu*) and the Southern Otomian languages (including Matlatzinca and Ocuilteco) (Bartholomew 1994: 1).[2]

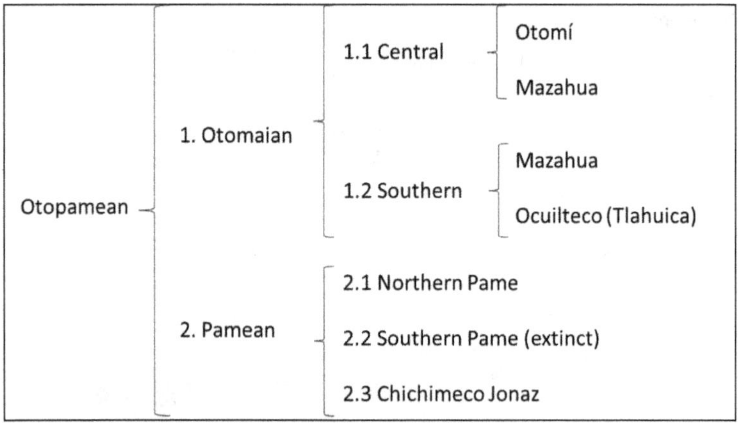

Figure 17.1: Otopamean linguistic group (from Bartholomew 1994: 1).

To understand the naming system in Mazahua, I will present some phonetic and lexical information. Mazahua is a tone language and the tone system "is an essential part of the grammar and lexical system of Mazahua, because through tones we can distinguish meanings in prefixes" (Romero Hernández 2010: 8, author's translation).[3] This language contains a high number of vowels: oral, nasal and glottal, as well as long and short allophonic variations. It is necessary to highlight that Mazahua does not have a writing system; however, several attempts have been carried out to develop one, taking into consideration the Spanish alphabet and

2 It is important to mention the self-denominations used by the community of speakers: Mazahua *-jñatrjo-*, Otomí *-hñähñu-*, matlatzinca *Bótuna* and Tlahuica or Oculiteco *-Pjekjakjo*.

3 In the original: "es parte esencial de la gramática y el léxico de la lengua mazahua, ya que a través de los tonos se distinguen significados en los prefijos".

some symbols taken from the International Phonetic Alphabet (IPA), although there is resistance among speakers and scholars to adopting it. The most accepted orthography is the one used by the Intercultural University from the State of Mexico, an institution which has been rescuing the language and teaching it at the higher level, as well as promoting research and the development of indigenous languages. They have supported the creation of dictionaries and alphabet regulations. The orthography presented below is the most developed so far and the one used to teach the language in schools.

Normales: a, e, i, o, u.

Nasales: a̲, e̲, i̲, o̲, u̲.

Glotales: a', e', i', o', u'.

Abiertas o guturales: u̸, u̸̲, e̸, a̸, o̸.

Alargadas: aa, ee, ii, oo, uu, a̸a̸, e̸e̸, o̸o̸, u̸u̸, a̲a̲, e̲e̲, i̲i̲, o̲o̲, u̲u̲, u̸̲u̸̲.

Figure 17.2: Vowels in Mazahua (López Marín 2010: 53).

López Marín (2010) suggests three groups of consonantal sounds, although the second and third lines are just diacritics or consonant clusters (Figure 17.3).

Consonants: b, ch, d, g, j, k, l, m, n, ñ, p, r, s, t, ts, x, y, z, zh.

Consonants with an apostrophe: b', p', d', ch', k', m', n', ñ', tr', t', s', ts'.

Consonant clusters: chj, jm, jn, jñ jy, kj, pj, sj, tsj, nd, ts, trj, tj, nz, nzh, mb, ng, dy, nr, zh, pj.

Figure 17.3: Consonants in Mazahua (López Marín 2010: 53).

2.1 Some lexical information about Mazahua

As proper names belong to the category of nouns (proper and common names) (López Franco 2010; Amaral and Seide 2020) I present a brief description of how Mazahua's lexical system works (especially noun morphology), following López Marín (2010) as a reference.

2.1.1 Noun

A noun designates an entity, be it an object, an animal, a person or an abstract concept. In this language we can find proper, abstract, personal, locative, animate and inanimate nouns. In the group of proper nouns, we find personal names. A major characteristic of this category is the addition of *e* as a marker of subject, which is reminiscent of the Japanese *ga* to refer to the subject. In (1) we can see some examples:

(1) a. *In-chuzgo* *e* *Xuba*
PRES-NAME SUBJECT PROP N
'My name is Juan'
b. ... *e* *Chico*
SUBJECT Francisco[4]

The particle *e* is considered an article (López Marín 2010: 66); it is commonly attached to proper names and indicates an ungrammatical Spanish use of proper names, like *e Xuba*, '*the John > John', *e Lipe* '*the Phillip > Philip'.

Toponyms are also contained in the group of proper names and are categorised as locatives, but they have the particle *a* attached to them (2) indicating place.

(2) a. *a* *Zumi*
LOC PROP N.
'in Toluca'
b. *a* *Mbaro*
'in Atlacomulco'[5]

2.1.2 Adjectives

Adjectives are of importance as they express characteristics or properties of nouns when attached to them. In Mazahua, the adjective works as a prefix (López Marín 2010: 66): *mbadyo* 'red dog' and *b'odyo* 'black dog'. This process of affixation is a compositional process as both adjective and noun merge into one word (with the prefixes *mba-* 'red' and *b'o* 'black').

4 Equivalents of John and Francis, respectively.

5 Two major cities in the State. Toluca is the capital and Atlacomulco an industrial municipality.

2.2 Some morphological aspects of Mazahua

Affixation is a productive process in Mazahua (López Marín 2010: 66). There are the augmentative prefixes *tr'a-*, *ta-* and *cha-* (they also depend on dialectal variation, thus: *tr'adyepjad'u* 'big needle', *tr'amuxa* 'big corn' or *Ta'migue* 'Miguelón < big Mike'. The diminutive prefixes are *ts'i-* and *ch'i-*, as in *Ts'imixi* 'small cat', *Ts'idyo* 'puppy – little dog' and *Ts'ingumu* 'small house'.

Mazahuan words are mostly disyllabic (except when there is augmentative or diminutive affixation), with words following the CVCV type. However, "Many Oto-Manguean languages permit complex rimes, especially in the Oto-Pamean and Zapotecan families" (DiCanio and Bennett 2017: 7). This structure is the one we'll refer below when classifying the naming system.

2.3 Onomastic systems

According to Fernández Juncal (2011: 142), an anthroponymic system is a "*diasistema*", or a double system, because of "the problems derived from the description of linguistic continuum borders presented as discrete units"[6]. These involve diastratic, diatopic and diachronic (in addition to diaphasic) variations.

There is a small amount of scholarly level research on names in Mexico; the pioneer paper is Peter-Boyd Bowman's (1970) work. In this study he collected name registrations in the Metropolitan Cathedral in Mexico City over a period of around 400 years so he could observe the historical development of names in the country. Gutierre Tibón's work comprises names and etymology in a comparative dictionary of names (1961, 1998) and a great collection of surnames in his dictionary of surnames from Hispano-America and the Philippines (1998). López Franco is currently the major referent for the study of Anthroponomastics in Mexico; she centres on comparative and descriptive studies. In her BA thesis, López Franco (1990) studies the distribution and choice of proper names among university students as a case study. López Franco (2003) is a study of the anthroponymic system followed by Arab migrants to the South of France during the second part of the twentieth century. Since 2005 she has specialised in two specific populations: Tlalnepantla de Baz, a municipality in the surroundings of Mexico City (López Franco 2005, 2006, 2009, 2010, 2020; López Franco and Jiménez Segura 2006), and Montpellier, France (López Franco 2013, 2015, 2016, 2017, 2019), also undertaking comparative studies between the two contexts (López

6 Original: "los problemas que plantea la descripción de zonas de continuum lingüístico presentadas como unidades discretas" (own translation)

Franco 2014a, 2020). In the same line, she has theorised about the semantics of names (2014b) and the sources for Anthroponomastics studies in Mexico (2019).

Regarding Anthroponomastics in indigenous languages, not many papers can be found. The website Lingmex (Barriga Villanueva, 2022) harbours more than 150 papers related to onomastics published in Mexico since the 1970s, however most of these are about toponyms. The ones related to Anthroponomastics are limited and hard to get hold of, as unfortunately they are only listed; the papers themselves are not available online and need to be digitalised for researchers. Based on the mention of the language in the titles of these papers, I highlight Pérez González (1970) and his work on the Chontal[7] patronymic system. Horcasitas (1973), Herrera Meza (1994, 2004, 2009) and Neaves (2021) study Nahuatl[8] anthroponymy. In his (1973) study, Horcasitas points out that names are studied from the perspective of ethnology; he analyses the structure and meaning of Nahuatl names and surnames collected over a time span of 400 years. Herrera Meza focuses on deverbal names[9] in her (2004) paper as she considers the metaphorical significance of the radical *poctli* 'smoke' in the formation process of ancient names; in her (2009) paper she devotes her efforts to clarifying the meaning of the names of Moctezuma.

Escalante Hernández (1994) focuses on Matlatzincas' nicknames, Hermann (2004) on Mixtecan anthroponyms, Mora Peralta (2008, 2012) on Mayan anthroponyms and Zúñiga (2018) on Mayan nicknames. Reyes Contreras (2017, 2018) focuses on names in Mazahuan areas, but not on indigenous names. In both papers he studies the way names are used in an indigenous-centred university in the central area of Mexico.

The effect of languages in contact affecting name systems is investigated in Prisacaru (2011: 90–93), who compares the Romanisation and Germanisation of names in Bucovina. The same phenomenon is found in Lawson's work, analysing Zulu and Maori (2016: 182–183, 189–190). Additionally, some other scholars have observed naming systems, such as Price and Price (1972), studying Saramaka onomastics, Cierbide Martinena (1996) studying the spread of Jewish names in Navarra, Spain and Jacinto Santos (2009) the names in Ashanti culture. Further north, Joalaid (2016) studies the Balto-Finnic name systems. Notzon and Nesom (2005) present the

---

7 Chontal is a language spoken in the states of Tabasco, Oaxaca and Guerrero. The paper only exists in its printed version.

8 Nahuatl, also known as Mexican or Aztec, mexicatl, mexcatl or mexicano tlajtol, is a southern language from the Uto-Aztecan family and it has more than 20 dialects. It is spoken by more than 1.5 million people in 16 states. Taken from: https://linguistica.inah.gob.mx/index.php/leng/92-nahuatl (accessed 2 March 2023).

9 Just taken from the title due to the fact that the paper is unavailable.

complexity of the Arabic system and Leibring (2016) makes a report on the European naming systems and their particular features.

Concerning the Mazahuan naming system, the earliest lexicographic work is the collection by Nágera Yanguas (1637) (re-edited by Knapp 2013), whose purpose was evangelisation, but who records many aspects of Mazahuan culture, such as the kinship system (Eusebio Maximiliano 2019). Tibón (1961) provides a register of Mayan, Purepecha, Nahuatl and Otomi surnames. It is hard to find names in Mazahua in colonial documents and nowadays we can find surnames only in the most widely spoken languages (Nahuatl, Mayan and Purepecha). Among Mazahuans, names did not persist but were merged with the Spanish names, and the grammar of this category merge with the Mazahuan phonological and lexical rules. In the coming sections I present a reflection on hypocoristics, as they are the basic term related to the Mazahua names; I then present the methodology and the account of the Mazahuan anthroponymic system.

2.3.1 Hypocoristics

The word hypocoristic is used to represent a name and other derived names. The term derives from the Greek verb *ὑποκοριστικός* 'to caress' or 'to name in an affectionate way' (Fernández and Palencia 2015: 13). The Spanish Royal Academy defines hypocoristics as "a special type of personal name in an abbreviated form which are used in the colloquial language as affectionate naming, such as Lola, Lupe, Nacho, Paco, Pepe, Pili, Tere"[10] (2022, author's translation). Do Couto (2000: 50) says they are "the familiar affectionate way of referring to people. In some cases, the word hypocoristic is considered as a personal name, usually (but not always) taking the stressed syllable and duplicating it" (author's translation).[11]

Lenz (1944, cited in Gutiérrez Santana 2009a) stated that they have been a morpho-phonological phenomenon since the early twentieth century, related to the diminutive, where "the dorso-prepalatal consonants ch, ñ ll and their phonetic substitutes (. . .) are frequent in affectionate abbreviations of personal names" (author's translation)[12]. Some other scholars, such as Pinto (1992), Do Couto (2000), Gonçalves

10 Original: "un tipo especial de nombres de pila [de] formas abreviadas que se usan en la lengua familiar como designaciones afectivas: Lola, Lupe, Nacho, Paco, Pepe, Pili, Tere"

11 Original: "o modo familiar, afetivo, de designarem as pessoas. Em alguns casos o nome hipocorístico é tirado do nome próprio da pessoa, frequentemente (mas nem sempre) tomando-se-lhe a silaba tónica e reduplicando-a".

12 Original: "las consonantes dorso-prepalatales ch, ñ, 11 y su sustituto fonético (. . .) son frecuentes en abreviaciones cariñosas de nombres propios de personas".

(2004), Suárez Rodríguez (2008) and Gutiérrez Santana (2009a, 2009b, 2014), have devoted time to studying them. Most of them agree with the reference to the language of children. Peter Boyd-Bowman (1970: 348–358), who studied a corpus of hypocoristics in Hispano-American areas, concludes that their main characteristics are:

1. Palatalisation of sibilants: *Anastacio* > *Tacho*
2. Rejection of -r: *Alejandro* > *Jando*
3. Loss of *-l* in final or interior consonant clusters: *Anselmo* > *Chemo, Luis* > *Wicho*
4. Fricative *-d* or *-r* > *ø, l* or *yod: Eduardo* > *Lalo, Yayo; Alfredo* > *Feyo*
5. Reduction of hiatus or diphthong: *Consuelo* > *Chelo, Octavio* > *Tavo*
6. Nasal consonant + oral consonant: *Concepción* > *Concha, Isabel* > *Chabela*
7. Fricative primitive exchange (child) > oclusive: *Alfonso* > *Poncho, José(f)a* > *Pepe (a)*
8. Diachronic evidence of language dominion: *Avelina* > *Minina, Santiago* > *Chago*
9. Immutability of vowels
10. Reduction to 8 basic consonants in the initial stage of learning. (author's translation)[13]

A phonological process that takes place in some words is the exchange of a phoneme or allophones, a subtraction of phonemes or a reordering of these processes of the assimilation-dissimilation of sounds. Morphologically, hypocoristics have the following characteristics:

1. Final vowel alters to indicate gender: *Concepción* > *Concho, Concha; Chon, Chona*
2. Masculine endings on female hypocoristics. *Rosario* > *Charo, Chayo.*
3. *-i* ending (adult form): *Alicia* > *Lichi*
4. Affectionate endings in *-s, -as, -is, -ix*: *Carlos* < *Carlangas, Josefina* > *Chepis*
5. Varied suffixes (*-ico, -ica, -tico, -uco, -uca, -in*, etc.): *Pedro* > *Perico; Apolinar* > *Polín.*
6. Abbreviation from suffix: *Adolfo* > *Adolfito* > *Fito*
7. Addition of unstressed suffix *-cho, -cha* to *-in, -on, -an*: *Juan* > *Juancho, Ramón* > *Moncho*

---

13 Original:

"1. Palatalización de las sibilantes: Anastacio > Tacho
2. Repugnancia por la -r: Alejandro > Jando
3. Pérdida de -l en grupos consonánticos, al final o interior: Anselmo > Chemo, Luis > Wicho
4. -d fricativa o -r > ø, l o yod: Eduardo > Lalo, Yayo; Alfredo > Feyo
5. Reducción de hiato o diptongo: Consuelo > Chelo, Octavio > Tavo
6. Solo cons nasal + cons oral: Concepción > Concha, Isabel > Chabela
7. Trueque primitivo (infantil) ficativo > oclusivo: Alfonso > Poncho, José(f)a > Pepe (a)
8. Evidencias diacrónicas del dominio del idioma: Avelina > Minina, Santiago > Chago
9. Inmutabilidad de las vocales.
10. Reducción a 8 consonantes básicas en la etapa inicial de aprendizaje."

8. Anglicisms and Galicisms: *Antonio* > *Toni*, *Jaime* > *Yimi.* (Boyd-Bowman 1970: 360–363, author's translation[14]; a summary of them is seen in Figure 17.4)

One of the phonological phenomena operating on hypocoristics is truncation or "copying the first two syllables of the base name – with some interesting restrictions (. . .) and movement of the stress to the first syllable, forming what we might call a trochaic pattern" (Prieto 1992, cited in Estrada 2014: 9). This author states that there are four levels in the formation of hypocoristics: "prosodic, segmental, syllabic and morphological".

Regarding indigenous languages and hypocoristics, Cerrón-Palomino (2016) is the only one so far to have studied them in Quechua.

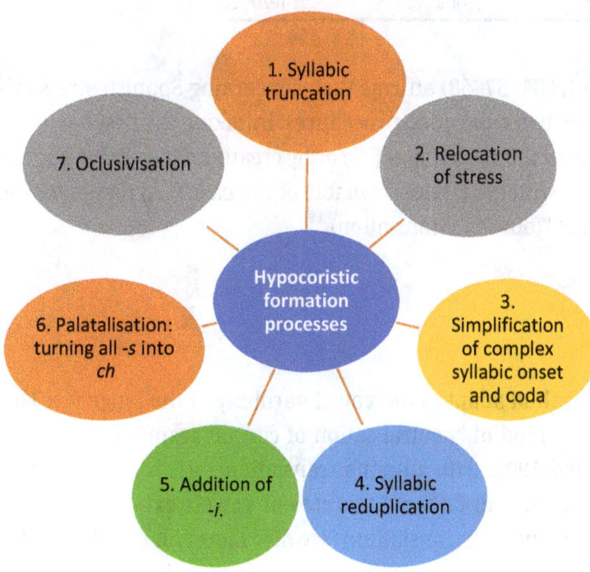

Figure 17.4: Hypocoristic formation processes (Reyes Contreras 2019b, adapted from Boyd-Bowman 1970).

14 Original:

"1. Alteración de la vocal fianl para indicar género: Concepción > Concho, Concha; Chon, Chona
2. Terminación masculina en hipocorísticos femeninos. Rosario > Charo, Chayo.
3. Terminación -i (forma adulta): Alicia > Lichi
4. Terminaciones cariñosas -s, -as, -is, -ix: Carlos < Carlangas, Josefina > Chepis
5. Sufijos varios (-ico. -ica, -tico, -uco, -uca, -in, etc.): Pedro > Perico; Apolinar > Polín, etc.
6. Abreviación con sufijo: Adolfo > Adolfito > Fito
7. Adición de sufijo átono -cho, -cha a -in, -on, -an: Juan > Juancho, Ramón > Moncho
8. Anglicismos y galicismos: Antonio > Toni, Jaime > Yimi."

Talking about truncation, “There are at least three types of truncations: the one that omits material from the right, the one from the left and, finally, one from both sides of the word”[15] (Gutiérrez 2014: 75–76, author’s translation; Grau Sempere, in Estrada 2014: 10).

Table 17.1: Types of truncations (adapted from Gutiérrez Santana 2014b: 76).

	Left	**right**	**Both sides**
Base	[. . . σ σ]	[σ σ . . .]	[. . . σ σ . . .]
Truncation	σ σ	σ σ	σ σ
Examples			
Base	Cuauhtémoc	Tonantzin	Moctezuma
Truncation	. . . Témoc	Tona . . .	. . . Tezu . . .

Ohannesian Saboundjian (2004: 57–58) affirms that, concerning Spanish stress syllables, “hypocoristics follow two truncation procedures: by taking the first two syllables, no matter the position of the stress mark (. . .) or by creating a bi-syllabic pattern stressed on the left starting with the stressed syllable of the base (. . .) no matter the position and syllabic weight” (author’s translation).[16]

2.3.2 Vowel harmony

The names in modern Mazahua adapt to the vowel harmony of the language. This phenomenon is known as a kind of “neutralisation of certain segments in a given vocalic system” (Tomcsányi 1992: 240, author’s translation)[17]; it is also an “assimilation phenomenon in which all or some features of vowels extend to others” (Jiménez and Lloret 2006: 1, author’s translation) (see also Lloret and Jiménez 2009: 300)[18]. Finally, vowel harmony is a pattern wherein vowels assimilate with respect to some feature (Heinz and Lai 2013: 55). Hypocoristics are generally bisyllabic or

15 Original: “Hay al menos tres tipos de truncamiento: el que omite material de la orilla derecha, el que lo hace de la orilla izquierda y, finalmente, el que corta a uno y otro extremo de la palabra”.
16 Original: “los hipocorísticos siguen dos procedimientos de truncamiento: cogiendo las dos primeras sílabas de la palabra, independientemente de la posición de la sílaba tónica (. . .) o formando una plantilla bisilábica acentuada a la izquierda a partir de la sílaba tónica de la base (. . .) y sea cual fuere la posición de su acento y su peso silábico”.
17 Original: “neutralización de ciertos segmentos en un sistema vocálico dado”.
18 Original: “un fenómeno asimilatorio por el cual todos o algunos de los rasgos de una vocal se extienden a otras vocales”.

bimoraic, as "the truncated version or *truncatum* must be monosyllabic, be it one or two moras long" (Avram, cited in Salaberri Zaratiegi and Salaberri Izko 2014: 191). For this reason, a hypocoristic is usually composed of two paroxytone syllables (see the example (3) taken from Salaberri Zaratiegi and Salaberri Izko 2014: 55).

(3) Roberto Verónica
CV CV CV CV
Be to Ve ro

One of the features of hypocoristics in Mazahua is the simplification of consonant clusters; for example, palatalization transforms a fricative sound like /s/ into the affricate /*ʧ*/ or /*lʧ*/ to /*lpj*/, as in *Adolfo* > *Dolpjo*, which seems opposite to the rule, since in Mazahua the phoneme /f/ is non-existent and it is articulated by the aspiration /p^{h}/ > /pj/. The rest of cases adapt to the optimal, i.e., combinations of CV (consonant-vowel) syllables, "the only universal syllabic model" (Do Couto 2000: 53–54, author's translation) (Figure 17.5).[19]

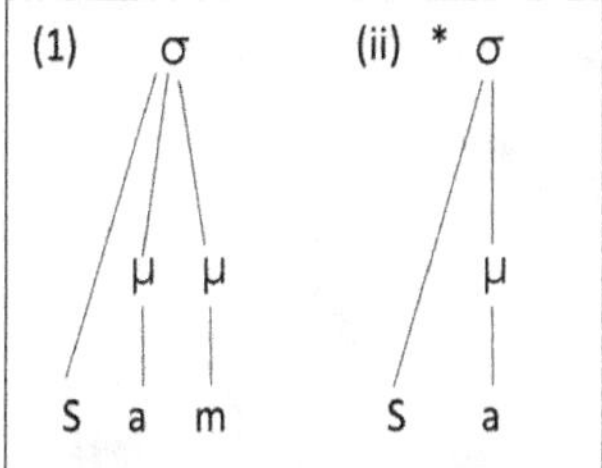

Figure 17.5: Hypocoristic optimal words (taken from Do Couto 2000: 53).

We can see that the structure of a hypocoristic sticks to the norm that every lexical word should have at least two moras.

19 Original: "o único modelo silábico universal".

3 Methodology

The study is divided into three different stages:

For data collection I selected a group of names taken from *Calendario de Galván* (2019).[20] These were read to a group of people (native and non-native speakers) from four municipalities in the State of Mexico, who were asked if they had heard or had acquaintances bearing such names, and a new list was made. The new list, comprising 364 names, was read to a couple of native speakers, who responded with the name in Mazahua. These responses were recorded and finally classified according to truncation patterns, vowel harmony patterns, (see Figure 17.6). Five different categories were found: initial, middle, final and truncation on both sides. The fifth category contains the special cases.

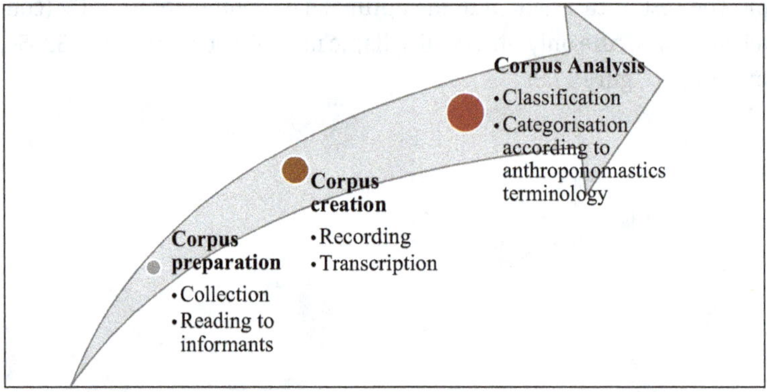

Figure 17.6: Methodological process.

4 Account of the Mazahuan name system

4.1 Vowel harmony

The data shows that some names in Mazahua assimilate to this pattern. In all the examples I write the Spanish first and then the Mazahuan equivalent. I have omitted the article *e* which, as mentioned before, should be attached to all names:

20 Galvan's Calendar. This is a Mexican Almanac which has been published since 1826. It contains the list of saints, catholic celebrations, astronomical features, etc. It can be found at https://www.calendariodelmasantiguogalvan.com.mx/.

(4)

Acacio	Kacho	Anastasia	Tachi
Adela	Dela	Angelina	Lina
Albina	Wina	Antolín	Tori
Alejo	Lejo	Antonia	Toña
Alicia	Lixa	Arturo	Turo
Amador	Mado	Aureliano	Lenu
Anacleto	Leto	Aurora	Lola

Long names are usually reduced to two syllables. There is a vowel harmony following CVCV patterns. In some other cases the reduction results in a monosyllabic name.

(5)

Aarón	Lon	Ezequiel	Kel
Abel	Bel	Eleazar	Sar
Abraham	Bram	Gabriel	Briel
Adán	Dan	Gil	Gil
Baltasar	Sar	Laura	Lau
Bernabé	Be	Leobardo	Leo
Darío	Lio	Ezequiel	Kel
Dorotea	Tea	Natalia	Lia
Ester	Ter	Mateo	Teo

4.2 Truncation

The phenomena found in the corpus include initial, middle and final truncation, as well as truncation to both sides; we can also see phonological phenomena such as palatalisation (e.g. *Alicia* > *Lixa*) or stress relocation (*Jacobo* > *Kobo*). A broader description of this process is found in Reyes Contreras (2019b).

4.2.1 Initial truncation

This means the elision of phonemes occurring at the beginning of the name. There is a loss of phonemes no matter the length of the name; the reduction results in a bi-syllabic pattern. This is the most productive group (6) in the corpus:

(6)

Macario	Kayo	j. Marcelina	Lina
Macedonio	Loñu	k. Ramiro	Miru
Maclovio	Nobio	l. Ricardo	Kalo
Magdalena	Lena	m. Rodolfo	Dolpjo
Marcelino	Linu	n. Rosendo	Sendo
Marcelo	Selo	o. Rufina	Pjina
Modesta	Desta	p. Regina	Jiña
Modesto	Desto	q. Rebeca	Beka
Marcela	Sela	r. Renato	Nato

4.2.2 Middle truncation

In the corpus there are only 7 cases of middle truncation. Names lose at least two phonemes and there is a loss or exchange of phonemes: *o* > *u Laureano* > *Lanu, Fausto* > *Pjatu.* Others examples are *Álvaro* > *Alo, Cándido* > *Cando, Carlos* > *Kalo, Leandro* > *Lendo, Lorenza* > *Lensa.*

4.2.3 Final truncation

This is the second most productive case and also follows the bi-syllabic pattern. In most cases, the assimilation to vowel harmony is CVCV but in cases like *Damián* > *Ndajmia, Odilón* > *Ndilo* and *Dimas* > *Ndima* there is an assimilation to Mazahuan consonant clusters, particularly the cluster *Nd* in a complex syllabic onset. Another case is *Salvador* > *Xaba* (*Chava*), in which /ʧ/ changes to /ʃ/, a characteristic sound of this language. Some other cases are as follows:

(7)

Valeria	Bale	e. Casilda	Kasi
Verónica	Bero	f. Constantino	Kosta
Judith	Judi	g. Cristóbal	Kito
Carina	Kari	h. Casilda	Kasi

4.2.4 Truncation on both sides

There are some names in the corpus which lose at least a phoneme on both sides, still assimilating to the CVCV syllabic pattern. Examples are:

(8)

Hilaria	Laxi	h. Isabel	Lina
Edgardo	Dy'argo	i. Estanislao	Miru
Adelaida	Lai	j. Constancio	Kalo
Eloísa	Lisa	k. Artemio	Dolpjo
Amador	Mado	l. Bartolomé	Tolo
Zenaida	Nai	m. Antolín	Tori
Oscar	Oka		

Notice, for example, how *Eloisa,* structured as [σ σ σ σ > e. lo. í. sa], turns into *Lisa* [σ σ > li . sa]; the same happens with the other names in this group.

There are some cases in which the modification is minimal and does not affect the syllabic structure but only the level of phonemes, that is, there is just an exchange of sounds, like *u* instead of *o* or *ch* instead of *s*. The following are examples of this:

(9)

a. Casio	Kacho	e. Gabino	Gabinu
b. Diego	Ndiego	f. Irma	Irjma
c. Albino	Albinu	g. Pedro	Pelo/Pegro
d. Flora	Pjlora	h. Sabino	Sabinu

Special cases are the ones which seem to contradict the rule of vocalic harmonisation. There are some names like *Caridad* > *Karidá, Melitón* > *Melitó, Zacarías* > *Sakaria* and *Salomón* > *Salomu*, which have a trisyllable pattern; however, there is an assimilation to the optimal structure: CVCVCV. *Francisco* > *Pancho* / *Chico* makes evident the imitation of Spanish hypocoristics.

Finally, some names suffer an almost complete change in the name, there is a syllable which seems out of place or there is an assimilation to the CVCV pattern. These include *Cándida* > *Landi*, which introduces an /l/ into the Mazahuan name. *Inés* > *Nesi* is an assimilation to the CVCV structure. There is a double palatalisation in *Celso* > *Checho* and *Isaac* / *Isaías* > *Chai*. There are complete changes in *Ariadna* > *Dei, María de Jesús* > *Lia* and *Manuel* > *Ngwame*. In cases like *David* > *Bili, Juan* > *Xuba, Crispín* > *Pimi, Raúl* > *Ralu* and *Everardo* > *Walo* it is clear that there is a change in structure and assimilation to the CVCV pattern.

5 Concluding remarks

The data collected prove the assumption that the anthroponymic system in Mazahua is a blending with Spanish and that names are a hybrid between Mazahuan phonology and morphology and the Spanish names, turning them into hypocoristics adapted to the bi-syllabic structure of the Mazahuan lexis incorporated to the vowel harmony of the Mazahuan language, as stated above.

A clear and consistent pattern can be seen in the adaptation of hypocoristic patterns into the phonology and morphology of Mazahua. I can also state that even when these data reveal consistent patterns, more research is needed in other areas and varieties of the language to have clearer evidence with more data to show that these patterns are consistent in the language. The most common phenomena observed are truncations, initial truncation being the most common; there is a consistent pattern in the vowel harmony CVCV as the major number of cases.

The optimal syllable, then, is the most common pattern, followed by monosyllabic words and more than one vowel. In adopting the hypocoristic system of Spanish, some of the names do not have clear boundaries and they are just adapted to the Mazahuan phonetic and phonological patterns. This paper intended to give an account of the shape of personal names in this indigenous language. Mazahua's modern naming system is a consequence of languages in contact, but it offers a rich and wide variety of possibilities for study.

References

Amaral, Eduardo Tadeo Roque & Marcia Sipavicius Seide. 2020. *Nomes próprios de pessoa. Introducao á antroponimia brasileira.* Saõ Paulo: Blucher.

Barriga Villanueva, Rebeca (coord.) con la colaboración de Valeria Chávez Granados. 2022. *Lingmex: Bibliografía Lingüística de México desde 1970. 28a. ed.* Mexico: El Colegio de México. https://lingmex.colmex.mx/

Bartholomew, Doris. 1994. Panorama of studies in Otopamean languages. In Leonardo Manrique & Yolanda Lastra (eds.), *Panorama de los estudios de las lenguas indígenas de México*, 335–377. University of Texas: Abya-Yala.

Boyd-Bowman, Peter. 1970. Los nombres de Pila en México desde 1540 hasta 1950. *Nueva Revista de Filología Hispánica* 19(1). 12–21.

CEDIPIEM. 2021. Ubicación geográfica de los Mazahuas. Available at: https://cedipiem.edomex.gob.mx/ubicacion_mazahua (accessed 2 March 2023).

Comisión Nacional para el Desarrollo de los Pueblos Indígenas (CDI). 2021. Mazahuans. State Government's official website: http://www.cdi.gob.mx/mazahuas_edomex/page2.html (accessed 5 May 2020).

Cerrón-Palomino, Rodolfo. 2016. Más allá de la función distintiva. La palatalidad con valor expresivo en el quechua. *Indiana* 33 (1). 27–37.

Cierbide Martinena, Ricardo. 1996. Onomástica de los judíos navarros (siglo XIV). *Nouvelle revue d'onomastique* 27–28. 97–108.

DiCanio, Christian & Ryan Bennett. 2017. Prosody in Mesoamerican languages. In Carlos Gussenhoven & Aoju Chen (eds.), *The Oxford handbook of language prosody*, 2–29. Oxford: Oxford University Press.

Do Couto, Hildo Honorio. 2000. Os hipocorísticos crioulos e o conceito de palavra ótima. *PAPIA* 10. 50–65.

Escalante Hernández, Roberto. 1994. Sobrenombres (apodos) matlatzincas. In Carolyn MacKay and Verónica Vázquez Soto (Eds.), *Investigaciones lingüísticas en Mesoamérica*, 197–207. Mexico: Universidad Nacional Autónoma de México.

Estrada, Juan Bernardo. 2014. La formación de los hipocorísticos en el español de México. *Anuario de Letras. Lingüística y Filología* 2 (2). 5–33.

Eusebio Maximiliano, Samuel. 2019. Un análisis contrastivo de los lexemas de parentesco de Nájera Yanguas (1637) con el uso actual en la comunidad de San Felipe Pueblo Nuevo (2016). In Iván Pedraza Durán & Miguel Reyes Contreras (eds.), *Estudios de las Lenguas y Culturas: Procesos Epistemológicos de los Pueblos Originarios*, 28–40. Toluca: Gobierno del Estado de México-Universidad Intercultural del Estado de México.

Fernández Juncal, Carmen. 2011. El sistema antroponímico como diasistema. *Nouvelle Revue d'Onomastique* 53. 141–150.

Fernández, Neiyelis & Gresmar Palencia. 2015. *Análisis del fenómeno fonético del apócope en los hipocorísticos utilizados por los estudiantes de segundo año de Educación Media del Liceo Bolivariano Pedro Gual.* Carabobo, Colombia: Universidad de Carabobo dissertation.

García Zúñiga, Antonio Hamlet. 2018. Apodos en Maya. Unpublished lecture during the *1st International Meeting of Onomastics Studies (June 2018)*. San Felipe del Progreso, Mexico: Intercultural University from the State of Mexico,

Gobierno del Estado de México. 2021. Map of the state. Estadísticas e indicadores. https://edomex.gob.mx/indicadores

Gonçalves, Carlos Alexandre. 2004. A morfologia prosódica e o comportamento transderivacional da hipocorização no português brasileiro. *Revista do Estudios Linguisticos* 12 (1). 7–38.

Gutiérrez Santana, Lucila. 2009a. *Procesos fonológicos utilizados en la formación de hipocorísticos. Una aproximación desde la fonología no-lineal.* Concepción, Chile: Universidad de Concepción dissertation.

Gutiérrez Santana, Lucila. 2009b. Procesos fonológicos en la formación de hipocorísticos. *Pre-textos* 3 (4). 90–102.

Gutiérrez Santana, Lucila. 2014. Hipocorísticos y truncamiento de nombres propios indoeuropeos y de la lengua náhuatl. *Temas Antropológicos* 36 (1). 73–84.

Heinz, Jeffrey & Regine Lai. 2013. Vowel Harmony and Subsequentiality. In András Kornai & Marco Kuhlmann (eds.), *Proceedings of the 13th Meeting on the Mathematics of Language (13)*, 52–63. Sofia, Bulgaria: Association for Computational Linguistics.

Herrera Meza, María del Carmen. 1994. Antropónimos nahuas con nombres deverbales. In Gerardo López Cruz & José Luis Moctezuma Zamarrón (eds.), *Estudios de lingüística y sociolingüística. I Encuentro de Lingüística en el Noroeste*, 123–132. Hermosillo: Universidad de Sonora-Instituto Nacional de Antropología e Historia.

Herrera Meza, María del Carmen. 2004. Valores metafóricos de po: c-tli 'humo' en los antropónimos nahuas. In Mercedes Montes de Oca Vega (ed.), *La metáfora en Mesoamérica*, 95–122. Mexico: Universidad Nacional Autónoma de México.

Herrera Meza, María del Carmen. 2009. Morfología en las escrituras de antropónimos de la Matrícula de Huexotzinco, *Diario de Campo. Boletín Interno de los Investigadores del Área de Antropología* 104. 12–24.

Horcasitas, Fernando. 1973. Cambio y evolución de la antroponimia náhuatl. *Anales de Antropología* 10. 265–283.

Jacinto Santos, Pablo Edwin. 2009. *Estudio del sistema de denominación antroponímica de la cultura asháninka*. Lima, Perú: Universidad Nacional de San Marcos dissertation.
Jiménez, Jesús & Maria-Rosa Lloret. 2006. Entre la articulación y la percepción. Armonía vocálica en la península ibérica. *Foncat UV*. 1–9.
Joalaid, Marj. 2016. Balto-Finnic personal name systems. In Carole Hough and Daria Izdebska (eds.), *Names and their environment. Proceedings of the 25th International Congress of Onomastic Sciences, Glasgow, Vol. 3*. 123–130. Glasgow: University of Glasgow.
Knapp, M. H. 2013. Doctrina y enseñanza en la lengua mazahua. Estudio filológico y edición interlineal del texto bilingüe de Nájera Yanguas. Mexico: Instituto Nacional de Lenguas Indígenas (INALI).
Lawson, Edwin D. 2016. Personal Naming Systems. In Carole Hough (ed.), *The Oxford handbook of names and naming*, 169–198. Oxford: Oxford University Press.
Leibring, Katharina. 2016. Given names in European naming systems. In Carole Hough (ed.), *The Oxford handbook of names and naming*, 199–213. Oxford: Oxford University Press.
Lloret, Maria-Rosa & Jesús Jiménez. 2009. Un análisis óptimo de la armonía vocálica del andaluz. *Verba, Anuario Galego de Filoloxía* 36. 293–325.
López Franco, Yolanda Guillermina. 1990. *La selección de los antropónimos en el nivel universitario. Estudio de un caso: la ENEP-Acatlán*. Mexico: Universidad Nacional Autónoma de México dissertation.
López Franco, Yolanda Guillermina. 2003. El sistema antroponímico de los hijos de inmigrantes de origen arabomusulmán en el sur de Francia, durante la segunda mitad del siglo XX. *Estudios de Asia y África* 38 (122). 617–655.
López Franco, Yolanda Guillermina. 2009. Mirada lexicológica a la atribución de los nombres de pila en Tlalnepantla de Baz, Estado de México, 1935–1955. *Multidisciplina* 2. 17–24.
López Franco, Yolanda Guillermina. 2010. *Un siglo de nombres de pila en Tlalnepantla de Baz. Estudio lexicológico y sociolingüístico*. Mexico: UNAM-Plaza y Valdés.
López Franco, Yolanda Guillermina. 2013. Les prénoms de ceux qui sont nés à Montpellier dans les années 1970. Approche socioanthroponymique. In Jean-Claude Bouvier (ed.), *Le nom propre a-t-il un sens ? Actes du XVe colloque d'onomastique, Aix-en-Provence, 2010*, 195–206. Aix-en-Provence, France: Presses universitaires de Provence.
López Franco, Yolanda Guillermina. 2014a. Comparaison des prénoms attribués en 1970 et 1975 dans deux comunes romanophones: Tlalnepantla de Baz au Mexique, et Montpellier en France. Une approche socioanthroponymique. In Joan Tort i Donada & Montserrat Montagut i Montagut (eds.), *Els noms en la vida quotidiana. Actes del XXIV Congrés Internacional d'ICOS sobre Ciències Onomàstiques*, 821–832. Catalunya: Generalitat de Catalunya, Departament de Cultura.
López Franco, Yolanda Guillermina. 2014b. En torno al semantismo de los nombres propios. Entre debate y síntesis teórica. *Revista Trama* 10 (20). 69–81.
López Franco, Yolanda Guillermina. 2015. Entre modèle traditionnel d'attribution et mode phénomène social: les prénoms des 25–30 ans nés à Montpellier, France. In Michel Tamine & Jean Germain (eds.), *Mode(s) en onomastique. Onomastique belgoromane*, 123–132. Paris: L'Harmattan.
López Franco, Yolanda Guillermina. 2016. Prénoms peu usités à Montpellier, France, de 1960 à 1985. Une étude socioanthroponymique. In Carole Hough & Daria Izdebska (eds.), *Names and Their Environment. Proceedings of the 25th International Congress of Onomastic Sciences*, 164–174. Glasgow: University of Glasgow.
López Franco, Yolanda Guillermina. 2017. Sacré et profane dans les prénoms donnés à Montpellier en 1990 et 1993. In Oliviu Felecan (ed.), *Nom et dénomination : actes de la conférence internationale d'onomastique nom et dénomination*, 224–233. Cluj-Napoca: Mega-Argonaut.

López Franco, Yolanda Guillermina. 2018. La question des sources dans les études anthroponymiques contemporaines. In *Noms de lieux, noms de personnes. La question des sources*, 125–133. Paris: Archives nationales.

López Franco, Yolanda Guillermina. 2019. Une enquete socioanthroponymique finiséculaire : la perception des prénoms dans huit communes de l'Hérault, France, en 1995. Une méthodologie toujours en vigueur. *Onomastica Uralica* 10. 209–227.

López Franco, Yolanda Guillermina. 2020. Las relaciones intercategoriales e intracategoriales en antroponimia. El caso de los nombres de pila en francés de Francia y en español de México. *Onomástica desde América Latina* 1 (1). 222–247.

López Franco, Yolanda Guillermina. 2020. Modelo de atribución tradicional: el calendario católico en las partidas de bautizo de la catedral de Tlalnepantla de Baz, Estado de México en 1960. *Onomástica desde América Latina* 1 (2). 144–164.

López Franco, Yolanda Guillermina & Selene Jiménez Segura. 2006. Análisis lingüístico de la atribución de los nombres de pila masculinos y femeninos en el municipio de Tlalnepantla de Baz, Edo de México, de 1901 al 2000. Avances de investigación. In María del Pilar Máynez & María Rosario Dosal (eds.), *V Encuentro Internacional de Lingüística en Acatlán*, 193–205. Mexico: Universidad Nacional Autónoma de México.

López Marín, Antonio. 2010. Introducción a la lengua *jñatjo* (mazahua). In José Francisco Monroy G. & Ildefonso Escobedo (eds.), *Diccionario español-otomí, mazahua, matlatzinca, tlahuica y náhuatl*, 61–72. Mexico: UIEM-CEDIPIEM-Plaza y Valdés.

Mora Peralta, Idanely. 2008. *Topónimos y antropónimos mayas en documentos coloniales del siglo XVII*, Disertation. Mexico: Universidad Nacional Autónoma de México, México.

Mora Peralta, Idanely, 2012. Hacia un análisis gráfico-fonológico de la antroponimia maya, en Emilio Montero Cartelle and Carmen Manzano Rovira (Coords.), *Actas del VIII Congreso Internacional de Historia de la Lengua Española: Santiago de Compostela, 14–18 de septiembre de 2009* vol. 2, 2605–2617. Santiago de Compostela: Meubook-Asociación de Historia de la Lengua Española.

Nágera Yanguas, Diego de. 1637. Doctrina y enseñança en la lengua maçahua, de cosas muy útiles, y provechosas para los ministros de doctrina, y para los naturales que hablan la lengua maçahua. Mexico: Juan Ruyz.

Neaves, Teresa. 2021. Glifo onomástico del segundo Motecuhzoma. Presentation at the bimonthly seminar organised by the Interinstitutional Seminar of Onomastics, 24 March 2021.

Notzon, Beth & Gayle Nesom. 2005. The Arabic Naming System. *Science Editor* 28 (1). 20–21.

Ohannesian Saboundjian, Maria. 2004. *La asignación del acento en castellano*. Barcelona: Universidad Autónoma de Barcelona dissertation.

Pérez González, Benjamín. 1970. Notas acerca de los patronímicos chontales. *Boletín Informativo de Escritura Maya.* 42. 10–13.

Pinto, Ana. 1992. Un ejemplo de contribución del lenguaje infantil a la lengua: el caso del sufijo inglés -ie, ey, -y. *Revista Española de Lingüística* 22. 77–86.

Price, Richard & Sally Price. 1972. Saramaka Onomastics: An Afro-American Naming System. *Ethnology* 11 (4). 341–367.

Prisacaru, Ana Maria. 2011. Interferenţe lingvistice româno-germane în antroponimia românească din Bucovina habsburgică (actualele teritorii românești). In Oliviu Felecan (ed.), *Numele și numirea. Actele ICONN 2011*, 89–93. Baia Mare: Editura Mega.

Ramírez, Irma. 2008. *Mazahuas del Estado de México.* Proyecto Perfiles Indígenas de México, Ms.

Real Academia Española. 2021. *Diccionario de la Real Academia Española (DRAE).* Online versión. https://dle.rae.es/?id=KT69on7 (accessed 12 January 2022).

Reyes Contreras, Miguel. 2017. Los antropónimos y patronímicos en la Universidad Intercultural. Estudio exploratorio en torno al nombre propio en la zona norte del Estado de México. In Varios Autores (editores), *XI conferencia Internacional Lingüística*, 1–25. La Habana: Instituto de Literatura y Lingüística.

Reyes Contreras, Miguel. 2018. Los antropónimos en la Universidad Intercultural del Estado de México. Exploración lexicológica y sociolingüística. In Arturo Fuentes (ed.), *Dinámicas y debates en la lengua actual desde las prácticas educativas*, 96–105. Mexico: Universidad de Ixtlahuaca CUI.

Reyes Contreras, Miguel. 2019a. Los antropónimos como parte de la identidad: la tradición, la iglesia y la ley civil. In Iván Pedraza & Miguel Reyes (eds.), *Estudios de las lenguas y culturas: Procesos epistemológicos de los pueblos originarios. Tomo 1.* 91–107. Toluca: Gobierno del Estado de México-Universidad Intercultural del Estado de México.

Reyes Contreras, Miguel. 2019b. Truncamientos de hipocorísticos españoles y antropónimos en mazahua: un fenómeno compartido. *Onomástica desde América Latina* 1(1). 141–171. DOI:10.48075/odal.v1i1.24164

Romero Hernández, Antonio. 2010. *El sistema léxico-segmental del mazahua.* Mexico: Universidad Autónoma Metropolitana.

Salaberri Zaratiegi, Patxi & Iker Salaberri Izko. 2014. A Descriptive Analysis of Basque Hypocoristics. *Fontes Lingvæ Vasconvm. Stvdia et docvmenta, Navarra* XLVI (117). 187–211.

Suárez Rodríguez, Luz A. 2008. Una mirada sociopragmática a las fórmulas de tratamiento entre niños escolares. *Cuadernos de Lingüística Hispánica* 11. 105–118. Tunja-Boyacá: Universidad Pedagógica y Tecnológica de Colombia.

Tibón, Gutierre. 1961. *Onomástica Hispanoamericana. Índice de siete mil nombres y apellidos castellanos, vascos, árabes, judíos, italianos, indoamericanos, etc.* Mexico: UTEHA.

Tibón, Gutierre. 1998. *Diccionario etimológico comparado de nombres propios de persona.* 3rd edition. Mexico: Fondo de Cultura Económica.

Tibón, Gutierre. 2001. *Diccionario etimológico comparado de los apellidos españoles, hispano-americanos y filipinos.* Mexico: Fondo de Cultura Económica.

Tomcsányi, Judith. 1992. Armonía vocálica y construcción simbolizadora en el lenguaje. *Letras* 25–26. 237–256.

Villegas Molina, María Elena y Rosa Brambila Paz. 2020. Antroponimia registrada en las Mercedes de Jilotepec, siglo XVI. *Onomástica desde América Latina* 1 (1). 122–144. DOI:10.48075/odal.v1i1.24162

Sambulo Ndlovu

Chapter 18
Gender intimations in the morphology of some Ndebele personal names

Abstract: Prior to gender advocacies, most human societies were patriarchal and the majority still are. The nature of patriarchal power matrixes is such that women are accorded lower social status than men; they are also treated as second to men. In a patriarchy, social systems are tailored to achieve male superiority. Sociolinguistic research has established that language is also gendered to disadvantage women and confine them to both linguistic and social subalternity. This chapter establishes that there are some Ndebele forenames for males and females which betray patriarchy and sexism within the Ndebele social culture. Ndebele personal naming conventions treat verb roots and noun stems as naturally being masculine; morphology is used to derive feminine names from these masculine bases. This gendered morphology creates male superiority and female subalternity. Primary data for this study were collected through observations and intuitions in the Silobela district of Zimbabwe. The data were further tested in nine other districts through questionnaires. The chapter engages sociolinguistic and gender theories to analyse the morphology of the Ndebele personal names collected. The research sought to answer the overarching question of why root lexis is affixed differently in the naming of males and females in Ndebele. The chapter deploys morphological analysis on the morpho-lexical operations and the affixations used to derive different names for males and females from the same word roots. The research establishes that morphological processes such as passive formation, applicative, tense and affixation are used to derive semantically subaltern names for females when compared to male names derived from the same roots. Gender inequalities in Ndebele social structure are mirrored in the linguistic structure of personal names.

Keywords: gender, Ndebele, personal names, othering, doing gender

---

Sambulo Ndlovu, University of Eswatini, Great Zimbabwe University, and University of Mainz, Germany, e-mail: matsilaneg@gmail.com

https://doi.org/10.1515/9783110759297-018

1 Introduction

Names and naming are part of language and Wa Thiong'o (1998) opines that language carries culture. This feeds into the Whorfian view of language as a mirror of social reality (Hussein 2012). Inequalities in society are reflected and reinforced in language. Patriarchal hierarchies can also be nuanced in language. Johnson (2007) identifies the link between language and patriarchy and gives English examples of how patriarchy has pejorated female terms such as *bitch*, *witch*, *crone* and *virgin* in order to disempower women and compromise their independence. He opines that in pre-patriarchal times, *bitch* referenced the goddess of hunting, who hunted with dogs, *crone* referred to an old and wise woman, *witch* was a woman with healing powers and a *virgin* was an unattached lady. All these terms have been pejorated through patriarchy to portray women as threatening, evil and sexually inexperienced. These examples demonstrate that language does gender. It also establishes the unequal gender hierarchies through pejorative references and meanings attached to terms used for women and girls. Fasold (1990: 113) postulates that:

> There is an imputation of sexual immorality to referents of the woman's term, with the man's term carrying very general and usually favourable implications . . . There are words like master and mistress, where the former would refer to an individual who is talented and skilled in a certain area while the latter would refer to sexual immorality or adultery.

In patriarchy, women are treated as subaltern, while language, which includes naming systems, reflects and maintains this patriarchy. Names and naming are part of language and they also reflect social realities, including the treatment of gender. Lake (2003: 2) observes that "the examination of names and naming draws attention to the fact that language not only gives us a medium to express our thoughts but also influences what we are capable of thinking". Pilcher (2017) opines that while names identify individuals, they also go beyond just referring to "doing gender". While gender is not a biological but a social and cultural construction, the gendering of language usually embodies biological differentiation. Cameron (1985) identifies sex differentiation and female subordination in language.

Ndebele personal names are analysed here within the precincts of theoretical linguistics and specifically at the levels of morphology and semantics. The forms and meanings of names are then further analysed within the context of cultural discourses to reveal gender intimations and how these names "do gender". While gender is outside the precincts of theoretical linguistics, it forms part of the extra-linguistic functions of language. Pilcher (2017: 813) avers that "whether normative and compliant, pragmatic, or creative and resistant, forenaming and surnaming practices are revealed as core to the production and reproduction of binary sex categories and to gendered identities, difference, hierarchies, and inequalities".

This study aimed to investigate how Ndebele names are differentiated for sex to establish why they are so treated and to understand the morphological and semantic connections between the structure of the names and the underlying patriarchal ideas and symbolism. The chapter was motivated by the fact that there has been a long tradition of feminist resistance to gender differentiation in Ndebele society but a slow uptake of androgynous names. The objectives of the study were to analyse the distribution of gender sensitive Ndebele personal names and to analyse the morphology of these names to reveal their pragmatic meanings and effects in gender hierarchisation. This chapter also looks at the conflation of gender into the meanings of root lexis based on gender stereotypes and ideals in Ndebele culture. It also identifies patronymic and metronymic prefixes used as markers of gender in Ndebele and how these play into patriarchal hierarchies. The analysis in this chapter then incorporates morpho-lexical processes and how these are linked to power indices in the verb argument structure and semantic role hierarchies. Critical discourse analysis (CDA) is engaged in the analysis of the gendered othering of females through forenaming. This is done within the precincts of othering and feminist theories.

2 Literature review

The nexus between language and culture has been widely researched. This includes names and naming in cultural contexts. This section reviews literature on gender and culture, naming and culture, gender implications in structural linguistics and the othering of women in language and society.

2.1 Gender in Ndebele culture

African societies and indeed many societies across the globe are run patriarchally. That is, they are structured to privilege men over women. Ndebele culture is no exception. While patriarchy has been defined and delimited variously, the common understanding is that it is not in individual actions but that it is a system that influences beliefs. It is not I, you, them or us, but it is an it (Johnson 2007). In Weber's (1947) classic definition, patriarchy is a system of government in which men rule society through their position as heads of households. This definition has been proven to be lacking in its coverage of what constitutes patriarchy as it has different levels of abstraction. Walby (1989) defines patriarchy as a system of social structures and practices in which men dominate, oppress and exploit women. This definition conveniently rides on biological determinism and generalises domination by all men and subordination by all women. Johnson (2007: 29) expands the definition and posits that "patriarchy's defining elements are its male-dominated, male-identified, and male-centred character. At its core, patriarchy is a set of symbols and ideas that make up a culture embodied by everything from the content of everyday conversation to literature and film".

In most African cultures, the control men have over women is based on marriage customs and expectations. Amoakohene (2004), describing patriarchy in Ghana, notes that there are distinct gender roles, with women expected to marry, bear children, keep the home and nurture children, whilst being available sexually for their husbands, while men are expected to work and provide materially for their families. Men are expected to take care of women, not the other way round. Ndlovu (2006) opines that the traditional Ndebele perception of marriage is that a woman marries so as to be looked after by her husband; she cannot provide for herself. To demonstrate his ability to take care of his wife, a man is expected to pay *lobola* ('bride price'). Ndlovu (2021) links the subordination of women in Ndebele culture to the custom of paying *lobola*, while Kambarami (2006) is of the view that *lobola* strips women of rights in exchange for marriage. Sikweyiya et al. (2020) further link patriarchy to the physical abuse of women by men as it empowers men with the privilege of owning and abusing women. Through family institutions and practices such as *lobola*, Ndebele society is inherently patriarchal. Sayi (2017: 246) confirms the existence of patriarchy in Ndebele thus:

> Literature and the prevailing conditions point to the patriarchal nature of Ndebele society, in which males dominate and women are subordinates. As such, men are *inhloko yomuzi* (the head of the family), holders of power and control, highlighting the central role that they play in the family set-up.

The family domination of women is spread to social structures outside the family. The patriarchal nature of Ndebele culture is also mirrored in the language. Ncube and Moyo (2011) postulate that the analysis of Ndebele proverbs and idioms confirms the society to be patriarchal and highly sexist. Names have also been proven elsewhere to be reflective of the patriarchal realities in society. In their study of Igbo personal names, Okagbue et al. (2017) argue that the names are gender sensitive because of the patriarchal nature of the Igbo culture. Ngubane (2013) also establishes that in Zulu culture, male children are the most desired and the naming reflects this societal preference. This chapter argues that the patriarchal nature of Ndebele culture is reflected in their personal names and naming conventions.

2.2 Naming and gender

Gender operates in naming just as it does in other aspects of culture and language. Gendered languages such as French, German and Swedish, for example, assign gender to proper nouns, whereby some are masculine, some feminine and others neuter. Fraurud (2011) studies the allocation of gender to proper nouns in Swedish between neuter and *uter* genders and discovers that the gender system operating on proper nouns tells of ontological distinctions underlying categorisation in general. In the case of personal names, gender distinctions are not only social but also embodied. Pilcher (2017: 812) concurs with the embodiment of gender in personal naming. She identifies re-naming as part of re-doing gender in transgender people. She opines that they change their names to match their re-done bodies. She further states that "forenames and surnames help in the embodied doing of gender and, likewise, that bodies are key to gendered practices of forenaming and surnaming, we have 'gendered embodied named identities'".

The embodiment of gender in naming people results in gender sensitive naming of newborns. For example, Alford (1988) reasons that it is a very strong cultural norm in the United Kingdom and the United States of America (as elsewhere) to give a newborn baby a sex-specific forename, according to the sex categorisation of the baby's body as male or female. Pilcher (2017) further states that androgynous or sex/gender-neutral forenames are rarely used in any human aggregates. Lieberson, Dumais and Baumann (2000) also establish that in the United States of America 97% of forenames regarded as female-appropriate are only given to children whose sex category is female. Likewise, 97% of forenames viewed as male-appropriate are only given to children whose sex category is male. Gender equality advocacy has not had a significant impact on gendered naming. Pilcher (2017) avers that despite the important changes in gender relations in the twentieth century, there was no significant increase in the use of androgynous forenames. Forenames are used to create gendered identities in society based on sex differentiation. Mkhize and Muthuki (2019), for example, reason that there is a connection between Zulu forenames and gender identity creation. Further, Ngubane (2013) avers that in Zulu culture, female names are usually derivatives from male names. This is an indication that males are the desired children. In the Ndebele naming system, verb roots and noun stems are also affixed and inflected differently to derive gender sensitive personal names.

2.3 Linguistic analysis and nomen gender differentiation

While gender is a domain of sociology, there has been significant interest in analysing gendered social structures through linguistic structures. Linguistic levels of analysis, which are phonology, morphology, syntax, semantics and pragmatics, have been deployed in the study of gender. Westbrook and Schilt (2014) posit that forenames are key to the social practice of determining gender. Social science researchers also use people's names to infer their sex. For example, Karimi et al. (2016) observe that computational social scientists rely on automated methods to infer gender from name information provided on the web. This is evidence that societies do use names to differentiate and determine gender and that there are linguistic methods of identifying people's gender from their names; these methods are applied across all levels of linguistic analysis. Online advertising also utilises gender prediction methods on forenames to customise commercial offers (Wais 2016).

Phonology has been linked to gender preferences and tastes in the advertising industry. Here, certain phonemes are identified as appealing to men and others to women. Guevremont and Grohmann (2015) actually establish that in French adverts, brand masculinity is enhanced by stop phonemes while fricatives enhance brand femininity. This affinity between certain phonemes and gender has also been established as operating in the naming conventions of many societies. There are some phonemes that are culturally conditioned to express gender differences in naming. The phonology of forenames has been identified as one of the levels of linguistic analysis that can betray gender differences (Slepian and Galinsky 2016; Slater and Feinman 1985). While this chapter does not focus on phonology, insights from phonological gender differentiation are key to understanding the morphological processes of gender differentiation which are discussed here.

Morphology and semantics are also deployed in naming conventions to derive gendered forenames. Ajíbóyè (2011) studies the morphosemantics of Yoruba forenames in Nigeria and establishes that the meanings of lexis used to derive proper nouns determine the gender of the names. He further posits that names which contain the words *baba* ('father'), *akin* ('valour'), *ogun* ('war'), *ja* ('fight') and *fe* ('like/love') are exclusively masculine; those formed from the words *iya/yeye* ('mother'), *ewa* ('beauty'), *ke* ('adorn') and *be* ('beg') are almost always feminine. Udu (2019) also looks at the morphology of personal names in Nigeria, focusing on the Tiv culture. He observes that Tiv forenames take the morphology of simple and compound nouns, and that gender prefixes derive and differentiate patronymic from metronymic forenames. Mojapelo (2009) researches the morphology and semantics of proper names in South Africa's Northern Sotho culture and notes that the morphological process of affixation is key in deriving proper nouns from appellatives and verbs. She further identifies the Northern Sotho prefixes *ma-* and *ra-* as derivational affixes for female and male forenames respectively. The prefixes are reflective of the gender differentiation prevalent in Northern Sotho culture. Ndebele also uses semantics and affixation to derive gender specific names and these processes are inclined to patriarchal conventions.

3 Theoretical framework

This chapter engages with the theories of othering, feminism, postmodernism and critical discourse analysis to disambiguate the gendered power asymmetries in the Ndebele personal naming system.

While othering theory originated with Hegel's (1807) Master-Slave Dialectic, it was popularised by De Beauvoir (1949), a feminist theorist who argued that the notion of the other opposes and helps create the self. According to Strani and Szczepaniak-Kozak (2018: 163), othering works to create dominance and subordination, whereby the dominant devalues others to a lesser category, creating a hierarchy. "This hierarchical categorisation leads to the assumption that difference from the dominant group signifies weakness or subordination" (Strani and Szczepaniak-Kozak, 2018: 163). Othering rides on other essentialising processes such as stereotyping, prejudice and discrimination (Celik, Bilali and Iqbal 2017). Names are also used to establish and reflect social hierarchies. Borkfelt (2011: 118) contends that "naming is thus not only the first and most basic of linguistic processes; it is also an excellent example of the power or control that is in many ways inherent to language use". The power to name others gives the namers authority to determine other people's social identities. Martinot (2011: 5) posits that "the power to define is the power to objectify, and thus inferiorise". The naming of women in Ndebele, and indeed in many cultures, reflects patriarchal ideas which have been a target of feminist reform. Mendoza (2015) alludes to the coloniality of gender in patriarchal social structures, which various feminist discourses seek to address.

This chapter engages with views on patriarchy from Marxist materialists (Dallas and James 1972), radical feminists (Firestone 1972) and postmodernists (Walby 1992). Materialists argue that women are confined to unpaid domestic work, and when they do get work outside the home, they get low paying jobs because they are socialised and structurally confined to such jobs. Patriarchy emphasises sex differentiation, and imagines superiority in masculinity. Johnson (2007: 29) observes that "to see the world through patriarchal eyes is to believe that women and men are profoundly different in their basic natures that hierarchy is the only alternative to chaos, and that men were made in the image of a masculine God". These social hierarchies are extended to access to material resources. Men are advantaged over women when it comes to the accumulation of materials. Materially, women become less valuable because of their unequal access to opportunities and they are in some cases named to reveal their lesser value in society. While materialists idealise women as belonging to a disadvantaged economic class, radical feminism argues that women are not an economic class but a sex class; their oppression stems from sexualisation and reproduction. In feminist theory, women suffer injustice in patriarchy because such a system is built on sexism, the objectification of women and misogyny (Jeffreys 2014). The nexus between naming and gender stereotyping is well captured in the tenets of postmodernist thinking. Postmodernists posit that the subordination of women is culturally constructed through language. They argue that language affects the psyche and helps construct gendered inequalities. Cameron (1992: 367) declares that "Feminist commentators on language have noted in many contexts that the world has been 'named' from a male and male-dominant perspective and that lexico-grammatical features in languages often reveal important underlying cultural (male) assumptions".

Feminist movements have sought to liberate women from social subalternities, and naming conventions have been their target too. Using naming trends in the USA as a case in point, Lieberson, Dumais and Baumann (2000) argue that the rise of the feminist movement, which militates against gender distinctions, saw an increase in parents giving their children names which do not mark gender. Such names are called androgynous names. However, they further note that parents who prefer androgynous names in the USA are parents of daughters. The fact that parents of daughters are the ones taking action to remedy the gendered naming practices is an indication that societies still prefer male children and that they name them to show this preference. In Ndebele culture, the uptake of androgynous names is also slow.

Analysing names as discourses of power engages onomastics at a critical level. Critical onomastics is a transition from traditional and scientific approaches to name studies, which have stayed clear of the politics of power (Palonen 1993). Critical onomastics is associated more with the study of toponyms and is called critical toponymy (Basik 2020). While power relations in forenames should be aptly named critical anthroponymy, critical discourse analysis suffices as an analytic tool. Discourse Analysis (DA) focuses on the purposes and effects of different types of language. According to Johnstone (2017), DA is an open-ended set of techniques which includes CDA, which, according to Fairclough (2012), subsumes a variety of approaches towards the social analysis of discourse. Johnstone (2017) established that discourse is shaped by the world, language, participants, prior discourse, medium and purpose, and that discourse, in turn, also shapes these factors. Fairclough (2013: 35) states that:

> CDA brings the critical tradition of social analysis into language studies and contributes to critical social analysis a particular focus on discourse and on relations between discourse and other social elements (power relations, ideologies, institutions, social identities, and so forth). Critical social analysis can be understood as normative and explanatory critique.

Earlier on, Fairclough (1995) established that non-linguistic social practice and linguistic practice constitute one another. He argued that power relations are established and reinforced through language use. As such, language can be used for manipulation and exploitation in situations of power asymmetries. CDA is a methodology for explicating how discourse reproduces (or resists) social and political inequality, power abuse or domination. This chapter treats gender sensitive names as part of language used within the hierarchical situations of patriarchy.

4 Research methodology

The research takes a qualitative approach framed within the interpretive paradigm to interrogate cultural meanings of names. It also uses limited quantitative data on the gender distribution of names to aid the qualitative analysis. Interpretive research does not have a single and absolute interpretation as the truth. Interpretivists believe in socially constructed multiple realities, and that truth and reality are not discovered but created. The researcher's worldview is important in interpretive research. Rehman and Alharthi (2016) characterise interpretive epistemology as subjective, whereby researchers bring their own worldviews and backgrounds to research. Blaikie (2000: 120) advises that "social researchers collect data from some point of view, and this point of view is influenced by their language, culture, discipline-based knowledge and past experiences". The researcher, in this case, is part of Ndebele language and culture, and is also competent in linguistic analysis.

The study adopted a descriptive survey as it sought to identify trends in the gendered naming of newborns within Zimbabwean Ndebele aggregates. Rehman and Alharthi (2016: 56) state that "interpretive researchers employ methods that generate qualitative data, and data collecting methods that yield qualitative data include open ended interviews in their various structures, observations, and discussions". The researcher used observations and intuitive knowledge to collect Ndebele gender sensitive names from their rural village in Silobela district. The names collected were then prepared into a questionnaire consisting of 33 gender sensitive names. The questionnaires were sent to purposively sampled teachers (most of them former college mates of the researcher) in the nine rural Ndebele speaking districts of Lower Gwelo, Zhombe, Nkayi, Bubi, Insiza, Lupane, Matobo, Tsholotsho and Umguza. Each of the nine districts had two respondents, one female and one male, making a total of eighteen. The respondents were to give the number of males and females they knew who bore each name from their villages. They were free to add other names of gender interest that were not among those listed in the questionnaire. All the respondents were either teachers or former teachers in the districts, as well as being locals. This gave them access to more names as they taught many children at school, and had access to documentation on the names of parents as well.

The main analysis of the names was done through linguistic analysis and CDA to identify their morphological make-up and how this reflects patriarchy. The analysis followed the tradition of content analysis, which, according to Krippendorff (1989: 403):

> . . . seeks to analyse data within a specific context in view of the meanings someone – a group or a culture attribute to them (. . .) Communications, messages, and symbols (. . .) reveal properties of their distant producers or carriers, and they have cognitive consequences for their senders, their receivers, and the institutions in which their exchange is embedded.

The names were analysed qualitatively to reveal their meanings and implications on patriarchal power indices. The morphological analysis fed into the CDA of the names.

5 Findings, analysis and discussion

The findings are presented, analysed and discussed thematically under the three sub themes of affixation, active and passive names, and agentic names. Under each section, names are numbered and analysed morphologically to reveal their meanings; below each analysis are statistical distributions of the names between male and female, as obtained from the data. The analyses are followed by discussions on the gender differentiations exhibited by each name as analysed through CDA.

5.1 Gendered nominal affixes and the othering of women

This section presents seven lexes used to derive gender sensitive Ndebele personal names through affixation. The lexes are numbered from (1a) to (1g) and the names they derive are numbered accordingly below their source lexis.

(1) a. ndlovu
elephant (surname, NS)
(i) **uNdlovu**
'Mr Ndlovu'
GD: only male
(ii) ma- ndlovu = u-**Ma-Ndlovu**
FP (daughter) – NS = POSS-N-daughter_of_Ndlovu 'Miss Ndlovu'
GD: only female

b. thalaz -a = thalaza
look_back -FV = 'look back' (V)
(i) um(u)- thalaz -ile = **uMthalazile**
NP-CL1 VR PFT = 'the one who looked back' (N)
GD: male – 1 female – 0
(ii) ka- mthalazile = u-**Ka-mthalazile**
POSS N = POSS-N-sister_of_Mthalazile
GD: male – 0 female – 1

c. -hle
'beautiful' (ADJ)
(i) ubu- hle = u**Buhle**
CL14 ADJ = 'beauty' (N)
GD: male – 3 female – 4
(ii) no- buhle = u-**No-buhle**
mother_of (FP) -N = 'mother of beauty' (COMP-N)
GD: male – 0 female – 15

d. um(u)- musa = umusa
CL3 kindness = 'kindness' (N)
(i) u**Musa**
N
GD: male – 5 female – 2
(ii) no- musa = **uNomusa**
mother_of (FP) kindness = 'mother of kindness' (COMP-N)
GD: male – 0 female – 7

e. thand -a = thanda
love -FV = 'love' (V)
(i) thand -o = u**Thando**
VR ND = 'love' (N)
GD: male – 6 female – 2
(ii) no- thando = u**Nothando**
mother_of N = 'mother of love' (COMP-N)
GD: male – 0 female – 11

f. azi
'know' (V)
(i) ulu- azi = u**Lwazi**
CL11 V = 'knowledge' (N)
GD: male – 4 female – 0
(ii) no- lwazi = u**Nolwazi**
mother_of N = 'mother of knowledge' (COMP-N)
GD: male – 0 female – 3

g. thandaz -a = thandaza
pray -FV = 'pray' (V)
(i) um(u)- thandaz -o = u**Mthandazo**
CL3- VR -ND = 'Prayer' (N)
GD: male – 5 female – 1
(ii) no- mthandazo = u**Nomthandazo**
mother_of N = 'mother of prayer'
GD: male – 0 female – 9

Ndebele uses patronymic and metronymic affixes to derive gender specific terminology, as in *seka-* and *naka-*, which prefix nouns to denote fatherhood and motherhood respectively. The gender markers *so-* and *no-*, for male and female respectively, derive from *u(yi)se ka. . .* 'father of. . .' and *u(ni)na ka. . .* 'mother of. . .'. Respectively, their grammaticalisation paths are *u(yi)se ka. . . < s(ek)a-. . . < sa/so*, and *u(ni)na ka. . . < -na(ka) < na/no*. However, in most cases the language drops the masculine affixes but the feminine ones are retained; for example, *umongi* ('nurse') is masculine, although it does not have any masculine affix attached to it, while *umongikazi* ('female nurse') is identified by the feminine suffix *-kazi*. It is worth noting that none of the examples in the data have any masculine affix, yet their feminine counterparts have the feminine affixes. While some may argue that the masculine affixes are now marked by zero morphemes -*Ø*-, it is clear that masculinity is the unmarked state of being. De Beauvoir (1949: 18) states that in patriarchy, "Humanity is male and man defines woman not in herself but as relative to him. She is not regarded as an autonomous being. She is defined and differentiated with reference to man and not he with reference to her". The use of surnames as forenames is common in the Ndebele pragmatics of respect, and these too are male centred. Surnames belong to men, and women can only be identified with the owners of the surnames, as in *MaNdlovu* for 'Miss Ndlovu', which means 'daughter of *Ndlovu*'. While daughters are called *MaNdlovu*, the sons are called by the surname without any reference to their father; they are *Ndlovu* ('Mr Ndlovu') just like their fathers and grandfathers. While forenames identify the individual from other individuals, surnames actually link people to each other as families and clans (Westbrook and Schilt 2014). However, the family connectedness in Ndebele surnames is such that women are connected to men and not the other way round. In some cases, women are actually identified through the forenames of their male relatives, as in the case of *Kamthalazile*. The name is a contraction of the phrase *dadewabo kaMthakazile* ('Mthalazile's sister'). *Mthalazile* cannot be identified through the sister because society grants him ownership of women through patriarchal structures, hence the possessive name *Kamthalazile*.

Gender differentiation in Ndebele is also achieved through the use of the prefixes *so-* and *no-*, which inflect the senses of 'father' and 'mother' respectively. The masculine prefix *so-* is generally excluded in the derivation of forenames from Ndebele words, but its feminine counterpart *no-* derives feminine forenames. In this way, Ndebele language is thought to be naturally masculine and this reinforces the patriarchal culture. According to Kirk and Okazawa-Rey (2004: 29), "patriarchal culture includes ideas about the nature of things, including men, women, and humanity, with manhood and masculinity most closely associated with being human and womanhood and femininity relegated to the marginal position of 'other'".

The marginality of femininity creates compound nouns for female forenames from natural words by prefixing them with the feminine prefix *no-*. Men are the natural species in a way and women are derivative; men are the knowledge, prayer, education, and women can only be mothers to these concepts. The prefix *no-* for 'mother of' is in fact sexist as it identifies women as instruments of reproduction used to produce men. For example, if *Lwazi* ('knowledge') is male and females can only be *Nolwazi* ('mother of knowledge'), women become important only as they reproduce men. It is interesting to note that the term *solwazi*, which is the masculine equivalent of *Nolwazi*, is the preferred Ndebele term for the translation of professor. The masculine prefix is used to create terminology describing knowledgeable people. Patriarchy imagines language to be masculine. It motivates the naming of women using appendages to the so-called masculine words. Ngubane (2013: 170) also identifies this trend in the naming of newborns in Zulu culture; he observes that:

> In the mind of the name giver, the concept starts with a male name, as males are the most desired children among most Zulu families. For example, the noun *imfundo* "education", which is in class 5 may be used to name a boy by changing it into class 1, *imfundo* thus becomes uMfundo. If the child happens to be a girl, a prefix *No-* will be added to the noun, which then becomes uNomfundo.

Suffice it to say that the Ndebele and Zulu languages and cultures are very close to each other, being sister Nguni languages. The Nguni world is idealised as belonging to men to the exclusion of women, and the naming conventions confirm this patriarchy. Note that the names *Thando* ('love'), *Buhle* ('beauty') and *Musa* ('kindness') are also given to females, although not as much as they are given to men. Their delegation to women also serves the patriarchal function of confirming the patriarchal stereotypes around women. Patriarchal stereotypes expect women to be loving, caring and beautiful (Ajíbóyè 2011). Concepts such as knowledge and prayer are seldom used without the feminine affix to name women. This can be interpreted to mean that women are believed to be without knowledge, and that they are not the desired children, hence they are not the parents' prayer. The significant dropping of masculine prefixes in the derivation of Ndebele personal names reflects the patriarchy in the culture. Women are the by-the-way in a male dominated society. It is possible that male names such as *Solwazi, Somfundo, Sobuhle, Sothando* and *Somusa* do exist, but none were found in the data. Such names are very uncommon, if they are there at all.

5.2 Active and passive voice in naming

This section presents six verb root lexes and demonstrates how the morpho-lexical process of passive formation is used to derive feminine names from active "masculine ones" in Ndebele. The verbs are numbered from (2a) to (2f) and the names they derive are numbered accordingly below their verb root.

(2) a. ph -a = pha
give - FV = 'give' (V)
(i) si- ph -o = **Sipho**
CL7- VR -ND = 'gift' (N)
GD: male – 8 female – 4
(ii) si- ph -iwe = **Siphiwe**
1PL- VR -PASS = 'we have been given'
GD: male – 0 female – 8
(iii) si- -mu- ph -iwe = **Simphiwe**
1PL- OC.CL1 VR PASS = 'she has been given to us'
GD: male – 0 female – 2

b. khulul -a = khulula
liberate -FV = 'liberate' (V)
(i) um(u)- khulul -i = u**Mkhululi**
CL1 VR ND = 'liberator' (N)
GD: male – 6 female – 0
(ii) isi- khulul -i = (i)**Sikhululi**
CL7 VR -ND = 'liberator' (N)
GD: male – 3 female – 0
(iii) khulul- -iwe = **Khululiwe**
VR -PASS = 'liberated one'
GD: male – 0 female – 3
(iv) si- khulul -iwe = **Sikhululiwe**
1PL- VR -PASS = 'we are liberated'
GD: male – 0 female – 4

c. hlen -a = hlenga
redeem -FV = 'redeem'
(i) um(u)- hleng -i = **uMhlengi**
CL1- VR -ND = 'redeemer'
GD: male – 2 female – 0
(ii) hleng -iwe = **Hlengiwe**
VR -PASS = 'the redeemed'
GD: male – 0 female – 6

d. same as (1e)
(i) same as (1e.i)
(ii) thand -iwe = **Thandiwe**
love -PASS = 'object of love' (N-PASS)
GD: male – 0 female – 4

e. Ondl/ong -a = ondla/onga
care -FV = 'care' (V)
(i) um(u)- ondl -i = **uMondli**
CL1- VR -ND = 'care giver'
GD: male – 2 female – 0
(ii) um(u)- ong -iwa = **uMongiwa**
CL1 VR -PASS = 'object of care (the one cared for)' (N)
GD: male – 0 female – 3

f. sindis -a = **sindisa**
save -FV = 'save' (V)
(i) um(u)- sindis -i = **uMsindisi**
CL1- VR -ND = 'saviour' (N)
GD: male – 2 female – 0
(ii) sindis -iwe = **Sindisiwe**
VR -PASS = 'the saved' (N)
GD: male – 0 female – 6

Children are believed to be a gift from God, hence the name *Sipho* ('gift'); the name references the bearer as the gift from God to the parents. The name is an active object of the verb 'give' and is used to name both men and women. The theta grid for the verb 'give' takes three arguments, the giver, the receiver and the gift. Naming a child *Sipho* is an expression of gratitude to the giver. The parents who name their children *Sipho* are beneficiary objects of a benevolent God. However, the passive forms, *Siphiwe* ('we have been given') and *Simphiwe* ('they have been given to us') do not express gratitude but acceptance. It is as if the parents wanted *Sipho* ('gift'), a boy, but they received a girl. In the data, the passive forms are only used to name girls. However, this does not rule out male *Siphiwes* and *Simphiwes* in Ndebele, but they will be few. The semantics of the two passive forms of the verb 'give' used, predominantly to name girls, changes the parents from the beneficiary object to a recipient one which has no choice but to accept what God has given them.

The other five verbs in (2), *khulula* ('liberate'), *hlenga* ('redeem'), *thanda* ('love'), *ondla/onga* ('care') and *sindisa* ('save') are used to derive exclusively masculine names in their active forms and exclusively feminine names in their passive forms. These verbs cover the meaning scopes of protection, care and liberation. They are deployed stereotypically in Ndebele forenaming to portray males as instigators and females as beneficiaries. Men are higher in the theta grids of the verbs as they come before the verbs in the agentic grid, while women have the lower theta roles of beneficiary objects after the verbs. This theta hierarchy is reflective of patriarchal hierarchies in Ndebele culture. Johnson (2007: 29) avers that "patriarchy is about standards of feminine beauty and masculine toughness, images of feminine vulnerability and masculine protectiveness, it is about defining men and women as opposites, about the naturalness of male aggression, competition, and dominance and of female caring, cooperation, and subordination". Women are named as the liberated, redeemed, saved, loved and objects of care because they are vulnerable and only men can protect them. The trend of using active verbs to derive masculine names and their passive forms for feminine names resonates with feminist protestations that femininity is stereotypically associated with being incompetent, characterised by being passive, illogical and emotional, while masculinity is stereotypically competent by being active and logical (Felmlee, Rodis and Zhang 2020; Ellemers 2018).

5.3 Norming agentic men in Ndebele personal naming

This section presents four lexes and demonstrates how the morpho-lexical operation of causative formation is used to derive agentic masculine forenames. It also demonstrates how women are excluded from the prime agentic thematic role of causer in Ndebele. The lexes are numbered from (3a) to (3d) and the names they derive are numbered accordingly below each lexis.

(3) a. fund -a = funda
learn -FV = learn (V)
(i) um(u)- fund -isi = **uMfundisi**
CL1- VR -CAUS = 'causer of learning (teacher)' (N)
GD: male – 2 female – 0

(ii) no- m- fund -o = **Nomfundo**
FP (mother)- CL9- VR -ND = 'mother of education' (COMP-N)
GD: male – 0 female – 2

b. lungis -a = lungisa
correct/fix -FV = 'correct/fix'
(i) um(u)- lungis -i = **uMlungisi**
CL1- VR -ND = 'corrector/fixer' (N)
GD: male – 7 female – 0
(ii) lungis -ile = **Lungi(si)le**
VR -PFT = 'correct/fixed' (ADJ)
GD: male – 2 female – 6

c. thokoz -a = thokoza
rejoice -FV = 'rejoice' (V)
(i) um(u)- thokoz -isi = **uMthokozisi**
CL1- VR -CAUS = 'causer of rejoicing' (N)
GD: male – 11 female – 0
(ii) thokoz -ile = **Thokozile**
VR -PFT = (V-PFT)
GD: male – 0 female – 8

d. and -a = anda
multiply -FV = 'multiply' (V)
(i) um(u)- and -isi = **uMandisi**
CL1- VR -CAUS = 'multiplyer'(N)
GD: male – 3 female – 0
(ii) a- ya- and -a = **Ayanda**
CL5- PRES-VR -FV = 'they are multiplying (girls/boys)'
GD: male – 1 female – 3

Men are named to be agentic and cause the events denoted by the verbs to happen or even cause other people to do these actions; these are powerful argument roles in verb argument structure. Women are not privileged to the agentic in the naming system. To avoid naming women as agents and causers, the verbs are inflated with the perfect tense or prefixed with the metronymic prefix *no-*. Ngubane (2013) describes how, in Zulu, a boy's name can be made feminine by adding the tense marker suffix *-ile*, and this is also true in Ndebele. The verbs 'teach' and 'fix' derive the professions of teaching and auto mechanics respectively; teachers teach people and auto mechanics fix cars. These are predominantly masculine roles in Ndebele culture, and it is not surprising that men bear the agentic names derived from these verbs. The feminine name deriving from the verb 'fix', for example, is a vivid reflection of the objectification of women. The suffix *-ile* on the verb *lungisa* derives the name *Lungile* ('fixed'), which is an adjective. In this case, women are fixed by men, who are named to be fixers, e.g. *Mlungisi.* It is as if men have a duty to keep "troublesome" women in check. The word *lungile* in Ndebele is a homonym as it also means good or obedient; this also speaks to the expected subservience in women. The name *Mthokozisi,* the causer of happiness to the parents, is exclusively masculine in the data; this confirms that parents prefer male children. Male children cause them happiness, and they name them thus. The name *Mandisi* testifies to the patriarchal role of men as heads of families and owners of homes; *Mandisi* means 'the multiplier of the clan'. Women do not multiply the clan but they are married away to help multiply other clans; only men can cause family and clan multiplication. The verb *anda-* ('multiply') is predominantly used in the perfect tense for girls' names; here, it has not much symbolic value other than describing that the girls are multiplying. Men are viewed as the essential agents for life and family processes. De Beauvoir (1949: 18) posits that in a patriarchal structure, "she is incidental, the inessential as opposed to the essential. He is the subject; he is the absolute – she the other". The Ndebele forenaming system sheds light on the patriarchal stereotypes which assert that men are the super agentic causers and women are the inessential and less desired others.

6 Conclusion

Ndebele culture is patriarchal and the language reflects this patriarchy. Men are accorded power, and the position of women is subaltern. The language is also structured to reveal this state of affairs. The morphology of Ndebele personal names betrays the gendered inequalities in Ndebele society. While the language uses affixes to differentiate masculinity from femininity, in the derivation of personal names, only feminine affixes are used to mark femininity, while the natural lexes are taken to represent masculinity. When surnames are used to name or address people, the metronymic prefix is used on the surname to denote women as daughters of the surname. The surname, even without the masculine prefix, is deemed to be masculine. This trend is extended to the derivation of gender sensitive names from general lexes. The patronymic prefix *so-* is generally not used to derive male names. The natural roots and stems are assumed to be masculine and only become feminised by prefixing them with the metronymic prefix *no-*. This process derives compound female forenames. The morpho-lexical operations of passive formation and the causative also differentiate male and female Ndebele forenames. Active verbs are used to derive male names whilst the passive forms derive female names. The active names are higher than the passive objects in the thematic hierarchy;

this mirrors the higher position accorded to men in Ndebele society and the subordinate one assigned to women. Active and passive names also confirm gender stereotypes of men as agentic and as protectors, while women are stereotypically weak and vulnerable. Men are also named to be super agentic as causers of action and as causing others to act. They are named as causers of happiness to the parents, and key to the survival of the clan, while women are not named using the causative construction in the data, and are seldom so named in Ndebele. The morphology and semantics of Ndebele gender sensitive personal names mirrors the othering of women in Ndebele culture.

Abbreviations

1PL	first person plural
ADJ	adjective
CL-1	class 1 (noun classes)
COMP-N	compound noun
FP	feminine prefix
FV	final vowel
GD	gender distribution noun
ND	nominative deverbative (affixes deriving nouns from verbs)
ND-CAUS	nominative deverbative causer (on verbs)
NP	noun prefix
NS	noun stem
OC	object concord
PASS	passive marker
PFT	perfective tense
POSS	possessive
PRES	present tense
SC	subject concord verb
VR	verb root

References

Ajíbóyè, Ọladiipo. 2011. The morphology, semantics and socio linguistics of Yorùbá names. *Alóre Ilorin Journal of Humanities* 20. 99–126.

Alford, Richard. 1988. *Naming and identity: A cross-cultural study of personal naming practices*. New Haven: HRAF Press.

Amoakohene, Margaret Ivy. 2004. Violence against women in Ghana: a look at women's perceptions and review of policy and social responses. *Social Science & Medicine* 59 (11). 2373–2385.

Basik, Sergei. 2020. Urban place names: Introduction. *Urban Science* 4 (80). 1–3.

Blaikie, Norman. 2000. *Designing social research*. Cambridge: Polity Press.

Borkfelt, Sune. 2011. What's in a Name? Consequences of naming non-human animals. *Animals* 1 (1). 116–125. http://dx.doi.org/10.3390/ani1010116

Cameron, Deborah. 1985. *Feminism and linguistic theory*. London: Macmillan Press.

Cameron, Deborah. 1992. *Feminism and linguistic theory*. 2nd edition. New York: St. Martin's Press.

Çelik, Ayşe Betül, Rezarta Bilali & Yeshim Iqbal. 2017. Patterns of 'othering' in Turkey: A study of ethnic, ideological, and sectarian polarisation. *South European Society and Politics* 22 (2). 217–238.

Dalla Costa, Mariarosa & Selma James. 1972. *The power of women and the subversion of the community*. Bristol: Falling Wall Press.

De Beauvoir, Simone. 1949. *The second sex*. London: Four Square Books.

Ellemers, Naomi. 2018. Gender stereotypes. *Annual Review of Psychology*, 69 (1). 275–298.

Fairclough, Norman. 1995. *Media discourse*. London: Edward Arnold.

Fairclough, Norman. 2012. Critical discourse analysis. *International Scientific Researchers* 7. 452–487.

Fairclough, Norman. 2013. Critical discourse analysis. *The Routledge handbook of discourse analysis* 35–46. Routledge.

Fasold, Ralph. 1990. *Language and gender. The sociolinguistics of language.* Cambridge: Blackwood.

Felmlee, Diane, Paulina Inara Rodis & Amy Zhang. 2020. Sexist slurs: Reinforcing feminine stereotypes online. *Sex Roles* 83 (1). 16–28.

Firestone, Shulamith. 1972. *The dialectic of sex*. London: Paladin.

Fraurud, Kari. 2011. Proper names and gender in Swedish. In Barbara Unterbeck, Matti Rissanen, Terttu Nevalainen & Mirja Saari (eds.), *Gender in grammar and cognition*, 167–220. Berlin: De Gruyter Mouton.

Guevremont, Amelie & Bianca Grohmann. 2015. Consonants in brand names influence brand gender perceptions. *European Journal of Marketing* 49 (1/2). 101–122.

Hegel, Georg Wilhelm Friedrich. 1807. *Phänomenologie des Geistes*. Frankfurt: Suhrkamp.

Hussein, Basel Al-Sheikh. 2012. The Sapir-Whorf hypothesis today. *Theory and Practice in Language Studies* 2 (3). 642–646.

Jeffreys, Sheila. 2014. *Beauty and misogyny: Harmful cultural practices in the West.* London: Routledge.

Johnson, A. G. 2007. Patriarchy: The System. In Gwyn Kirk & Margo Okazawa-Rey(eds.), *Women's Lives: Multicultural Perspectives*, 28–37. 4th edition. New York: McGraw-Hill.

Johnstone, Barbara. 2017. *Discourse analysis*. Massachusetts: Blackwell Publishers.

Kambarami, M. 2006. Femininity, sexuality and culture: Patriarchy and female subordination in Zimbabwe. Presentation in: *Understanding Human Sexuality Seminar Series.* Africa Regional Sexuality Resource Centre and University of Fort Hare. http://arsrc.org/downloads/uhsss/kmabarami.pdf (accessed 2 March 2023).

Karimi, Fariba, Claudia Wagner, Florian Lemmerich, Mohsen Jadidi & Markus Strohmaier. 2016. Inferring gender from names on the web: A comparative evaluation of gender detection methods. In Jacqueline Bourdeau (ed.), *Proceedings of the 25th International Conference Companion on World Wide Web*, 53–54. Montreal: WWW 16 Cmpanion. https://doi.org/10.1145/2872518.2889385- (accessed 2 March 2023).

Kirk, Gwyn & Margo Okazawa-Rey. 2004. *Women's lives: Multicultural perspectives*. 3rd edition. New York: McGraw Hill.

Krippendorff, Klaus. 1989. Content analysis. In E. Barnouw, G. Gerbner, W. Schramm, T.L. Worth & L. Gross (eds.), *International Encyclopedia of Communication*, 403–407. Oxford: Oxford University Press.

Lake, Obiagele. 2003. *Blue veins and kinky hair: Naming and color consciousness in African America*. Westport: Greenwood Publishing Group.

Lieberson, Stanley, Susan Dumais & Shyon Baumann. 2000. The instability of androgynous names: The symbolic maintenance of gender boundaries. *American Journal of Sociology* 105 (5). 1249–1287.

Martinot, Steve. 2011. *The coloniality of power: Notes toward de-colonization*. San Francisco: San Francisco State University. https://www.ocf.berkeley.edu/~marto/coloniality (accessed 2 March 2023).

Mendoza, Breny. 2015. Coloniality of gender and power: From postcoloniality to decoloniality. In Lisa Jane Disch & Mary E. Hawkesworth (eds.), *The Oxford Handbook of Feminist Theory*, 100–121. Oxford: Oxford University Press.

Mkhize, Zamambo & Janet Muthuki. 2019. Zulu names and their impact on gender identity construction of adults raised in polygynous families in KwaZulu-Natal, South Africa. *Nomina Africana: Journal of African Onomastics* 33 (2). 87–98.

Mojapelo, Mampaka L. 2009. Morphology and semantics of proper names in Northern Sotho. *South African Journal of African Languages* 29 (2). 185–194.

Ncube, Bhekezakhe & Thamsanqa Moyo. 2011. Portraying women as the other: Ndebele proverbs & idioms in the context of gender construction. *Africana* 5 (3). 126–142.

Ndlovu, Sambulo. 2021. Mutation of lobola and "othering" of women in Ndebele culture. In Lovemore Togarasei & Ezra Chitando (eds.), *Lobola (Bridewealth) in contemporary Southern Africa*, 185–200. Cham: Palgrave Macmillan.

Ndlovu, Tommy Matshakayile. 2006. Perpetuation of colonial stereotypes in Ndebele fiction writing by women: Its importance on the changing roles of women in modern society. In Zifikile Mugnai, Munashe Furusa & Rubby Magosvongwe (eds.), *Womanhood in Zimbabwean literature: A critical perspective on women's literature in Zimbabwe languages*, 138–152. Harare: Weaver Press.

Ngubane, Sihawukele. 2013. The socio-cultural and linguistic implications of Zulu names. *South African Journal of African Languages* 33 (2). 165–172.

Okagbue, Hilary I., Abiodun A. Opanuga, Muminu O. Adamu, Paulinus O. Ugwoke, Emmanuela C. M. Obasi & Grace A. Eze.. 2017. Personal names in Igbo culture: A dataset on randomly selected personal names and their statistical analysis. *Data in brief* 15. 72–80.

Palonen, Kari. 1993. Reading street names politically. In Kari Palonen & Tuija Parvikko (eds.), *Reading the political*, 103–121. Helsinki: The Finnish Political Science Association.

Pilcher, Jane. 2017. Names and "doing gender": How forenames and surnames contribute to gender identities, difference, and inequalities. *Sex Roles* 77 (11). 812–822.

Rehman, Adil Abdul & Khalid Alharthi. 2016. An introduction to research paradigms. *International Journal of Educational Investigations* 3 (8). 51–59.

Sayi, Sanelisiwe. 2017. Gender sensitivity in Isichazamazwi sesiNdebele. *South African Journal of African Languages* 37 (2). 245–250.

Sikweyiya, Yandisa, Adolphina Addoley Addo-Lartey, Deda Ogum Alangea, Phyllis Dako-Gyeke, Esnat D. Chirwa, Dorcas Coker-Appiah, Richard M. K. Adanu & Rachel Jewkes. 2020. Patriarchy and gender-inequitable attitudes as drivers of intimate partner violence against women in the central region of Ghana. *BMC Public Health* 20. 1–11.

Slater, Anne Saxon & Saul Feinman. 1985. Gender and the phonology of North American first names. *Sex Roles* 13 (7). 429–440.

Slepian, Michael L. & Adam D. Galinsky. 2016. The voiced pronunciation of initial phonemes predicts the gender of names. *Journal of Personality and Social Psychology* 110 (4). 509–527.

Strani, Katerina & Anna Szczepaniak-Kozak. 2018. Strategies of othering through discursive practices: Examples from the UK and Poland. *Lodz Papers in Pragmatics* 14 (1). 163–179.
Udu, Titus Terver. 2019. Names as repositories of worldview: Empirical evidence from the morphological and semantic analysis of Tiv personal names. *International Journal of Language and Linguistics* 6 (4). 100–108.
Wais, Kamil. 2016. Gender prediction methods based on first names with genderizeR. *The R Journal.* 8 (1). 17–37.
Walby, Sylvia. 1989. Theorising patriarchy. *Sociology* 23 (2). 213–234.
Walby, Sylvia. 1992. Post-post-modernism? Theorising complexity. In Michèle Barrett & Anne Phillips (eds.), *Destabilising theory: Contemporary feminist debates*, 108–128. Cambridge: Polity Press.
Wa Thiong'o, Ngugi. 1998. Decolonising the mind. *Diogenes* 46 (184). 101–104.
Weber, Max. 1947. *The theory of social and economic organisation*. New York: Free Press.
Westbrook, Laurel & Kristen Schilt. 2014. Doing gender, determining gender: Transgender people, gender panics, and the maintenance of the sex/gender/sexuality system. *Gender & society* 28 (1). 32–57.

Notes on contributors

Prof. Dr. Antje Dammel (University of Münster, Germany) is a linguist interested in grammar and pragmatics of Germanic languages from variationist, diachronic, and typological perspectives. Within this field, she is co-editor-in-chief of the *Oxford Encyclopedia of Germanic Linguistics*. One of her research interests is onomastics, especially anthroponyms, in interplay with other means of person reference. Together with colleagues, she edited publications such as *Zoonyme* (*Beiträge zur Namenforschung* 50 [1–4] 2015), *Grammar of Names* (*Language Typology and Universals* 72 [4] 2019), and *Anthroponyms in Motion* (*Beiträge zur Namenforschung* 56 [1–2] 2021) on phenomena of bearing multiple names across social domains and changing names in social transitions. A recently completed project (2018–2021) investigated structures and socio-pragmatic functions of unofficial person names in dialects of German. A current project explores reference with the human indefinite pronoun *man* from a diachronic perspective within the research group *Practices of Person Reference.*

Prof. Dr. Sambulo Ndlovu is Professor of linguistics at Great Zimbabwe University and the University of Eswatini. He is also a Humboldt research fellow in the Department of Anthropology and African Studies at the Johannes Gutenberg University in Mainz, Germany. He holds a PhD in linguistics from the University of Cape Town, and his research areas are onomastics, socio- and anthropological linguistics, and cultural studies. He is the editor in-chief of the *Nomina Africana Journal of African onomastics*, and his latest book is *Naming and othering in Africa: Imagining supremacy and inferiority through language*.

Dr. Svenja Völkel (University of Mainz, Germany) is a linguist with an anthropological, typological, and cognitive focus on the Pacific region, where she has conducted extensive fieldwork. Among other topics, she has a particular interest in person reference, including honorifics, kinship terminology, and anthroponyms in Tongan, a Polynesian language and culture. Within this field, she has published the monograph *Social structure, space and possession in Tongan culture and language* (John Benjamins, 2010), and the articles *Tongan kinship terminology and social stratification* (Berghahn, 2015), *Tongan-English language contact and kinship terminology* (World Englishes, 2016), *Tongan honorifics and their underlying concepts of mana and tapu – a verbal taboo in its emic sense* (Pragmatics & Cognition, 2021). Furthermore, she is co-author of the book *Introducing linguistic research* (Cambridge University Press, 2021), and co-editor of the new book series *Anthropological linguistics* (de Gruyter Mouton) and its first volume *Approaches to language and culture* (2022).

Dr. Sara Petrollino is Assistant Professor at the Leiden University Centre for Linguistics. Her main research interests are in the field of anthropological linguistics and language description with a focus on East Africa. She has worked on language contact and attrition in Tanzania, and she has published descriptive work on Hamar, a South Omotic language spoken in South West Ethiopia. She is currently carrying out a research project funded by the Dutch Research Council on the visual systems of pastoralists' lingua-cultures.

Dr. Angella Meinerzag received her doctorate in anthropology at Heidelberg University. She lectured there several years. She worked moreover as teacher for languages and cultural integration. Her contribution to this chapter emerged out of 14 months of fieldwork in Papua New Guinea in the years 2000/2001 and 2004. Based on this work, she wrote her monograph *Being Mande: Person, Land and Names among the Hinihon in the Adelbert Range* (Universitätsverlag 2015). Her chapter

https://doi.org/10.1515/9783110759297-019

Foreign Confidants. A Field Diary Narrative in *Facets of Fieldwork. Essays in Honor of Jürg Wassmann* (Universitätsverlag 2017) gives personal insights during fieldwork.

Prof. Dr. Márcia Sipavicius Seide holds a Ph.D. in Philology and Portuguese Language from the University of São Paulo. She is an associate professor at the Western Paraná State University (UNIOESTE), where she teaches undergraduate and graduate courses in Philology and Portuguese Language. She is a member of the International Council of Onomastic Sciences (ICOS). She co-authored the book *Personal Names: an introduction to Brazilian anthroponomy (2022)*, and the article *"Name-giving motives in Lithuania and Brazil: A comparative view (2021)*, another of her key publications is *Interdisciplinary definition of proper name (2021) and Comparative Anthroponomastics (2021).* She is editor-in-chief of the journal *Onomástica desde América Latina* (Onomastics from Latin America) (whose first issue was published in 2020 being the first one on Onomastics in the region. Through her research interests in comparative onomastics, she is developing and coordinating the project "*Spanish names and Brazilian names: exploring comparative onomastics*" in collaboration with Professor Carmen Fernández Juncal from Salamanca University.

Dr. Ilona Mickienė is Associate Professor at the Vilnius University (Lithuania). Their reseach interests are lexicology, onomastics, and word derivation. Their key publications in onomastics include: Male personal names in the 1813–1814 church register of births of the Church of the Nativity of the Blessed Virgin Mary in *Radviliškis.Lituanistica* (co-authored, 2019), Personal names in baptismal records of Seredžius of the early nineteenth century (1802–1803). *LITUANISTICA* (co-authored, 2019), Forest names of proper name origin: West Aukštaitian Region *LITUANISTICA* (2019). They also did the project: "Modern geo-linguistics research in Lithuania: optimization of the network of points and interactive dissemination of dialect information (VP1-3.1-ŠMM-07-K-01-028), 2011–2014" funded by the EU program "Support for the scientific activities of scientists and other researchers (global grant)".

Dr. Rita Baranauskienė is Associate Professor at the Vilnius University (Lithuania). Her reseach interests are syntactic semantics, functional grammar, and pragmatics. Her key researches include; Urbanonyms as the semiotic signs of language teaching and learning. *EDULEARN* (co-authored, 2020), Toponyms from appellative personal names in the Southern Highlands region. *Respectus Philologicus* (co-authored, 2019), Structure of Lithuanian nicknames. *Onomastica Uralica* (co-authored, 2019), Nicknames as a fun game for foreign language learning. *EDULEARN* (co-authored, 2019). She is also a database expert ofor "*Lituanistika*" (LDB) international research database, and COST (European Cooperation in Science and Technology). She was also part of the research project "Modern geo-linguistics research in Lithuania: optimization of the network of points and interactive dissemination of dialect information (VP1-3.1-ŠMM-07-K-01-028), 2011–2014" funded by the EU program "Support for the scientific activities of scientists and other researchers (global grant)".

Dr Shlomit Landman is the head of the program of teaching Hebrew as an additional language to native Arabic speakers in „Achva Academic College". Landman's research deals with socio-linguistic processes that can be identified through changes of onomasticons in the Jewish communities in modern Israel & in the world. Her book „I am the only Lishaz in the world: naming newborns', (in Hebrew) was published in 2020. The book presents qualitative research among 45 Israeli parents regarding their choices of names to their children.

Prof. Dr. Susan Kus is Professor of Anthropology, Rhodes College, Memphis, Tennessee U.S. Research interests include the archaeology, and ethnohistory of early state origins in Madagascar. Most current research involves ethnographic fieldwork with ritual specialists in central Madagascar. Among other skills these specialists' orient houses and tombs in space and time to foster life and contain death to its proper domain, and who foster destiny and correct problematic destiny of individuals in their local society. Recent publications include: (2016) "'Concerning contributions to this volume," in The Archaeology of Anxiety: The materiality of anxiousness, worry, and fear, *Fleisher and Norman* (eds.) New York: Springer, pp. 187–211, and (2015) with Victor Raharijaona, "The 'dirty' material and symbolic work of 'state' building in Madagascar: From indigenous state-crafting to indigenous empire building to external colonial imposition and indigenous insurrection," in Materializing Colonial Encounters: Archaeologies of African Experience, F. Richard (ed.) New York: Springer, pp. 199–227.

Dr. Victor Raharijaona is Doctor III Cycle University of Civilizations and Oriental Languages, Paris, France, Associate Researcher University of Fianarantsoa, Madagascar (Docteur III Cycle Université de Langues et Civilisations Orientales, Paris, France, Chercheur Associé Université de Fianarantsoa, Madagascar). Current research interests include ethnohistory and ethnographic research in central Madagascar concerning *mpanandro* ("makers-of-days"), in particular, the role that primary orality plays in the poetic and analytic skills of these specialists. Recent publications include: (2015) with Susan Kus, "The 'dirty' material and symbolic work of 'state' building in Madagascar: From indigenous state-crafting to indigenous empire building to external colonial imposition and indigenous insurrection," in Materializing Colonial Encounters: Archaeologies of African Experience, F. Richard (ed.) New York: Springer, pp. 199–227, and (2014) with Rasoamampionona, and Kus: "Rakelimalaza, can the Powers-That-Be "take a joke"? Some (a)musings on human encounters with powerful "things" and on the poetics of non-anthropomorphic forces in the highlands of Madagascar," in *Autour des entités sacrées. Approches pluridisciplinaires et nouveaux terrains à Madagascar*, Etudes Océan Indien, Paris, nos, 51–52, pp. 101–128.

Dr. Jill Vaughan is a sociolinguist at the School of Languages, Literatures, Cultures & Linguistics at Monash University. Her research focuses currently on the sociolinguistics of multilingualism, and has involved published work on Australian Indigenous languages of northern Australia, the Irish language in the diaspora, online language use, and variation in Australian English. Since 2014, she has worked with community members in the Maningrida region of Arnhem Land documenting local languages and conducting sociolinguistic research. Jill is a co-founder of the Linguistics Roadshow.

Dr. Ruth Singer is a linguist who researches multilingual language practices in collaboration with Warruwi Community, an Indigenous community of Arnhem land (Australia). She has a book on the topic coming out with Routledge and has published in linguistics and anthropology journals on the topic. Ruth Singer also creates digital language resources with Warruwi community including producing films with young people and two dictionaries of Mawng. Her language documentation work has involved building archival collections of Mawng and other Indigenous languages of Warruwi in their multilingual context. She has published an earlier book on nominal classification and also writes about collaborative approaches to linguistic research with Indigenous communities. Ruth Singer is an Australian Research Council Future Fellow at The University of Melbourne.

Prof. Dr. Willie Lungisani Chigidi holds a PhD in African Languages and Literature from the University of South Africa and is a Professor of African Languages and Literature at Midlands State University (MSU) in Zimbabwe. He is a former chairperson of the Department of African Languages and Culture and a former Chairperson of the Editorial and Publications Committee at MSU. Professor Willie Chigidi is a member of the International Society of the Oral Literature of Africa (ISOLA) and a member of the African Language Association of Southern Africa (ALASA). His research interests lie in the areas of African oral and written literature, indigenous knowledge systems and African culture. He has published a number of book chapters, a number of articles in peer-reviewed journals, and has also published several Shona text books for secondary schools. Professor Willie Chigidi is also a renowned Shona playwright with six published plays to his credit.

Dr. Danson Sylvester Kahyana holds a PhD in English Studies from Stellenbosch University, South Africa. He is an Associate Professor in the Department of Literature at Makerere University, Uganda, where he teaches courses on orature, poetry, creative writing studies, and East African studies, among others. His critical work has appeared in refereed journals like *English in Africa*, *Journal of African Cultural Studies*, *Social Dynamics*, and *Matatu*. He has also published a children's novel and edited and co-edited anthologies of poetry, special issues of journals, and an edited volume of critical essays. He is a recipient of the African Peace building Network Individual Award (2022), Fulbright Postdoctoral Research Fellowship (2021), the Andrew W. Mellon Early Career Postdoctoral Fellowship (2018), and the African Humanities Programme (AHP) Postdoctoral Fellowship (2015), among others.

Dr. Xu Duoduo is a postdoctoral fellow from the School of Humanities, Nanyang Technological University, Singapore. She received her Bachelor's Degree and Master's Degree from Tsinghua University, and PhD from NTU, Singapore. Her research interests include Oral Traditions, Philology, Grammatology, Tibeto-Burman Linguistics, Dongba and Daba Cultural Studies. Her recent publications include "Noun-Epithets of Dongba and Daba Oral Traditions" in the *Linguistics of Tibeto-Burman Area* and "Naish Languages and Dongba/Daba Oral Traditions" in the *Routledge Handbook of Asian Linguistics*.

Prof. Dr. Eyo Mensah teaches in the Department of Linguistics, University of Calabar, Nigeria and is currently a Guest Professor of Anthropological Linguistics and Senior Research Fellow at the Merian Institute for Advanced Studies in Africa (MIASA), University of Ghana, Legon. He is the pioneer president of Nigerian Name Society (NNS). His research interests include morphosyntax, pragmatics, identity and naming, sexuality and gender, youth language and African studies. He is AHP/ACLS Postdoctoral Fellow, Leventis Postdoctoral Researcher (University of London), and Firebird Anthropological Research Fellow. He is also a Senior Research Fellow in FRIAS, University of Freiburg, Germany. He is the General Editor of *Journal of Linguistic Association of Nigeria* (JOLAN). His latest publications have appeared in *Names: A Journal of Onomastics* (Routledge), *International Journal of Language and Culture* (John Benjamins), *Poznan Studies in Contemporary Linguistics* (De Gruyter), *English Academy Review* (Routledge), *Anthropological Quarterly*, *Sexuality and Culture* (Springer), *African Studies* (Routledge), *Language Sciences* (Elservier), *Sexualities* (Sage), *English Today* (Cambridge), *Southern African Linguistics and Applied Language Studies* (Routledge), *Language Matters* (Routledge), *Gender Issues* (Springer), *Communicatio* (Routledge) and *Journal of Religion in Africa* (Brill).

Dr. Philip Manda Imoh is a lecturer in the Department of Languages and Linguistics at Nasarawa State University, Keffi, Nigeria. His research interests are in morphology, syntax and African linguistics. His recent publications include: Àbachà, ugbò ùwẹ̀ dẹ́: A structural study of Ígálâ death prevention names. *Preorc Journal* 4 (1) forthcoming (co-authored, 2022), Recounting history through pristine settlements: A Study of Selected Basà Toponyms. *International Journal of General Studies* (IJGS). 2(2), 130–152 (co-authored, 2022). He has also guest edited the following journals: (2020) *Jos Journal of the English Language*, 2(2). University of Jos, (2017). *Journal of Linguistics Association of Ghana:(LAG)*(vol. 6, 7& 9), Ghana. He is also part of the research teams on the following projects: *Documenting the linguistic* *profile of languages in Nasarawa State*, and Ideologies in personal naming practices of selected languages in Nasarawa State.

Dr. Reyhan Habibli is Associate Professor of linguistics at Baku State University, Azerbaijan. He is also chairperson of the department of Azerbaijanian Linguistics. In 2021 he successfully defended his PhD thesis on Azerbaijani applied onomastics. His research interests are onomastics, and lexicology of the Azerbaijani language. Some of his key publications in onamastics include: *Azerbaijanian onomastics dictionaries* **(**Monograph**).** Baku (2020), *The problems of applied onomastics* **(**Monograph**).** Baku (2018), Onomastic units and social factors the Turkic world. *Journal of Language and Literature* (2011), The role of the proper names on the internet-communication *Journal of Critical Reviews* (2020).

Prof. Dr. Chia-Jung Pan obtained his PhD degree in anthropological linguistics from the Language and Culture Research Centre, James Cook University, Australia in 2012. He is Professor of Linguistics at the Center for Linguistic Sciences of the Institute of Advanced Studies in Humanities and Social Sciences, Beijing Normal University, China. His research interests include linguistic anthropology, linguistic typology, morphosyntax and pragmatics. He has published articles in *International Journal of American Linguistics*, *Oceanic Linguistics*, *STUF-Language Typology and Universals*, and *Asian Languages and Linguistics*, and book chapters in Oxford University Press, The Australian National University Press, Routledge, Brill, and De Gruyter Mouton. He is the sole author of the two monographs *The Grammatical Realization of Temporal Expressions in Tsou* (2010) and *A Grammar of Saaroa* (2018, in Chinese), the co-author of *A Grammar of Tsou* (2018, 2nd edition, in Chinese) and the editor of *Explorations in Basic Linguistic Theory – Evidentialtiy* (2021, in Chinese).

Miguel Reyes Contreras holds a B.A. in English and an M.A. in applied linguistics from the Universidad Autónoma del Estado de México (UAEM), Mexico, and currently, he is a Ph.D. student at Universidad Autónoma Metropolitana Iztapalapa, Mexico City. He holds a diploma in Discourse Analysis and was part of the Scholar in Residence Program as a Fulbright fellow grantee at the Institute of American Indian Arts (IAIA) (Santa Fe, New Mexico). He researches the areas of Language Teaching (Literacy), Onomastics, Paremiology and Discourse Analysis. He has participated in several national and international congresses and has published some research papers in these areas. He is part of SIO, Interinstitutional Seminar of Onomastics and has been a local chronicler in the Historical association in Ixtlahuaca Mexico.

Index

https://doi.org/10.1515/9783110759297-020

www.ingramcontent.com/pod-product-compliance
Lightning Source LLC
Chambersburg PA
CBHW071729270326
41928CB00013B/2605

* 9 7 8 3 1 1 2 2 1 3 9 8 8 *